LATIN AMERICAN URBAN POLICIES

AND THE SOCIAL SCIENCES

Latin American
Urban Policies
and the Social Sciences

edited by
JOHN MILLER
and
RALPH A. GAKENHEIMER

SAGE Publications   Beverly Hills · London

Portions of Chapters 3, 5, 7, and 8, appeared
(in earlier versions) in the May-June, 1969, issue of
The American Behavioral Scientist (Volume XII, Number 5),
published by Sage Publications, Inc.

For information address:

SAGE PUBLICATIONS, INC.
275 South Beverly Drive
Beverly Hills, California 90212

Printed in the United States of America

International Standard Book Number 0-8039-0056-2

Library of Congress Catalog Card No. 70-103481

First Printing

CONTENTS

LIST OF FIGURES

LIST OF TABLES

Preface

... without municipal support a sordid barrio *has risen up. Its streets are dusty in the summer, muddy in the winter, strewn with rags, scraps from the table, discarded slippers and decaying rats. One can guess that the* barrio *is new like those that break forth like mushrooms everywhere in the cities of America. . . . One senses the country; one notes that the contact with the true part of the city is scarce. . . . But, in spite of the excessive vitality, of the rapid change that visually assaults the viewer, one notes in that* barrio *an indefinable aspect of fatalism and fatigue stamped on the features and things as if a mask of decay and sadness covered it all.*

—Joaquin Edwards Bello (1920) El Roto

The Jahuel Seminar on the Social Sciences and Urban Development in Latin America, cosponsored by the Ford Foundation and the Pontifical Catholic University of Chile, was the temporary convening body that brought together a group of academic and practicing social scientists for a four-day retreat in the Chilean pre-Cordillera during April 22-25, 1968. Papers from that meeting form the core of the present volume.

The Seminar itself was the latest sequel to a series of international conferences spawned by the problems and potentials of an accelerated pace of urbanization in Latin America. Three such conferences had preceded it in Chile in the previous decade. Unlike prior conferences, however, which were almost exclusively concerned with the internal structure and functions per se of the Latin American city, the Jahuel Seminar placed emphasis on (1) the national significance of urban growth, (2) nationwide urban systems, (3) the socio-economic and political integration of urban areas with surrounding national regions and those of other nations, and (4) on the role of the social sciences in suggesting national policies and areas of research which would assist the complementary processes of urbanization and modernization to advance national development. Like most such meetings, a multidisciplinary attack on these emphases formed an invigorating, occasionally polemical, and, frequently, coalescing (interdisciplinary) approach to the issues raised.

Social scientists, whether in the universities and private research institutions or in government (where they are engaged directly in pragmatic tasks), have increasingly become preoccupied with the use of the social sciences for understanding and guiding urbanization and the process of national modernization which parallels urban growth. The four invited papers to the Seminar included here reflect this concern. Accordingly, they are addressed to various policy issues related to urban development in Latin America at the international, national, and local levels and from the points of view of the separate social sciences.

Each of these papers has been written in such a manner as to offer various probing analyses into areas helpful to theoretical formulation and model and typology construction at each of these urban policy levels. The editors have supplemented this search for possible schemes in which to formulate urban policy by the inclusion of editorial material with a number of objectives. The first is to provide a review of additonal related research in the social sciences that bear on urban policy in the Latin American context. A second objective is to familiarize the reader with certain historic and recent events, and government strategies, programs, and projects which are illustrative of many of the issues dealt with by the authors of the Seminar papers.

A further objective, in the opening chapter, has been to place urbanization among the countries of Latin America within a framework of an urban development hierarchy that is related to a number of socioeconomic variables. Additionally, this chapter attempts to aid the uninitiated who are not familiar with the evolving process of urbanization in Latin America to grasp a modicum of comprehension of what is occurring in that cultural region. Another objective, in the closing chapter, has been to examine the intriguing interface between the social sciences and the societal pressures of urban Latin America, which beg increasingly for the attention of the social disciplines, as a means of alerting the disciplines to the practical use of their knowledge and talents.

A final objective has been to assemble modest bibliographical material on the different themes of the book which will provide the basis for more extensive reading.

Organization of the combined Seminar papers and editorial material within the book has been made in such a way that one is guided from the overall topic of urban development in Latin America through the social questions and urban policy areas of bi- and multi-national integration, the role of cities as integral parts of national urban systems and the political implications of national urban policies, to metropolitan policy for squatter settlements. It concludes with policy and action roles for the social scientist.

Specifically, PART I: THE NEW URBAN ERA IN LATIN AMERICA: A CHALLENGE sets forth, through editorial material in Chapter 1: The Urban Phase: Raison d'être for Policy, a regional basis for subsequent presentations.

PART II: INTEGRATING URBAN-REGIONAL POLICIES AMONG NATIONS includes two chapters. Chapter 2: The Rapprochement of Nations with Contiguous Regions, by one of the editors, reports some of the successes and experiences in practical terms of certain bi-national and multi-national integration agreements and examines briefly some of the results and implications for spatial and urban systems integration. Presence and lack of urban policy as part of these integration efforts is discussed. This is followed by the Seminar paper of Professors Poul Ove Pedersen and Walter Stöhr, "Economic Integration and the Spatial Development of South America," which examines various interrelations between transportation-communication structures and urban regional development within the context of the overall South American economy. Among the proposed policies discussed by these authors are basic growth poles and transportation-communication policies for the spatial development of South America, and policies for intermetropolitan and corridor development, resource complex exploitation, depressed and border areas, and river basin development.

PART III: URBAN GROWTH POLICIES FOR THE NATION combines an editorial chapter, Chapter 4: Channeling National Urban Growth in Latin America, with Chapter 5, which brings together the Seminar paper by Professor John Friedmann, "The Role of Cities in National Development," a critique of that paper by Professor Richard M. Morse, "Planning, History, Politics: Reflections on John Friedmann's 'The Role of Cities in National Development,' " and John Friedmann's "Rejoinder to Richard M. Morse." Basically, the Friedmann paper has set forth a set of six leading issues for urban policy in underdeveloped countries which he considers necessary for serious reflection. These are:

(1) the optimum rural-urban balance for successive phases in a process of national development;

(2) the optimal rate of urbanization at successive phases of the development process;

(3) the optimal patterns of spatial organization at successive phases in the development process;

(4) the optimal transformation paths in shifting from one type of spatial organization to another;

(5) the criteria for determining the proper timing in shifts from one kind of urban development strategy to another; and

(6) the criteria to be applied in determining the optimal balance between centralization and decentralization in administrative and political decisions for urban development.

In critique, Morse has offered less a refutation of Friedmann's emphasis on spatial aspects of development than he has presented what he calls a "lens correction," a concern less with theory than with morphology, and more with "the enduring recurrences and ironies of the human condition than with its ultimate purification"—as seen by the historian. In rebuttal, Friedmann argues that a theory of urbanization is possible, a view that Morse seemingly declines to accept readily. Accordingly, Friedmann asserts that "theory in the social sciences is ahistorical, in the sense that its validity is always circumscribed by a number of explicitly formulated assumptions. What is to be predicted," he continues, "is not future history but the behavior of certain variables under conditions that are held constant. It is only in this sense that a theory of urbanization appears possible."

To these arguments and counterarguments have been appended the Seminar participant comments of Professor Jorge Hardoy, Dr. Antoni R. Kuklinsky, and of the Senior Advisor on Regional Development to the United Nations, Ernest Weissmann.

PART IV: POLITICAL DEVELOPMENT VIS-A-VIS URBAN GROWTH presents, again, an editorial chapter, Chapter 6: The Distribution of Political and Government Power in the Context of Urbanization, a brief review of some of the issues involved in this growing field of interest as they are reflected by historic past and current events in Latin America, together with the Seminar paper by Professor Robert T. Daland, "Urbanization Policy and Political Development in Latin America." Daland points out a little discussed aspect of urbanization, which is that greater consideration should be given to the political development implications of national urban growth policies. Certain issues of political development that are engendered by urbanization are identified by Daland, who attempts to link the "evidence" in the social sciences with respect to these issues to models of the relationships between urbanization and political development. In conclusion to Part IV the Seminar participant comments of Professors José A. Silva Michelena and Gideon Sjoberg add critical statements about certain elements of Daland's model which, while not necessarily invalidating it, keep an examination of its future development open to study.

PART V: METROPOLITAN POLICY FOR SQUATTER SETTLEMENTS presents the Seminar paper of Professor Carlos Delgado entitled "Three Proposals Regarding Accelerated Urbanization Problems in Metropolitan Areas: The Lima Case." This contribution to the Seminar is devoted primarily to the formulation of criteria for systematically describing and analyzing the problems which have their origin in the accelerated rate of urbanization in Lima. Principal focus is placed on a classification of "marginal" residential settlement types as an initial step in research leading to the development of policies for improving the quality of the communities considered. This chapter is concluded by the Seminar participant comments of José A. Silva Michelena which broaden the scope of Delgado's paper by examining some of the effects of urbanization-modernization on groups (other than those of the marginal settlements) within the cities of Venezuela.

In PART VI: A FUTURE ROLE FOR THE SOCIAL SCIENCES: POLICY AND ACTION, Chapter 9 provides an examination, through editorial material, of the social sciences and public policy, of traditional research areas of the various disciplines regarding urban processes and of new directions for research, and a brief description of existing Latin American centers for education and research in urban affairs. It is complemented by the Recommendations of the Seminar Work Group on Urban and Regional Research.

The foregoing has been augmented, in the APPENDIX, by a Summary of the Jahuel Seminar made by Dr. Kalman H. Silvert who has ably summarized some of the "different oppositions or dichotomies" present in the Seminar, polarities which are basic, probably, to any gathering of practitioners and theorists, or academicians. Further, he presents the "core" themes which flow in a current of intriguing ideas throughout the Seminar papers and discussions. Although his summary has been appended to the book, the reader interested in the interaction of separate social sciences within a major policy topic would be benefited by reading his comments before launching on an examination of the book itself.

This is perhaps the point to state that this is neither a book of social science research nor one exclusively focused on urban policies. In this sense it will probably fail the purer intellectual interests of some social scientists and the purely pragmatic focus of the decision maker who too frequently must rely on an intuitive political "wisdom" rather than on guidelines from the behavioral sciences for action. To postulate either of these positions as lacking in worth is obviously incorrect. Few would want to govern or be governed exclusively from either position under complex social conditions. The middle ground, however, which brings the two together, is an area demanding greater attention and understanding. The political and elitist core (whether that be located in the historic "metropolitan" nations of Spain and Portugal with rule by edict and fiat or in the modern national metropolis of the maturing and now independent Latin American nations) could not and cannot govern adequately without a better understanding of the forces of change, especially those symbolized by the burgeoning urban centers. These forces are little likely to decline in importance as national issues and the contrary is almost certain. It behooves, therefore, both the social scientist and the policy maker in seats of government to grope for a rapprochement in which the work of social science may be better made to fit policy questions and in which the receptivity of the policy centers in the use of social science research is heightened.

It can be pointed out that the issues of social science research and policy planning as two separate, but complementary, activities are basic to the underlying content of the volume. In sum, this publication recognizes the justifiably strong interest of social scientists in the testing and elaboration of hypotheses leading to the formation of theory related to urbanization processes and the continuing value of research for this purpose. It also recognizes the *possibility* that this may be useful for policy formulation. It further concedes that the personal interests of researchers and research funding institutions may or may not involve the usefulness and relevance of research for policy purposes.

Finally, it assumes that there is probably some potential input to policy-making in most urban research, but where resources are scarce, as in Latin America, concern should be for maximum impact. The argument is often made that the benefits of research undertaken for "basic" knowledge may be unknown at the time research is undertaken; certainly this is true of the natural and physical sciences. The social sciences, however, have not been able to demonstrate as readily as the other sciences that their research findings are useful for social purposes (including economic ones), with the consequence that funding from the private sector has been negligible. Basic social research in financing has, therefore, derived from government sources and nonprofit foundations. Since Latin American governments are potentially substantial users of the results of social investigation, the economic position of social research would, unquestionably, be enhanced by improved contributions to policy areas in Latin America.

No apology is necessary for the geographic parochialism in the content of this volume. It goes without saying that Latin America, culturally and physically, conforms to a major research area which is intriguing by reason of its many similarities and differences. The number of Americans interested in the problems of that vast region among social scientists is pitifully small. The number of those committed to work on those problems is smaller. A growing corps of Latin American social scientists, however, is being trained and is gaining experience in policy formulation within government.

An improved social approach to problems, including those of the urban sector, and the setting of policy for these problems by government is providing the opportunity for this experience. The recently accelerating move for greater economic and physical integration through improved transportation and communication, free trade agreements, and industrial integration schemes is creating an increasingly sophisticated approach to policy issues within, between, and among nations. These policies as they are extended and made more detailed will have a growing influence on policies for coping with the urbanization process. Too, there is a movement under way among Latin American social science research and teaching institutes for collaboration and mutual assistance in seeking better knowledge about and solutions for problems involved in urban growth.

It might be unfair to launch the reader into a discussion of urban policy in the main body of the book without somehow making a brief statement about policy itself. Accordingly, we will rely on a recent work by Robert R. Alford (1967) which is helpful in this respect. Alford has said, for example, that "a *policy* is a series of decisions of a certain type (where *decisions* are particular acts of government agencies or other authoritative groups), any one of which has a certain probability determined by the consistency of the policy, its legality, and support by political and economic forces." It is, he says, *the role of government* to be committed "to certain types of policies, established formally by law or informally by means of the dominance of groups in a community holding certain political values and goals."

As Alford has demonstrated in this same article, there are four broad classes of factors which explain or show the consequences and correlates of decisions, policies, and governmental roles: *situational* (sequence of events and balance of political and social forces bearing upon and determining a particular decision), *structural* (long-term "situations" and relatively unchanging elements of the society and polity), *cultural* (value commitments of groups within the community as a whole, expressed through laws and policies), and *environmental* (factors which operate outside the boundaries of the particular political system although affecting it).

It is the structural and cultural factors which impinge most upon community life (national or local) and produce events which, if they occur with sufficient frequency, may convert into processes of various types (high abortion rates as a birth control measure, rural-urban migration as a process tending toward spatial and socioeconomic equilibrium and rapid urbanization, and so on). Depending upon situational factors (i.e., the balance of political and social forces which view this as an important decision and policy area *or not*), the "process" will or will not be advanced publicly for action (decisions) and policy formulation as one of the concerns of government. When it is, it becomes "the problem area," not only a "process." When it isn't, it is merely viewed, if at all, as a "process," either with mere intellectual interest or indifference.

It can be the role of the social scientist, then, to identify the "process," to detail its elements and their interrelationships and to point out that the process has sufficient merits to deserve the attention of government for taking decisions and that these decisions, because of their "linkage," form an identifiable policy area. Government itself, of course, must decide that they do form such a policy area, and that decision derives, basically, from the nature and strength of situational pressures brought to bear on the political representatives. Almost without exception, it may be said, Latin American governments are actually engaged in taking a series of decisions, dispersed though they may be and without any central direction, which do constitute *implicit* urban policy due to their actual effect upon the urbanization process. In other words, a lack of purposeful (conscious) policy may be present, but the effects that derive from the uncoordinated decisions actually coalesce in influencing the urbanization process and altering the direction it might have taken if government had much less power over finances and the control of decisions in the private sector than it does. In the end, the implicit policy is no less real than the explicit one. The failing of an implicit—one can hardly call it a laissez faire—policy about the urbanization process is that a lack of *explicit* attention to the implications of the presence of a continuing flow of "effecting" decisions may accentuate the problems growing out of the process. In any event, the decisions forming implicit policy typically tend to become oriented toward paliation of the symptoms rather than toward a channelling of the process and toward a change in the causes which produce the problems within the process. Until the effects on the process of the implicit policies are identified (as well as their origin in government and private decisions) and until it can be shown how the decisions reinforce or cancel each other out in given directions, many such decisions will actually work counter to what a consciously conceived (explicit) policy for the given "process" would produce.

In concluding these prefatory remarks, the editors wish to state that, although the Jahuel Seminar on the Social Sciences and Urban Development in Latin America was cosponsored by the Pontifical Catholic University of Chile through the Interdisciplinary Center of Urban and Regional Development (CIDU) and by the Ford Foundation, and funds for this purpose were made available by the Foundation, neither of these institutions are responsible for the viewpoints of the authors of invited papers to the Seminar or for any other content of this book, nor do they hold any position with respect to the topics discussed.

The editors, personally, wish to extend their thanks to the myriad of individuals who participated in the Jahuel Seminar and later, and who have, thereby, made this final product possible. Warm thanks are due, of course, to authors and participants (especially those who submitted detailed comments on the papers); their patience in preparing their work for publication was constant. (A complete list of the participants is included in the Appendix.) John Friedmann, chairman of the program committee for the Seminar, later guided the editors in the initiation of the editorial work. Sonia de Jordán, Coordinator of the Secretariat, and her staff, Lucía de Royo, María Teresa Alvarez, Raquel Velasco, Sergio Bravo, Andrea Ratinoff, and Isabel B. de Ducci provided invaluable assistance prior to, at the time of, and immediately after the Seminar. Subsequently, Carmen Yañez, Mary Bartok, and Jean McBeth labored in the typing of manuscripts for publication. And, finally, only the editors will ever know what merited thanks are due to their publisher, Sara Miller McCune, and her staff.

It would be blatantly erroneous to assume that certain errors may not have crept past the best intentions of the editors, but only because imperfect knowledge or momentary editorial oversights blurred their vision. Such inadequacies, we hope, can be overlooked in the general objective of making the material available to a wider audience.

JOHN MILLER
RALPH GAKENHEIMER

REFERENCE

ALFORD, R. R. (1967) "The comparative study of urban politics," p. 264 in Leo F. Schnore and Henry Fagin (eds.) Urban Research and Policy Planning. Beverly Hills, Calif.: Sage Publications.

Part **I**

The New Urban Era
in Latin America

A Challenge

Chapter 1

The Urban Phase

Raison d'être for Policy

JOHN MILLER

Urbanization[1] **constitutes one of the principal change** phenomenon of contemporary Latin America. And, it may not be an exaggeration to say, as Felipe Herrera (B, 1966) has, that the recent development of Latin America is the development of its urbanization. In fact, changes under way there in most countries since 1940 constitute sufficient reason, perhaps, to refer to the present epoch as a second urban era in Latin America—with the first being that of Spanish colonial town founding in the sixteenth century.

Not since that earlier period of a deliberate and carefully developed pro-urban policy has there been such a dramatic shift in the rural-urban structure. The "colonial urban era," however, was characterized principally by the fact that the basically rural indigenous population structure of the region (excepting certain important religious-cultural and government centers) was altered through the founding and maintenance of a widely spread European "town" system. Actually, of course, the founding of towns in colonial Luso-Hispanic America continued throughout the sixteenth and up to the early nineteenth century in certain regions of the continent. Chile was especially characterized by late town founding due to the belligerence and tenacity there of the Mapuches in defense of their territory to the south of the Río Bío Bío. They were successful, in fact, in holding the Spanish and Creoles at bay for three hundred years and in causing the destruction of town sites which subsequently had to be abandoned. Although a number of villages were established during the eighteenth century in this frontier region, many fell to the fire and ravage of the native defenders (Guarda, 9: L, 1968).

3

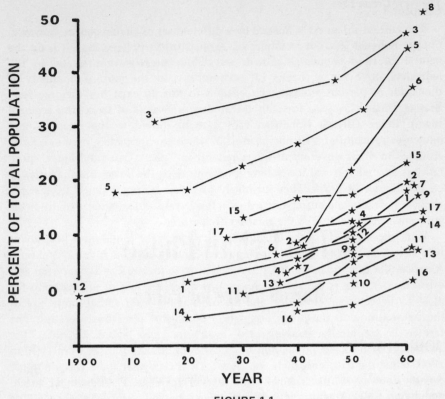

FIGURE 1.1
**Urban Level of Selected Latin American Countries,* 1900-60
(Localities of 20,000+)**

*Selected countries are numbered as in Tables 1.4-1.10 as follows: (1) Brazil, (2) Mexico, (3) Argentina, (4) Colombia, (5) Chile, (6) Venezuela, (7) Peru, (8) Uruguay, (9) Ecuador, (10) Guatemala, (11) El Salvador, (12) Bolivia, (13) Paraguay, (14) Nicaragua, (15) Panama, (16) Honduras, and (17) Costa Rica.

SOURCE: Miró (B: 1968), Table 8, 17-18.

TABLE 1.1
**Increases in Urban and Rural Population in Latin America,
1920-1960, By Decades (rough estimates by percentage)**

	1920-30	1930-40	1940-50	1950-60
Urban[a]	40	39	61	67
Rural and small town	17	17	16	19

SOURCE: United Nations. Bureau of Social Affairs, Population Division (A, 1966b) as presented by Browning (B, 1967: 95).

a. Cities of 20,000 or more inhabitants.

The New Urban Era

The current urban era is marked by a different set of circumstances, however. Change is based less, for example, on explicit urban policies than it is on the natural forces of population growth and rural-urban migration released by the individual drive for a change of environment on the part of hundreds of thousands of persons annually. Exceptions to this do exist but they are few: Brasilia, Ciudad Guayana (actually the modern equivalent of an existing regional town), Belize (British Honduran capital to be moved to the interior), and numerous agricultural settlements, most of which are completely rural in nature. Aside from these government-sponsored urban "plants" in rural areas, spontaneous new villages and towns have sprung up along the Belem-Brasilia highway on the interior of Brazil. They seemingly owe their existence almost exclusively to sheer necessity and entrepreneurship in the private sector rather than to direct government intervention in the creation of new *urbes*.

While the extension of the urban network through the founding of new towns is a strong possibility in the next quarter-century on the interior of South America, the new urban era in Latin America up to the present derives from two other factors. One is the abrupt change upward in the rate of urbanization for most Latin American countries, and the other is the sheer and absolute size of the net addition to the urban population during the past three decades. The former is graphically demonstrated in Figure 1.1, which illustrates the percentage of the total population in localities of 20,000 or more from 1900 to 1960. While the data shown are incomplete, it is clear that there was a notable change upward in the rate of urbanization (percentage increase in urban population between census periods) beginning for many countries about 1940 or 1950. Only Paraguay and Costa Rica show rather poor performance in this respect. This sudden change is also borne out in Table 1.1, which shows that for all of Latin America there was an almost straight-line increase of forty percent in the size of the urban population in the decades between 1920 and 1940. During the decade 1940 to 1950, however, the increase in the absolute size of the urban population rose to sixty-one percent and, subsequently, to sixty-seven percent in the decade 1950 to 1960.

Even an examination of the urban population (as defined as living in localities of 20,000 or more) when separated into two city-size classes of 20,000 to 99,999 and 100,000 and over shows a similar pattern with the exception that there was a substantially greater acceleration in the latter group (see Figures 1.2 and 1.3). Chile and Venezuela were two nations which showed a trend towards the reinforcement of towns in the size class 20,000 to 99,999, a trend which, if continued, could assist in the development of a more balanced urban system in those countries over the next quarter-century. An actual decrease in the percentage of total population in localities of 20,000 to 99,999 in the cases of Panama, Costa Rica, El Salvador, and Honduras is due to the fact that one or more cities passed into the class 100,000 and above with little or no growth at all in the smaller city class during the period where decline was evident.

It is to be noted that four of the five nations (Argentina, Chile, Venezuela and Uruguay) listed in Table 1.4 as countries with a single metropolis of a million inhabitants or more are also the countries which have long maintained the

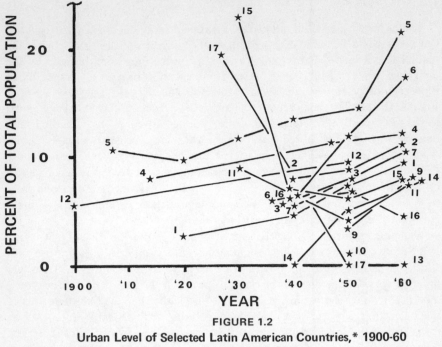

FIGURE 1.2
Urban Level of Selected Latin American Countries,* 1900-60
(Localities of 20-100,000)

*Selected countries are numbered as in Tables 1.4-1.10 as follows: (1) Brazil, (2) Mexico, (3) Argentina, (4) Colombia, (5) Chile, (6) Venezuela, (7) Peru, (8) Uruguay, (9) Ecuador, (10) Guatemala, (11) El Salvador, (12) Bolivia, (13) Paraguay, (14) Nicaragua, (15) Panama, (16) Honduras, and (17) Costa Rica.

SOURCE: Miró (B: 1968), Table 8, 17-18.

highest level of urbanization as measured by the proportion of the total population in localities of 20,000 and above (see Figure 1.1).

Dramatic Shift in the Absolute Size of the Urban Population

While the graphs show that there was a significant change in the rate of urbanization around 1940 or 1950, the absolute numerical increase in urban population levels is also evidence of major quantitative shifts in the past quarter-century. It is estimated, for example, that there was a net addition of twenty million people to the cities and towns of Latin America in the brief five-year span 1960 to 1965. Further, in the period 1965 to 1975 an estimated augment of fifty-five million more will join their immediate predecessors and the ninety million who were resident there in 1960. When one compares these fifty-five million new urban dwellers now in the midstream of their arrival with the mere sixty million who lived in localities of 2,000 or more in 1950, the scale of change becomes more easily perceptible. In fact, when one compares the estimated 1970 urban population of one hundred fifty million with the sixty million urban inhabitants of 1950, there appears to be an additional justification

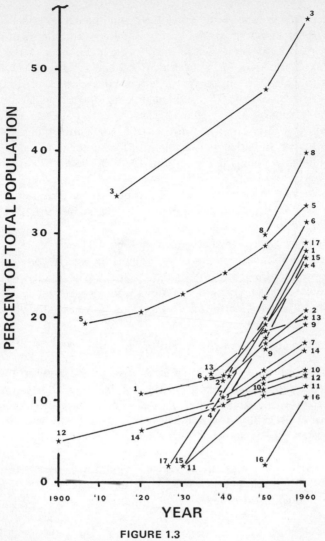

FIGURE 1.3
Urban Level of Selected Latin American Countries,* 1900-60
(Localities of 100,000+)

*Selected countries are numbered as in Tables 1.4-1.10 as follows: (1) Brazil, (2) Mexico, (3) Argentina, (4) Colombia, (5) Chile, (6) Venezuela, (7) Peru, (8) Uruguay, (9) Ecuador, (10) Guatemala, (11) El Salvador, (12) Bolivia, (13) Paraguay, (14) Nicaragua, (15) Panama, (16) Honduras, and (17) Costa Rica.

SOURCE: Miró (B: 1968), Table 8, 17-18 and Davis (A: 1969), Table C, 120-25.

for denoting the present epoch as a new urban era in that part of the hemisphere.[2]

Urban vis-à-vis Rural Population Growth

These abrupt changes are not without their background in the general process of demographic growth. Current statistics, for example, on the demographic growth rate for nations in Latin America indicate, on a continental basis, one of the highest growth rates in the world, 2.9%, and there is no evidence that it may be decelerating significantly. Moreover, overall population growth has been, for the most part, increasingly concentrated in the urban areas. Although the total population increase was 32.2% between 1950 and 1960 in all of Latin America, the total population increase in the urban zones (cities of 20,000 or more inhabitants) was 67.0%. The rural and small town populations grew by a considerably smaller rate, 19.0%. These coupled trends (a high overall population growth rate and an urban growth rate almost four times that of the rural rate) raised the urban population in cities and towns of 2,000 or over from 39.0% of the total population in 1940 to 49.0% in 1960.[3] As a result, cities grew at an average annual rate of 4.5% (some grew at 6.0% or more) compared with a rural growth rate of 1.4%. By 1975 it is expected that eleven countries in Latin America will have an urban population in excess of 60% of total national population; in 1960 there were four.

As mentioned before and as shown in Table 1.1, a strong rise in the rate at which the absolute size of the urban population was growing was noticeable between the decades of 1930-1940 and 1940-1950, while the rural growth rate per decade remained practically stationary at sixteen and nineteen percent. These two differential facts form a third reason for viewing the present period as a new urban era.

Latin America Compared with Other World Regions

When contrasted with the other lesser-developed regions in the world, the proportional urban level in Latin America in 1960 (thirty-two percent as measured by population in places of 20,000 or more inhabitants) was substantially higher than for all other such regions. Even Central Europe had a lower proportional urban level (twenty-seven percent). Furthermore, estimated projections reaching to the year 2000 indicate that the differences between Latin America and other lesser-developed regions with respect to proportional urban level would continue to widen. While only nineteen and fifteen percentage points separated Latin American urban levels from those of Africa and Asia, respectively, in 1960, the difference between Latin America and Africa, South Asia, and East Asia would rise to thirty-two, thirty-five, and twenty-nine,

TABLE 1.2
Percentage of the Total Population in Places of 20,000 or More Inhabitants, 1960

World			24-25
Lesser developed regions		17-18	
Latin America		32	
Argentina, Chile, Uruguay	56		
Rest of Latin America	28		
Africa		13	
North Africa	26		
Africa south of Sahara	9		
Asia		16-18	
Continental China	10-15		
Rest of Asia	19		

SOURCE: United Nations (A, 1969).

respectively, by 1980. By 2000 they would be forty-one, forty-five, and forty for the same sequence (see Table 1.3).

Projected Levels of Urban Population

In terms of the absolute change in total urban population between 1960 and that projected for the year 2000 in Latin America, it will be little short of astounding if projected urban levels and total population figures become future historic facts. In 1960 there were approximately 102 million urban dwellers; by 2000 this is projected to increase to 608 million, just over a half billion more in the relatively short span of forty years!

There should be little question by now that events are rapidly creating urban situations on a scale with which national and local governments have not hitherto dealt and that this new urban era is creating a major challenge which will have to be met by directed and planned government intervention. Such intervention will derive from a concern in the maintenance of political stability and social justice on a par with past concerns regarding industrialization for the promotion of economic growth. Urbanization has largely occurred in the recent past as a parallel and consequent result of industrialization. As a separate policy area, it has been largely ignored except as it served the purposes of industrialization or has had to be channeled to conform to traditional images of the city or of the elite classes within it. This period is rapidly drawing to a close. The recent experience of São Paulo in attempting to retrieve itself by massive planning and extensive urban surgery from a fathomless pit of chaos and seemingly permanent discontinuities in its social and physical structure is an example of what must occur elsewhere if the challenge is to be met. While many smaller and medium-sized cities can unquestionably continue to grow without strongly directed guidance, as did São Paulo, the opportunity will soon be lost to make these cities more livable, more functional, before correction is impossible or extraordinarily costly. The challenge to government is to make the necessary investment in planning now for the growth which is coming.

Finally, where will these half-billion people make their homes, work out their lives, and enjoy the companionship of family and friends? In 1960, 27.7 million Latin Americans out of a total of 101 million urbanized people there lived in ten cities of one million or more. If the same proportion (27.4%) of the expected 608 million urban dwellers of the year 2000 were to live in these same ten

TABLE 1.3

Proportion of Urban to Total Population in 1960 and Projections for 1980 and 2000, World and Geographic Regions (in percentages)

Region	1960	1980	2000
World	33	46	51
Latin America	49	60	80
Africa	18	28	39
South Asia	18	25	35
East Asia	23	31	40
North America	70	81	87
Europe	58	65	71

SOURCE: United Nations (A, 1969).

metropolitan areas, each would contain an average of 16,660,000 persons—almost eight times their 1960 average of 2,767,000. Actually, many of the smaller cities are growing at a faster rate than the metropolitan areas but, since metropolitan cities are relatively so much larger, they are gaining absolutely much faster than the lower-order centers. They could, therefore, conceivably even be larger than 16 million.

While it may be that cities of 16 million or more are possible, the real question is whether they are desirable. Increasing evidence would suggest that they aren't, either in advanced industrialized countries or in the lesser-developed regions of the world.

There were also 34 cities in Latin America in 1960 between 250,000 and a million. This represented 14.5% of the total urban population in that year. Their proportionate share of the projected year 2000 urban population would be an average 2,590,000 each. Only four of the ten metropolitan areas of 1960 were larger than this! The next city-size class, 100-250,000, included 63 cities in 1960 and they represented 9.7% of the total urban population. A proportionate share of the projected turn-of-the-century population would be an average of 936,000 persons each. If anything, these simple projections suggest that as much emphasis as possible should be given now to the development of cities in this latter class in order to draw to them some of the population which appears slated for the larger cities because of present urban investment patterns and location of economic production there.

The future of these smaller cities, however, many of which will equal or exceed one million within 40 years, is more than the simple addition of population. Many of them have a relatively weak urban economy with low levels in the use of technology and a serious lack of the social institutions which provide the necessary institutional infrastructure for development. If national governments do not intervene—and intervention should begin with serious direction in the next decade—many of these cities could well represent little more than a shadow economically, socially, and physically of what cities of one million presently are. Almost all of the cities which were metropolitan (over one million) in 1960 were capitals (eight of the ten). Consequently, there was a concomitant greater attention given to these cities for urban investment (on a per capita and need basis) than was given to provincial cities. With the expected continued attention that they will receive as they grow in size and as they require more expensive and better transportation, potable water, and sewerage systems (relative to the smaller cities), it does not bode well for the creation of new cities of one million or more with an equal infrastructure to those of that size now.

If these problems are to be averted or ameliorated, national governments will have to intervene forcefully with explicit urban policies and the power and will to carry them out, especially during the next fifteen to twenty years. In contrast, the growth of large cities in the last half-century has not been accompanied by a political appreciation for the national implications of rapid urbanization since this growth was defined as metropolitan, not national. It is not unlikely that in less than a half-century Latin America will see the addition of an urban population equal to that in seventy metropolitan cities the size of Buenos Aires in 1960 (seven million). National preoccupation with urban development will not necessarily replace present concern for economic development, but there seems little question that it will become a preoccupation.

This, then, is the new urban era; this is the challenge; this is the urgent raison d'être of an urban policy conceived at the national level for the purpose of guiding this astounding social phenomenon as surely as metropolitan Spain guided the New World's first urban era. It may be fortunate in the final analysis that the centralist tradition of Castile has hung on with such tenacity in most nations, since there seems to be little question that any serious guidance will require a gargantuan degree of national purpose.

A Typology Based on an Urban Systems Hierarchy of Nations and Urban Population Sizes: A Device for Exploring National Urban Policy Areas

As a means of demonstrating possible national urban policy issues at fairly generalized levels, and for showing certain similarities among nations grouped together by classes, a hierarchy of Latin American nations based on the level of development of their urban systems was prepared.

The hierarchy was established on the general assumption that all nations, given an indefinite period of time for population growth and urbanization, would proceed through a series of urban stages involving an urban system:

(1) with a single medium-sized city of 250,000 to one million;

(2) with multiple medium-sized cities;

(3) with a single metropole of one million or more; and

(4) with multiple metropoles.

Each nation was assigned to one of these classes in accordance with the size of cities in 1970 as estimated by Davis (A, 1969). Using 1960 census data, each country was then ranked according to the absolute numerical size of its urban population on the general assumption that the total urban population level should bear a close relation to a hierarchy of national urban systems, which in fact it does (see Table 1.4). The ranking of all nations proceeds in perfect descending order from one hierarchical class to the next with the exception of Argentina. By urban population level, Argentina ranks third and should come between Mexico and Colombia in the top urban system hierarchy class, that of multiple metropole nations. Instead, it falls in the single metropole category. Before 1980, however, the urban system of Argentina is expected to convert into a multiple metropole system. Guayaquil, Ecuador, too, will exceed one million by 1980, and Ecuador will pass into the single metropole class. As a result, there will be complete congruence between ranking by urban population size and urban system hierarchy within the next ten years, and the rankings of nations by urban population size will descend in perfect numerical order.

An additional comment is required with respect to ranking "7A– FEDERATED CENTRAL AMERICA." This "nation" has been included in order to speculate about possible national urban policies with respect to a federated Central American nation, as well as various socioeconomic variables associated with it in Tables 1.4 to 1.10. A hypothetical Federated Central America includes Guatemala, El Salvador, Nicaragua, Panama, Honduras, and Costa Rica. Based on their combined urban population, it would fall between Peru and Uruguay among the ranked nations. But, since there is no single metropolis in any one of the present nations, a federated nation of Central America would be classed just ahead of Ecuador in the urban system hierarchy class of nations with multiple medium-sized cities. During the 1970s, however, Guatemala City is likely to pass the one million mark, and this fact would advance such a federated nation to its proper position just ahead of Uruguay when ranked by urban population size.

There is no intended mystique about the significance of the typology. Typically, nations are grouped and ranked in accordance with their levels of economic development. This volume is focused in large part on national urban systems and national urban policies. Grouping and ranking of nations in accord with this central concern and with a natural progression of urban systems through a hierarchy of increasing complexity makes possible, therefore, certain contrasts and comparisons not as easily evident with the use of a rank order based on level of economic development.

Basically, the urban system hierarchy and the ranking of nations by the size of their urban populations are compared with several groups of variables, as follows:

Table 1.4: total population, proportional urban level, and era of urbanization (basic urban population data);

Table 1.5: number of cities and population by size class (urban system);

Table 1.6: total city population (100,000 plus) and size of largest city (urban primacy);

Table 1.7: gross national product, level of socioeconomic development, and dependency ratio (economic);

Table 1.8: national crude birth rate, illiteracy, and use of newspapers (social and communications);

Table 1.9: economically active male population in various urban activities (urban economy and urban services); and

Table 1.10: level of electoral participation, centralization of budget, proportion of university students to population, and number of inhabitants per hospital bed (political development and government services).

Discussion will proceed by reference to each table in sequence with occasional comments about variables and relationships in other tables.

Basic Urban Population Data and the Urban System and
Urban Primacy (Tables 1.4, 1.5, and 1.6)

An examination of the urban system hierarchy categories relative to ranking by total population, proportional urban level, and era of urbanization (columns 4, 5 and 6 of Table 1.4) demonstrates a remarkable degree of similarity within each category with an occasional variant nation. Uruguay, for example, exhibits a basic distortion (relative to the other nations in its category) by ranking first in proportional urban level, but eleventh in size of total population. This distortion is exaggerated even further by the fact that it contains not a single city greater than 100,000 population save the capital, Montevideo, of 1,500,000 (Table 1.5, col. 7 and Table 1.6, col. 11). All other nations in this class, on the other hand, contain anywhere between three and fifteen cities of 100,000 to a million.

On the basis of the presumed gradual development of nations through an urban systems hierarchy, this suggests that Uruguay might appropriately promote the development of some of its towns below 100,000, especially in view of the expected urban population increase during the next half-century. Since Montevideo already contains 53.7% of Uruguay's total urban population (Table 1.6, col. 12), any policy for promoting the development of cities or towns less than 100,000 would have to be applied quite severely with incentives attractive enough to ensure rapid and continued growth in the face of the gravitational pull of Montevideo. In essence, what appears to be called for is the diversion of new economic production facilities to a planned regional growth pole, perhaps linked with proposed infrastructural projects in the Río La Plata Basin development scheme. Further, since central government is such a major factor in Montevideo, a policy should be promoted, perhaps, to deconcentrate certain government activities to the new growth pole. Some of these might include agricultural planning and services, transportation planning, certain record-keeping activities (statistics, social security, national archives), new universities and technical institutes, national research centers in health, specialized hospitals for long-term treatment, and the like.

Urban policy suggestions, such as the above, do not imply that any other variable, such as economic growth, would be necessarily affected favorably. Further analysis would have to be made of the expected consequences of new urban policies, and the objectives which they are intended to serve would have to be weighed against certain economic objectives. The latter would not, in all cases, govern, however.

In the same hierarchy category, single metropole, Peru is shown to rank low relative to its class members in terms of its proportional urban level. This suggests that a policy of promoted and stepped-up urbanization would be called for in order to provide better "fit" with its class. This policy proposal contrasts, actually, with the general cry of alarm with respect to the rate of urban growth experienced in Lima in the past three decades. (Lima actually contained 92.2% of Peru's city population in 1960: Table 1.6, col. 11.) An examination of Table 1.5, col. 7, would indicate that every effort might be made, especially, to promote the development of Arequipa, Chiclayo, and Trujillo (the three cities in the city size class 100-250,000) and of the regions which they serve, as well as cities less than 100,000 where they lie in regions more favorably disposed to regional development.

It is no coincidence, perhaps, that, with the exception of Peru, all nations in the single metropole class are the most urbanized (between 62.4 and 72.0%), and, excepting Peru and Venezuela, they were the only nations which reached an urban level of 25.0% by 1920 in all of Latin America.

The nations with multiple metropoles (Brazil, Mexico, and Colombia), in contrast, all rank in a middle-level position with respect to their proportional urban levels (Table 1.4, col. 5). While the sum of their ranked positions by size of urban population comes to seven, the sum of their ranked positions with respect to proportional urban level comes to eighteen. The exact reverse is true for the sum of ranks in the single metropole category—twenty-nine for rank by size of urban population and nineteen by proportional urban level. This illustrates that the single metropole nations are not only more highly urbanized, but they are more highly urbanized *with respect to the actual size of their urban populations* than is true for the group "multiple metropoles."

First, by their total population size (ranks 1, 2, and 4) and, second, by the proportion of the total population yet to be urbanized (fifty-five percent or more in 1960), Brazil, Mexico, and Colombia are notable in the potential they contain for the sheer size of rural-urban population shifts in the future. Fortunately, they all contain a reasonable distribution of cities among metropoles and medium- and small-sized cities (6—15—15, respectively, in the case of Brazil; 3—6—14 in Mexico; and 2—5—8 in Colombia; Table 1.5, col. 7). Even the population spread among these cities is not unreasonable when other nations are contrasted with them (Table 1.5, col. 8). Finally, the percentage of total city population (population in cities of 100,000 or more) and the percentage of total urban population found in the largest (capital) cities are the lowest of all nations. This makes the potential gravitational force they exert, on the basis of relative size, much less serious than in other national cases. The percentage of total city population in Brazil, Mexico, and Colombia found in Rio de Janeiro, Mexico City, and Bogotá, for example, was 25.4, 43.5, and 33.2% respectively in 1960. The percentage of the total urban population in each of these nations residing in the capital cities, in the same order, was 14.8, 16.0 and 17.4% (Table 1.6, cols. 11 and 12).

Perhaps for these reasons it may be appropriate to advance the suggestion that serious efforts aimed at achieving a degree of balance between regions through regional development planning and the use of the existing urban system is more suitable to these nations than it might be for other nations. The opportunities exist, also, of building upon these more complex and extended urban networks in such a way that expected urban population growth can be more evenly distributed. This can be contrasted, for example, with Uruguay, where only dictatorial fiat and the massive armed enforcement of a national urban policy would be capable of creating a more balanced distribution of urban population among several city size classes. Brazil and Colombia, particularly, due to an unexploited and unsettled interior, have the opportunity to divert future rural and urban population growth into virgin regions, thereby assuring a given level of future rural-urban migration to new urban places rather than to existing cities and towns.

Argentina, too, may be included in this general policy framework in view of its present urban system and the expectation that it will join the class "multiple metropoles" within the present decade. It has the serious disadvantage, however, that its primate city, Buenos Aires, contained 64.5% of Argentina's total city population in 1960 and 52.2% of the total urban population (Table 1.6, cols. 11 and 12). Rosario and Córdoba both can be expected to top the one million mark during the 1970s, however. By virtue of Rosario's location as a transport node and shipping point and thanks to Córdoba's industrial base, they both make seemingly rational spatial, economic, and urban extensions of metropolitan Buenos Aires. Mendoza, too, by 1980, could exceed one million in which case its proximity to Chile's metropolitan central valley and Santiago suggests an analysis of the two urban economies for the possible reinforcement of economic links between the two. The existence of an additional twelve cities between 100,000 and 500,000 inhabitants in 1970 spread fairly evenly over the upper two-thirds of Argentina provides a reasonably good urban systems base for regional development throughout the area. South of Bahia Blanca, on the Atlantic Ocean, however, there is no city greater than 100,000 population in an extension of over 1,200 miles, a fact which calls forth special settlement and resource exploitation policies—perhaps even an international immigration policy. Implementation of the former two has actually been attempted in recent times.

Chile, it would appear, might profitably try to divert the narrowing proportion that the rural population bears to the whole in that country (35.3% in 1960) into its one medium-sized city (Valparaiso) and its four smaller cities (Concepción and Talcahuano, twin cities, Antofagasta, and Viña del Mar, twin city of Valparaiso). When one notes that Santiago contained 77.9% of Chile's total city population in 1960, it seems evident that a more balanced urban system calls for the promotion and strengthening of second-order cities through economic development and the provision of social infrastructure. Actually, in all of these cases, with the exception of Antofagasta, there are some rather severe constraints on the spatial growth of these cities which could mean excessive densities if growth continues unabated for the next half-century. Spatial expansion in terms of linear growth along coastal areas and penetrations into coastal cordilleras in the case of Concepción-Talcahuano and Valparaiso-Viña del Mar create special physical development problems not found in the Central Valley. There satellite cities close to Santiago could be promoted, and in more distant valley regions cities such as Talca, Chillán, Temuco, and Valdivia could very easily be expanded into extremely pleasant medium-sized cities of up to a million population by 2000. In the case of Antofagasta, water in that desert region could prove to be an extremely costly growth problem unless sea water conversion or subsurface water technology costs can be lowered.

Ecuador, while it ranks ninth in total urban population, actually ranks fourteenth in proportional urban level. This indicates that an increased rural-urban migration pattern would be justified (under present assumptions) to

TABLE 1.4

Comparison of Ranking by Size of Urban Population in Selected Latin American Nations (1960) With Total Population and Urban Level (1960) and With Era of Urbanization

(1) Rank by Size of Urban Pop.	(2) NATIONS[a]	(3) Urban Population[b] (millions)	(4) Total Population[c] (millions)		(5) Proportional Urban Level[d] (percentage) (3) ÷ (4)		(6) Era of Urbanization[e]
MULTIPLE METROPOLES (million+) 1970[f]							
1	BRAZIL	32.0	1	71.0	7	45.0	II
2	MEXICO	17.7	2	34.9	5	50.7	II
4	Colombia	7.1	4	15.4	6	46.3	II
(7)			(7)		(18)		
SINGLE METROPOLE (million+) 1970							
3	ARGENTINA	13.4	3	20.0	2	67.0	I
5	Chile	5.0	6	7.8	3	64.7	I
6	VENEZUELA	4.6	7	7.3	4	62.4	II
7	Peru	4.5	5	11.0	9	40.9	II
8	Uruguay	1.8	11	2.5	1	72.0	I
(29)			(32)		(19)		
MULTIPLE MEDIUM-SIZED CITIES (250,000-1 million) 1970							
9	Ecuador	1.4	8	4.4	14	33.0	II
SINGLE MEDIUM-SIZED CITY (250,000-1 million) 1970							
10	Guatemala	1.2	9	3.8	15	30.7	III
11	El Salvador	0.9	12	2.5	11	38.1	III
12	Bolivia	0.8	10	3.5	16	22.8	III
13	Paraguay	0.6	14	1.8	13	34.4	III
14	Nicaragua	0.6	15	1.4	10	39.3	III
15	Panama	0.4	17 -	1.1	8	41.4	II
16	Honduras	0.4	13	1.9	17	21.6	III
17	Costa Rica	0.4	16	1.2	12	34.8	III
(108)			(106)		(102)		
7A	FEDERATED CENTRAL AMERICA	3.9	4A	11.9	14A	32.2	III
	CONTINENTAL SYSTEM	89.9		191.5		47.0	II

a. Only continental nations are included, and among these, British Honduras, French Guiana, Guyana and Surinam have been excluded for a lack of comparable data in all variables. Country names which have been capitalized have federal forms of government while all others are governed by a central unitary system. "FEDERATED CENTRAL AMERICA" assumes that Guatemala, El Salvador, Nicaragua, Panama, Honduras and Costa Rica form a single federal system of government. "CONTINENTAL SYSTEM" includes only those nations given in the table.

b. SOURCE: Davis (A, 1969), Table A: 57. Figures are derived from official censuses, official estimates, or estimates of the Institute of International Studies at the University of California, Berkeley. Generally, most official definitions in Latin America define urban population as that population living within closely settled communities of 2,000 or more—with some minor additional inclusions. A few exceptions to this general rule include Colombia, Panama and Honduras which use 1,000 as the low-limit for definition.

c. SOURCE: Davis (A, 1969) Table A: 57.

d. Derived from data given by Davis (A, 1969) Table A for (3) and (4). Due to rounding of numbers in (3) and (4), the percentages as given in (5) are based on data before rounding.

e. Era of urbanization refers to the period in which each nation reached an urban level of 25% as follows: I (by 1920); II (between 1920-1960); III (still below 25% in 1960). Taken from Rabinovitz (B, 1969) and based on a classification from United Nations, Bureau of Social Affairs, Population Division (A, 1966a).

f. The classification "Multiple Metropoles (million+) 1970" refers to the fact that countries listed under this class all had two or more metropolitan cities in excess of 1,000,000 population in 1970. Nations included in class "Single Metropole (million+) 1970" had only one city of this size in 1970. Only one country, Ecuador, is classified in the group "Multiple Medium-Size Cities (250,000-1 million) 1970" which means that it contained more than one city in this range and none larger. The "Single Medium-Size City (250,000-1 million) 1970" class contains all those nations with one city of this size and none larger. Derived from Davis (A, 1969) Table E.

TABLE 1.5

Comparison of Ranking by Size of Urban Population in Selected Latin American Nations (1960) With Number and Population of Cities in Each Nation by Size Class (Estimated 1970)[a]

a (1) Rank by Size of Urban Pop.	(2) NATIONS	(7) Number of Cities in Each Nation by Size Class			(8) Population in City Classes with Ranking by Nation (millions)					
		(a) million+	(b) 250,000-million	(c) 100,000-250,000	(a) million+		(b) 250,000-million		(c) 100,000-250,000	
MULTIPLE METROPOLES (million+) 1970										
1	BRAZIL	6	15	15	1	22.0	1	6.8	1	2.9
2	MEXICO	3	6	14	3	5.9	4	2.4	2	2.4
4	Colombia	2	5	8	4	3.6	3	2.5	3	1.4
					(8)		(8)		(6)	
SINGLE METROPOLE (million+) 1970										
3	ARGENTINA	1	8	7	2	9.4	2	4.2	4	1.1
5	Chile	1	1	4	5	2.6	14	0.3	6	0.6
6	VENEZUELA	1	2	4	7	2.1	6	1.0	5	0.7
7	Peru	1	0	3	6	2.5	–	–	7	0.5
8	Uruguay	1	0	0	8	1.5	–	–	–	–
					(28)					
MULTIPLE MEDIUM-SIZED CITIES (250,000-1 million) 1970										
9	Ecuador	0	2	0	–	–	5	1.3	–	–
SINGLE MEDIUM-SIZED CITY (250,000-1 million) 1970										
10	Guatemala	0	1	0	–	–	7	0.8	–	–
11	El Salvador	0	1	1	–	–	12	0.4	8	0.1
12	Bolivia	0	1	1	–	–	8	0.5	9	0.1
13	Paraguay	0	1	0	–	–	9	0.4	–	–
14	Nicaragua	0	1	0	–	–	13	0.4	–	–
15	Panama	0	1	0	–	–	10	0.4	–	–
16	Honduras	0	1	0	–	–	15	0.3	–	–
17	Costa Rica	0	1	0	–	–	11	0.4	–	–
7A	FEDERATED CENTRAL AMERICA	0	6	1	–	–	2A	2.7	7A	0.1
	CONTINENTAL SYSTEM	16	47	57	–	49.6	–	22.0	–	9.8

a. Derived from Davis (A, 1969) Table E.

TABLE 1.6

Comparison of Ranking by Size of Urban Population in Selected
Latin American Nations (1960) With Total City (100,000+) Population,
Size of Largest City, and Percentage of Total City Population and
Total Urban Population in Largest City (1960)[a]

(1) Rank by Size of Urban Pop.	(2) NATIONS	(9) Total City (100,000+) Population (millions)		(10) Size of Largest City (millions)		(11) Percentage of Total City Population in Largest City		(12) Percentage of Total Urban Population in Largest City	
MULTIPLE METROPOLES (million+) 1970									
1	BRAZIL	1	18.1	2	4.7	1	25.4	1	14.8
2	MEXICO	3	6.5	3	2.8	3	43.5	2	16.0
4	Colombia	4	3.7	7	1.2	3	33.2	3	17.4
(7)		(8)		(12)		(6)		(6)	
SINGLE METROPOLE (million+) 1970									
3	ARGENTINA	2	10.9	1	7.0	6	64.5	14	52.2
5	Chile	5	2.5	4	1.9	7	77.9	9	37.8
6	VENEZUELA	6	2.2	6	1.3	5	59.4	5	27.9
7	Peru	7	1.6	5	1.5	8	92.2	7	33.7
8	Uruguay	8	1.0	8	1.0	9	100.0	15	53.7
(29)		(28)		(24)		(27)		(50)	
MULTIPLE MEDIUM-SIZED CITIES (250,000-1 million) 1970									
9	Ecuador	9	0.8	10	0.4	4	58.9	6	31.4
SINGLE MEDIUM-SIZED CITY (250,000-1 million) 1970									
10	Guatemala	10	0.5	9	0.5	10	100.0	11	40.6
11	El Salvador	15	0.2	15	0.2	11	100.0	4	23.9
12	Bolivia	11	0.4	11	0.4	12	100.0	12	50.7
13	Paraguay	12	0.3	12	0.3	13	100.0	13	51.6
14	Nicaragua	16	0.2	16	0.2	14	100.0	8	35.5
15	Panama	13	0.3	13	0.3	· 15	100.0	16	60.4
16	Honduras	17	0.2	17	0.2	16	100.0	10	37.8
17	Costa Rica	14	0.3	14	0.3	17	100.0	17	63.1
(108)		(108)		(107)		(108)		(91)	
7A	FEDERATED CENTRAL AMERICA	6A	1.9	9	0.5	—	25.0	—	12.1
	CONTINENTAL SYSTEM		49.6		7.0		15.4		7.8

a. Derived from Davis (A, 1969) Tables A and E.

raise the proportional urban level for better fit with a staged urban development pattern as posited in this typology. During the 1970s the port city of Guayaquil will become a metropolitan city of over one million and Ecuador will then be classified as a single metropole nation. Column 7 of Table 1.5 would suggest that greater emphasis, therefore, should be given to building up towns less than 100,000 so that a more balanced distribution of cities across the size classes would be ensured.

Finally, an examination of the Central American republics shows an amazing degree of parallelism with respect to urban population data, urban systems, and urban primacy with a few slight variations. Ranking within the group according to total urban population, total population, proportional urban level, and era of urbanization (Table 1.4, cols. 3-6) are almost totally congruent within their urban system hierarchy category. The principal variation is found in the case of Panama, which achieved a moderate level of urbanization earlier than the rest (see Figure 1.1).[4] El Salvador, too, is distinguished by the fact that it has one medium-sized and one small-sized city, whereas no other Central American nation has any city in the class 100,000-250,000 (Table 1.5, col. 7 and Table 1.6, col. 12). Guatemala, on the other hand, is differentiated by the estimated 1970 size of its capital city, which is almost twice as large as any other capital on the Isthmus. Panama and Costa Rica, too, had a rather substantial part of their total urban populations in their national capitals in 1960, 60.4 and 63.1% respectively (Table 1.6, col. 12), which indicates higher primacy in their urban systems relative to all other Central American countries where between 23.9 and 40.6% of the total urban populations were domiciled in the capital cities.

The principal interest in examining these countries, however, is presented when they are considered as a single federated nation. On this basis, such a nation would be classed with Ecuador as a multiple medium-sized cities nation in the urban systems hierarchy. By both total urban population and total population ranking, however (Table 1.4, cols. 1 and 4), they should be classed in the single metropole category. As Table 1.5, col. 7 indicates, however, a Federated Central America would contain only six medium-sized cities and a single small-sized city. In order to create "fit," then, with its category, such a federated nation would need to promote the development of a single center so that it could pass into the single metropole category which its total urban population and total population levels would suggest. Guatemala City is actually the only city (an estimated 770,000 in 1970) even remotely approximate to the metropolitan level of one million (Table 1.5, col. 8b).

Even if such a federated nation should achieve "fit" in the single metropole class, one outstanding fact would distinguish it from other nations in that category. This would be its relatively low proportional urban level (32.2%) in contrast with 62.4-72.0% for the others, excepting Peru with 40.9%. It, like Peru, could conceivably benefit by a directed attempt to step up the rate and level of urbanization. In this it might be more successful given that it has five medium-sized and one small city whereas Peru has only three small cities (Table 1.5, col. 7). There is close fit, however, between it and the single metropole category with respect to the size of its total city (100,000+) population which would rank a Federated Central America 6A after Venezuela (Table 1.6, col. 9).

TABLE 1.7

Comparison of Ranking by Size of Urban Population in Selected
Latin American Nations (1960) With Gross National Product (1967),
Per Capita Income (1961), Adelman-Morris Index of
Socioeconomic Development, and Dependency Ratio

(1) Rank by Size of Urban Pop.	(2) NATIONS	(13) Gross National Product Per Capita[a] 1967 (US$1960)		(14) Per Capita Income[b] 1961 (US$)		(15) Adelman-Morris Index[c]		(16) Dependency Ratio[d]	
MULTIPLE METROPOLES (million+) 1970									
1	BRAZIL	12	302	10	186	8	0.79	6	83.5
2	MEXICO	4	611	7	279	10	0.75	11	91.6
4	Colombia	9	331	8	222	13	0.66	7	84.2
(7)		(25)		(25)		(31)		(24)	
SINGLE METROPOLE (million+) 1970									
3	ARGENTINA	1	825	3	378	1	1.91	2	57.7
5	Chile	6	585	4	377	3	1.39	4	78.6
6	VENEZUELA	2	750	1	671	4	1.37	10	90.8
7	Peru	8	385	14	145	12	0.68	9	89.0
8	Uruguay	3	634	2	450	2	1.59	1	56.2
(29)		(20)		(24)		(22)		(26)	
MULTIPLE MEDIUM-SIZED CITIES (250,000-1 million) 1970									
9	Ecuador	14	283	15	143	14	0.54	13	93.8
SINGLE MEDIUM-SIZED CITY (250,000-1 million) 1970									
10	Guatemala	10	330	13	151	15	0.35	5	81.2
11	El Salvador	11	306	12	176	11	0.71	12	92.3
12	Bolivia	17	179	16	113	17	0.35	3	78.3
13	Paraguay	15	255	17	113	5	0.97	14	96.5
14	Nicaragua	13	295	9	213	6	0.88	17	104.9
15	Panama	5	603	5	367	7	0.84	8	88.0
16	Honduras	16	223	11	182	16	0.26	15	102.8
17	Costa Rica	7	500	6	291	9	0.78	16	103.3
(108)		(94)		(89)		(86)		(90)	

a. SOURCE: Sociedad Interamericana de Planificación (B, 1969b).

b. Derived from figures in United Nations (A, serial) 1968.

c. SOURCE: Adelman and Morris (A, 1967), Table IV-5: Grouping of Countries by Factor Scores on Factor Representing Level of Socioeconomic Development, p. 170.

d. Derived from population distribution by age groups in United Nations (A, serial), various years. Dependency ratio is equal to population in age group 0-14 plus that in group 65+, the sum of which is divided by population in age group 15-64 and multiplied by 100.

Socioeconomic Variables (Table 1.7)

One of the most obvious discrepancies in the relationship between the socioeconomic variables and ranking by size of urban population and location in the urban systems hierarchy is that, taken as a group, the single metropole nations and single medium-sized city nations lie on a socioeconomic level higher than might be expected by their position in the urban systems hierarchy continuum. The sum of the national rankings by size of urban population for the single metropole category, for example, is twenty-nine while the sums of rankings for the socioeconomic variables are twenty, twenty-four, twenty-two, and twenty-six. For the single medium-sized city category the sum of national rankings by size of urban population is one hundred eight and the summed rankings for the variables are ninety-four, eighty-nine, eighty-six, and ninety. On the other hand, the multiple metropoles class lies considerably below on the socioeconomic variables (twenty-five, twenty-five, thirty-one, twenty-four) in contrast to what its sum of rankings by size of urban population (seven) and location in the urban systems hierarchy would suggest it might be.

Within classes, a substantial number of variations is also noted. Mexico, for example, had a gross national product per capita (1967) almost double that of Brazil and Colombia (Table 1.7, col. 13), and it ranked slightly better in per capita income (1961). The Adelman-Morris Index of factor scores for level of socioeconomic development and dependency ratios for each country were relatively close among the multiple metropoles nations. Peru and Argentina, within the single metropole class, represent the primary variants within that group, with Argentina ranking higher in the socioeconomic variables than urban population size rank would suggest. Peru, on the other hand, showed an extremely weak socioeconomic position relative to the other members in the class with a gross national product per capita and a per capita income roughly half that of other class member nations. This was also reflected in the Adelman-Morris Index. These measures of economic level were no doubt partially affected by higher dependency ratios. This would mean, for example, that a greater proportion of the population was economically inactive and that government services, such as education, would have to be spread more thinly, a condition that would adversely affect economic development in the long run. Ecuador, too, in the multiple medium-sized classification, also places lower in the socioeconomic variables than its ranking by size of urban population would indicate appropriate.

Within the single medium-sized city category, Panama and Costa Rica are notable for their considerably higher socioeconomic levels when contrasted with their ranking by size of urban population. Bolivia, on the other hand, is somewhat lower.

The clearest conclusion that can be drawn from this cursory examination is that there is little apparent correlation between ranking by size of urban population and these socioeconomic variables. Within the single metropole class there is a fair degree of congruence and, excepting Panama and Costa Rica, this is true of the single medium-sized city class. In this latter case, the relatively stronger economic positions, as measured here, of Panama and Costa Rica, would favor them over Guatemala, for example, as the best location of the

TABLE 1.8

Comparison of Ranking by Size of Urban Population in Selected Latin American Nations (1960) With National Crude Birth Rate, Illiteracy of Population 15 Years and Over, Consumption Per Inhabitant of Newsprint, and Newspaper Circulation Per Thousand Persons

(1) Rank by Size of Urban Pop.	(2) NATIONS	(17) National Crude Birth Rate[a]		(18) Illiteracy of Population 15 Years and Over[b] (percentage)		(19) Consumption Per Inhabitant of Newsprint 1960[c]		(20) Newspaper Circulation Per 1,000 Inhabitants, 1960[d]	
MULTIPLE METROPOLES (million+) 1970									
1	BRAZIL	8	40.0	7	32	4	3.2	10	54
2	MEXICO	16	44.3	8	32	7	2.8	7	79
4	Colombia	6	35.7	11	35	8	2.4	9	56
(7)		(30)		(26)		(19)		(26)	
SINGLE METROPOLE (million+) 1970									
3	ARGENTINA	1	21.4	1	6	1	8.2	2	155
5	Chile	4	30.6	3	15	5	3.1	3	131
6	VENEZUELA	12	42.3	9	32	3	3.5	4	96
7	Peru	3	30.1	12	37	12	1.7	13	39
8	Uruguay	2	21.4	2	9	2	7.1	13	185
(29)		(22)		(27)		(23)		(23)	
MULTIPLE MEDIUM-SIZED CITIES (250,000-1 million) 1970									
9	Ecuador	11	41.5	10	32	10	2.0	11	54
SINGLE MEDIUM-SIZED CITY (250,000-1 million) 1970									
10	Guatemala	15	44.2	14	55	14	1.0	14	31
11	El Salvador	17	45.4	16	59	11	1.9	12	45
12	Bolivia	5	33.5	17	60	15	1.0	15	27
13	Paraguay	10	41.0	5	22	16	0.7	17	12
14	Nacaragua	13	43.0	13	47	13	1.2	8	66
15	Panama	9	40.0	6	25	9	2.2	6	89
16	Honduras	14	44.0	15	55	17	0.4	16	21
17	Costa Rica	7	38.1	4	15	6	3.1	5	92
(108)		(90)		(90)		(101)		(93)	

a. SOURCE: United Nations (A, serial) 1968. Crude birth rate is live births per 1,000 population.

b. SOURCE: Population Reference Bureau (A, 1968).

c. SOURCE: United Nations (A, 1966), Table 40: 544-551. Consumption of Newsprint per inhabitant, 1960 (kilograms).

d. SOURCE: United Nations (A, 1966), Table 38: 526-534. Daily General Interest Newspapers: Estimated Total Circulation per 1,000 Inhabitants.

metropolitan city for a Federated Central America—if it can be assumed that their better economic positions are associated with higher degrees of education, technological performance, entrepreneurship, and modernization. According to Table 1.8, cols. 18-20 (illiteracy of population fifteen years old and over, consumption per inhabitant of newsprint, and newspaper circulation per 1,000 inhabitants), Table 1.9, cols. 21, 22, and 24 (economically active male population in urban activities, professional-clerical, and services sector), and Table 1.10, cols. 25 and 27 (level of electoral participation and number of university students per 1,000 persons), these rough measures of a more modern urban economy and society all indicate a more favorable urban social, institutional, and social infrastructural basis for a dynamic regional metropolis than Guatemala.

Assuming a Federated Central America and given that Guatemala City will become metropolitan under the demographic and change forces present there anyway in this decade, some argument might be made for giving a strong push to the development of San Jose or Panama City as secondary metropolitan centers for the region. Since Panama and Guatemala (plus dynamic El Salvador) lie at the extreme ends spatially of a potential federation, the polar positions, competition, and intervening flows of commerce between two major population centers could possibly help to create a corridor of development that would gradually bring economic growth to the lesser-developed intervening subregions. Free population flow to these centers from the entire region would be an essential ingredient of this policy.

Social and Communication Variables (Table 1.8)

Much the same pattern already noted among the socioeconomic variables is also present in the social and communications variables. The multiple metropole group of nations rate lower in these variables when their rankings are contrasted with their rankings by size of urban population, while the single metropole and single medium-sized city nations rate somewhat higher. Given that the national crude birth rates are especially high (33.5 to 45.4), it appears obvious that Brazil, Mexico, Colombia, Venezuela, Ecuador, and all the single medium-sized city nations can expect substantial net additions (relatively) to their national populations, much of which will come to be urbanized in the next half-century. This is especially true in Central America, where the proportional rural level varies between 60.7 and 78.4% with substantial opportunities, consequently, for major rural-urban migration flows based on high birth rates and a present low urban to rural ratio.

Urban Economy and Urban Services (Table 1.9)

The proportion of the economically active male population engaged in urban activities, and the professional-clerical, manufacturing-construction, and services sectors has been used in an attempt to make a rough comparison among the countries and by category with respect to the urban economy and urban

TABLE 1.9

Comparison of Ranking by Size of Urban Population in Selected Latin American Nations (1960) With Percentage of Economically Active Male Population in Urban Activities, Professional-Clerical Activities, Manufacturing-Construction, and the Services Sector

(1) Rank by Size of Urban Pop.	(2) NATIONS	(21) Urban Activities[a] (percentage)		(22) Professional-Clerical[b] (percentage)		(23) Manufacturing-Construction[c] (percentage)		(24) Services Sector[d] (percentage)	
MULTIPLE METROPOLES (million+) 1970									
1	BRAZIL	12	32.0	10	7.8	15	12.3	9	19.7
2	MEXICO	7	38.9	7	8.9	5	18.3	8	20.6
4	Colombia	13	31.5	5	9.9	12	14.2	12	17.3
(7)		(32)		(22)		(32)		(29)	
SINGLE METROPOLE (million+) 1970									
3	ARGENTINA	2	63.8	2	n.a.	3	26.3	2	37.5
5	Chile	3	54.2	3	16.3	4	24.9	4	29.3
6	VENEZUELA	4	53.6	4	10.1	6	17.7	3	35.9
7	Peru	8	38.5	11	7.6	8	16.3	6	22.2
8	Uruguay	1	68.9	1	17.0	2	26.7	1	42.2
(29)		(18)		(21)		(23)		(16)	
MULTIPLE MEDIUM-SIZED CITIES (250,000-1 million) 1970									
9	Ecuador	11	33.4	13	5.3	9	15.8	11	17.6
SINGLE MEDIUM-SIZED CITY (250,000-1 million) 1970									
10	Guatemala	16	n.a.	15	3.8	16	n.a.	16	n.a.
11	El Salvador	14	28.0	14	4.6	10	15.4	15	12.6
12	Bolivia	6	39.7	16	n.a.	1	26.8	14	12.9
13	Paraguay	10	34.0	6	9.2	11	15.4	10	18.6
14	Nicaragua	15	28.0	12	5.4	13	14.2	13	13.8
15	Panama	9	34.5	9	8.0	14	12.6	7	21.9
16	Honduras	17	19.2	17	n.a.	17	8.6	17	10.6
17	Costa Rica	5	40.6	8	8.6	7	17.4	5	23.2
(108)		(87)		(97)		(89)		(97)	

a. SOURCE: United Nations (A, 1967), Table 44: 484-498. Urban activities category includes manufacturing industries; construction; electricity, gas, water and sanitary services; commerce; transport, storage and communications; and other services. This category groups columns (23) and (24). Data derive from 1950 for Bolivia and Paraguay; 1951 for Colombia; 1960 for Argentina, Brazil, Chile, Mexico and Panama; 1961 for El Salvador, Honduras, Peru and Venezuela; 1962 for Ecuador; and 1963 for Costa Rica, Nicaragua and Uruguay.

b. SOURCE: United Nations (A, 1967), Table 45: 499-512. Professional-clerical category includes professional, technical, administrative, managerial and clerical. Data derive from 1950 for Brazil, Guatemala, Panama and Paraguay; 1951 for Colombia; 1952 for Chile; 1960 for Mexico; 1961 for El Salvador, Peru and Venezuela; 1962 for Ecuador; 1963 for Costa Rica, Nicaragua and Uruguay.

c. SOURCE: United Nations (A, 1967), Table 44: 484-498. Manufacturing-construction category includes manufacturing industries and construction. Year of data is as given in note (a).

d. SOURCE: United Nations (A, 1967), Table 44: 484-498. Services sector category includes electricity, gas, water and sanitary services; commerce; transport, storage, and communications; and other services. Year of data is as given in note (a).

services. Column 23 in Table 1.9, "manufacturing-construction," includes those employed in manufacturing and construction industries which are considered here to be urban goods production activities. Column 24, "services sector," includes all males actively engaged in electricity, gas, water, and sanitary services; commerce; transportation, storage, and communications; and other services. This would yield some rough measure of the scale of urban services on a national basis. Column 21 is the combined total of columns 23 and 24. Column 22 presents a fair impression of the level of urban leadership and supporting staff, as it includes all males in the professional, technical, administration, and clerical categories who are actively employed.

Again, it can be appreciated that the multiple metropoles category is less favored in the summation of rankings for the urban economy and services variables when contrasted with the summed rankings based on size of urban population—i.e., thirty-two, twenty-two, thirty-two and twenty-nine versus seven. Brazil shows the greatest variation in this respect, with Colombia a close second. Furthermore, as with national socioeconomic variables, the categories "single metropole" and "single medium-sized city" generally are slightly favored in the summation of the rankings for these variables when contrasted with their summed rankings by size of urban population.

Peru, within the single metropole category, shows least congruence with its class members as it has generally in most other variables. The percentage of economically active males in all urban activities (38.5) is almost exactly equal to its proportional urban level (40.9). This is not the case for Brazil, Mexico, and Colombia. Although they have proportional urban levels of 45.0, 50.7 and 46.3%, respectively, they have much lower percentages of all economically active males employed in urban activities (32.0, 38.9, and 31.5%). Whether this actually represents a poorer position of urban economies and services with respect to actual urbanized levels or it reflects the possibility that their definitions of urban actually include a good many localities which depend upon agriculture for their livelihood is uncertain. In the latter case the rather moderate proportional urban level would be even smaller if these localities were excluded from the urban sector.

Political Development and Government Services (Table 1.10)

Generally speaking, the category of multiple metropoles rates substantially lower, as measured by the sum of rankings of the dependent variables of electoral participation level, number of university students per 1,000 population, and number of inhabitants per hospital bed (i.e., thirty-one, thirty-six and thirty-two) when contrasted with the sum of their rankings by size of urban population (seven). There is close congruence, actually, between degree of budgetary decentralization (col. 26) and rankings by size of urban population. Ranking for budgetary decentralization was based on the assumption that, as size of urban population increases and as a nation comes to have more and larger metropolitan and medium-sized cities, there will be greater necessity for a central government to share the responsibilities for urban development with local government, a fact which would be reflected in budgetary allocations to the cities.

TABLE 1.10

Comparison of Ranking by Size of Urban Population in Selected Latin American Nations (1960) With Level of Electoral Participation, Level of Regional-Local Government Expenditures, Number of University Students Per Thousand Inhabitants, and Inhabitants Per Hospital Bed

(1) Rank by Size of Urban Pop.	(2) NATIONS	(25) Level of Electoral Participation[a] (ca. 1960) (percentage)		(26) Level of Regional-Local Government Expenditures[b] (percentage)		(27) Number of University Students per 1,000 Persons[c]		(28) Number of Inhabitants per Hospital Bed[d]	
MULTIPLE METROPOLES (million+) 1970									
1	BRAZIL	9	19.1	1	42.0	11	1.2	8	350
2	MEXICO	7	23.0	8	9.5	13	0.9	17	590
4	Colombia	15	9.8	3	29.4	12	1.0	7	330
(7)		(31)		(12)		(36)		(32)	
SINGLE METROPOLE (million+) 1970									
3	ARGENTINA	2	44.8	2	31.1	1	7.7	1	170
5	Chile	10	17.8	16	2.5	3	3.9	4	260
6	VENEZUELA	3	43.1	6	12.9	9	1.3	6	300
7	Peru	14	12.3	11	4.4	7	1.8	13	460
8	Uruguay	1	57.9	4	n.a.	2	5.2	2	180
(29)		(30)		(39)		(22)		(26)	
MULTIPLE MEDIUM-SIZED CITIES (250,000-1 million) 1970									
9	Ecuador	12	14.4	5	19.0	8	1.4	15	520
SINGLE MEDIUM-SIZED CITY (250,000-1 million) 1970									
10	Guatemala	13	13.5	7	10.3	17	0.1	9	420
11	El Salvador	11	16.0	13	3.2	16	0.3	10	420
12	Bolivia	16	4.4	17	2.2	6	2.0	14	480
13	Paraguay	17	n.a.	14	n.a.	10	1.3	12	440
14	Nicaragua	4	30.6	10	4.8	14	0.7	11	420
15	Panama	6	25.0	15	n.a.	5	2.6	5	280
16	Honduras	8	19.2	9	9.5	15	0.7	16	550
17	Costa Rica	5	28.6	12	4.4	4	3.9	3	220
(108)		(80)		(97)		(87)		(80)	

a. SOURCE: Labelle and Estrada (B, 1963) as given by Rabinovitz (B, 1969: 117). Level of electoral participation is the percentage of total population voting.

b. SOURCE: Stöhr (B, 1969). Level of regional-local government expenditures is the percentage of total government expenditures of all levels expended by governments below the central (national) level. As such, it measures budgetary centralist tendency.

c. SOURCE: Germani (B, 1965).

d. SOURCE: United Nations (A, 1967), Table 17: 206-213.

Since two of these countries, Brazil and Mexico, are constituted as federal systems, it is not too surprising that this group should rank relatively high in the decentralization of government budgets. What is surprising is the degree of budgetary centralization actually present in Mexico. Data for 1958 indicates that the central government spent 90.5% of all public expenditures in that year while state governments disbursed 7.1%, and the municipalities struggled along with 2.4% (Stöhr, B, 1969). Fiscally, at least, it presents a condition of budgetary centralization no different with respect to the municipalities than practically all the nations with a unitary form of government.

It might not be inappropriate to suggest, at least tentatively, that a national urban policy scheme in Mexico include the assignment to the municipalities of a larger proportion of the total fiscal resources of government. As a nation with an extensive urban network of six metropolitan cities, fifteen medium-sized (250,000 to 1 million), and fifteen small-sized (100,000 to 250,000) cities in 1970, it seems unbalanced fiscally, to say the least, when they account for as little as 2.4% of all government expenditures. An examination of the economic efficiency and effectiveness of federally directed and implemented programs in the urban sector in Mexico and its alternatives would make an interesting analysis in view of the foregoing. Perhaps the present system is efficient and effective, or more so than alternative patterns—especially where urban development projects are planned and implemented by decentralized offices of the central government.

Finally, with regard to this category, it is also surprising, in view of the general pattern throughout Latin America, that municipalities in Colombia, which has a unitary form of government, had access to and disbursed 12.0% of all public expenditures.

As demonstrated previously and almost consistently, Peru is the principal variant nation in the single metropole category. It rates lower on all the variables (excepting number of university students per 1,000 population) when compared with its ranking by size of urban population and with class members. Generally throughout, then, Peru has been shown to be most in need, perhaps, of major social and economic improvement relative to the size of its urban population than all other nations. Uruguay, in contrast, ranks very much higher on the political development and government services variables (one, four, two and two) than its rank by size of urban population (eight).

Finally, Panama and Costa Rica, among the Central American nations, rank substantially higher on all variables excepting budgetary decentralization, than they do on their ranking by size of urban population and in comparison with other class members.

Concluding Comments and a Proposal for the Creation of National Urban Systems Planning Units

The presentation of a typology of selected Latin American nations within the idea of an urban systems hierarchy has been used primarily as a device to expose some of the possible national urban policy questions. Any actual conclusions which have been drawn from this device are only suggestive. More concrete policies should depend upon much more precise and extensive analysis involving many more socioeconomic variables. Even in this cursory treatment, however, it has been possible to illustrate generally, in the opening essay, many of the more probing and specific policy questions which are exposed in the remainder of the volume.

Touched on lightly have been Central American federation and the integration of separate national urban systems and economies into one, with the resultant question of where urban development should be encouraged within an urban systems and regional development strategy. Other policy questions have included the use of existing urban networks as the spine and catalyst for regional development; the colonization and settlement of uninhabited or sparsely settled areas for extending the urban system and for absorbing the growth of a vastly enlarged urban population into a larger urban system during the next forty years; the question of budgetary centralization and efficiency when dealing with the urban sector (is it efficient and effective or not?); discrepancies between national ranking in the size of urban population and ranking for various socioeconomic and political variables and the possible need for achieving greater congruence between the two; better balance within nations in the distribution of cities among various city size classes and the possible need to promote the development of certain classes of towns;[5] and the like.

The use of the urban system hierarchy as a device has served, therefore, to raise many potential policy questions; many more could be raised either here or through a deepening of the analysis. Statements about policy in particular national cases have been made more as an exercise in demonstrating the type of policy questions which may be relevant at the national level. This emphasis on national urban policies, too, must be complemented by the full recognition of the impact of a half-billion people on urban Latin America by the year 2000. To doubt that preoccupation about the guidance of this phenomenon is a matter of national concern in this still incipient stage of the new urban era is to ignore the social and political tinder of an urban population some ten times greater than that of 1950 a mere half-century later. The patterns of national urban networks, of the relative importance of different urban centers, and of utilized or unutilized national spaces is being engraved more deeply into the economic, social, and political structures of national life each day. Furthermore, the fine net of functional relationships is extraordinarily difficult to change once the absolute size of societal elements becomes quite large and fixed by tradition and location. In essence, explicit policy, serious guidance, and concrete action are increasingly imperative. The essays by Pedersen-Stöhr, Friedmann, Daland, and Delgado, particularly, illuminate some of these more important policy areas. Whether social scientists can actually provide the kinds of concrete, careful analysis and the answers useful to urban policy in many of these areas soon enough is questionable. In some cases only theoretical posturing and educated intuition from the academic world will guide government. The Spanish Crown launched the culture of the peninsula and the power of its governmental institutions into the American hemisphere three centuries ago for the purposes of urban development and national glory with less guidance from its universities. But, it did have a plan and a set of policies, and it was aware of the future.

A situation of greater awareness on the part of governments to the implications of urban change on a national scale is perhaps one of the most critical concerns of the present time. Awareness of the potential for altering the future favorably, of course, is insufficient. It must be followed, as it was in the sixteenth century, with concerted policy and directed government intervention in conformity with those policies and explicitly formulated urban objectives on a par at least equal to other national concerns. In an epoch when nations and their urban networks are more evidently merging as one and the same basic structure than ever before, it seems rather illogical to continue to ignore the structural-functional fusion of the two. When a nation is ninety percent or more urban, and the foods production sector (formerly referred to as the rural-agricultural sector) is merely one of the technological activities of the urban-national sector, mechanisms and structures for the guidance of the urban system would appear appropriate. Some Latin American nations could reach that situation within a half-century.

It may not be untimely, then, to begin to suggest that future national planning offices there will have planning sections for national urban systems on an equal footing with global economic planning. And, just as sectoral plans must be examined and adjusted for their impact on global economic objectives, so will they be analyzed for their impact on the national urban structure. Furthermore, national urban objectives and policies will, themselves, set some of the priorities of sectoral plans much as global economic planning objectives now do. Finally, global economic planning and national urban systems planning will be made more congruent and, on occasions, economic planning objectives may have to be diminished in their importance so that urban objectives can be met in semi-crisis and crisis conditions.

Conscious efforts might well be made now to create such a planning section in certain Latin American countries. Brazil, for example, would appear to be one particularly good candidate, due to the combined importance of an extensive existing network, a relatively large rural population yet to be urbanized, and the imminent colonization of the interior on a more extensive scale than heretofore through the penetration of the interior with modern highways. Other nations, for varied reasons, include Uruguay, Venezuela, Peru, Mexico, Colombia, and Argentina.

The proposal of a national urban systems planning body equal in importance to global economic planning is made for the same basic reasons that have created global economic planning. All the economic sectors function within a single system with important functional links and overlaps, and a proper understanding of any one sector involves a better understanding of the whole (global) system. This is also true of the various subsectors within the complete urban system. Housing, urban utility systems, urban economic activities, education, health, transportation, communications, the supply and flow of people, government—all form part of a national urban system, and the best understanding of any one subsector ultimately depends upon knowledge about the others *within the complete (global) system of urban places.* Agriculture as an economic sector and the constituent elements of institutions, physical infrastructure, location, inputs, and so forth associated with it have had special recognition in national government planning in the majority of Latin American nations for several decades. Given the relative importance (and this is growing) of the urban sector, it is astounding that at least equal consideration has not been given to it as a specialized national policy area—with an appropriate institutional structure dealing with the national issues, not with projects at the local level with thought only of their local implications.

It may be noted that regional planning was not mentioned. This omission was not without intent. Basically, it is suggested that the urban system is the principal organizer and catalyst for regional development in urban societies. The pampas of Argentina and Uruguay, for example, may continue indefinitely as extensively used agricultural areas for the production of beef. (In the beginning of their "exploitation" it was urban England which largely induced this form of development.) In contrast, if one were to create by decree, by government investment, and by government-directed private sector activity a metropolitan zone in the midst of this vast area, this city would organize the surrounding pampa. It would do it largely without government intervention (if capital were available) and on a scale that traditional regional development planning would find inconceivable—provided soil, climate, and topographic conditions were favorable. This is the magic and vision of Brasilia and Ciudad de Guayana. Just as the economic complexity and staged development of a nation depend upon the increasing size of its urban population to help in the organization of the economy, so does regional development often depend on the growth of important urban places within each region as the catalyst for regionally staged development. To attempt regional development and regional development planning seriously while permitting the continued concentration of net population growth to occur in one or two geographic points outside the region is to ignore one of the prime movers of regional growth and change. This was one of the functions of cities which the Spanish understood only too well, and they made every effort to ensure a regional distribution of their "town system," not alone for the pacification of the indigenous populations.

Regional development planning, therefore, might well be made an integral part of the national urban systems planning body with primary emphasis still remaining on the urban network. One of the shortcomings of economic planning has been that, in the pursuit of easily quantified economic objectives, too little attention has been given to other elements of a complete social structure and of objectives related to them. A national urban systems planning function would serve, in this sense, much more broadly, and it would set forth and aim for the attainment of objectives other than those of the economy—although posing it in this fashion would not prevent the inclusion of economic objectives. Accordingly, the global economic planning body would, also, have a division dealing with the regional implications of global-sectoral planning, as well as serving to monitor regional growth. Perhaps both regional divisions might be organized technically as one. As one division guidance and demands on its services would come from both global economic and urban systems planning bodies, much as any private service organization serves several clients and manages to economize in the use of its inputs thereby and to optimize the use of the knowledge and broader understanding it gains by serving more than one master. In this sense, its function would be less in setting objectives than it would be in serving as a technical arm.

Can urban societies actually manage themselves efficiently, effectively, and provide environments for the human organism, physically and psychologically, with a modicum of satisfaction and enjoyment in the living out of life *without* planning and guidance on the national level? What is the "minimum modicum" to which a society can sink before complete social chaos renders the social institutions incapable of functioning? Can the optimism of sixteenth-century Spain with respect to an urban society be revived? If so, will that optimism drive men to act on their faith?

This chapter was initiated with a brief description of the current and expected meteoric unfolding of the urbanization process in Latin America to the year 2000, and the scale of this change was presented as a challenge to government policy makers and social scientists. This was followed by a general exposé of possible national urban policy areas through the artificial device of an urban systems hierarchy. It has ended on a proposal for the creation of a new national planning function within an urban systems planning group parallel and equal to global economic planning. Three elements have been shown to be present now with respect to an urban society in Latin America—a new urban era, a challenge, and a raison d'être of a national urban policy. One important element is lacking: a new planning structure adequate to the era and the challenge and one capable of developing the policies. If this structure is established, given political support and the power to direct and guide the present toward the future, Latin America's new urban era will contain, in this one sense at least, the principle of centrally guided direction which accompanied the Spanish colonial urban era. An opportunity was once offered to Isabella and the immediate occupants of the Spanish throne after her; another opportunity of staggering proportions in contrast is now being exposed. How will the future judge the evolving present? Was it seized forcefully and ably or fumbled and lost?

NOTES

1. "Urbanization" is used throughout this chapter in the stricter etymological sense of the suffix "-tion" to indicate action or a process involved with action. In the present case this process is associated with the root word "urbanize" which means "to cause to be, or to become, urban." This is taken to mean the "urbanization" of the rural immigrant by his incorporation physically and culturally to an urban place. *Urban growth,* as a process implying the mere numerical increase of urban population, although often used interchangeably with urbanization, should probably be reserved to refer only to the change process involving a numerical increase of population in geographic units which are already totally urban, such as the individual city.

A metropolitan area, however, might be said to be still undergoing the process of urbanization so long as there remained an agricultural population within its limits which was being "urbanized." Even this becomes difficult definitionally, however, when the life style associated with the population deriving its income from agriculture is basically urban. It might be appropriate, actually, to refer to the "urbanization" of a population still engaged in agricultural pursuits as a second form of urbanization to be distinguished from the first, where the rural immigrant is "urbanized" within the city and engaged in urban activities. In any event, the distinction in advanced economies of agricultural as a rural pursuit is fast giving way to the concept of agriculture as an urban pursuit—managerially, technologically, financially, and even socially.

In sum, urbanization, derived from its root word and suffix, means "the process of causing to be, or to become, urban." It is a meaning which is dynamic rather than static, although it is not infrequently used for a static condition, or level. More appropriately, the static condition, or the process at any one time, might better be referred to as *urban level, urbanized level* or *level of urbanization.* Kingsley Davis (A, 1965), for example, has defined urbanization as "the proportion of the total population concentrated in urban settlements, or else a rise in this proportion." In this he refers to urbanization first as a static condition, the level at any given time, and, secondly, as a changing, dynamic process. *Urbanism,* too, is occasionally used interchangeably with urbanization, but the concept of urbanism, deriving from Louis Wirth's work, is basically a qualitative concept which, because of its elusive and definitionally extended nature and due to its difficult application cross-culturally, has not led to any rigorous quantitative work. Urbanization, in its demographic meaning, on the other hand, yields readily to quantitative, empirical analysis.

Specifically speaking, then, *urbanization* is used here in a demographic (not spatial or strictly cultural) sense to denote the process resulting in a change (rise) in the urban (urbanized) level of the population within a given population unit. The urban (or urbanized) level or level of urbanization refers to the static condition at which the process of urbanization may be found at any given time. It is measured as an absolute numerical condition or as a proportional (percentage or ratio) relationship of the urban to total population. The first definition of urban level, as absolute numerical size, is merely the total urban (urbanized) population included in the given definition of urban in a given population unit. It is usually given as the urban population level (or size) in this essay. The second definition of urban level, the proportional relationship of the urban to total population, is referred to as the proportional urban level. Although it could be given as a ratio, it is almost exclusively percentage.

An explanation of urbanization as a process could be made exclusively in descriptive, nonquantitative terms, but as soon as quantification is desired, it must be measured through rates of urbanization. There are two principal ones which derive from the separate definitions of urban level given beforehand. The first rate of urbanization is the *percentage increase in the urban population level* (or size) over a given period of time. The second rate is the *percentage increase in the proportional urban level,* also expressed over a given time span. Whenever a given population unit becomes totally urbanized, any further increase could only be expressed as a percentage increase in the urban population level, or more strictly, as the *rate of urban growth* (change in the absolute population size expressed as percentage).

A final measure of urbanization would be one which indicated whether there was a decreasing or increasing tendency to urbanize. This is referred to as the *change in the rate of urbanization* which, again, is more commonly expressed by two measures deriving from the separate definitions of urban level. The first is the *change in the rate of the increase of the urban population level.* This expresses the actual tendency of the rate of urbanization (increase in the urban population level) to accelerate or decelerate when two or more adjacent time spans are compared. The second is the *change in the rate of the increase of the proportional urban level.* This denotes the actual tendency of the rate of urbanization (proportional urban level) to accelerate or decelerate when two or more adjacent time spans are compared.

These terms can be illustrated by the following artificial example:

Terms	Point in Time		
	1900	1910	1920
1. *Urbanization:* Process denoting change in urban levels.			
2. *Urban level* (or level of urbanization): Static condition.			
a. *Urban population level* (absolute numerical size)	50,000	80,000	160,000
b. *Proportional urban level* (percentage or ratio of total population which is defined as urban)	10%	20%	35%
3. *Net addition to urban population level*	-	30,000	80,000
4. *Rate of urbanization* (change in urban level over time)			
a. *Percentage increase in urban population level* (when totally urbanized, this becomes *rate of urban growth*)	-	60%	100%
b. *Percentage increase in proportional urban level* (when totally urbanized, this rate no longer applies)	-	100%	75%
5. *Change in the rate of urbanization*			
a. *Change in the rate of increase of the urban population level* (when totally urbanized, this becomes *change in the rate of urban growth*)	-	-	66.7%
b. *Change in the rate of increase of the proportional urban level* (when totally urbanized, this measure no longer applies)	-	-	-25%

The foregoing has been offered in order to clarify usage, at least for the purposes of this essay. It emphasizes, particularly, the use of the word "urbanization" as a dynamic process and complements the process with measures of change, rates of urbanization. The static condition is replaced by "urban level," "urbanized level," or "level of urbanization." Additional measures, or the rates of change in the rates of urbanization, are offered to illustrate whether urbanization is accelerating or decelerating.

2. A recent monograph by Francis Violich (B, forthcoming) gives a review in depth of the formation and growth of metropolitan areas and urbanization in Latin America and of critical metropolitan problems. It also presents metropolitan studies of Santiago, Bogotá, Caracas, and São Paulo, and advances an approach to planning for metropolitan growth in Latin America.

3. This is similar to the urbanization process experienced in the United States between 1900 and 1920 at the same urban level. In 1900 the proportional urban level was 39.7% (population in localities of 2,500 or more). This had risen to 50.9% by 1920. In 1940, the proportion of population in localities of 2,500 or more 55.6% (4.7% above 1920), but it increased 14 percentage points by 1960 to a level of 69.6%.

4. It should be noted that column 5 of Table 1.4 and Figure 1.1 do not correspond, since Figure 1.1 is based upon an urban definition which includes only localities of 20,000 or more, while Table 1.4 data are based on national definitions of urban which includes localities between 1,000 to 2,000 and above.

5. See Parviz S. Towfighi (B, 1970) for a recent study on the strategy of concentrated decentralization for regional growth which is specific to the Venezuelan and Italian cases.

REFERENCES

A. Urbanization: General

ADELMAN, I. and C. T. MORRIS (1967) Society, Politics and Economic Development. Baltimore: Johns Hopkins Univ. Press.

ANDERSON, N. (1963) "Aspects of urbanism and urbanization." International J. of Comparative Sociology 4: 101-106.

ARRIAGA, E. E. (1970) "A new approach to the measurements of urbanization." Economic Development and Cultural Change 18 (January): 206-218.

AXELROD, M. (1956) "Urban structure and social participation." Amer. Soc. Rev. 21 (February): 14-18.

BREESE, G. (1969a) Modernization and Urbanization: Existing and Potential Relationships in the "Third World." Exchange Bibliography 70. Monticello, Ill.: Council of Planning Librarians.

--- [ed.] (1969b) The City in Newly Developing Countries. Englewood Cliffs, N.J.: Prentice-Hall.

--- (1966) Urbanization in Newly Developing Countries. Englewood Cliffs, N.J.: Prentice-Hall.

DASGUPTA, P. S. (1969) "On the concept of optimum population." Review of Economic Studies (July).

DAVIS, K. (1969) World Urbanization, 1950-1970. Vol. I: Basic Data for Cities, Countries, and Regions. Population Monograph Series. Berkeley: University of California, Institute of International Studies.

--- (1965) "The urbanization of the human population." Scientific American 213 (September): 41-53. (Republished as Chapter 1 in Cities. New York: Alfred A. Knopf.)

--- and H. H. GOLDEN (1954) "Urbanization and the development of pre-industrial areas." Economic Development and Cultural Change 3 (October): 6-26. (Reprinted in 1957 in Hatt and Reiss [eds.] Cities and Society. Glencoe, Ill.: Free Press. Concludes that there is an "appropriate" rate of urbanization in relation to industrialization.)

DUNCAN, O. D. (1957) "The measurement of population distribution." Population Studies 21 (July): 27-45.

GIBBS, JACK P. (1966) "Measures of urbanization." Social Forces 45 (December): 170-177.

GREER, S., D. L. McELRATH, D. W. MINAR, and P. ORLEANS [eds.] (1968) The New Urbanization. New York: St. Martin's Press.

HAUSER, P. M. (1965) "Urbanization: an overview," pp. 1-47 in P. M. Hauser and L. F. Schnore (eds.) The Study of Urbanization. New York: John Wiley.

--- [ed.] (1955) Special Issue: "World Urbanism." Amer. J. of Sociology 60 (March).

KAHL, J. A. (1959) "Some social concomitants of industrialization and urbanization." Human Organization 18 (Summer): 53-74.

KAMERSCHEN, D. R. (1969) "Further analysis of overurbanization." Economic Development and Cultural Change 17 (January): 235-253.

LAMPARD, E. E. (1965) "Historical aspects of urbanization," pp. 519-554 in P. M. Hauser and L. F. Schnore (eds.) The Study of Urbanization. New York: John Wiley.

--- (1963) "Urbanization and social change," pp. 225-247 in O. Handlin and J. Burchard (eds.) The Historian and the City. Cambridge, Mass.: MIT Press and Harvard Univ. Press.

LASUEN, J. R. (n.d.) Urbanization and Development.

LEE, R. H. (1955) The City: Urbanism and Urbanization in Major World Regions. Philadelphia: J. B. Lippincott.

LUBOVE, R. (1967) "The urbanization process: an approach to historical research." J. of the Amer. Institute of Planners 33 (January): 33-38.

MACURA, M. (1961) "The influence of the definition of the urban place on the size of the urban population," pp. 21-31 in J. P. Gibbs (ed.) Urban Research Methods. Princeton, N.J.: D. Van Nostrand.

MEADOWS, P. and E. H. MIZRUCHI [eds.] (1969) Urbanism, Urbanization and Change: Comparative Perspectives. Reading, Mass.: Addison-Wesley.

MEHTA, A. (1967) "The social impact of urbanization as a universal process," pp. 25-34 in Urban Development: Its Implications for Social Welfare. New York: Columbia Univ. Press.

Population Reference Bureau (1968) World Population Data Sheet–1968. Washington, D.C.

REISS, A. J. Jr. (1964) "Urbanization," p. 738 in Julius Gould and William L. Kolb (eds.) A Dictionary of the Social Sciences. New York: Free Press.

REISSMANN, L. (1965) "Urbanism and urbanization," pp. 37-38 in Julius Gould (ed.) Penguin Survey of the Social Sciences 1965. Hammondsworth, England: Penguin Books.

——— (1964) "Urbanization: a typology of change," pp. 212-236 in The Urban Process. New York: Macmillan.

SCHNORE, L. F. (1964) "Urbanization and economic development: a demographic contribution." Amer. J. of Economics and Sociology 23 (January): 37-48.

——— (1963) "Some correlations of urban size: a replication." Amer. J. of Sociology 62 (September): 185-193.

SJOBERG, G. (1965) "Cities in developing and in industrializing societies," pp. 213-263 in P. M. Hauser and L. Schnore (eds.) The Study of Urbanization. New York: John Wiley.

SOVANI, N. V. (1964) "The analysis of 'over-urbanization.'" Economic Development and Cultural Change 12 (January): 113-122.

TILLY, C. (1967) "The state of urbanization: review article." Comparative Studies in Society and History 10 (October): 100-113.

TISDALE, H. (1942) "The process of urbanization." Social Forces 20 (March): 311-316.

TRIVEDI, H. R. (1969) "The 'semi-urban pocket' as concept and reality in India." Human Organization 28 (Spring): 72-77.

United Nations (1967) Compendium of Social Statistics 1967. New York.

——— (1966) Statistical Yearbook 1965. New York.

——— (1963) Monthly Bulletin of Statistics (May). New York.

——— (serial) Demographic Yearbook. New York.

——— (n.d.) World Survey of Urban and Rural Population Growth. New York.

——— Bureau of Social Affairs, Population Division (1966a) "Urbanization and economic and social change." Presented at the Inter-Regional Seminar on Development Policies and Planning in Relation to Urbanization, University of Pittsburgh, October 24-November 17. New York.

——— (1966b) "World urbanization trends, 1920-1960. An interim report on work in progress," Working Paper 6, Inter-Regional Seminar on Development Policies and Planning in Relation to Urbanization, University of Pittsburgh, October 24-November 17. New York.

United Nations. Secretary-General (1969) Housing, Building and Planning in the Second Development Decade. New York.

WESTPHALEN, J. (1969) "Population explosion and development policy." Inter-economics (April): 112-117.

WIRTH, L. (1938) "Urbanism as a way of life." Amer. J. of Sociology (July): 1-24. (Reprinted in 1957 in Hatt and Reiss [eds.] Cities and Society. Glencoe, Ill.: Free Press.)

ZELINSKY, W. (1966) "The geographer and his crowding world: cautionary notes toward the study of population pressure in the 'developing lands.'" Revista Geográfica 65 (December): 7-28.

B. Urbanization in Latin America

ANDRADE LLERAS, G. (1968) "El proceso de urbanización en Latinoamérica," pp. 26-49 in Asociación Colombiana de Facultades de Medicina. Urbanización y Marginalidad. Bogotá.

BAZZANELLA, W. (1960) Problemas de Urbanização na América Latina: Fontes bibliográficas. Rio de Janeiro: Centro Latino-Americano de Pesquisas em Ciência Sociais.

BEALS, R. L. (1953) "Urbanism, urbanization and acculturation," pp. 172 ff. in O. E. Leonard and C. P. Loomis (eds.) Readings in Latin American Social Organization and Institutions. East Lansing, Michigan.

BEYER, G. H. (1967) "Resumé: themes and issues," pp. 302-335 in G. H. Beyer (ed.) The Urban Explosion in Latin America. Ithaca, N.Y.: Cornell Univ. Press.

BROWNING, H. L. (1967) "The demography of the city," in G. H. Beyer (ed.) The Urban Explosion in Latin America. Ithaca, N.Y.: Cornell Univ. Press.

––– (1958) "Recent trends in Latin American urbanization." Annals of the Amer. Academy of Pol. and Social Sci. 316 (March): 117 ff.

CALDERON, L., A. CALLE and J. DORSELLEER (1963) Problemas de Urbanización en América Latin. Bogotá: FERES.

DAVIS, K. and A. CASIS (1946) "Urbanization in Latin America." Milbank Memorial Fund Q. 24 (April): 186-207.

DORSELLEER, J. and A. GREGORY (1962) La Urbanización en América Latina. Bogotá: FERES.

DUCOFF, L. J. (1968) "La brecha entre el desarrollo rural y el urbano." Revista Mexicana de Sociología 30, 2.

DURAND, J. D. and C. A. PELAEZ (1965) "Patterns of urbanization in Latin America." Milbank Memorial Fund Q. 43 (part 2, October).

ELIZAGA, J. C. (1964) "Urban-rural pattern of population distribution in Latin America and changes in this pattern during the last ten decades." Series A, No. 14. Santiago: Centro Latinoamericano de Demografía.

––– (1960) Distribución Espacial de las Poblaciones. Series B, No. 9. Santiago: Centro Latinoamericano de Demografía.

FRIEDMANN, J. (forthcoming) The Future of Urbanization in Latin America. Studies in Comparative International Development 059. Beverly Hills, Calif.: Sage Pubns.

FUNES, J. C. (1968) "Aspectos económicos." Revista de la Sociedad Interamericana de Planificación 2 (March-June): 52-60.

GERMANI, G. (1965) "Estrategia para estimular la movilidad social," in J. A. Kahl (ed.) La Industrialización en América Latina. Mexico City and Buenos Aires: Fondo de Cultura Económica.

GUADARRAMA, L. (1967) "El crecimiento de la población y el crecimiento urbano." Revista de Economía (México, D.F.) 30, 8: 243-249.

HARDOY, J. E. (1966) "Aspectos de la urbanización en América Latina." Cuadernos del Centro de Estudios Urbanos y Regionales 6. Buenos Aires.

––– and R. P. SCHAEDEL (eds.) (1968) El Proceso de Urbanización en América Hasta el Presente. Buenos Aires. Centro de Estudios Urbanos y Regionales.

HARDOY, JORGE E. and CARLOS TOBAR (eds.) (1967) El Proceso de Urbanización en América Latina. Buenos Aires: Centro de Estudios Urbanos y Regionales.

HERRERA, F. (1966) "Progreso y urbanización," Desarrollo Económico 3, 1.

Inter-American Development Bank. Social Progress Trust Fund (1968) 1968 Annual Report. Washington, D.C. (Especially the entire section devoted to a study of the dimensions and correlated problems of urban development in Latin America.)

LABELLE, I. and A. ESTRADA (1963) Latin America in Maps, Charts and Tables. Cuernavaca, Mexico: Center for Inter-Cultural Formation.

LAMBERT, D. (1964) "Urbanisation et développement économique en Amérique latine." Caravelle 3.

MIRO, C. A. (1968) La Población de América Latina en el Siglo XX. Series A, No. 48. Santiago: Centro Latinoamericano de Demografía.

––– (1964) "The population of Latin America." Demography 1: 15-41.

RABINOVITZ, F. F. (1969) "Urban development and political development in Latin America," in Robert T. Daland (ed.) Comparative Urban Research. Beverly Hills, Calif.: Sage Pubns.

REINA, R. E. (1964) "The urban world view of a tropical forest community in the absence of a city: Petén, Guatemala." Human Organization 23 (Winter): 265-277.

SMITH, T. L. (1968) "Aspectos demográficos." Revista de la Sociedad Interamericana de Planificación 2 (March-June): 46-51.

——— (1964) "Why the cities? Observations on urbanization in Latin America," pp. 17-33 in P. L. Astuto and R. A. Leal (eds.) Latin American Problems. Thought Patterns No. 12. Jamaica, N.Y.: St. John's Univ. Press.

——— (1963) "Urbanization in Latin America." International J. of Comparative Sociology 4 (September): 227-242. (Reprinted in 1970 in T. L. Smith, Studies of Latin American Societies. Garden City, N.Y.: Doubleday.

Sociedad Interamericana de Planificación (1969a) América en el Año 2000. Vol. 1: Situación Social de América Latina en el Año 2000, H. Godoy (ed.); Vol. 2: Prospección de la Política Nacional e Internacional, K. Silvert (ed.); Vol. 3: La Integración y el Desarrollo, C. Veliz (ed.); Vol. 4: La Nueva Cultura, H. Perloff and J. E. Hardoy (eds.); and Vol. 5: Demografía y Planificación, J. Donaire (ed.). Lima: Editorial Universo, S.A.

——— (1969b) Newsletter (July-August): 7.

STOHR, W. (1969) Materials on Regional Development in Latin America: Experience and Prospects. Presented at the United Nations Seminar on Social Aspects of Regional Development, Santiago, Chile, November 3-14. Santiago: United Nations, Economic Commission for Latin America.

STYCOS, M. (1966) "Problemas demográficas de América Latina." Revista Latino-americana de Sociología 2 (March): 20-26.

TOWFIGHI, P. S. (1970) The Strategy of Concentrated Decentralization for Regional Growth. Ph.D. dissertation. MIT.

United Nations (1957) Report on the World Social Situation. New York. (Contains a section on urbanization in Latin America.)

——— Economic and Social Council (1963) Urbanization in Latin America. New York.

United Nations. Economic Commission for Latin America (1968) "La urbanización en América Latina." Boletín Económico de América Latina 13 (November): 211-229.

United Nations. Economic Commission for Latin America (1963) "Geographic distribution of the population of Latin America and the regional development priorities." Economic Bull. for Latin America 8 (March): 51-63.

VIOLICH, F. (forthcoming) Metropolitan Urban Planning in Latin America. Franklin K. Lane Series on Comparative Studies of Planning and Urban Growth in Metropolitan Regions in the United States and Other Nations. Berkeley: University of California, Institute of Governmental Studies.

WINGO, L., Jr. (1967) "Recent patterns of urbanization among Latin American countries." Urban Affairs 2 (March).

WONDERLY, W. L. (1960) "Urbanization. The challenge of Latin America in transition." Practical Anthropology (September-October).

C. Urbanization in Latin America: Country and City Studies

(See also Chapter 9: Reference L: Urban History in Latin America.)

ARRIAGA, E. E. (1968) "Components of city growth in selected Latin American countries." Milbank Memorial Fund Q. 46 (part 1, April): 237-252.

BAZZANELLA, W. (1963) "Industrialização e urbanização no Brasil." América Latina 6 (January-March): 3-28.

BIRD, R. (1963) "The economy of the Mexican Federal District." Inter-American Economic Affairs 17 (Autumn): 50-51.

BOLLENS, J. C. and H. J. SCHMANDT (1968) "The metropolitan trend in London, Ibadan, Tokyo, and São Paulo," pp. 525-540 in S. F. Fava (ed.) Urbanism in World Perspective. New York: Thomas Y. Crowell.

BORAH, W. and S. F. COOK (1969) Conquest and Population: A Demographic Approach to Mexican History. Proceedings of the American Philosophical Society (April 17).

BROWNING, H. L. (1962) Urbanization in Mexico. Ph.D. dissertation. University of California.

CARRILLO BATALLA, T. E. (1967) Población y desarrollo económico. Caracas: Banco Central de Venezuela. (Study of the impact of demographic growth on economic development in Venezuela covers problems of urbanization, the occupational structure, development of the service industries, and so on.)

DELORENZO NETO, A. (1959) "O aglomerado urbano de São Paulo." Revista Brasileira de Estudos Políticos 3 (July): 121-127.

DOLLFUS, O. (1966) "Remarques sur quelques aspects de l'urbanisation péruvienne." Civilisations 16: 338-353.

DOTSON, F. and L. O. DOTSON (1956) "Urban centralization and decentralization in Mexico." Rural Sociology 21 (March): 41-49.

DUPREE, L. (1968) City and Nation in the Developing World: Five Case Studies from Asia, Africa, and Latin America. Vol. II. New York: American University Field Staff.

FRIEDMANN, J. R. and T. LACKINGTON (1967) "Hyperurbanization and national development in Chile: Some hypotheses." Urban Affairs Q. 2 (June): 3-29.

HURTADO RUIZ-TAGLE, C. (1966) Concentración de Población y Desarrollo Económico: El Case Chileno. Publication 89. Santiago: University of Chile, Institute of Economics.

International Urban Research (1959) The World's Metropolitan Areas. Berkeley: Univ. of California Press.

LENERO OTERO, L. (1968) "The Mexican urbanization process and its implications." Demography (no. 2).

LUNA, G. (1967) "Megalopolis trends in Mexico." Ekistics 24 (July): 15-20.

MORSE, R. M. (1958) From Community to Metropolis: A Biography of São Paulo, Brazil. Gainesville: Univ. of Florida Press.

PEARSE, A. (1961) "Some characteristics of urbanization in the City of Rio de Janeiro," pp. 191-205 in P. M. Hauser (ed.) Urbanization in Latin America. New York: International Documents Service.

PEREZ RAMIREZ, G. (1965) "La urbanización y el cambio social en Colombia." Revista de Ciencias Sociales (Rio Piedras, P.R.) 9, 2: 203-220.

POSADA, R. (1967) "El desarrollo urbano en Colombia." Revista de la Sociedad Interamericana de Planificación 1 (June): 45-47.

RAMA, C. M. (1962) "De la singularidad de la urbanización en el Uruguay." Revista de Ciencias Sociales 6 (June): 177-186.

RAMIREZ, T. E. (1968) "El proceso de urbanización en Colombia." Revista Geográfica 58 (June): 19-32.

RATINOFF, L. A. (1966) "La urbanización en América Latina: el caso Paraguay." Revista Paraguaya de Sociología 3 (May-August).

REIS FILHO, N. G. (1968) Contribuição ao Estudo da Evolução Urbana do Brasil (1500-1720). São Paulo: Liv. Pioneira e Ed. da Universidade.

RIVAROLA, D. M. and G. HEISECKE [eds.] (1969) Población, Urbanización, y Recursos Humanos en el Paraguay. Asunción: Centro Paraguayo de Estudios Sociológicos. (Especially, L. A. Ratinoff, "La urbanización en el Paraguay.")

RODRIGUEZ LAMUS, L. R. (1967) El Desarrollo Urbano en Colombia. Bogotá: Ediciones Universidad de los Andes.

SMITH, T. L. (1970) "Urbanization and socio-cultural values in Brazil," pp. 360-371 in Studies of Latin American Societies. Garden City, N.Y.: Doubleday.

UNIKEL, L. (1968) "El proceso de urbanización en México: distribución y crecimiento de la población urbana." Demografía y Economía (Guanajuato) 2, 2.

URQUIDI ZAMBRANA, J. (1967) La Urbanización de la Ciudad de Cochabamba: Síntesis del Estudio, Documentos y Antecedentes. Cochabamba, Bolivia: Editorial Universitaria.

WALSH, A. H. (1969) The Urban Challenge to Government: An International Comparison of Thirteen Cities. New York: Frederick A. Praeger.

D. Population Movement: Concentration

(See also Chapter 4: Reference G: Population Movement: Diffusion [Colonization])

ADAMS, N. A. (1969) "Internal migration in Jamaica: an economic analysis." Social and Economic Studies 18 (June): 137-151.

CAMARGO, J. F. (1960) Exodo Rural no Brasil: Formas, Causas e Conseqüências Econômicas Principais. Rio de Janeiro: Conquista.

CARDONA GUITERREZ, R. (1968) "Migración, urbanización y marginalidad," pp. 63-87 in Asociación Colombiana de Facultades de Medicina, Urbanización y Marginalidad. Bogotá: Asociación.

CHEN, C. (1968) Movimientos Migratorios en Venezuela. Caracas: Instituto de Investigaciones Económicas de la Universidad Católica Andres Bello.

COMBETTO, R. (1968) Las Migraciones Internas en la Argentina. Buenos Aires: Universidad de Buenos Aires.

DUCOFF, L. J. (1965) "The role of migration in the demographic development of Latin America." Milbank Memorial Fund Q. 43 (October).

ELIZAGA, J. C. (1966) "A study of migration to Greater Santiago." Demography 3, 2: 352-377.

――― (n.d.) "Migración a las áreas metropolitanas de América Latina." PRB (Bogotá, Colombia).

FLINN, W. L. (1968) "The process of migration to a shantytown in Bogotá, Colombia." Inter-American Economic Affairs 22 (Autumn): 77-88.

FLORES COLOMBINO, A. (1967) "Reseña histórica de la migración paraguaya." Revista Paraguaya de Sociología (Asunción) 4, 8-9: 89-107.

HANSON, R. C. and O. G. SIMMONS (1968) "The role path: a concept and procedure for studying migration to urban communities." Human Organization 27 (Summer).

HERRICK, B. H. (1966) Urban Migration and Economic Development in Chile. Cambridge, Mass.: MIT Press.

JACKSON, J. A. [ed.] (n.d.) Migration. Sociological Studies 2. New York: Cambridge Univ. Press. (Articles develop theory of both long- and short-distance migration, including migration and motivation, rural-urban migration, assimilation, and the sociology of migration in industrial and postindustrial societies.)

LOPEZ T., A. (1968) Migración y Cambio Social en Antioquia Durante el Siglo Diez y Nueve. Monografía 25. Bogotá: Universidad de los Andes, Centro de Estudios sobre Desarrollo Económico.

MARGULIS, M. (1968) Migración y Marginalidad en la Sociedad Argentina. Biblioteca América Latina, Serie Menor, 10. Buenos Aires: Paidós.

MARGULIS, M. (1967) "Sociología de las migraciones." Aportes (no. 3): 5-23.

McGREEVEY, W. (1968) "Causas de la migración interna en Colombia," in Empleo y Desempleo en Colombia. Bogotá: Universidad de los Andes, Centro de Estudios sobre Desarrollo Economico (CEDE).

MONTOYA ROJAS, R. (1967) "La migración interna en el Peru: un caso concreto." América Latina 10 (October-December): 83-108.

SAHOTA, G. S. (1968) "An economic analysis of internal migration in Brazil." J. of Pol. Economy 76, 2: 218-245.

SMITH, T. L. (1960) "Rural-urban migration," chapter 4 in Latin American Population Studies. Social Sciences Monographs 8. Gainesville: Univ. of Florida Press. (Reprinted in 1970 in T. L. Smith, Studies of Latin American Societies. Garden City, N.Y.: Doubleday.)

TESTA, J. (1966) "Migraciones internas y proceso de urbanización." Cuadernos del Centro de Estudios Urbanos y Regionales (Buenos Aires) (no. 6).

TOBAR, MARGOT (n.d.) Las Migraciones Internas y la Expansión Urbana. Buenos Aires: Centro Editor de América Latina.

E. Bibliographies, Directories, Sources

BAYITCH, S. A. (1968) Latin America and the Caribbean: A Bibliographical Guide to Works in English. Dobbs Ferry, N.Y.: Oceana Pubns.

BRAITHWAITE, S. N. (1968) "Real income levels in Latin America." Rev. of Income Wealth 14 (June): 113-182.

Latin American Center (1968) Latin American Urbanization: A Guide to the Literature, Organizations and Personnel. Reference Series 6. Los Angeles: Univ. of California Press.

––– (1967) Statistical Abstract of Latin America, 1966. Los Angeles: Univ. of California Press.

LORENZ, R., P. MEADOWS, and W. BLOOMBERG (1964) A World of Cities: A Cross-Cultural Urban Bibliography. Publication 12. Prepared for the Cross-Cultural Project. Syracuse, N.Y.: Syracuse University, Maxwell Graduate School, Center for Overseas Research.

MORSE, R. M. (1965) "Recent research on Latin American urbanization: a selective survey with commentary." Latin American Research Rev. 1 (Fall).

Pan American Union (serial) Inter-American Review of Bibliography (Revista Interamericana de Bibliografía). Washington, D.C.

RABINOVITZ, F. F. et al. (1967) Political Systems in an Urban Setting: A Preliminary Bibliography. Gainesville: University of Florida, Center for Latin American Studies.

SABLE, M. H. (1967) A Guide to Latin American Studies. Los Angeles: University of California, Latin American Center.

––– (1965) Master Directory for Latin America. Los Angeles: University of California, Latin American Center.

STREET, J. and G. WEIGEND (n.d.) Urban Planning and Development Centers in Latin America. New Brunswick, N.J.: Rutgers University, Department of Geography.

WEAVER, J. L. [ed.] (1969) Latin American Development: A Selected Bibliography, 1950-1967. Bibliography and Reference Series 9. Santa Barbara, Calif.: American Bibliographical Center–Clio Press.

Part **II**

Integrating Urban-Regional Policies Among Nations

Chapter 2

The Rapprochement of Nations with Contiguous Regions

JOHN MILLER

As the result of concerted mutual effort, the nations of Latin America began to move modestly toward the goal of a more closely integrated economy during the latter part of the 1960s. While absolutely outstanding examples of triumph and success would be difficult to cite, new means of overcoming the difficulties of both the structural and functional similarities and differences which weigh against greater complementarity were being offered. The "industries integration scheme" such as those of the Central American Common Market and the one proposed by the signatories to the Cartagena Agreement (the Andean countries of Colombia, Ecuador, Peru, Bolivia, and Chile) was one such means. By agreeing to divide the projects of an integrated petro-chemical complex, for example, each nation of the Andean group will be able to construct one or more units of the integrated industrial scheme. Economic feasibility in terms of the minimum production size of plant will be assured by the market size provided by the combined demand in all five countries. Without such an arrangement, no one nation could have afforded the risk of finding external markets for the excess production over and above the internal demand which the consideration of scale economies would have imposed upon them. The objective, however, of wider continental integration based on the "logic of unity" continues to be elusive, and the slow, although steady, integration process initiated by the Latin American Free Trade Association concept still struggles toward the attainment of its potential.

Fortunately, the difficulties encountered in lowering barriers to free trade, in arranging industrial integration, and so forth, on a continental basis, are partially ameliorated by occasional binational efforts aimed at achieving national development through mutual cooperation in the creation of an infrastructure (social overhead capital) which furthers the process of physical integration. In fact, an improved physical infrastructure in the peripheral frontier regions of some nations is almost a prerequisite for economic integration with adjacent nations and their contiguous regions, much as it has been essential in the social and economic integration of the individual nations themselves. If economic integration between adjacent nations depended upon commercial flows between them by way of the coastal ports, as it has in the past, then some of the finesse and potential of integration would be largely missing. Just as ease of access to the coastal transfer points has been essential for the integration of national space in all three economic development phases (resources exploitation, import substitution, and national integration) described by Pedersen and Stöhr in Chapter 3, so is greater ease in the flow of products, services, and people between contiguous national regions and between the nations themselves now important for integration between and among Latin American countries.

That the physical approach to economic integration is as widely accepted as it is should come as no surprise, since the construction of most of the projects related to this approach are deemed, somehow, to benefit the nation and region in any event. It becomes much simpler, therefore, to coordinate common projects in energy and communications, river basin-regional development, and transport, for example, since national integrity and separate position can usually be maintained, a much more difficult task when it comes to complementary industrial development. Even so, the criteria which are used by the individual governments in making an evaluation of multinational project benefits and costs can be sufficiently different that mutually acceptable criteria or convergence of purpose and commitment becomes a matter of no small consequence, an important detail pointed out by one author concerned with this problem (Casas Gonzalez, C, 1969).

The purpose of the Pedersen-Stöhr paper in the following chapter has been to examine the economic implications of free trade and complementary agreements and the physical implications of infrastructural development on the spatial development of the South American continent. Further, the authors are interested in whether the creation of a common market and the construction of an internal transport system leads to further economic concentration in and around the present core regions, or whether they will work toward diffusion of growth into the interior of the continent. They ask, "Will these measures be able to bring about economic integration? " or, "If not, what complementary policies for changing the spatial structure will be required? " The examination of these questions has been made on a continental basis in which flows of goods between nations, transport connections and frequency of movement, division of the continental metropolitan hinterlands, market potentials, and the like have played an analytical part in attempting to answer the questions posed.

A presentation at the level of description is set forth in this chapter for some of the actual attempts in Latin America at the spatial integration of contiguous national regions or, as in the case of Central America, of an entire group of nations. In practical, rather than theoretical, terms, these attempts range all the way from the multi-national spatial integration of social, economic and political spheres (Central American Common Market) to multi-national river basin development (Río de la Plata); transport links stretching across interior voids of the continent from populated, developed coastal regions to other national boundaries (Brazil); a continental-scale highway linking the undeveloped regions of Colombia, Ecuador, Peru, and Bolivia; and a binational scheme for the economic development of an indigenous group whose cultural territory spans the boundary between Colombia and Venezuela.

Each effort at bi- or multi-national collaboration involves one or more of the varied aspects of integration: spatial-physical, economic, demographic-cultural, and political. Spatial integration in some cases, for example, depends upon the simple provision of *lineal* forms (transport and communications) which tie one national political body to another without necessarily aiming at the development of adjacent national regions. "Umbilical" in nature, they are intended rather to provide for the flow of products, services, persons, and information between two countries. These may or may not lead to further concentration in and around present core regions, a potential effect which is of interest to Pedersen and Stöhr. While such projects are lineal in form, others are *areal* in scope and are intended to bring about the mutual development of river basins and regions which cross two or more national boundaries. Whether intended or not, both of these forms of spatial integration also frequently involve a third, the *point* integration of urban elements in the binational system of cities. Whether areal and point integration result in greater impact on national core regions or upon the periphery will very much depend upon the particular circumstances.

Economic integration providing for a greater and freer flow of raw materials, products, and services between participating nations, for industrial and other sectoral integration schemes, and for common tariffs and joint measures towards other nations are usually thought of in terms of entire national economies. There is reason to suspect, however, that this global vision of the integration of economic activities might well undergo further analysis in the future with regard to the more remote interior regions. Why not, for example, make it possible for free trade arrangements to exist within the eastern Andean regions of the proposed Carretera Marginal de la Selva? The free flow of certain products and materials between nations might not be, for one reason or another, feasible at the national level but they could provide substantial support in the common development of the Amazon and Orinoco regions and hasten the day of wider economic integration at the national level. This points up the fact that economic integration schemes can be developed for contiguous regions as well as for entire nations.

Demographic-cultural and political integration is nearly always the most difficult to achieve. The latter, especially, goes considerably beyond economic integration, per se, as it deals with the coming together of entire, separate social-political bodies or collectivities, whereas the union of economic activities can occur piecemeal. Demographic integration, whether planned or not, whether a matter of international agreement or not, is frequently a matter of fact. The presence of a quarter-million El Salvadoreans in Honduras and an equal number of Chileans in the Argentine Patagonia without legal basis is testimony to this unplanned, nonnegotiated form of integration. In both these cases, contiguous areas are involved. The demographic movement is basically a rural-rural process in the case of El Salvador and Honduras, although some rural-urban and urban-urban movement is present. In the case of Chile and Argentina, it is both rural-rural and rural-urban in somewhat the same degree. The tragic events of the so-called Central American "football war" are testimony to the need for a mutually agreeable population integration (migration) policy, as well as the need for a population (control) policy in high density, high demographic growth areas. Additional policy questions involved in this particular situation are those of agrarian reform in El Salvador, which would provide for a more equitable distribution of agricultural lands so as to make migration to Honduras less necessary, and of transport investment and regional development programs in the Honduran region occupied by the El Salvadoreans in order to integrate it spatially and economically into the national structure.

Discussion in the remainder of this chapter will focus on some of these policy questions and present brief examinations of a few of the present integration schemes which involve a degree of spatial integration between and among nations.

The Central American Common Market

Historical Basis

As Karnes (D, 1961) has documented so very well, the idea of the reintegration politically of the Central American nations, which were originally constituent parts of the Reino de Guatemala during the colonial epoch, has been a permanent concern since 1821 of the governments of that region. It is probably not appropriate to speak of their social, economic, and spatial reintegration since there was relatively little contact between the separate parts of the colonial kingdom. All such was seriously discouraged and directly proscribed by the crown, although topographical features were a natural deterrent in any event. In view of historic developments, then, it is best to speak of their social, economic, and spatial (physical) integration. Even at the political level, except for their relation to Spain, there was no actual political cohesion during the period before independence. Each section of the colony acted without regard for the others, and the development of regional interests around major urban centers and economic interests in each region effectively prevented the formation of a common nation when independence did come.

A letter from the U.S. Minister in Central America to the Secretary of State dated 1873 reports some of the difficulties of political union, which only recently and only in certain respects have been overcome. Among the factors prejudicing union were: the memories of past regional struggles which made friendship and alliances practically impossible; the extraordinary degree of local prejudice against neighboring countries; lack of identity of interest even among big landowners; the absence of communication even between major centers which prevented cooperation and stymied favorable interaction; and the fact that one of the nations (Costa Rica) had always followed a policy of isolation (Karnes, D., 1961).

Even so, they were like the separate parts in search of the whole, and some twenty-five formal attempts were made at reintegration, a remarkable average of one failure every five years for a century and a quarter. Although Spain exerted central control over the region as a unit, internally there were no urban centers or local groups which functioned as dominant elements over the rest, nor was any one center large or powerful enough to assert dominance. The model of a centrally ineffective federal system suited regional agrarian interests best, but the federation, or United Provinces of Central America, established after independence, could not survive a weak executive, strong regional rights, and a paucity of economic and administrative resources. It collapsed in 1838. They were basically, writes Karnes, "a league of towns, suspicious of each other and linked only by a common concern for protection."[1]

Towards Integration

One should, perhaps, pause and consider the criticism of some about the presumed parasitic, dominant position of certain national capitals in Latin America in light of the absence, at the time of independence in Central America, of a single city sufficiently capable of exerting a political, social, and economic influence over the region to weld it together into a single nation. One can only speculate, of course, that such a union would have produced at the present time a single national economy greater than the combined economies of the separate nations or that levels of social and physical well-being would have been higher. It is possible, however, to say that the social and economic costs of waging regional wars, including the most recent one, could have been avoided. It is also possible to assert (based on the almost sevenfold increase in eight years[2] in the level of intraregional trade with the elimination of various trade barriers) that the regional economy would have been advanced over what it is now if federation had been successful.[3] In any event, it makes a substantial argument for centralist proponents. On the other hand, regions within the federation (such as Nicaragua and Honduras) might not have been so well off economically.

Adverse effects on the degree of integration which has been achieved were rudely felt as a result of the forceful interruption in trade brought on by the football war of 1969 between El Salvador and Honduras, and it demonstrates the economic strength that integration actually provides. Although disagreement over a football match was the spark which set off this conflict, it was actually due to much more serious and deeper reasons. The issue was one primarily of the continuous current of migration to Honduras from El Salvador that has been underway for a half-century, as well as a certain degree of resentment over the influence of the more economically aggressive El Salvadoreans in Honduras. Migration derives from the fact that population density in the rural areas of El Salvador is at the saturation level, the natural growth rate continues high, and virgin lands were accessible across the border in Honduras. El Salvador has a population density of 160 persons per square kilometer, for example, and that of Honduras is only 22.[4]

Due to the war and the consequent closure of Honduran highways to vehicles originating in or going to El Salvador, trade between those two countries (and between the two most southernmost nations, Costa Rica and Nicaragua, and El Salvador) was halted by terrestrial means. With one simple act, commerce totalling thirty-two million, two hundred thousand United States dollars annually ceased between the two contenders. Another twenty to twenty-five million United States dollars represented the possible annual loss in interchange between El Salvador and Nicaragua and Costa Rica, respectively, and another ten million United States dollars between Honduras and Guatemala. This interruption in trade on an annual basis represents more than twice the total intraregional trade in 1960 (see E, [1969] "Mercomún: Cómo poner la casa en orden"). For these reasons many observers find it difficult to imagine that economic interchange will not be resumed, repeating, thereby, the centuries old drive towards unification even in the face of latent and evident hostilities.

Population, International Migration, and Urban Growth

The recent belligerent episode points up, nonetheless, the pitfalls potentially present in the road leading to economic integration which derive from problem areas outside economics that either have not been considered or are difficult to resolve. As Nye (D, 1967) has succinctly phrased it, "ready agreement on the free mobility of persons, e.g., has been more difficult than opening the frontiers for the passage of potatoes and cows." Various schemes even for a freer labor market at the professional level have not been successful in the Central American Common Market. Hildebrand (D, 1967) has suggested that the demographic problem could be ameliorated by a more even distribution of population in Central America, a solution which might, at the same time, raise the regional product of certain areas such as in Honduras. Juan C. Elizaga (E, 1967), speaking on this issue, has written that the basis of a regional policy concerning migration between nations, capable of relieving demographic pressure in the most affected areas, cannot depend on the isolated development of each of the affected countries. It should be, he says, based on some form of cooperation for the development of particular aspects of the economies, especially through the exploitation of natural resources where they are more abundant, including presently unexploited areas. Equally important, countries of potential emigration should contribute with technical and financial resources to the development of programs located in the countries of potential immigration. Further, international organizations should support such mutual endeavors. As a result of the El Salvadorean-Honduran conflict, the ministers of the OAS have proposed an unprecedented demographic research program related to socioeconomic development plans in the Central American region. By so doing they have openly recognized the urgent necessity of a regional focus with respect to growing demographic "afflictions" in Central America (Alfred, D, 1969).

It should be fairly obvious that the degree of freedom for population movement across boundaries has considerable potential for affecting the urban growth, as well as the rural growth, of the involved countries. The fact that as many as 300,000 El Salvadoreans were living in rural Honduras, e.g., meant that the urban growth in El Salvador was effectively reduced by some considerable proportion of the total, since the opportunities for absorption in the rural sector in that country are negligible. This would have been a net addition to urban El Salvador, possibly on the order of the size of the capital (239,000) in 1960! It is to be noted that in expectation of the influx of up to 60% (or 180,000) of the 300,000 citizens of El Salvador to Honduras, the El Salvadorean government announced special measures to help deal with this repatriation. Two of these measures would have been directly influential in urbanizing the returning nationals. The first involved the construction of hospitals, low-income housing, schools, and highways for combating unemployment. The second was directed toward urban development capable of "modernizing the cities and principal urban places."

These two measures are, perhaps, not out of keeping with the tacit recognition that population for El Salvador is on the verge of becoming a major urban question in significant ways which has not been true to the same extent up until now. The ability to cope with what is now an excess rural population through agrarian reform is questionable, based on traditional attitudes which have delayed effective action in this area. Now that continued migration to Honduras seems to have been halted and a reverse flow initiated, a not insignificant spurt of urban growth may be inevitable. To this national, demographic-sectoral structure one must also add the relatively low level of urbanization (38.1%) which existed in 1960. Further, industrial growth in El Salvador which, with that of Guatemala, is the best in Central America, exerts a gravitational force from the principal urban centers and becomes a powerful influence on migration. Coinciding as these facts do with limited opportunities for employment absorption in the agricultural sector, they point out the urgent need for a migration policy in the Central American Common Market and for a national urban policy in El Salvador closely associated with one for the agricultural sector.

Industrial Location and Urban Growth in Central America

If the urban system of the Central American Common Market countries plus Panama is examined as a single network of urban places within a federated union, it reveals a system unique in Latin America when contrasted with other areas. All other nations either have a scattering of urban places across the city-size classes 100,000-250,000, 250,000-1,000,000, and 1,000,000 plus or, as in the case of Uruguay, Ecuador, Bolivia, and Paraguay, they have one or two cities only above 100,000 in size (see Table 1.5, Chapter 1). Due to the small size of each nation, a low level of urbanization and industrialization, and restraints on the movement of population across national boundaries, no nation in Central America had more than one city in the grouped class 100,000 and larger in 1960, and there was relatively little difference in size among these cities with the exception of Guatemala City. They were: Guatemala City (474,000); Panama City (273,000); San Jose, Costa Rica (257,000); San Salvador (239,000); Managua, Nicaragua (197,000); and Teguci-galpa, Honduras (159,000). By 1970, one additional city had grown to the city-size class 100,000-250,000, in El Salvador (Davis, 1: A, 1969).

It can be seen from Table 1.5 that a federated Central American nation would follow directly after Peru in nations ranked according to total urban population size. In terms of the urban development hierarchy, however, it would be out of phase in this ranking since this would place it in the class of nations with a single metropolis of 1,000,000 or more people. Actually, it should precede Ecuador in the urban development hierarchy class of nations with two or more cities of medium size (250,000-1,000,000). If it can be assumed, as it has been in Table 1.5, that the level of urbanization-industrialization and a growing complexity in the national network of cities (in terms of a distribution of cities in each of the city-size classes above 100,000) are closely linked in a staged growth toward a more diverse and modern economic maturity, then a federated Central American nation would need to accelerate and favor the growth of one or, at the most, two of the present development centers. It could then pass into the urban development hierarchy class with a single metropolis of 1,000,000 or more where the total size of its urban population suggests it should be. In terms of an urban hierarchy strategy this would place it roughly in the same position as Ecuador although, unlike this latter nation, it would then have a more complex overall urban system due to the larger number of medium-size cities existing in Central America.

In effect, actual and present circumstances mean that there is almost no single, overly dominant point in the urban system for a presumed federated Central America including Panama. In one overall sense, this has probably been favorable to the idea of economic integration, since no one nation has been so urbanized or industrialized that it has prevented the others from participating in the integration scheme. It can be imagined, for example, that if San Salvador or Guatemala City had been cities of 1,000,000 or more with a more varied and larger industrialization level, that agreement for economic integration might never have occurred. Actually, however, the almost parallel urban growth has not been quite so equal among the five nations that Honduras and Nicaragua, being differentially slightly less urbanized, have not been completely eager about the creation of a more integral Central American system. Costa Rica, El Salvador, and Guatemala, even under the general conditions of underdevelopment in Central America, have certain potential advantages over the other two with respect to possible gains from integration. In terms of major city sizes and preintegration industrial growth within their national boundaries, the first three nations have developed the basis for a few miniscule development centers. The fear has existed, therefore, that they might attract new investment out of proportion to the other two common market members, a situation which would lead, unquestionably, to greater intraregional disparities. Even so, a 1950s study by ECLA suggested that the potential combined market of the five countries (3,487,000 population in 1960) would not make possible the development of large industrial complexes or the efficient production of machinery and heavy equipment in the foreseeable future. It would, nonetheless, be of an adequate size to support the output of many intermediate and durable consumer goods.[5]

This all too real apprehension about where growth would occur, then, has been the basis for the development of the industrial integration scheme by mutual agreement of the five signatory countries in 1960. Basically, this converted the original limited zone of free trade association of 1958 into the Central American Common Market and dedicated more attention to a "balanced" attempt at industrialization. Closely connected with this was the establishment of the Central American Bank of Economic Integration (BCIE) as an instrument of finance and promotion of integrated economic growth *on the basis of regional balance,* or the equitable spread of industry in the region.

The principal purpose of this industrial integration effort, and of the regional bank in financing it, has been to prevent what Gunnar Myrdal has described as the *backwash effect* of industrialization in integration agreements. According to him, an imperfect price system, primitive transportation facilities, and an uneven distribution of social-economic overhead in the more backward regions tend to give greater importance to agglomerative tendencies. The result is a movement of capital and skilled labor toward the more advanced centers and the concentration in these centers of new industries, a situation which only exacerbates regional disparities. The growing strength of markets at the center and low cost inputs there, plus gradual improvements in the exchange of technological information and induced technical change, accelerate the process.[6]

It has been pointed out that the tendency for new investment to concentrate in the more-developed centers of an integrated area, at least in the short run, is highly relevant to the Central American Common Market (Hansen, D, 1967). As a result, the lesser-developed Central American nations have resisted mutual efforts which would allow the location of new industries to be wholly determined by "market forces." One author (Cable, D, 1969) asserts, however, that backwash effects are probably very small in Central America because there is little factor mobility of capital, technology, and skills between the nations. Overseas investment, due to insufficient common market planned control, is going to the historically developed centers, rather than to Honduras and Nicaragua, a situation which can actually be labelled a spread effect from developed nations outside the common market to the less-developed Central American region.

This opposite trend, the *spread effect,* as described by Myrdal, includes an increased demand on the part of the more-developed centers for the products of the less-developed members as well as the transmission to the latter of technical knowledge and improved skills. While the amelioration of the backwash effect is a matter of concern in Central America, much less attention has been given to increasing the influence of the spread effect within the region. It would seem that this should be the concern, especially, of international organizations working to assist the Central American Common Market. As has been pointed out by Cable, most large new projects appear to have been set up in El Salvador, Guatemala, or Costa Rica with a few exceptions (a modern textile factory in Honduras and a caustic soda and insecticide complex in Nicaragua). Major projects which were earmarked unofficially for Honduras, a pulp and paper factory for one, have been difficult to implement due, in part, to poor roads, a lack of skilled labor and slow project preparation. Honduras, however, has enjoyed some spread effects in the form of increased agricultural exports to its partners. It is expected that Nicaragua's intraregional position will improve as exports of milk products and caustic soda plants increase.

Actually, the Integration Industries Agreement (1958) and the subsequent Special Industries Agreement (1963) giving concessions and national monopoly positions to important growth industries have had limited effects to date. Under the first agreement only a few industries have been designated, the caustic soda complex mentioned before (established), a fertilizer plant in Nicaragua, and a tire and tube factory (established) in Guatemala. A fourth one, a plate glass industry in Honduras, although authorized, has not yet been established, which is also true of a second tire plant in Costa Rica producing different tire sizes. These "designated" plants are allotted by mutual consent, which specifies the location, minimum capacity, the conditions of growth in terms of regional demand, production quality norms, measures for "consumer protection," regulations relative to the participation of Central American capital, and the level of common external tariff duties related to the product of the designated plant (for a discussion, see Cochrane, E, 1965). Meanwhile, industrial growth otherwise has proceeded largely through national efforts and external financing in El Salvador, Guatemala, and Costa Rica.

As a strategy of balanced regional development, and given almost parallel urban systems among the five nations, it will be interesting to observe the consequences of global economic development in the region if some semblance of balance can be maintained. The contrast with other Latin American nations having more extreme regional disparities and much larger distortions in the structure of national urban systems (large dominant centers and considerably smaller second order urban places) will make comparison a matter of theoretical interest in terms of the arguments of the protagonists and antagonists of the balanced theory of growth.

Physical Integration

As late as the 1930s there were no all-weather roads, paved or otherwise, which connected the Central American capitals. This can now be contrasted with the fact that the first stage of the Central American Highway Plan will be completed in 1972. This is a major improvement plan which will permit the free and efficient movement of persons and products among the countries.[7] The Agency for International Development alone has granted loans of $85 million to the Central American Fund for Economic Integration, most of it destined for infrastructural projects in the region, particularly of transportation, communications and others that contribute to the region's physical integration.

These transportation schemes are not only providing easier access between the countries; (see Figure 2.1) in certain cases they are also opening up agricultural areas so that products can flow directly to newfound markets. The Western Highway in Honduras, for example, which is being reconstructed and paved, links Tegucigalpa, the capital, with the bustling manufacturing center of San Pedro Sula and reduces driving time from eight to two-and-one-half hours. Its continuation from San Pedro Sula to Puerto Cortés, an expanding Honduran port, and to the border with El Salvador will traverse an isolated territory containing forty percent of the population of Honduras and connect with San Salvador, which has the largest manufacturing center in Central America. When national differences are resolved sufficiently, it will provide the people of the area with additional urban markets. Accordingly, there is an emergence of interest in expanding agricultural production which will, undoubtedly, gradually evolve into a fuller integration with the national and Central American economies (Fulton, C, 1969).

Further, an agreement has been signed for the linking of the electrical and telecommunications systems. A telecommunications network will connect the five capitals with world facilities in Mexico and Panama. Planned for this electronics facility is eventual capacity of 960 circuits for telephone, telegraph, telex, radio, and television.

Considering the fact that intraregional trade increased sevenfold between 1960 and 1968, it can be expected that the improved means for the flow of trade, ideas, and persons through new transportation and communications modes will be a significant major addition to integration.

While many important steps have been taken to link Central America through economic agreements and physical infrastructural investments, political integration remains a distant goal. Perhaps some of the pitfalls to agreement in this area will be gradually overcome as the advantages of economic and physical growth together become dominant as national issues. Wionczek has argued

SOURCE: T.S.C. Consortium (1969) Map IV-C I, 164-165.

FIGURE 2.1

Proposed Central American Common Market Highway System

(B, 1966b), however, that, when markets are small, entrepreneurs scarce, and infrastructure weak, the reduction of tariffs, reliance on competitive market forces, and so on must be supplemented by bureaucratic measures that involve a greater infringement of state sovereignty. The establishment of a regional planning function, for example, which would work to assist member nations to mutually plan and develop adjacent national regions, might be one step in this direction. Technical assistance teams, perhaps, reinforced by international assistance, could also be established to work on a mobile basis for the resolution of certain sectoral problems and for project planning and implementation. In the area of urban development, it would seem appropriate and useful to attempt the development of urban planning on a regional basis so that the principles involved in successful projects in the individual countries could be disseminated more broadly. Even at the legal level, it may not be unrealistic to suggest that legislation might be formulated and enacted so that the growth of legal parallels in certain juridical areas would gradually ensue.

In many respects, the ferment set loose, even with the difficulties which are ever-present, by the Central American Common Market is an exciting and challenging area for planning professionals and social scientists who view the experiment as an important new force in Latin America.

The Andean Common Market

A recent study by Perloff (A, 1969) suggests that one key area needed for improvement within the concept of the Alliance for Progress objectives for social and economic progress in Latin America is the encouragement of regional development programs that would involve several countries. One such program, the Andean Common Market, has been recently proposed in South America. It will eventually link a subregional grouping of five countries for greater economic integration. The Andean Group (Ecuador, Colombia, Peru, Bolivia, and Chile) contains 55,000,000 inhabitants (23.5% of the population of the nations within the Latin American Free Trade Association). Spatially, the nations also form a single geographic area, but far more extensive that that of Central America, since their combined territories span the South American continent from the Caribbean to the Straits of Magellan and Tierra del Fuego. In area, the Andean Common Market will comprise a region equal to half that of Brazil.

The industrialization process which will be engendered by the opportunities opened up by the Cartagena Accord, which is a committed statement of intent to initiate the common market, is bound to provide a substantial increase in the need for capital goods, equipment, intermediate industrial products, raw materials, and so on. Many of these will be available for commercial interchange within the zone. The integrated development of various dynamic industries (at this stage of common economic development) will include those of chemical, petro-chemical, electronics, metals and machinery, motors, and the like. That these particular economic activities will lead to greater spatial (terrestrial) integration is questionable, because the bulk of goods transfer will probably be by sea. The gradual relaxation of trade restrictions which successful initial efforts may suggest, however, could produce closer ties in other commercial areas which would bring about heightened land-transfer flows, especially between adjacent nations.

Further, as regional planning attains a more respected status and a technical-professional base in each of the participating nations, common programs of regional development across national boundaries will probably occur with greater frequency. In many cases there are often stronger reasons for economic contacts in the border areas than there are between the remaining portions of each nation.

The Multi-National Río de la Plata Basin Plan

Perhaps the most ambitious proposal in Latin America for the spatial and infrastructural integration of nations with common boundaries is that based on a recent study concluded by the Inter-American Development Bank. The proposed development region covers over one million square miles of the Río de la Plata basin (roughly one-sixth the area of the continental United States) in Argentina, Bolivia, Brazil, Paraguay, and Uruguay. This river basin is comprised of four principal rivers and has a population of fifty-three million persons, one-fourth of whom live in the metropolitan areas of Buenos Aires, São Paulo, and Montevideo, and the capitals of Bolivia and Paraguay—La Paz and Asunción. Development projects already begun or proposed include the construction of various highways, ports, hydroelectric plants, and electrical distribution systems in an area containing substantial quantities of natural resources, many of them little used. Such large-scale serious schemes give additional importance and vitality to the ideas advanced by Pedersen and Stöhr in Chapter 3 concerning the spatial implications of improved accessibility through free trade and transportation policies and the practical achievements of South American integration policies.

The Río de la Plata basin proposal is essentially different from other regional plans in that it is less concerned with full economic integration and more interested in the opportunities offered by the proximity and common geographical features of the five countries for international cooperation, mainly of infrastructural projects.

The Guajira Peninsula Regional Project (Colombia-Venezuela)

This project, although much smaller in scope than the Río de la Plata proposal, is especially important in terms of the social implications of binational, regional development. While the Central American Common Market is both economically and physically oriented in its integration and the Río de la Plata proposal is principally infrastructurally determined, a sociocultural objective and orientation forms the basis for the joint Colombian-Venezuelan effort.

The Guajira Peninsula of Colombia and Venezuela has been a region of common concern on the part of these two countries for a number of years. As a result, an interinstitutional program including the International Labour Office, the United Nations, UNESCO, FAO, and the two respective governments was initiated in 1969. The objective of the project is to assist Colombia and Venezuela to elaborate a common development plan of the upper and central regions of Guajira and to promote the participation of the inhabitants. Especially important will be the objective of incorporating the economic and social life of the Guajiras, including some 80,000 Indians, into their respective national communities. It is proposed that new resources will be exploited and cattle-raising and agriculture improved so that the present trend toward depopulation due to child mortality and emigration can be reversed. To this end, both governments have promised to form a council including Colombians and Venezuelans who will work for the development and integration of Guajira through regional communities in each nation. Research and planning will span three years and culminate in a regional development plan. According to a community development expert in the Administrative Department of Planning in Colombia, the plans will respect the customs and traditions of the Guajira Indians. Economic integration, not "cultural genocide" is its purpose. Although the peninsula is a semi-desert area, there appear to be possibilities that it can be converted into a fertile and productive

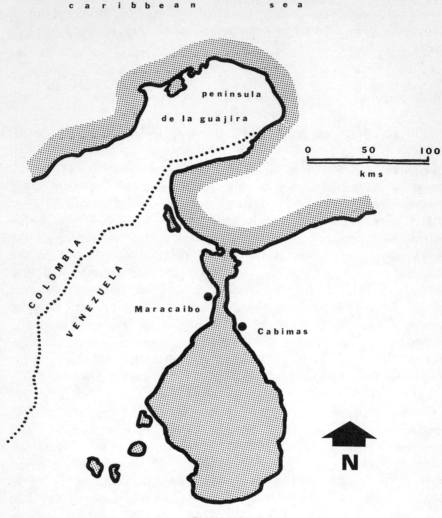

FIGURE 2.2
Guajira Peninsula Regional Project

.area. There are many such subcultural areas in Central and South America which cross international boundaries and provide, by multi-national cooperation, the opportunity to bring about a rapprochement between governments through their regional development. (See Figure 2.2.)

Multi-National Transportation Links

The foregoing joint efforts of various Latin American nations to achieve a degree of economic, physical, and social integration, with overtones of political integration in the Central American case, are basically integration attempts which are multi-directional and complex in their forms. Such straightforward and simplistic projects as major new highway proposals and projects linking nations across virgin, little-populated, and isolated regions on the interior of the South American continent can hardly be ignored, however, in the implications which they have for future, more complex integration schemes. Especially important in this sense are the Carretera Marginal de la Selva (Marginal Highway of the Forest) and new highway projects spanning the interior of Brazil and reaching out towards the frontiers with Paraguay, Bolivia, and Peru.

The Carretera Marginal de la Selva

Although still fraught with fantastic problems of financing, engineering, and construction, and though competing with other national priorities, the Carretera Marginal de la Selva is the most dramatic highway proposal of recent times in South America. When completed at some vague future time, the proposed project would stretch 3,300 miles from the Colombian border with Venezuela in the Northeast to the city of Santa Cruz in south-central Bolivia. It would follow, for the most part, the eastern side of the Andes through Colombia, Ecuador, Peru, and Bolivia. (With the exception of Chile, these are the signatories of the Cartagena Accord to establish the Andean Common Market.) The region it will traverse will include a vast area of one of the world's last frontiers, the Amazon and Orinoco river plains in the center of the continent.

Economically, the feasibility studies claim that it will yield substantial benefits in excess of its cost. Initially, at least, there would be an increase in agricultural production from areas that are now negligible contributors to national gross domestic product. An increase in income from auxiliary processing activities can also be

SOURCE: Snyder (D: 1965), 114.

FIGURE 2.3
Carretera Marginal De La Selva

expected as the entire region develops. According to Stokes (C, 1969) more than 1,590,000 people will be affected directly. Some 7,400,000 hectares will be brought into production, and major new colonization areas will be made available. (See Figure 2.3)

It is estimated that within Peru alone as many as half a million Peruvians could find new land and economic opportunities *during* the period of development. In Colombia substantial migration has already begun into the llanos (plains) in this general region and approximately twelve in every one thousand Colombians would be able to take advantage of location there. In Ecuador this rises to twenty-five of every one thousand Ecuadoreans. Already agronomists are seeking appropriate crops, techniques, and land-use patterns which would be especially adaptable to the climatic, geological forms, and soils of the region.

As has been pointed out beforehand, projects of this type may have relatively little importance in the short run on the integration of existing national economies, but the possibility of opening up and releasing latent potentials in distant national regions and of tying these up to the adjacent regions of other nations is not inconsequential. Movement among La Paz, Lima, and Bogotá would hardly be affected, for example, but movement between the Colombian llanos to the Ecuadorean sierra, or from the Peruvian Department of Madre de Dios to La Paz, Bolivia, would be potentially significant as the economies began to flourish. It is generally recognized that the flow of commerce would be relatively large and significant at the regional level, and that the development of this vast zone depends, in the end, on making land transport possible.

A Caribbean Coastal Highway: Panama-Brazil

On the periphery of the South American continent coastal transportation has not been everywhere equally available for the movement of trade and persons. This has been especially true across the southern edge of the Caribbean Sea spanning the northwest bulge of the continent beginning in Panama and extending to and along the coast in Brazil. The recent initiation of construction of new, and the improvement of existing, sections in the coastal highway connecting Panama, the Colombian and Venezuelan coasts, the Guayanas, and the Brazilian coast augurs a change in opportunities for multinational exchanges that are now effectively prevented by a lack in ease of movement along this route. The project will be especially important in the development of the Colombian Atlantic coast as it will provide direct communication between ports and towns there

SOURCE: (D: 1969) "Monumental programa de carreteras en Brasil."

FIGURE 2.4
Brazilian National Highway Plan

and the western region of Venezuela where rapid growth is under way. Connection will also be made with the national highway network of Colombia that leads to Bogotá, Medellín, and Cali.

National Highway Penetration of the Interior

A previously little-noticed alteration in the lines of access and communication by land in Brazil has recently begun to receive wider notice. That it has gone unnoticed in contrast to other news from that nation is due to the speed with which it has occurred and to the dispersed nature of the change itself. In 1965 a National Highway Plan was approved by law and a National Department of Expressways was established to execute the plan. As a result of nationally determined priorities and a major input of financial and technical resources, some 7,200 miles of new highways were constructed and 4,800 miles were paved in the four-year period 1967-1970. In this period alone, the paving itself constituted almost sixty percent of the paved federal network which had existed at the start of the program. New highways represented, on the other hand, almost double those that existed in 1967 (see Figure 2.4).[8]

What is most astounding is the potential future effect that the program has for opening up Brazil's interior and connecting that nation with its remote frontiers with Bolivia and Peru. Improved connections with Paraguay also place that nation within easier and more rapid reach of an Atlantic port on Brazil's coast.

Eliseu Resende, director of the National Department of Expressways (DNER), has observed that the works terminated or in execution will mean that in 1970 "we will be provided with interconnections by paved highways between all the state capitals of the northeast, east and central south, and this interconnection will extend to Argentina, Uruguay and Paraguay." And, he added, "new routes are advancing in the direction of the frontiers of Guyana, Venezuela, Peru and Bolivia" (see "Monumental programas de carreteras en Brasil," D, 1969). A complete plan to be carried out over a period of twenty-five years would provide Brazil with a federal highway system of almost 50,000 miles in length.

Related to this physical infrastructural plan has been the preparation of a study aimed at establishing a development level and plan for each of the Brazilian regions, perhaps the first such attempt linked to a major national improvement program within this hemisphere.

The most immediately significant single project for social and economic integration of the nation itself has been the Belem-Brazilia project, which links the Amazonia with the developed southeastern states. Amazonia, although it occupies an approximate fifty percent of the total area of Brazil, has a population of only four percent that of the total national population. Until the completion of the highway, Belem, an important growth center on the Amazon river, and its region were practically isolated from the rest of the country. The only prior link was by coastal (water) transport and air. It was, according to one observer, a region existing under "conditions similar to those of an overseas colony." Now, however, commerce between the markets in the southeast of Brazil and Belem have all the characteristics of a genuine explosion with an interchange similar to that produced between developed and underdeveloped areas. Industrial products flow north to Belem, and agricultural and extractive materials flow to the south; the population flows in both directions. In the state of Pará only five percent of the transport was formerly carried by highway; now such transport is almost ninety percent of the total. New agricultural and cattle-growing areas are being brought rapidly into existence in the Guajarina forest area, and benefits are extending as far as Baixo and Medio Amazonas, where the cattle industry is advancing rapidly with the introduction of zebu cattle appropriate to the climate.

Numerous new towns and settlements have also sprung up along the length of the Belem-Brazilia land trajectory, and many existing ones, formerly vegetating in their isolation, have sprung to life—among them the city of Imperatriz. One spokesman of DNER has said that more than one hundred towns have been founded and, in the state of Goiás alone, sixteen new "cities" have been established.

With respect to links with other nations, a number of projects under study or construction are altering the concept of communication with other Latin American nations. A technical and economic study is under way for the construction of a 450-mile highway connecting Rio Branco in the state of Acre with the Peruvian frontier. Improvements are being made in the transport net between Uruguay and Brazil which will contribute to the closer integration of these two countries. Expected benefits include a drop in transport costs and an increase in tourist movements favoring, especially, the Uruguayan economy. The widening and paving of 400 miles of highway connecting Puente de la Amistad over the Rio Iguaçu on its frontier with Paraguay with the Brazilian port of Paranaguá will permit a greater flow of commerce between the two countries and provide an Atlantic coast outlet for Paraguayan products. Finally,

BR-363 is planned to link the state of São Paulo with the border of Peru and will pass close to Bolivia.

Argentina, during the period 1961-1968, carried out construction, reconstruction, widening, and paving of highways that connect Buenos Aires with the Bolivian, Paraguayan, Brazilian, and Chilean frontiers. In Chile, the major improvement of the Carretera Trans-andina will shorten transport time and eliminate difficulties over the Andean spine for travel to Argentina. Much better access to the Chilean port of Valparaiso will also be provided to Mendoza, Argentina, for the export of agricultural products to the Pacific.

In sum, it can be said that the three-centuries-old transport orientation of the Spanish toward the sea is under serious alteration. The idea of the historic and inward-looking Inca road network which was designed to link distant valley provinces to the imperial capital on the interior of the continent is in resurgence. While Latin American nations are yet looking outward toward international markets and economic opportunities through the coastal interface, a new parallel and supporting orientation is emerging. What appears to be important about these new transportation developments is not only their supportive role to overseas commerce by their penetration of remote areas and their ties to the ports, but, also, the possibility that new opportunities will arise for integrating certain aspects of the interior regional economies of the nation with those adjacent in the border areas of other nations.

The potential influence on the process and direction of urbanization can only be surmised, but any guess as to what it may be could easily be conservative. The rural-urban migration brought on both by industrialization and severe rural population pressures in conditions of traditional latifundia and minifundia structures could be shifted, for example, to a migration pattern flowing from the traditional agricultural areas to the rural frontier. And, as population builds in the remote regions, the need for new commerce-serving urban places will arise. A degree of agricultural processing is also sure to occur in them and, due to vast distances to coastal areas, many new consumer product activities are likely to be initiated. Modest in individual size, perhaps, in the first half-century, there seems to be little question that their total effect upon urban patterns will be substantial.

How many would have expected, for example, two centuries ago that Chicago, St. Louis, and Kansas City on the edge of urban America would come to be what they are today or that Denver, Salt Lake City, Albuquerque, Phoenix, and points west would ever be more than way stations on the land route to the Pacific coast? If the present population of the urban West in the United States were today collapsed into the urban system of the East one might have an impression of what would occur in Brazil, Peru, Bolivia, Colombia, and Venezuela if the future population of the interior were to be collapsed into the coastal urban systems of the respective nations. Improved transportation, regional development, and the creation of a more complex and extended urban network as these are now developing and will develop in many Latin American countries constitute factors in national development which, in retrospect, will perhaps seem as important socially and economically as the present emphasis given to industrialization within the developed and urbanized areas of Latin America.

NOTES

1. A historic examination of the common and separate paths and attempts at unification in Central America is given by Herrarte (E, 1964); Stranger (E, 1932); and Facio (E, 1949).

2. Intraregional trade in 1960 when the Central American Common Market was inaugurated was US$32,676,000. By 1966 it had grown to US$173,600,000 and was US$260 million in 1968. This is an astounding annual median rate of increase of 36 percent! In 1961 intraregional exports amounted to 8 percent of total Central American exports; by 1966 the proportion was 21 percent (see J. B., B, 1968).

3. For an examination of the relationship between economies and size of nations, see Robinson (B, 1960).

4. Population pressure in El Salvador upon agricultural land during the 1950s brought about an increase in the number of farms of less than eight acres (minifundios) from 125,000 to 176,000, while overall the average size of minifundios actually decreased. The number of farmers with no recognizable legal title to or status on their land rose from 33,000 to 81,000 (Hansen, D, 1967).

5. The studies did indicate that the Central American market could support various industries producing, for example, such products as glass containers, sheet glass, light bulbs, caustic soda, chlorinated insecticides, petroleum derivatives, razors, tires and tubes, fertilizers, and copper wire and cable. Other more substantial production, it was felt, would only become feasible as economic growth increased the purchasing power of the market.

6. For an examination of this in the general and the Central American case, see Belassa (B, 1961; B, 1965).

7. This has been reported upon in the Boletín de la Integración of the Instituto para la Integración de América Latina, of Buenos Aires. See the July 1969 issue.

8. In the three-year period 1968-1970, federal highway construction totalled approximately forty percent of the total investment program of the federal government. This included extra funds made available by the Brazilian Coffee Institute, the Brazilian Institute of Agrarian Reform, and the National Bank of Economic Development.

REFERENCES

A. Political-Institutional Integration: Latin America

ALDUNATE UNDURRAGA, JOSE M. (n.d.) "Verdadero orígen de la política de integración total latinoamericana en lo cultural, económico y político." Santiago.

BRUCK, N. K. (1969) "Higher education and economic development in Central America." Rev. of Social Economy 27 (September): 160-180.

DEUTSCH, KARL et al. (n.d.) Integración y Formación de Comunidades Políticas. Buenos Aires: Instituto para la Integración de América Latina (INTAL).

ELAC, JOHN C., FELIX PENA, and JAIME UNDURRAGA (1969) "Investigación sobre las fórmulas jurídica administrativas para proyectos multi-nacionales de infraestructura física." Derecho de la Integración. Buenos Aires (April).

GLASSNER, MARTIN IRA (1970) "The Río Lauca: dispute over an international river." Geographical Rev. 60 (April): 192-207. (Political difficulties in the unilateral development of an international river for agricultural and industrial purposes without consultation between riparian users.)

HAAS, ERNST B. and PHILIPPE C. SCHMITTER (1964) "Economics and differential patterns of political integration: projections about unity in Latin America." International Organization 18 (Autumn).

HILTON, RONALD [ed.] (1969) The Movement Toward Latin American Unity. New York: Frederick A. Praeger.

Instituto para la Integración de América Latina (n.d.) Series in Revista de la Integración. Buenos Aires.

LAREDO, IRIS MABEL (1968) "Integración regional y política internacional: acción de los factores externos en todo proceso integrativo." Foro Internacional (México) 9 (July-September).

LEWIS, S. and T. G. MATTHEWS (1967) Caribbean Integration: Papers on Social, Political, and Economic Integration. Third Caribbean Scholars' Conference, Georgetown, Guyana, April 4-9, 1966. Rio Piedras, Puerto Rico: Institute of Caribbean Studies.

MARTINEZ-MONTERO, HOMERO (1967) "Historical roots of Latin American integration." Américas 19 (April): 17-23.

MITCHELL, CHRISTOPHER (1967) "The role of technocrats in Latin American integration." Inter-American Economic Affairs 21 (Summer): 3-30.

O'CONNELL, DE ALURRALDE, LILLIAN (1966) "Intégration politique en Amérique latine: une idéologie pertinente? " Tiers-Monde 7 (January-March): 49-71.

PERLOFF, HARVEY S. (1969) Alliance for Progress: A Social Innovation in the Making. Baltimore: Johns Hopkins Press.

RUSSETT, BRUCE M. (1967) International Regions and the International System: A Study in Political Ecology. Chicago: Rand McNally.

SIDJANSKI, DUSAN (n.d.) Dimensiones Institucionales de la Integración Latinoamericana. Buenos Aires: Instituto para la Integración de América Latina (INTAL).

VON LAZAR, ARPAD (1969) "Multi-national enterprises and Latin American integration: a sociopolitical view." J. of Inter-American Studies 11 (January): 111-128.

B. Economic Integration: Latin America

BALASSA, BELA (1965) Economic Development and Integration. México: Centro de Estudios Monetarios Latinoamericanos.

––– (1961) The Theory of Economic Integration. London: George Allen & Unwin.

CLARK, J. W. (1966) Economic Regionalism and the Americas. New Orleans: Hauser Press.

COLE, J. P. (1965) Latin America: An Economic and Social Geography. Washington, D.C.: Butterworth.

DELL, SIDNEY (1966) A Latin American Common Market? London: Oxford Univ. Press.

GRUNWALD, JOSEPH and PHILIP MUSGROVE (1970) Natural Resources in Latin American Economic Development. Baltimore: Johns Hopkins Press.

Instituto para la Integración de América Latina (1968) La integración económica de América Latina: Realizaciones, problemas y perspectivas. Buenos Aires: Instituto and Banco Interamericana de Desarrollo.

J. B. (1968) "Central America: the progress of integration." B.O.L.S.A. Rev. 2 (June): 323-332.

MARSDEN, K. (1969) "Integrated regional development: A quantitative approach." International Labour Rev. 99 (June): 621-646.

NEEDLEMAN, L. [ed.] (1968) Regional Analysis: Selected Readings. Baltimore: Penguin Books.

NOURSE, HUGH O. (1968) Regional Economics: A Study in the Economic Structure, Stability, and Growth of Regions. New York: McGraw-Hill.

PORTNOY, LEOPOLDO (1966) "Les pôles de développement et l'integration latino-américaine." Tiers-Monde 7 (January-March): 15-24.

RAMSETT, DAVID E. (1969) Regional Industrial Development in Central America. New York: Frederick A. Praeger.

ROBINSON, E. A. [ed.] (1960) "Economic consequences of the size of nations." Proceedings of the Conference held by the International Economic Association. London: Macmillan.

ROBINSON, HARRY (1967) Latin America: A Geographical Survey. New York: Frederick A. Praeger.

STEIN, STANLEY J. and BARBARA H. STEIN (1970) The Colonial Heritage of Latin America: Essays on Economic Dependence in Perspective. New York: Oxford Univ. Press.

TAMAMES, RAMON (1968) La República Dominicana y la Integración Económica de América Latina. Buenos Aires: Instituto para la Integración de América Latina (INTAL) and the Banco Interamericano de Desarrollo.

WINIARSKI, B. (1969) "Le processus spatial de croissance économique." Economies et Sociétés 3 (January): 125-165.

WIONCZEK, MIGUEL S. [ed.] (1969) Economic Cooperation in Latin America, Africa, and Asia: A Handbook of Documents. Cambridge, Mass.: MIT Press.

——— (1966a) "Integración económica y la distribución regional de las actividades industriales." El Trimestre Económico 33 (July-September): 469-502.

——— (1966b) Latin American Economic Integration. New York: Frederick A. Praeger.

WOODRUFF, WILLIAM and HELGA WOODRUFF (1969) "The illusions about the role of integration in Latin America's future." Inter-American Economic Affairs 22 (Spring): 69-79.

C. Physical Integration: Latin America

ALEXANDER, TOM (1968) "A Pan American waterway? " Américas 20 (July): 14-19.

BROWN, ROBERT T. (1966) Transport and the Economic Integration of South America. Washington, D.C.: Brookings Institution.

CASAS GONZALEZ, ANTONIO (1969) "Evaluación de proyectos multi-nacionales de integración." Temas del BID (April): 1-7.

FULTON, DAVID C. (1969) "A road to the west." Finance and Development 3: 2-7.

HILTON, RONALD [ed.] (1969) The Movement Toward Latin American Unity. New York: Frederick A. Praeger. (Authors discuss the integration prospects of transportation, communications systems, electrical power, and educational television.)

Inter-American Development Bank (1968) Las Inversiones Multi-nacionales en el Desarrollo y la Integración de América Latina. Washington, D.C. (Bibliography on regional integration in Latin America; also available in English.)

LEPAWSKY, ALBERT (1963) "International development of river resources." International Affairs 39: 533-550.

PERROUX, FRANCOIS (1968) "Les investissements multinationaux et l'analyse des pôles de développement et des pôles d'intégration." Tiers-Monde 9 (April-June): 239-265.
PREST, A. R. (1969) Transport Economics in Developing Countries. New York: Frederick A. Praeger.
REYNER, ANTHONY S. (1970) "Which route for the Isthmian Canal? " Current History 58 (February): 102-106, 113-114.
STOKES, CHARLES J. (1969) Transportation and Economic Development in Latin America. New York: Frederick A. Praeger.
United Nations. Special Fund (1964) Estudio Sobre la Red Regional de Telecommunicaciones entre las Repúblicas del Istmo Centroamericano. 2 vols. New York.

D. Latin American Integration: Case Studies

ALFRED, RICHARD (1969) "Explosión de población y la guerra: el sistema interamericano se enfrenta al problema de población forzado por el violento conflicto entre Honduras y El Salvador." PRB Comunicado de Prensa. Bogotá (August).
AMAYA LECLAIR, MANUEL, FRANCISCO MALAVASSI, and FERNANDO IRIGOYEN (1969) Hacía la Integración Física de Centro América. Tegucigalpa, Honduras: Banco Centro-americano de Integración Económica.
Banco Centroamericano de Integración Económica (n.d.) Carta Informativa Series. Tegucigalpa, Honduras.
BRADBURY, ROBERT (1961) "Trade and transportation: dynamic factors in Central American development." In A. Curtis Wilgus (ed.) The Caribbean: The Central American Area. Gainesville: Univ. of Florida Press.
CABLE, VINCENT (1969) "Problems in the Central American Common Market." B.O.L.S.A. Rev. 3 (June).
CASTILLO, CARLOS M. (1966) Growth and Integration in Central America. New York: Frederick A. Praeger.
Congreso Centroamericano de Estudiantes de Derecho Sobre Integración Política del Istmo (1966) Integración política de Centroamérica. Guatemala.
HANSEN, ROGER D. (1967) Central America: Regional Integration and Economic Development. Washington, D.C.: National Planning Association.
HILDEBRAND, JOHN R. (1967) "The Central American Common Market: economic and political integration." J. of Inter-American Studies 9 (July): 383-395.
Inter-American Development Bank (1966) Hacía un Programa de Integración Fronteriza Colombo-Ecuatoriana. Washington, D.C.
――― (1964) Posibilidades de Integración de las Zonas Fronterizas Colombo-Venezolanas. Washington, D.C.
KARNES, THOMAS L. (1961) The Failure of Union: Central America, 1824-1960. Chapel Hill: Univ. of North Carolina Press.
MARTZ, JOHN D. (1959) Central America: Crisis and Challenge. Chapel Hill: Univ. of North Carolina Press.
McCAMANT, JOHN F. (1968) Development Assistance in Central America. New York: Frederick A. Praeger.
MILLER, THEODORE R. (1969) Graphic History of the Americas: Prehistory to the Present. New York: John Wiley.
"Monumental programa de carreteras en Brasil." (1969) Progreso (November-December).
NYE, JOSEPH S., Jr. (1967) Central American Regional Integration. International Conciliation 562. (Reprinted in 1968 in Joseph S. Nye, Jr. [ed.] International Regionalism. Boston: Little, Brown.
RAMSETT, DAVID E. (1969) Regional Industrial Development in Central America: A Case Study of the Integration Industries Scheme. New York: Frederick A. Praeger.
SANDERS, THOMAS G. (1968) "Andean economic integration." American Universities Field Staff Reports 15 (August).
SNYDER, DAVID E. (1967) "The 'Carretera Marginal de la Selva': a geographical review and appraisal." Revista Geográfica (December): 87-100.

T.S.C. Consortium (1969) Central American Transportation Study. 2 vols. Tegucigalpa, Honduras: Central American Bank for Economic Integration. (Also available in Spanish.)

WIONCZEK, MIGUEL S. (1968) "The Central American common market." Intereconomics (August): 237-239.

――― (1967) "Central American integration." B.O.L.S.A. Rev. 1 (March): 127-136.

E. Integration Through Population Movements

COCHRANE, JAMES D. (1965) "Central American economic integration: the 'integrated industries' scheme." Inter-American Economic Affairs 19 (Fall).

ELIZAGA, JUAN C. (1968) "Internal migration in Latin America: components of population change in Latin America." Milbank Memorial Fund Q. 43 (Part 2, October).

――― (1967) Population and Migration: Latin America and the Caribbean. Submitted to the West Indies University Conference on "Political and Economic Relations of the Caribbean and Latin American States," Kingston, Jamaica, March. Series A 66. Santiago: Centro Latinoamericano de Demografía (CELADE).

FACIO, RODRIGO (1949) Trayectoria y Crisis de la Federación Centroamericana. San José, Costa Rica: Imprenta Nacional.

HERRARTE, ALBERTO (1964) La Unión de Centroamérica: Tragedia y Esperanza. Guatemala City: Ministerio de Educación Pública.

MARCENARO BOUTELL, ROBERTO (1967) "La inmigración de los países limítrofes." Inmigración (Buenos Aires) 9, 12: 5-16.

MARMORA, LELIO (1968) Migración al Sur: Argentinos y Chilenos en Comodoro Rivadavia. Buenos Aires: Ediciones Libera.

"Mercomún: cómo poner la casa en orden." (1969) Progreso (November-December): 33-36, 98-101.

MINKEL, CLARENCE W. (1967) "Programs of agricultural colonization and settlement in Central America." Revista Geográfica (June): 19-49.

NIETOROA, GUSTAVO (1970) "Guajira: 'aguachando' un desierto." OIT Panarama (January-February): 2-13.

STRANGER, FRANCIS M. (1932) "National origins in Central America." Hispanic American Historical Rev. (February).

Chapter 3

Economic Integration and the Spatial Development of South America

POUL OVE PEDERSEN and WALTER STOHR

The present spatial pattern on the South American continent[1] is dominated by a number of coastal core regions surrounded by narrow strips of integrated periphery, while the interior of the continent constitutes a largely nonintegrated periphery.

This structure has come about through a development process in which we can distinguish three broad phases: the resources exportation phase, the import substitution phase and the national integration phase. In the natural resources exportation phase most of the national income originated from extraction of natural resources for European and North American markets, from which in turn practically all manufactured goods were imported. In this period most larger South American cities were either terminals for foreign trade or administrative centers. Trade among South American countries was minimal. The cities that grew rapidly were, with few exceptions, seaports with good access to overseas markets.

Under the economic crises between the world wars, when the demand for natural resources suddenly decreased drastically, the dominance of natural resources as a source of income proved clearly unsatisfactory. Resource extraction was, therefore, supplemented by policies for strengthening the already slowly developing manufacturing industry, through import restrictions and protective tariff walls. These policies favored the largest of the shipping and administrative centers that contained most of the national buying power for manufactured goods. This led to further concentration in a few of the existing centers.

As the possibilities for industrial expansion within the limited markets of the main cities became exhausted, policies for economic development were turned towards national integration, i.e., the incorporation of the national peripheries in the national market. These policies have, since the middle of the thirties and especially since World War II, manifested themselves in industrial development programs for provincial towns, regional development programs, as well as national transportation development plans in many of the South American countries. Generally, however, the national integration policies have been a success only in part, and they are presently being supplemented by policies for continental integration. It may take many years before common market policies will be realized completely but it is likely that development in Latin America over the next few decades will be guided primarily by policies for integration—economically through free-trade and complementary agreements, and physically through infrastructure development. How will such policies influence the spatial development of the South American continent? Will the creation of a common market and the construction of an internal transport system lead to further economic concentration in and around the present core regions, or will they work towards diffusion of growth into the interior of the continent? Will these measures be able to bring about economic integration? If not, what complementary policies for changing the spatial structure will be required? These are the main questions we shall try to answer in this paper.

The South American Transportation and Trade Pattern

The Transport Modes in South America

The most frequently given characteristics of foreign trade involving the countries of South America (see, for example, Brown, 1966) are:

> —an apparently small proportion of the total foreign trade, namely about 10 percent, takes place *within* South America;
>
> —more than 95 percent of the goods involved in foreign trade, even within South America, are transported by ship;
>
> —about 90 percent of export, even within South America, consists of unprocessed and semiraw materials.

These characteristics of South American foreign trade, which have been used as major arguments in pushing for the Latin American common market, compare the foreign trade between South American countries to the foreign trade out of the continent. If, however, we wanted to see the trade and transportation situation of an integrated South America, national borders would be treated as unimportant divisions of the continent, and the foreign trade out of South America would have to be compared to the total amount of goods transported within South America, both within and across national boundaries. Exact data for such a comparison are not available and the data on inland transportation, presented in Table 3.1, are admittedly little more than qualified guesses. Weak as they are, however, they indicate two aspects of the trade and transportation pattern that have not yet received attention.

First, although South American countries trade about ten to twenty times more with the rest of the world (152-276 million metric tons) than they do among each other (13 million metric tons), the sum of these figures amounts to only half of the total of South American trade, nationally and internationally (345 million metric tons). Still, foreign trade dominance is probably greater than in the more developed continents. This can be explained, at least in part, by the very long distances between the main economic centers of the South American countries, and the generally low level of economic development. Policies supporting trade among the South American countries, therefore, will be of little value unless they are combined with policies of national and regional[2] economic development.

Secondly, if we compare the distribution of weight among transport modes within South America for total trade, national and international combined, with the equivalent distribution for the large, developed countries, we see (Table 3.2):

> —that although 95 percent of the international trade is carried by water transport, this is the case for only 60-65 percent of the total (including national) trade within South America. However, this is still more than the corresponding portion in the large, developed countries (11-31 percent).

> —that road transport (measured in metric ton-km.) plays about the same role in South America as it does in Europe and the United States.[3] This is perhaps the most surprising finding and indicates that the imbalance among transport modes in South America, as compared to other continents, is between the modes for bulk transportation (maritime and rail) rather than between the water and surface transportation in general (including roads).

From this we can conclude that total South American transportation is not nearly as dependent on maritime transport as one

TABLE 3.1

Distribution, by Mode, of the Total Transportation Within South America, National and International, 1960

	Weight		Weight-distance		Average trip length, km.
	10^6 metric ton	%	10^9 metric ton-km.	%	
Road[a]	200	58	40	22	200
Rail[b]	99	29	32	17	325
Coast and river[c]	33	9	33	18	1000
Maritime foreign trade within South America[d]	13	4	79	43	5900
Total	345	100	184	100	530
Foreign trade into and out[f] of South America	152-276	-	-	-	-

[a] On the basis of data for a number of Latin American countries given in *El Transporte en América Latina*, (New York: United Nations, 1965), it is assumed that each truck transports an average of 30,000 ton-km. per year. The average trip length is a guess. (A smaller average trip length, which is probable, would increase the dominance of road transport in the distribution of tons transported.)

[b] Data compiled from *El Transporte en América Latina*.

[c] Data on tons transported is compiled from *El Transporte en América Latina*. The average trip length is a guess.

[d] Data on tons transported is compiled from Robert T. Brown (1966). Average trip length is computed under the assumption that all foreign trade within South America is transported between the capitals.

[e] The distribution of ton-km. is more reliable than the distribution of tonnage.

[f] The weight of intercontinental trade is computed from data for dollar value of the foreign trade, assuming that foreign trade out of South America has the same weight per dollar value as foreign trade within South America. In the first of the figures shown it is assumed that the imports to the continent, which are higher valued manufactured good, have zero weight. In the second the figure both imports and exports are counted as equal. The true weight will be somewhere in between. Data compiled from Robert T. Brown (1966).

TABLE 3.2

**Percentage Distribution of Transportation by Transport Mode
(in Weight-Distance) in Some Countries Outside South America**

	U.S.A. 1958	France 1960	West Germany 1960	South America 1960
Road	22	31	26	22
Rail	58	58	43	17
Inland Waterways	20	11	31	61
Total	100	100	100	100

SOURCE: *El Transporte en América Latina* (New York: United Nations, 1965).

NOTE: The international comparability of the data given is rather poor, but the data do suggest direction. The shipping data for the U.S.A., France, and West Germany refer to inland waterways only and do not include coastal shipping as do the South American data. The inclusion of coastal shipping would reduce the percentage of total transportation allocated to road traffic.

might expect looking at the foreign trade data alone, because road transport plays an important role in national transportation. This difference in transport modes between national and international transportation is likely to be increased in the near future because most national transportation development programs feature important road development and railroad renewal programs, at the same time that integration policy is practically concerned with maritime shipping only.

The present dominance of maritime transportation in the foreign trade within South America is, however, to a great extent, due both to the predominance of trade in raw materials and to the lack of sufficient international surface transportation links. Therefore, when the continent develops economically and trade in manufactured goods assumes weight, the significance of a continental surface transportation system will grow in importance. To concentrate policies for Latin American integration on maritime transportation because present international transportation is dominated by maritime shipping might thus prove to be based on circular reasoning, and serious consideration should be given to the optimal timing of the development of an international surface transportation system.

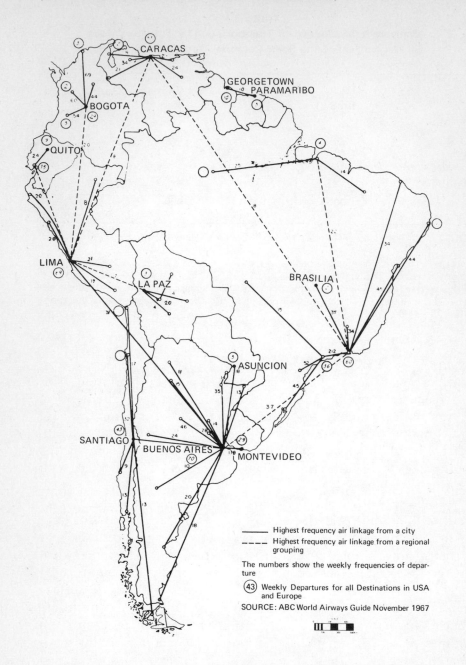

Highest frequency air linkage from a city

Highest frequency air linkage from a regional grouping

The numbers show the weekly frequencies of departure

(43) Weekly Departures for all Destinations in USA and Europe

SOURCE: ABC World Airways Guide November 1967

FIGURE 3.1

Most Frequent Airline Linkages From South American Cities, November 1967

The Geographical Pattern of Flows

To give a geographically more detailed picture of the flow patterns in South America, we shall distinguish between: (1) passenger flows among urban centers, (2) freight flows among urban centers, and (3) flows between the urban centers and their hinterlands.

Passenger flows will be represented by data on the airline frequencies among cities in South America. Though the airline frequencies do not say anything directly about the transport capacity or about the actual passenger flows, they probably give a much better picture of the quality of the service than passenger flow information would.

Figure 3.1 shows for each city the airline route which has the highest frequency of scheduled flights. The figure indicates the existence of eight relatively isolated regions in the route network that have higher relations internally than with the seven other regions. The eight regions are: (1) Argentina, Uruguay, Paraguay, Chile, and Peru, centered around Buenos Aires; (2) Brazil, except the Amazon area, centered on Rio de Janeiro; (3) the Amazon area, centered on Belém; (4) the Guayanas; (5) Venezuela, centered on Caracas; (6) Colombia, centered on Bogotá; (7) Ecuador; and (8) Bolivia, centered on La Paz. That Colombia, Venezuela, Ecuador, and Bolivia show up as independent national systems in the network may result from the high frequencies found on internal airline routes, which reflect poor land connections. This explanation, however, is only partially valid, because the frequency of international routes from these countries is also much smaller than from the other countries. This can be seen from the dotted lines in Figure 3.1, which shows the highest frequency air route from each of the "isolated" regions to any of the others.

Taking both kinds of air routes into account, we can identify the following main centers in the network: Buenos Aires, with Santiago and Lima as "satellites"; the axis Rio de Janeiro-São Paulo, with the loosely associated satellite of Belém; Lima, with La Paz, Guayaquil, and Bogotá as loosely associated satellites; and Caracas, with equally loose connections to Rio de Janeiro and Lima.

The freight flow pattern among urban centers can be illustrated by international trade flows, assuming that all the trade takes place exclusively among the most important single trading cities in each country. In Figure 3.2 are indicated the most important South

UNPROCESSED RESOURCES

MANUFACTURED GOODS

Only flows constituting more than 20% of a country's export of the commodity group to other South American countries are shown

SOURCE: Donald W. Baerresen, Martin Carnoy and Joseph Grunwald, *Latin American Trade Patterns* (Washington, D.C.: Brookings Institution, 1965).

FIGURE 3.2
International Trade Structure Within South America, 1959-61

American export flows for each of the countries (i.e., all flows that represent more than 20 percent of the country's export to other South American countries). Flows of trade involving unprocessed raw materials and manufactured goods are shown separately. At present, the trade with raw materials is much more important than trade with manufactured goods (unprocessed goods 54 percent, semiprocessed goods 34 percent, and manufactured goods 12 percent of the international trade within South America in 1959-1961)[4] but in the future the role of trade with manufactured goods will probably increase. The difference in trade structures for raw materials and manufactured goods, therefore, gives us an idea of the direction of future changes in the overall trade pattern. The two maps in Figure 3.2 show that raw materials from all of the South American continent flow to the main core regions of Buenos Aires and southern Brazil, i.e., distance-decay in the pattern of trade with raw materials is quite limited, while manufactured goods flow primarily over short distances between neighboring countries.

This is paradoxical inasmuch as traditional location theory would lead one to expect greater distance-decay for heavy, bulky goods than for highly valued manufactured goods. The explanations for this must be partly that raw materials are dependent chiefly on sea transport, where cost is influenced very little by the distance moved, while manufactured goods rely much more on inland transport, where cost depends much more on distance;[5] and partly that raw materials are consumed by a relatively small number of big industries, which are easily informed about market possibilities, while the diffusion of information about market possibilities for manufactured goods is much more difficult and insufficient; and this diffusion of information probably has a strong distance-decay.[6]

Commodity flows between urban centers and their hinterlands at present are, with few exceptions, dominated by the flows between the national territory and the capital city in each country. This situation, however, is artifically supported by the existence of national boundaries, and their removal, as envisaged for an integrated South America, might very well lead to a change in the hinterland borders so that they would no longer correspond to the national borders.

To get an impression of the changes in hinterland borders that can be expected to occur in a fully integrated South America, we have shown (Figure 3.3) national boundaries and the hinterlands of all cities with more than 250,000 inhabitants in 1960. In marking the hinterland borders, we have assumed that the drawing power of each

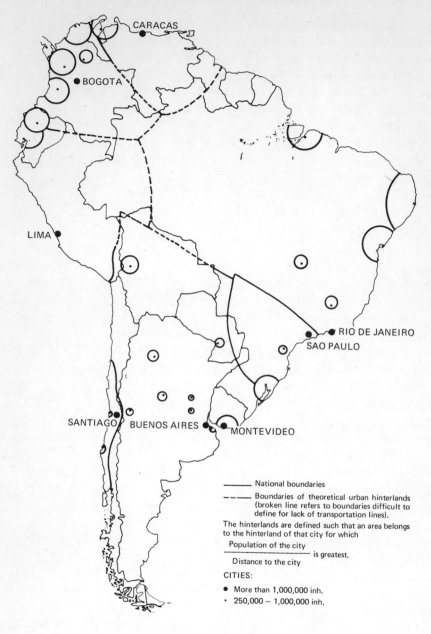

FIGURE 3.3
Metropolitan Hinterlands and National Borders in
South America, 1960

urban center is proportional to its population, and that the decay of the urban field is reciprocally proportional to the road travel time from the center, i.e., an area is allocated to the hinterland of that city for which the population of the city divided by the distance between the area and the city is largest. These assumptions are admittedly crude, but they are the best that can be done at this time without extensive research.

The map reveals that very few short-run changes in the hinterland borders can be expected to take place as a result of international integration. The only important differences between the borders of nations and of urban hinterlands are: (a) that the hinterland of Buenos Aires also seems to extend into the extreme ends of Chile (this, however, is probably due to the fact that sea transport has not been taken into account on the map); (b) that the hinterland of Buenos Aires also extends into most of the areas of the smaller neighboring nations, Bolivia, Paraguay, and Uruguay (so far as any conclusions on the map can be drawn at all, this indicates that the insistence of the smaller nations on preferential treatment in the Latin American common market may not be unwarranted); and (c) that the hinterland boundaries in the Amazon area are largely meaningless as, for much of the area, neither population nor surface transportation exists at the present time.

In evaluating long-run changes in the hinterlands it must be realized that present urban sizes may well represent an adjustment to the present national boundaries. If this is the case, removal of the national boundaries would probably lead to changes in the growth patterns of the cities, tending to change their relative size distribution and therefore also their hinterlands. Such changes may occur because full utilization of modern transportation technology is presently hampered by national boundaries, and because the possibilities of increasing export to areas outside the hinterland, when entering the common market, will differ from city to city, depending on industry mix and access to foreign markets.

On the basis of the above, we can draw the following characteristics of the geographical patterns of flows in South America:

(1) With regard to passenger flows, the southern part of the continent constitutes an integrated system, centered on Buenos Aires, while the northern countries constitute a set of only loosely interrelated subsystems.

(2) Raw materials flow from the whole continent to the main core regions of Buenos Aires and southern Brazil.

(3) Manufactured goods tend to flow between neighboring countries over relatively short distances.

(4) The national areas correspond closely to the present metropolitan hinterlands defined as simple urban gravitation fields.

Spatial Implications of Improved Accessibility— Free Trade and Transportation Policies

Both in the literature on regional economic development and in the literature on common markets, there is general agreement that improvements in accessibility are a necessary condition for economic development, because only through increased trade can that specialization among regions take place that is necessary to diversify the national and regional economies. However, only if the economic opportunities created by the improvements in access are seized will the transportation investments and the common market policies lead to economic development. Some scholars believe that this will happen automatically as a result of the work of market forces, but it is most likely that at least some active planning will become necessary. In this part, we shall assume that the opportunities created are utilized in full, and that the specialization and diversification process will take place. Given this assumption, we shall try to see how improvements in the transportation network and removal of customs barriers can be expected to change the distribution of economic activity on the Latin American continent.

Economic Development on the Basis of Maritime Transport

In the rate structure for maritime transportation, it is not unusual that the terminal costs (i.e., that part of the transportation cost that is independent of the distance) make up between 50-70 percent of the total cost of shipment (Brown, 1966: 149).[7] Variations in the terminal costs are therefore much more important than variations in the distance over which goods are shipped, and the city whose harbor has the lowest terminal cost will also be the one that has the highest accessibility. Low terminal costs will usually be found in the biggest harbors, because these will have the highest frequency of regular freight route arrivals, and often also the most modern loading and unloading facilities. Exceptions to this are the specialized mineral ore and petroleum export harbors, which have very little importance outside the special activities they serve.

Emphasis on maritime transportation will, therefore, give the existing urban agglomerations locational advantage over both the interior of the continent and the less developed coastal regions. Planned development of the maritime transportation network being attempted by the LAFTA and the Andean Group might eventually result in an improved locational situation for the less developed coastal regions, but current shipping policies seem mainly geared towards improvements for the largest harbors.

Removal of customs barriers will be of greater importance where transportation costs are smallest. When reliance is placed on maritime transport, it will therefore strengthen the tendency towards geographic concentration.

Development of Latin America based only on maritime transport will thus lead to a concentration of economic opportunities; an integration of Latin America relying only on maritime transportation will mean little to the 75 percent of the population who live away from the principal harbors. (Only 20-25 percent of the population in South America lives within 150 km. from harbors with more than one regular freight route arrival a week.)

Economic Development on the Basis of Surface Transport

If full integration of Latin America is to take place, surface transportation must be improved as well. In the rate structure for surface transportation, the terminal cost is of much less importance than for maritime transportation and the accessibility of a point on a surface transportation network will, therefore, depend partly on the geographical location of the potential markets and partly on the quality of the links in the network. We know from empirical studies in many parts of the world (see, for instance, Linnemann, 1966; Haggett, 1965) that the ability of a region, i, to sell its products in another region, j, will, on the average, decrease as a function of the transportation cost between the regions, r_{ij}, and increase with the size of the buying power of the region j, I_j. We can therefore express the accessibility A_i from the region i to the region $j = 1,2,\ldots,n$ as

$$A_i = \sum_{j=1}^{n} \frac{I_j}{f(r_{ij})}$$

To get an impression of the accessibility differences in South America due to the structure of the inland transportation system, we have computed the above index for seventy three points in South

America. For lack of sufficient data on the regional incomes we have used data for the urban population instead. This should be permissible because per capita income and degree of urbanization are highly correlated. The distance is set to $f(r_{ij}) = r_{ij}$. Though empirical analysis from other parts of the world shows that more complicated functions often fit better to reality, such a complication would not change the qualitative conclusions reached here, as long as the distance function is monotone decreasing, which has always shown to be the case. The distance, r_{ij}, is measured as estimated travel cost where the travel cost on hard surface roads is set at twice the cost on a gravel road and four times the cost on a dirt road.[8] Where international borders are crossed, customs and cost of delays should be added to the travel costs. For simplicity we shall assume that these border-crossing costs are infinitely larger before integration and that after integration they will disappear completely.

Figure 3.4 shows iso-accessibility lines (assuming existence of the road network in the beginning of the 1960s and assuming further that the customs barriers are prohibitive for any trade over the borders). The map shows that the highest accessibility exists around the big urban agglomerations, especially in the area around and between Buenos Aires, São Paulo, and Rio de Janeiro. This, of course, is not surprising. It is more interesting, however, to see what changes are brought about by improvements in the transportation network. To do this, we have shown in Figures 3.5, 3.6, 3.7, and 3.8 the increase in accessibility resulting from a complete removal of the customs barriers (Figure 3.5), improvements in the road network[9] after the customs barriers have been removed (Figures 3.6 and 3.7), and the joint effect of free trade and improved transportation (Figure 3.8).

The map in Figure 3.5 indicates that removal of the customs barriers would, first of all, increase accessibility in the small nations of Uruguay and Paraguay, both of which would gain access to the big markets of Argentina and Brazil. The potential growth corridor between Santiago and Buenos Aires also gets big improvements in access, while the bordering areas between the Andean countries get medium-sized increases.

Improvements in the transportation network (see Figure 3.7) result in a relatively greater increase in accessibility in the peripheral regions than in the urban centers, i.e., there would be a decrease in the difference in accessibilities. The reason for this is that the peripheral regions get closer to the large markets in the center regions, while the center regions get closer only to the relatively

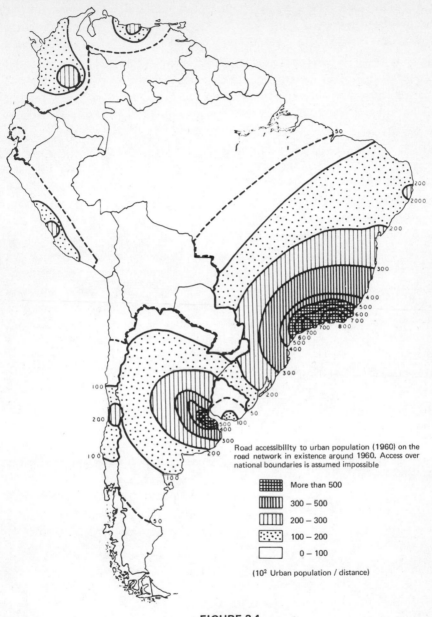

Road accessibility to urban population (1960) on the road network in existence around 1960. Access over national boundaries is assumed impossible

More than 500

300 – 500

200 – 300

100 – 200

0 – 100

(10² Urban population / distance)

FIGURE 3.4
Market Potential—1960

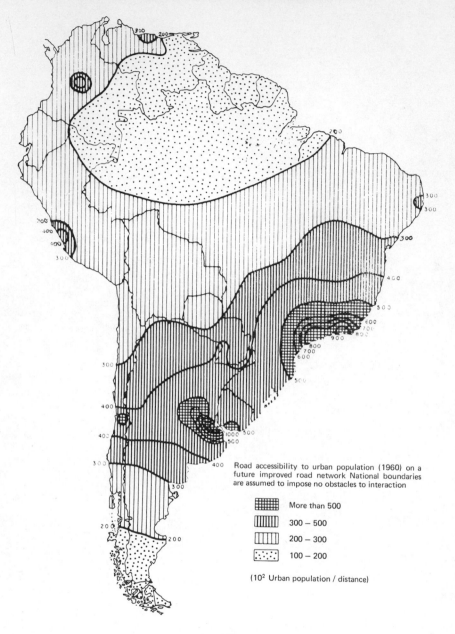

Road accessibility to urban population (1960) on a future improved road network National boundaries are assumed to impose no obstacles to interaction

▦	More than 500
▥	300 – 500
▥	200 – 300
∴	100 – 200

(10^2 Urban population / distance)

FIGURE 3.5
Market Potential—Future

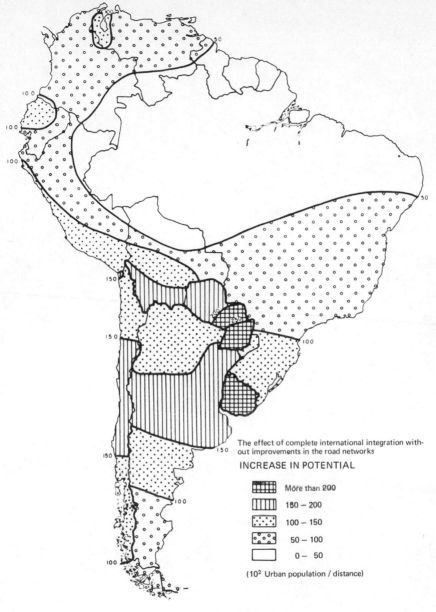

The effect of complete international integration without improvements in the road networks

INCREASE IN POTENTIAL

More than 200

150 − 200

100 − 150

50 − 100

0 − 50

(10^2 Urban population / distance)

FIGURE 3.6
Changes in Market Potential—I

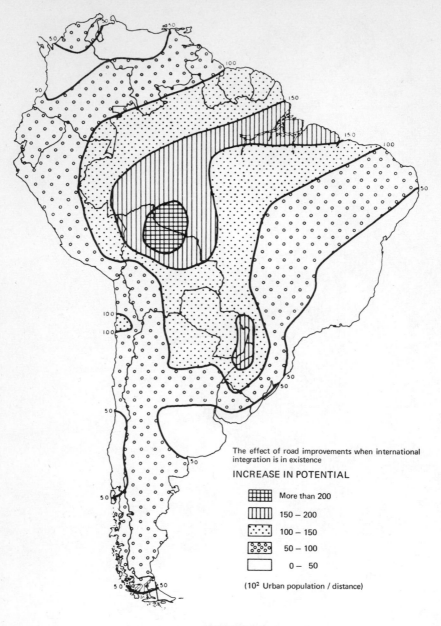

The effect of road improvements when international
integration is in existence

INCREASE IN POTENTIAL

More than 200

150 – 200

100 – 150

50 – 100

0 – 50

(10^2 Urban population / distance)

FIGURE 3.7
Changes in Market Potential—II

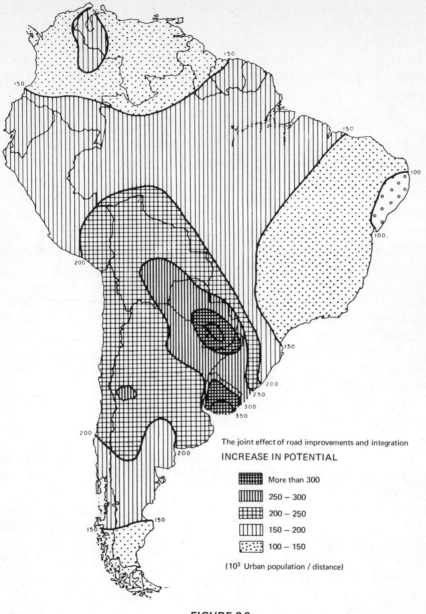

The joint effect of road improvements and integration

INCREASE IN POTENTIAL

More than 300
250 – 300
200 – 250
150 – 200
100 – 150

(10² Urban population / distance)

FIGURE 3.8
Changes in Market Potential—III

smaller markets in the periphery. The areas along the Bolivian-Brazilian border and in eastern Paraguay and the Argentine Misiones area especially receive improved access. The joint effect of free trade and improved road transport will be greatest in a band stretching from Uruguay through northern Argentina and Paraguay into Bolivia (see Figure 3.8).

Accessibility and Economic Development

If accessibility is decisive for the existence of economic development opportunities, as is assumed here, it would be relevant to draw an accessibility-production curve. The effect that the observed decrease in accessibility differences between the centers and the peripheries will have on the distribution of the economic activities depends on the shape of the accessibility-production curve. If the curve is a straight or downward-bending line, corresponding to an assumption of diseconomies or only small economies of agglomeration, a decrease in the accessibility differences will lead to a geographic spread of economic activities (Figure 3.9a). If the curve is upward-bending, corresponding to strong agglomeration economies, improvements in the transportation network will lead to a concentration of the economic activities in the large urban centers, even though their increase in accessibility is smaller than that of the periphery (Figure 3.9b).

Which form the accessibility-production curve actually has, we do not know. But a recent investigation of a large number of countries all over the world shows a tendency for the regional per capita income differences to increase with development in the less developed countries, and to decrease in the more developed countries (Williamson, 1965). Such changes in regional differences of per capita income can be explained either by regional accessibility differences, which increase in the first part of the development process and decrease during the later parts, or by the existence of an S-shaped accessibility-production function, with the less developed countries located below the inflection point and the more developed countries located above the inflection point (Figure 3.9c).

As we have found (in Figure 3.5 and 3.7 and in the preceding section of this paper), transportation investment and common market policies alone would lead to decreasing accessibilities differences in South America, hence the changes in the regional differences in per capita income will, if the above hypothesis is true, depend partly on the development level and partly on the shape of the accessibility-production curve. We should thus expect the regional income differences to increase in countries with low levels of

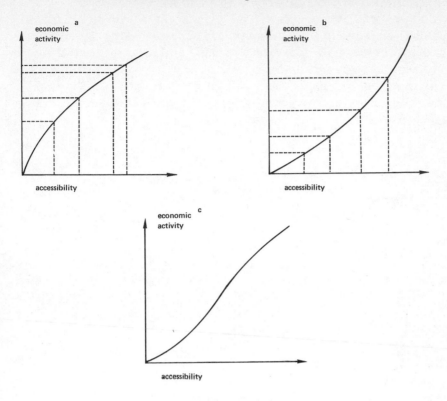

FIGURE 3.9
Accessibility-Production Curves

development. Only when the countries reach the inflection point on the accessibility-production curve would income difference start to decrease. This means that we must be very careful in evaluating the effect of transportation investments or common market policies on the economic development in a low-income region. The usual criterion for success is that the per capita income has increased more rapidly in the region than in the country as a whole and, therefore, has improved its situation relative to the country as a whole. If, however, the accessibility-production function is S-shaped, we should not expect such a development to take place before the country has reached the inflection point on the curve; we should be satisfied with an increase in the growth even if it does not match the national average.

We must thus conclude that integration in the short run can be expected to reinforce the existing trend towards geographic concentration, when it is based on both maritime and on surface transportation. Therefore, if wider geographic spread of the growth process is thought to be desirable, other means, as discussed in the following parts of this paper, will have to be applied. When higher levels of economic development are reached, the effect of integration should reverse itself if it is based on surface transportation, and thus support other policies for achieving a wider spread of economic activities.

Practical Achievements of South American Integration Policies

The basic strategies that have been applied so far to achieve South American integration in the frame of Latin American integration policies have been tariff reduction, complementary agreements for specific economic sectors, and subcontinental regional integration schemes. By far the most dominant approach has been that of tariff reduction as part of the free-trade concept. This is clearly indicated by the fact that the Montevideo Treaty of 1960 stipulates as its first aim the establishment of the Latin American Free-Trade Association. In the preceding part we have therefore analyzed the general spatial implications of a free-trade policy in South America. In the following paragraphs we shall briefly review the main integration instruments used so far.

Continent-wide Free-Trade Policy

The free-trade concept consists fundamentally of the improvement of mutual accessibility to markets. In the traditional method, borrowed from the model of European integration, LAFTA was putting its principal attention on a mutual reduction of tariffs on a continent-wide scale. Results on the whole have been disappointing; first, because administrative obstacles in part were shifted from tariffs to quantitative restrictions (quotas); and, second, because little was done to promote accessibility by positive means such as the overcoming of physical barriers and the reduction of the cost of overcoming distance. Recently, some agreements to coordinate maritime transport have been reached, but a common internal transport policy has barely begun to take shape.

The second weakness in applying the European integration model was the fact that, unlike integration within a developed continent, integration in Latin America does not automatically bring about development. A first step towards development would be increased foreign trade. But neither pure tariff reduction nor transport policies are sufficient to bring about increased foreign trade, because there is little to be interchanged due to limited industrialization and the absence of specialization within existing industry in South America.

Commercial expansion accordingly is disappointing and unable to respond to the tariff reductions because it is composed almost entirely of traditional primary products (Dell, 1966: 108; Ferrero, 1967). Integration is currently oriented towards a change in the direction and composition of trade rather than towards a change in the structure of production (French-Davis and Griffin, 1967: 198). A change in the structure of production, however, would require planned and coordinated action in a series of fields such as specialization of economic activity and infrastructure investment. It has therefore been maintained that the absence of a common development program assigning specific functions and permitting a fairly "just" participation of all countries in the benefits of growth, are among the principal bottlenecks standing in the way of continental growth and integration (Dell, 1966: 117).

Sectoral Complementarity

With the limited impact of economic planning, even within nations, comprehensive planning for all of Latin America evidently is a premature objective at this initial stage. An approach in planning for greater complementarities among economic sectors across national frontiers therefore seemed a reasonable way to reduce planning efforts to manageable proportions. But it turns out that for the entire LAFTA area it is impossible to reach complementary agreements for more than a very few and extremely narrow industrial sectors. The development of large-scale industries, based on access to all continental markets, as well as continent-wide agreements to specialize among similar industries operating in different countries, is almost completely lacking (Dell, 1966: 183). It may be that sectoral complementarity can have only very limited feasibility for an entire continent like South America. Complementarity by broad sectors tends to create political problems, since very often only one country would benefit to the exclusion of all others; complementarity by intrasectoral specialization might require a higher degree of industrial specialization than is feasible at the present stage of South American development.

Subcontinental Regional Integration

In geographic terms, integration in Latin America has, from the beginning, aimed at the entire continent. After an initial major participation of countries in the southern "cone," the Montevideo Treaty of 1960 has become effective for all Latin American countries, except for Central America and the Guayanas. Evidently it was extremely difficult to design a common development policy for countries of not only greatly varying market size and development levels, but also with very few channels of intercommunication. Internal surface transportation routes exist only in certain limited areas (an interrelated system has been established only among the Pacific coast states via the Pan American Highway, whereas the big Atlantic coast states, Venezuela, Brazil, and Argentina, are still lacking intercommunication by road); maritime transport contributes little to integration since rates are often more expensive between Latin American states than with European ports, in spite of the considerably shorter distances involved (Dell, 1966: 147).

Subcontinental regional integration has developed along three lines:

(1) *Grouping of geographically contiguous national units with limited differences in market sizes and development levels and a fairly efficient common transport infrastructure.* The case in point is the subcontinental integration agreement of the "Andean Group" (comprised of Venezuela, Colombia, Ecuador, Peru, Bolivia, and Chile) which, as shown in Figure 2, already has a relatively large internal trade in manufactured goods. It is characteristic of the favorable preconditions of this group that, beyond the traditional instruments of tariff reductions and foreign exchange compensation (Cámara de Compensación), considerable advances have also been made towards sectoral complementary agreements, the establishment of a common development corporation, a common transportation policy, and international border development schemes.

(2) *Grouping of countries of relatively lower economic development levels.* At first these countries avoided integration agreements for fear of possible negative effects, but more recently they have allied into a pressure group striving for preferential treatment in Latin American integration (United Nations, 1967b). The purpose behind this alliance is less that of mutual integration than the insistence on special policies towards countries with specific develop-, ment characteristics.[10] These special policies, in essence, boil down to a preferential status in receiving resources (technical assistance, capital, etc.), in shielding themselves against the import of commodities, and in obtaining preferential rights to improve accessibility among themselves. That such special policies will be necessary is supported by Figure 3.3, which shows that large parts of the small countries would fall within the gravity fields of the big continental core regions once integration takes place.

(3) *Border areas of adjacent countries* are the only subnational units that at present are receiving major attention in relation to South American integration. In these areas the reduction of

economic barriers will have an especially large impact (see Figure 3.5 and this paper, above). International development schemes have been formalized, however, in a few instances where the mobilization of evident resources or the solution of specific problems can be reached only by concerted efforts on both sides of the border. Such schemes might be most feasible where gravity fields do not coincide with national borders (see Figure 3.3) or where pure tariff reductions will create considerable improvements in accessibility (see Figure 3.5).

Evaluation of Integration Policies

Undoubtedly, South America encounters much greater obstacles to economic integration than a more developed continent such as Europe. This is primarily to be ascribed to the industrial homogeneity, but also to the great heterogeneity in development levels of countries and regions within the continent, and difficulties of access between them. It is mainly because of these reasons that continent-wide integration efforts have encountered great obstacles and until now have had rather disappointing results.

Due to these facts, a simple lowering of tariff barriers therefore must have very different and sometimes even contradictory consequences in various parts of a given country. In fact, preparedness for international integration among regions of similar development levels in different countries may be much better than for the countries as a whole. This suggests that certain aspects of integration policy might need to be "subdivided" by types of areas and by other regional criteria not necessarily following national boundaries. This would require a considerable shift in policy instruments for integration away from the heavy preponderance of tariff reductions to more diversified instruments in fields like infrastructure policy, growth pole policy, natural resources policy, and interarea coordination. Some of these policies will be suggested in the following section.

Implications for the Spatial Development of South America

From the preceding parts of this paper it has become clear that neither increased physical accessibility nor economic integration will necessarily bring about the incorporation of the large interior areas of the continent that today are undeveloped. Such an "internationalization" of development will depend on a series of factors, the most important of which are: (1) the existence of sufficiently worthwhile natural resources in the interior of the continent to justify opening these areas with given technology; (2) the limited potential for change in the present spatial distribution of population and economic activity concentrated in fringes along the coasts; (3) future changes in the economic structure of the continent that will bring about different locational requirements for economic activity and changed transportation demands (a major source of such changes will be the full realization of the Latin American common market); (4) the economic ability to provide an international surface transportation network; (5) the economic ability to provide new external economies, including urban infrastructure, in the interior of the continent; and finally (6) the political and social ability to allocate investments to long-term targets rather than to short-term needs. While the first two of these factors are essentially incapable of being changed by human intervention, the remaining four are to a considerable extent subject to planned influence.

For the opening of new areas to development, different types of policies are being applied.

Pure settlement policy is the most rudimentary of them. Its main instrument is the improvement of accessibility by the opening of new roads or air connections. The creation of other developmental factors such as the identification of natural resources and the creation of urban infrastructure is left to the initiative of the new settlers. Cases in point are many of the colonization efforts in the interior of Brazil and Peru, in Aisén of Chile, etc. Such policies offer a testing ground for keeping up the long-standing pioneer tradition of Latin America and for initiating spontaneous social organization. In most cases it goes along, however, with very low levels of living and great personal sacrifices. Such sacrifices seem justified only if natural resources have been identified in advance, to assure that the initial hazards of colonization are not being undertaken without rewarding economic prospects. Modern aerophotogrammetric techniques and field surveys permit a fair evaluation of natural resources before settlement actually takes place, so it is no longer necessary to settle a territory merely to find out what its resources are. Justification for a pure settlement policy usually has to be derived from political objectives, such as the strengthening of national sovereignty over peripheral zones. The extent to which such political objectives, rather than economic ones, can be afforded will depend on the level of development of the country and on the availability of financial resources.

Resource extraction policies go one step further in that they are based on already existing knowledge of natural resources, the utilization of which is facilitated by inputs in accessibility (road, railroad, ship). Urban infrastructure will be limited to the locations directly related to the extraction process and they will usually come to be islands within their undeveloped surroundings. Cases in point are the copper and lead mining areas and most of the plantation-type agricultural areas of the continent. Unless different resources can be combined to produce an industrial complex, the lack of a regional market will usually not permit major elaboration or self-sustained development within the area, but will tend to relegate the area to "colonial" dependence on the major elaborating or consumption centers in other parts.

Both of these policies for spatial development—directed at settlement and resource exploitation—open new areas by making accessibility inputs; by themselves they do not produce self-sustained development, mainly because they do not contain a systematic effort to create external economies in the form of growth poles.

Integral development policies, in turn, attempt to create and diffuse self-sustained growth. This is achieved by joining natural and human resources from the area (or adjoining ones) with capital and know-how from the continental or world system of cities at a strategic point in the area—the growth pole—so as to produce goods and services for the area itself and for other markets accessible from the growth pole. Such policies thereby tend to relate the development of a new growth pole to its surrounding area and to a larger system of information, production factors, and goods. Conditions for promoting integral development and for the creation of growth poles do not exist equally in all parts. They depend on locational criteria such as accessibility to existing markets, availability of human resources and urban infrastructure (or the feasibility of obtaining them), and the availability of natural resource complexes.

Two basic strategy alternatives have been discussed regarding the spatial development of South America: "vertical" development as following, in principle, the existing spatial pattern of development; and "horizontal" development as incorporating essentially new areas into the development process (United Nations, 1967a). These two important strategy alternatives can be considered as different combinations of inputs between capital (the scarcest factor) and natural resources (the most abundant factor of production in Latin

America). We shall define *vertical development* policy as concentrating inputs on the production factors of capital, labor, and know-how without increasing the factor of land. It is basically equivalent to economic growth without spatial growth. *Horizontal development* policy, on the other hand, emphasizes the incorporation of natural resources of not yet colonized, or thinly populated, areas, and, basically, signifies economic growth relying to a considerable extent on spatial growth.

It is clear that neither of these two alternatives can serve exclusively as a strategy for Latin American development. But in combining the two concepts, four major fields for spatial development in the short and medium run can be identified. As regards vertical development policy, major emphasis might be put on two types of regions where good accessibility to markets, human resources, and urban infrastructure exists or can easily be provided — the metropolitan regions and certain types of densely populated depressed regions.

For the metropolitan regions of Latin America a major vertical development potential lies in a closer interaction among them, a kind of *intermetropolitan integration*. This would knit major cities that today are only loosely related to each other into a highly interrelated system of urban centers, among which information, capital, and products can be rapidly diffused. When considering that existing metropolitan centers of Latin America taken together have a population superior to that of any Latin American country except Brazil and, at the same time, contain the greater part of Latin American purchasing power and intellectual capacity, one can imagine what possibilities for achieving complementarity of production, services, and knowledge this might offer. Such an interrelated system of Latin American metropolitan centers would, in fact, constitute a highly potent motor for creating the economic and intellectual basis for incorporating the rest of the continent into a process of economic growth and social development. It would mean aggregating the major external economies existing on the continent. Concrete programs toward this end might be: (1) the creation of efficient communication and transportation linkages, (2) the institutionalization of information exchange on a continental basis, (3) a systematic exchange of professionals, and (4) international collaboration among research and training institutions.

Vertical development for *densely populated but depressed regions* might require giving preferences to areas in which (due to short distances) accessibility to major core regions can easily be established, or to those where the internal market can be expanded to facilitate economies of scale. In some cases this may be achieved by enlarging a regional market across national borders (border area integration schemes). The main instruments would be improving external or internal accessibility and creating external economies in one or more suitable locations. In some cases an initial transfer of purchasing power through public funds may be necessary to initiate self-sustained growth in a potentially large but poor consumer market.

As regards horizontal development, the most promising areas to be incorporated into economic development would seem to be those where external economies can be introduced in connection with good accessibility to two or more existing metropolitan centers and/or based on a complex of natural resources. The first would mean establishing *growth corridors* along existing or new transportation routes between metropolitan centers. Priority candidates for this policy might be areas between metropolitan centers at relatively short distances from each other, and where basic infrastructure and economically dynamic towns already exist. Cases in point might be many of the gaps in the present coastal development fringe and relatively short inland penetrations such as the Santiago-Buenos Aires axis, for which Figures 3.6-8 show that transport investment and free market policies are likely to give the highest benefit. Investment in infrastructure and production would be directed into these areas which would be considered as units rather than as a series of separate locations. They would have favorable chances, next to the metropolitan centers themselves, of becoming preferential locations for new industries that would produce goods for the continental market. Since most of the major metropolitan areas are today separated from each other by national boundaries, such growth corridors will as a rule have to be developed through multinational efforts.

The other focus of horizontal development policy would be the identification of *natural resource complexes* in peripheral areas. The aim would be to create self-sustained growth based on complementary natural resources in areas with potentially low-cost accessibility. It would be desirable in such cases to attempt the creation of a new growth pole by concerted investment in resource processing, industrialization, and urban infrastructure. There exist very few examples of industrial complexes based on interrelated resource use in Latin America. A classic example is the Guayana project in Venezuela; another one is being studied in Bahia, Brazil. As accessibility is an important factor, the area of the central part of the La Plata tributaries might be, potentially, an interesting one; this would be the only interior region with transportation costs to continental markets as low as some of the major metropolitan areas, both under present and foreseeable conditions of the inland transportation system.

NOTES

1. In most parts of this paper we shall be concerned with South America rather than with Latin America in its entirety. As we are interested in the interrelations between economic integration and spatial transformations, South America appeared to be the more significant test case. Though Mexico from the start has been a member of LAFTA, and Central America may join it in the future, their participation is likely to have only secondary consequences for the transformation of continental spatial structures. A major reason is that due to geographic location their trade relations with South America wil! be based primarily on maritime and air routes rather than on terrestrial ones.

2. Wherever the term "regional" is used it refers to subnational units and not, as has been common in economic literature on Latin American integration, to the whole continent. For South America we shall use the term "continent."

3. The same conclusion for Colombia is drawn in Charles T. Stoke (1967).

4. Data computed from Donald W. Baerresen et al. (1965).

5. How large a part of the international trade with manufactured goods is actually transported by inland transportation is difficult to estimate from the available statistics. R. T. Brown (1966: 44) writes that probably less than five percent of the total trade between the South American countries goes by road and rail transportation. For the manufactured goods alone, however, the percentage must be larger. If we leave petroleum, minerals, and grain in bulk out of the sea transport, and to United Nations data on the road transport make some additions due to unregistered trade (which the Interamerican Development Bank [1964] estimates to be twelve times the size of the registered trade between Colombia and Venezuela), we get the following distribution by transport made of the international trade with manufactured goods within South America around 1960:

	10^3 ton	Percent
Road	200	7
Rail	250	9
Ship	2360	84
Total	2810	100%

6. For references, see Gunnar Olsson (1965) and P. Haggett (1965).

7. This does not cover the interest loss due to waiting time and slow transportation, which is likely to be very big in Latin America where interest rates are high; nor does it include the cost for breakage and theft, reflected in freight insurance rates, which, in Latin America, is the highest in the world.

8. Information on the road network was obtained from gasoline companies' roadmaps (editions from the first half of the 1960s).

9. All roads existing in 1960 are assumed to be asphalted and the following connections are assumed to be constructed, all with asphalted surfaces: Brazilia-Belém, Brazilia-Fortaleza, São Paulo-Corumba-Santa Cruz, Rio de Janeiro-Puerto Velho-Lima, Puerto Velho-Manaus, Manaus-Caracas, Manaus-Bogotá, Santa Cruz-Trinidad (Bolivia), Brazilia-Asunción. These are connections suggested in Robert B. Keating (1967).

10. A limited diversification of industrial base, reduced possibilities for mobilizing capital, insufficiency of external sector, relatively narrow internal market, low gross product, low income per inhabitant, etc.

REFERENCES

BAERRESEN, DONALD W. et al. (1965) Latin American Trade Pattern. Washington, D.C.: Brookings Institution.

BROWN, ROBERT T. (1966) Transport and the Economic Integration of South America. Washington, D.C.: Brookings Institution.

DELL, SIDNEY (1966) Experiencias de la Integración Económica en América Latina. México: CEMLA.

FERRERO, ROMULO A. (1967) El Comercio Exterior de América Latina. CICYP (September).

FRENCH-DAVIS, R. and K. GRIFFIN (1967) Comercio Internacional y Políticas de Desarrollo Económico. México: Fondo de Cultura Económica.

HAGGETT, P. (1965) Locational Analysis in Human Geography. London: Arnold.

Interamerican Development Bank (1964) Posibilidades de Integración de las Zonas Fronterizas Colombo-Venezolanas. Washington, D.C.

KEATING, ROBERT B. (1967) "Regional transport for Latin American economic integration." Paper presented at a meeting arranged by the International Development Bank, October, Washington, D.C.

LINNEMANN, HANS (1966) An Econometric Study of International Trade Flows. Amsterdam: North-Holland.

OLSSON, GUNNAR (1965) Distance and Human Interaction: A Review and Bibliography. Philadelphia: Regional Science Research Institute.

STOKE, CHARLES T. (1967) "The freight transport system of Colombia, 1959." Economic Geography 43 (January): 71-90.

United Nations, CEPAL-ILPES (1967a) Discusiones sobre el Desarrollo del Interior de América Latina. Santiago.

United Nations, Economic Commission for Latin America (1967b) Noticias de la Cepal. (No. 8) Santiago.

WILLIAMSON, J. G. (1965) "Regional inequalities and the process of national development." Economic Development and Cultural Change 13 (July).

Part III

Urban Growth Policies for the Nation

Chapter 4

Channeling National Urban Growth in Latin America

JOHN MILLER

The termination of the Decade of Development auspiciously launched by the United Nations in 1960 brought with its conclusion a growing interest in the elusive complexities and nature of development itself, a phenomenon which somehow had seemed relatively simpler ten years previously. No longer is "development" posited solely in terms of nationally aggregated economic growth rates and certain "critical" indices of education, health, employment, and other global evidence of social improvement. Although simple means of measurement were originally necessary in keeping with the level of statistical knowledge, the objectives of development were also simpler than at present. In many respects, indices showing change in gross national product, average national per capita income, and measures of social improvement are secondary indications only of what is occurring in a qualitative and distributive sense, socially and spatially, in processes such as those of urbanization.

Kenneth E. Boulding writes (H, 1970) that he has "been arguing for years [and nobody has paid the slightest attention] that the real measure of economic welfare is not income at all. It is the state or condition of the person, or of the society." In essence, attention is merited and overdue which goes beyond gross measures of economic welfare. A better view of what is occurring—which qualitatively, as well as quantitatively, affects the individual and larger social groups in the processes of change and which cannot be measured by GNP—is much needed. Economic development, it should be no surprise by now, has had unexpected social consequences which are not being entered in the society's ledger book of costs and benefits. It is generally accepted that the urbanization process has more plus than minus marks in its favor and that, therefore, the pattern of urban settlement, local rates of growth, urban economic mix, urban patterns of social ecology, and other evidence of the process is somehow beneficial overall, regardless of how dysfunctional they may seem to be in the particular. What this attitude ignores is that important improvements can still be made and that these improvements can be valued as objectives of greater importance in fact than the mere measure of increase in material wealth.

This is a theme which is becoming increasingly more current in economic literature. One French economist, Roger Dehem (B, 1968), has gone so far as to distinguish three main objectives of economic planning which go beyond mere production: unemployment prevention, economic growth through regional development *(amenagement regional),* and redistribution of wealth (individual and regional). It is to be noted that economic growth as an objective is conditioned by the further objective of regional development, an objective which has important consequences for the growth of a national urban system and is crucially instrumental in the way in which that growth is channelled spatially.

It is issues of these kinds which government planning, economic policy, and the aggregated social attitudes of individuals and production firms, who control private planning and policy, have ignored in large part in the past. Crisis is frequently the only means of forcing some sense of balance, but processes which reach this stage are usually faced with costly remedial action. The urban process, especially, is critically subject to this defect of correction.

While it has been true that economic development planning has achieved a limited degree of success in most areas, there is now a finer appreciation of the existence of changes accompanying and deriving from economic growth which need critical analysis and government policy guidance. This is even shown to be the case in developed countries as the loss of environmental quality has gradually accompanied the emergence of the affluent economy and population. In the words of one social scientist (Ponsioen, D, 1968), even economists have come to question "what kind of a process is actually going on in developing," and it may be added, developed, "countries that is to be labeled development?"

In retrospect, there have been global payoffs from basic policies for economic advance and social betterment in many nations as measured by certain indices of change. Yet a more sophisticated awareness and changing definition of "development" is bringing a clearer identification and a basic reexamination of some of the multiple processes involved in development. The urban process is one of these. While economic growth may occur, mere measures of its total change do not reflect in what sense it may be badly distributed in terms of personal income and spatial location (urban and regional). Since sectoral imbalance has been and is easily incorporated into economic development planning as a part of that planning itself, policy moves in this area are constantly under revision. The development of the national space and urban system, on the other hand, has been a Johnny-come-lately only during the last half of the Development Decade. Yet given the urban growth projected for the seventies in Latin America, the issue has not yet reached the level of policy attention which it is almost certain to have in this decade.

A recent document of ECLA (9: C,1969) that synthesizes available information on the processes of social change which have accompanied recent economic trends in Latin American nations points out that there is a continuing imbalance between the great cities, the smaller urban centers, and the rural areas even though satisfactory rates of increase in per capita income are being experienced as a national average. Along with a growing dependence on the world market and foreign investment, and a growing penetration, through the great cities, of foreign influence on culture and consumption patterns, this imbalance is producing a "partial development," "internal colonialism," and the "concentration of technical process." ECLA notes, however, that there is a growing tendency among planning organizations to use a combined analysis of social and economic structures as a basis for evaluating the viability of policies serving to define development strategies. Among the problems now being considered more intensely in terms of development is rapid and concentrated urbanization. The document concludes that there is a growing consensus that a development policy limited to the instruments and techniques employed up until now can only foment a certain type of economic growth that is inherently limited to itself; that this is unjust; and that it contributes to a marginalization of vast stratas of the population—much of which is located in the periphery. In effect, the famed development gap occurs not only at the international level; it is also present at the national level. There have not only been sectoral imbalances in growth patterns; there have also been spatial imbalances.

As John Friedmann has demonstrated in the essay included here, there is an urban process, one of several (economic, social, political, institutional, and regional), which make and contribute to "national development." If urban change as evidenced by size, location, distribution, mix, and quality is to develop positively, new policies and the change of old ones will be required in order to channel future urban growth. When development is thereby viewed more broadly than that related to quantifiable economic development alone, new planning problems arise. Urban processes (and objectives which could be associated with the urban growth process) which have been largely ignored in the past may appear to be in conflict with normal production objectives. Thus any adventurous alteration of the existing urban pattern as a policy measure may be objected to as a threat to economic growth since guided change seemingly goes against the urban pattern as it has developed "freely" and, presumably, efficiently in the past. The difficulty with this defense of the status quo is that this pattern has not necessarily developed freely in that government decisions, not necessarily efficient in the short or long run, have played an important role in the location of urban places and in the level of their physical and service infrastructures. Government construction of rural infrastructure has also made possible modern agricultural production and aided in the growth of certain regional cities. Further, the particular mix of economic activities in given cities has been determined in part through control over who gets what state credits, tax assistance, import licenses for machinery, and the like, for industrial expansion.

This has been most clearly so in the last three decades. The growth of an urban system and its distributed characteristics is not necessarily one which happens because the free market has determined it. Government intervention through investment and the use of financial and other controls are increasingly more influential. There is nothing startlingly new about this. Urbanization in Latin America from its initial phase has been closely associated with political-administrative prerogatives. Nonetheless, subtle changes have been underway in the role of national government with respect to patterns of urbanization, especially through economic intervention and investment in the industrial sector, a sector which is basically determining urban growth patterns in the new urban era of Latin America. Before discussing what the influentials are in this new era, it would be worthwhile to review some of the historic reasons for urbanization and the limited functional role of the Latin American city prior to the early and middle parts of the twentieth century.

Historic Urbanization and the Latin American City

Industrialization in the latter part of the nineteenth century for some Latin American countries and in this century for others has brought with it a new sense of the words urban and urbanization. It was preceded, however, by a long period in which the Latin American city from the time of the conquest was basically a residential, regional-commercial, administrative, and political center. As Richard Morse (A, 1962a: 474) has described it, the Latin American city was the source of energy and organization for the exploitation of natural resources, while the Western European city represented a movement of economic energies away from extractive pursuits toward those of processing and distribution.

Metropolitan Spain early recognized and furthered the policy that a highly centralized colonial administration was best assured by a few powerful urban centers and a network of subserviant secondary towns. Mexico and Lima each, for example, maintained a grip over a territory greater in size than the region from Georgia to Massachusetts in the English colonies, an extended administrative domain based on a policy considerably at variance with that of the English crown.

The centralized political function was one already firmly established in metropolitan Spain, one which was slavishly followed in the New World colonies, and one which continued in the newly independent nations later. Portugal's policy was little different and extended more easily to its colony because of the physical contiguity of all the territories in its claim in the Americas.

The location of the urban functions of residence and commerce paralleled closely the site of the political-administrative powers, with some variations. Actually, other than the capital and port cities and a very few regional centers, commerce was not too important until relatively late. Much of the needs of the countryside and towns was met by individual, family, and rural estate production, including that provided by limited cottage (*hacienda* estate) industries formed to satisfy the demand for given semi-industrial products.[1] The lingering effects of poor design and fabrication deriving from the low level of technology which was associated with this estate industry can still be seen in such items as basic tools in a number of Latin American countries. Unlike circumstances in the United States where the design and production of hand tools became industrialized and highly specialized early, leading thereby to the growth of a number of modest industrial urban places, especially in New England, almost no urban effects were produced in Latin America.

Further, the original organization of *municipios* as the source of energy and organization for the exploitation of natural resources, especially of agriculture and minerals, militated against the growth of the idea of an urban industrial economy. A particularly well-functioning economic structure, or one which was at least understood and could be manipulated for personal gain, involved a fine sense of control over these resources and the human energy to work them. The existing structure was also favored by world demand in the intensely industrializing environment of Western Europe and the United States for the raw materials of this urban-directed rural production. After independence, an insatiable desire among the Latin American social elites for the industrial and cultural objects of the foreign marketplace continued to favor importation; certainly little comparable was available locally. There were strong arguments then against breaking with traditional economic patterns. As Jacques Lambert (B, 1968) has indicated, particular "feudalistic-type" socioeconomic structures were so thoroughly and firmly implanted in Latin America during the colonial era that they survived the wars of independence intact and successfully resisted changes for long afterwards. Under the circumstances, the rise of the modern industrial city was inevitably delayed.

Urban places were, economically speaking, basically the center for the production and market management of local prime materials and the locus for the consumption of the material marvels of foreign industry and the much-esteemed style of the haute couture of Europe.[2] Even such items as quality furniture were not produced until the past decade or so in many countries, since past consumption patterns based on importation had continued to hold down the growth of local skills.

With a social, economic, and political structure so closely intertwined and oriented toward the maintenance of institutions that would assure the continuance of the traditional forms of this structure, it is little wonder that truly urban economies based on manufacture and distribution were so long delayed. Further, the use of private savings was strongly supportive of this tradition. In the nineteenth century, according to Smith and Marchant (B, 1951), the capital accumulated in Brazilian cities was used, even before the establishment of banks, to extend the dominion of the city over the country in the form of loans. This was a practice later adopted by the new banks and, as such, it forged a close banking-agricultural link prejudicial to other sectoral development that has lasted until the present time in certain countries.

This almost complete reliance upon a rural-based economy has had a particular kind of influence over the growth of regional urban centers. It has been precisely the basic dependence upon primary materials production and exportation and shifts in world demand which have led to abrupt changes in the importance of regions and to dynamism or decay in the New World urban outposts. This has, undoubtedly, given additional economic value to the importance of the national capital and major multifunctional regional centers as they came into existence. A nation of investors soon learns that returns on one's capital investment are most likely to be favored in the metropolis as opposed to urban centers whose dynamism or decadence depends on fickle shifts in the monoculture and minerals economies.

Certain urban centers have been favored not only in the private management and investment of rural-based savings, but also in the government collection of agriculturally derived taxes and their subsequent distribution. Hutchinson (E, 1968) asserts, for example, that the manner in which the major tax on sugar is collected and redistributed in Northeastern Brazil highly favors the capital city rather than the agricultural area and the towns where production occurs. This arises from the fact that absentee landlords prefer residence in the major centers, especially the capital city, and these centers are also the location of the business offices of the sugar enterprises. As taxes are collected where the paper transactions occur and since the tax receipts are distributed on a prorated basis to the *municipios* where the tax collection occurs, the capital city has profited greatly from transactions based on wealth produced elsewhere. Over the centuries, Hutchinson maintains, this system has drained off agricultural wealth and impoverished local municipal governments, thereby eliminating any possibility for the provision of public services, roads, welfare, and so on for the local plantation and small towns where the sugar mills are located. This is a situation not uncommon throughout Latin America.

The growth of urban centers based on industrial activities was also early stymied since Latin America's industrialization efforts overall, even in the simplest forms of industrial production, were seriously hampered by the mercantilist policy of Spain. Industrialization was forbidden as a matter of economic policy in order to create a monopolistic environment for Spanish merchants. Even the industrial processing of agricultural products was prohibited as, for example, in the case of sugar and the making of brandy from 1618 to 1794 in Peru. Attempts were also made to suppress grape cultivation and the manufacture of wine, a product which would have competed with imports from Spain (Moses, H, 1908: 77-79). Even though Spain's level of technology and economic organization didn't permit it to export many industrial products to the New World, the Spanish merchants and the Crown did profit from their intermediate position between the more industrial nations and the colonies.

The prohibition of manufacturing activity in Brazil was established by decree in 1785, but, as Furtado (B, 1963: 87) reports, there was so little reaction to it that it was more or less obvious that the growth of manufacturing had been practically nil prior to that in spite of the existence of major urban centers and demands in the rural and mining areas for such simple items as horseshoes. Furtado speculates that the main cause of this inactivity was the technical inability of immigrants to initiate industrialization on any major scale—as defined by the structure of industry at that time. Actually, Portugal had experienced incipient manufacturing development at the end of the seventeenth century as the result of an active policy encouraging the importation of skilled manpower. The Methuen Treaty of 1703, which made Portugal an agricultural dependency of England, destroyed this early start and left the Portuguese colonists without the technological basis for even simple industrialization. Furtado also speculates that the flow of Brazilian gold, which provided the Portuguese elite with the wherewithal to enjoy life through the importation of English industrial products without becoming industrial entrepreneurs themselves, undoubtedly prevented the establishment of Portuguese industry.[3] This is a consequence which would also have been felt in Brazil since no knowledge of technology and industrial organization, nor of the spirit of industrial opportunism, would have been available for exportation to the colony. Again, later in the nineteenth century, industrialization was weakened by the fact that, just at the point when Brazil might have begun the industrialization of certain products, such as textiles, lower prices for imported products made their manufacture in Brazil a precarious venture.

According to Chapman (H, 1933: 146-147), this low level of industrialization also derived from Spanish social attitudes towards the mechanical arts which had become institutionalized as part of the national value system. These attitudes were major impediments to industrial development in both Spain and the Americas and revolved around an aversion to the mechanical industries, even among artisans in the colonies who had come from Spain.

Further Background to Urban Growth

With the incipient initiation after independence of industrialization (textiles, footwear, basic processing of agricultural products for exportation, and the manufacture of sugar and wine, for example), the first urban consequences of the industrial era in Latin America began to be felt in a few select locations. São Paulo obtained its first factory-size cotton spinning and weaving mill in 1872 and fifteen years later there were two mills with three hundred fifty looms. By 1881 there was a ceramics plant, five large foundries, a factory for calicos, four plants for wood manufacture, a furniture factory, a rendering plant, one match and two hat factories. This is amazing when one considers that its population was only 45,000—apparent evidence that its industrial production was already serving a wide hinterland and laying the base for the industrial giant it is today. Such early industrial vigor is the exception and, although other centers began to show evidence of the new urban era, none were so obviously moving into it as São Paulo at the turn of the century.

Prior to late nineteenth century industrial growth and aside from the towns containing residential, commercial, and political-administrative functions, there were also isolated mining centers like Potosí (120,000 inhabitants in 1650 and probably the largest urban center in the Americas at that time), Tijuco (Diamantina) and Villa Rica (Ouro Preto). Transportation nodes and break-of-bulk points, too, provided justification for the rise of other bustling centers. After independence in Chile and before the opening of the Panama Canal, Talcahuano, for example, became a thriving port for the transshipment of goods brought through the Straits of Magellan by boat. In the Bay of Concepcion the cargo was unloaded and reshipped, according to the travel routes of departing vessels, to the entire Pacific.

Under colonial fiat the development of certain logically placed ports was held up until the nineteenth century by Spanish and Portuguese control over where trade with the exterior was permitted. This was the case in Brazil, for example, where ports were closed to trade with non-Portuguese nations until 1808. The royal decree opening Brazilian ports and the exportation of the then existing or later regional production of cacao, rubber, rice, tobacco, and sugar to other nations (principally England) aided in the growth of Bahia, Recife, and Belem as important transportation and marketing centers to the exterior and for the country. In Argentina the closure of the port of Buenos Aires to trade for two hundred years following its founding forced all trade with the Plata region to arrive by way of

Panama, Lima (where the viceroyalty for all of South America was located), and the Andean passes. The development of the potentially productive pampa region was, thereby, delayed. Buenos Aires was not made a viceroyalty with political and economic powers until 1776 and, since it served such limited functions before then, its population had not grown past 25,000 by 1770, two centuries after its founding. New York City in the same length of time had accumulated 150,000 people (Davis, A, 1960: 53).

Urbanization or urban growth, under these circumstances, was a quite different phenomenon than it was to be later during the rise of modern industrialization in the twentieth century—in the new urban era of Latin America. Most of the earlier development of specific urban centers and the growth of true urban systems in each nation had derived primarily from the location of political power and government, from an export agricultural and minerals economy, and from locational advantages for transportation. Most of the location decisions for firms in the incipient industrial economy of materials transformation and basic consumer products were linked by necessity to proximity of prime materials and to transportation points to the exterior. In some cases these locations also happened to coincide with the location of the national capital as well. Buenos Aires and Montevideo, especially, can be cited. In the case of São Paulo, it was also linked to the existence of an entrepreneurial group with capital which sought, perhaps, to ease the recurrent crisis situation of a purely agricultural economy by production in the industrial sector for markets beyond the São Paulo region. Any government influence over location, even if it had been possible, would have been seriously circumscribed by the economic considerations of location.

The promise of urbanization which one might have expected from the urban-oriented beginnings of the colony was not fulfilled, in effect, because the crown did not permit the growth of complex urban functions and industrial economies necessary for urbanization. The continued reliance on monoculture and the export of primary materials after independence was long assisted by the development of social, political, economic, and religious institutional structures which functioned well enough for those few who could control them that no change was favored.

Subtle but Certain Shifts Evidenced after Independence

The delay in the establishment of a more complex industrial structure based on an internally oriented, urban-directed consumption pattern did not mean, however, that urban growth was stymied.

Growth in most nations was continuous and steady, although not spectacular in later twentieth-century terms, until 1940 (see Figures 1.1, 1.2 and 1.3). This slower rhythm can be attributed to the continuing ability of the rural areas to absorb population growth, to a lack of urban employment opportunity (industrialization) in many nations, and to the higher mortality rate generally prevalent throughout Latin America prior to the provision of improved health services by the government. Exceptions to this were those cities and towns suddenly hit by the onslaught of external immigration, such as Buenos Aires, or the development of a major new economic activity, such as mining.

The industrial development of São Paulo, as a regional capital, has been a development especially favored by a chain of complementary events and fortuitous circumstances. Although it was occasionally affected adversely by changing conditions, new activities and functions always helped to maintain the momentum necessary to achieve the present level of metropolitan gigantism. The exploitation of rural resources through the development of a monoculture based on coffee and aided by the radiation from São Paulo of four principal railways with promotion-minded directorates, plus the entrepreneurial skill to centralize all the marketing processes in São Paulo and Santos, the port, to the exclusion of the interior cities, established São Paulo early as preeminent in the accumulation of capital and wealth. This capital and the free time of the ambitious and the motivated gave impetus to early industrialization beginning about 1870. Following the coffee crises of the first quarter of the twentieth century, according to Morse (9: L, 1951), a new cadre of leaders began to emerge—traditionless, opportunist, generated by the city. The almost continous drive to seize every opportunity and to shift with events readily, which indicates an early presence of the Parsonian pattern variables of universalism, diffuseness, and the like, gave to São Paulo a leadership in the attitudes of modernization and industrialization that is now an instrumental factor in the growth of one of the world's largest metropolitan areas.

These new attitudes and forms of social structure in São Paulo represent in the specific case what Lambert (B, 1968) has argued for the general case in Latin America—that is, that these new attitudes and forms which began to appear in the mid-nineteenth century were a gradual response to developments in technology, industry, and commerce. This was accompanied, as has been seen, by a migration to the newly developing urban areas. These new social patterns were unlike those which had existed previously in the rural areas and, even, in the cities themselves, and they were expressed through the establishment of a reformist-minded, literate, urban middle class, the creation of a number of important labor unions, the appearance of a growing industrial leadership, and the birth of a variety of new political parties and several new sociopolitical ideologies.

Following Lambert's thesis that there was a development of a progressive social and economic structure in the cities (the center) alongside rural areas (the periphery, including rural-dominated regional towns) with entrenched archaic social structures dominated by conservative estate owners and caudillos, it is possible to speculate that this has been one of the principal factors in the growing disparity between the center and the periphery.[4] The urban elites in the center have attempted, according to this idea, to optimize their opportunities for economic and political gain by concentrating their attention on development in the center and to avoid confrontations and power struggles with the periphery by abandoning the modernization of the periphery, or, alternatively, by continuing the traditional exploitation of the periphery where it was possible and convenient. If so, it explains, at least in part, the continued impoverishment of the regions and the imbalance in the growth of national systems of urban settlements. Lambert sees one indication of this policy of abandonment in the intriguing polarity of centralization of government in urban areas (the center) controlled by the new elites and contrasted by decentralization and local autonomy in the countryside.

In this sense, the urban system is centralized and dominated by the capital or by regional metropolitan cities socially, politically, and economically. Accordingly, the growth of the national urban system is withheld except as it suits the limited objectives of the center. Regional towns, lacking sufficient strength in terms of the necessary elements of modernization and surrounded and influenced by a morass of rurally decentralized personal autonomy in the form of the traditional agrarian aristocracy, have continued to fulfill historic functions moderated only by certain limited service roles to the center. That this is changing is certain since many of these regional centers are now favored by economic criteria of location for the establishment of new industries (steel, petroleum refining, chemicals, and so on) over the capital and, thereby, now serve the interests of the central elite for development purposes. This factor, plus a growing awareness of the need to stabilize, colonize, and develop frontier regions and "integrate" national space may be thought of as the economic and politico-psychological background to what could be, in Latin America, a new cognizance of the role of cities and a national urban system in modern national development. Not since original efforts at colonization were based on a well-defined urban system has there been a similar period. It is a phase which can be said to have truly begun about 1940, which has been called the "new urban era in Latin America" here, and which, it is believed, will become increasingly evident in the decade of the seventies.

This new awareness was present to a degree in the inaugural address of the Minister of Housing and Urban Development in Chile to the Jahuel Seminar in which he placed emphasis on the role of cities in the development strategy of that nation. "If we are capable of utilizing," he said, "the irreversible flow of population towards the great urban centers, in place of trying to ignore the obstinate fact of human concentration, the power deriving from deliberate utilization will further the accelerated 'modernization' of the population and the role of the cities will be decisive in the development strategy of the nation."

National development is now more than ever before, perhaps, also the development of the periphery in Latin America and this, necessarily, implies a given degree of gradual decentralization of the economy (or better said, the concurrent development of the regions and the center) and, eventually, of resources and administrative decisions. It would be counter-productive for the modernized central elite, however, under Lambert's thesis, to permit this to occur through the political, social, and economic structures of the rural-based elites in the regions. The proper channel would logically be through regional urban centers with modernizing social groups and institutions, veritable social growth poles, which would contain outside the capital those qualities which have given a degree of dynamism to the national metropolis itself. In many respects, a substantial basis for the more rapid extension of the new urban era in Latin America has been set in the past quarter century. But, as the decade of the seventies begins, that extension can now be based upon a greater awareness of the modern role of the city, both individually and as part of a more dynamic and better functioning and interrelated urban system, and upon directed policy measures for achieving channelled and balanced urban growth complementary both to national development, broadly construed, and regional growth.

The New Urban Era in Latin America

It is possible to identify the first significant beginning of the new urban era in Latin America as evidenced by a major shift in 1940 for most Latin American nations to a steeper slope in the line plotting the level of urbanization in each nation since 1900—when measured by urban population as a percentage or total population (see Figures 1.1, 1.2 and 1.3). Also, about much the same time, changes in the fundamental nature of the region's cities began to be much more evident. As T. Lynn Smith (1: B, 1963) has pointed out, the Spanish American and Brazilian cities had come to resemble those of other parts of the western world much more closely by 1960 than they did what they themselves were as late as 1925, and the functions they began to perform more extensively in the second half of the twentieth century are vastly different from what they were during the first quarter of this century. For some nations, the 1940s also marked a period of significant shifts in the relative composition of sectoral employment with a trend towards greater employment in the "harder" urban sectors, such as industry, and away from such heavy reliance on marginal services—principally domestic. This is discussed in the Mexican and Chilean cases in the following section: "Shifts from Overurbanization to Balanced Industrial-Urban Growth."

Prior to this century, as Smith indicates, and from the earliest days of their founding, the Spanish American cities, and more especially the national capitals, have specialized to the greatest degree in administrative and other governmental functions and as centers for the residential location of the upper social strata. The Brazilian upper class, on the other hand, tended to live out life on rural estates until quite late in the colonial period, unlike their Spanish American counterparts who concentrated in the cities and towns for much of the year and left *fundo* management to overseers. This changed in nineteenth-century Brazil, according to Gilberto Freyre (B, 1951), when the planter class moved from the rural *casa grande* to the *sobrado*, or town house of the developing urban bourgeoisie. Even a full hundred years after independence, however, the basic functions of political-administrative and residential nature had really changed very little for most cities.

Only with changes in this century has the degree of specialization been altered; but, largely because of the prior specialization of the capital in socioeconomic and political power, much of the development in this century has occurred where this power has been centered—in the national metropolis. This has been less so in the cases of Buenos Aires, Rio de Janeiro, Havana, and Montevideo. As national capitals, they have also been located favorably for trade and transportation, but their power as national political and social centers has been secondary as a reason for growth with respect to their locational advantages for economic purposes.

As this century approaches its last quarter, it is evident that there have been profound changes underway in the roles and functions of many Latin American cities since 1925. A growing specialization among cities is now much more obviously the pattern. The first thrusts of modern industrialization have left behind the simpler classification of cities based on political-administrative, regional commercial, mining, and transportation functions. The days when the development of towns and cities were not dependent upon the establishment of national industries, the provision of services and materials to them, and the shipment of national industrial products to internal or international markets has yielded considerably to a growing dependence on this type of urban economy. Historical functions still linger, but they are tempered now by a new recognition of the function of the urban center as a processor of products and the provider of new kinds of services which are to be sold elsewhere for the products and services of other national centers. Consumption is beginning to be viewed increasingly as a mutual process among urban centers, rather than due to the more exclusive and fortuitous circumstance of residency in the capital.

This is basically a development of the last two decades and, as a development, it is uneven among countries, since industrialization has proceeded at differing paces. Opportunities for industrial growth due to internal market size, availability of technology, entrepreneurs, and natural resources and capital are not the same everywhere. Even without it, however, it is surprising how much evidence of commerce can be seen on new, improved roads between urban places in countries like Peru and Bolivia where industrialization is low and where communications between urban places was extremely difficult until recent years. Nonindustrial crafts and agricultural production exchange is always favored, necessarily, in those countries where there are commercially important variations between regions in the types of agricultural produce and artisan end-products available. Improved transportation systems within nations and the decline in restraints over trade between them through common market arrangements are also beginning to demonstrate the value of physical and political-economic links within Latin America. Recognition of this is proving to be one more important means of building up and taking advantage of complementary functional relationships among the differently specialized urban centers and regions.

New steel and chemical complexes (Ciudad Guayana, Concepcion, Monterrey); modern recreational-resort centers (Viña del Mar, Acapulco) based on an attractive topography and climate and on an increasing middle-class clientele made affluent by the benefits of industrialization; specialized heavy industry (Oroya, Volta Redonda); and new national capitals established or being established to develop remote national areas beyond the edges of urban life (Brazilia, Belize) are introducing the awareness of new kinds of urban functions. And, particular places now serve in major functional roles within the national urban system which were not enjoyed or imagined in simpler epochs. As colonization proceeds in the interior of the continent and along the frontiers of long-settled lands, "new" towns, such as Santa Cruz, Bolivia, are experiencing the type of commercial and service growth based on agricultural development which preceded such industrial cities as Montevideo in Uruguay[5] and St. Louis and Kansas City in the United States. Too, other existing centers have been able to incorporate various new functional roles along with those which preceded them in a less dramatic and more multifunctional pattern. But these functional roles are more than functions as classified by economic sectors. Perhaps more important, and making possible the growth of new economic activities, urban specializations and a greater richness in the internal and external relations of the cities, has been the growth of an urban culture that has and is serving as a vehicle for changing values and beliefs. It is the changes in these values and beliefs themselves which is largely instrumental in providing the base for the new economic activities.

Shifts from Overurbanization to Balanced Industrial-Urban Growth

A number of analysts have described continuing urban growth without an equal growth in industrial activity as over- or hyperurbanization (Friedmann and Lackington, 4: 1967; and Sovani, 1: A, 1964). In many respects, the hyperurbanization of Latin American countries has existed for several decades; indeed, it postdates World War I by a half-century. The large, dominant city containing a well-organized bureaucracy, both national and municipal, an agglomeration of nonindustrial service occupations, and a highly valued bureaucratic and professional tradition preceded the first evidence of significant industrialization by almost a century. In fact, given the low levels of education, limited knowledge of technology, land-based social elitism, political stability, and the like, it may be assumed that hyperurbanization in the Latin American context may have been a necessary precursor of an urban culture that would make modernization and industrialization possible. By a curious paradox in the historical process, "industrial" reformism, imported from Europe during the nineteenth century, actually preceded the coming of industry by close to one hundred years (Veliz, H, 1965: 3-5).

Usually a rise in the overurbanization phenomenon in underdeveloped countries brings with it a rise in the size of the services sector relative to other sectors.[6] The shift in employment in the services sector in such circumstances, principally personal and domestic services, is well demonstrated in the case of Chile. In 1940 before the main impact of modern industrialization brought about by the effects of World War II and a forced reduction in imports of manufactured goods had occurred, there were 886,000 persons employed in nonspecified services. There were only 593,000 employed in other urban sectors (industry, construction, transportation, and commerce). Twelve years later, in 1952, and after an expansion of industry for the production of formerly imported products, there were 576,700 persons in nonspecified services, a decline of 309,300 or 35%. Santiago experienced approximately the same percentage decline. During the same period, the remaining urban sector rose 236,100 to 829,200, an increase of almost 40%. Fifty-nine percent of this occurred in Santiago. Part of the drop in employment in the nonservice sector could be attributed to a lower employment rate in the younger age group as the data is based on 12 years or more and the employment of the youngest in this age group has been steadily declining.

Even so, it must be concluded that there was a major shift away from marginally productive, nonspecified service employment to employment based on industry and industrially related urban services—transportation, construction, and commerce. One basis for this change is due to the creation of new industries for national import substitution which occurred during this period. According to Anibal Pinto (H, 1962), there was an extraordinary process of substitution, a process which would have been felt in urban population growth and employment shifts among the sectors. This is dramatically shown in fact in Table 4-1.

TABLE 4.1
Products Whose Importations Were Reduced in Chile:
Variation Between 1925-29 and 1948-52 (percentages)

Thread, yarn, and textiles	- 78
Metals and their manufactured products	- 21
Pulp, paper, and cardboard	- 12
Stones, ores, and glass	- 65
Woods and wood products	- 79
Furs, skins, and so on	- 78
Oils and edible fats	- 79
Diverse	- 80

SOURCE: Anibal Pinto (1962) Chile: Un Caso de Desarrollo Frustrado. Santiago: Editorial Universitaria.

It is notable that much of the new production and employment (seventy-three percent) engendered by this early industrialization by substitution occurred in the central province in and around Santiago. This tendency continued in the period 1952-1960 during which time sixty-five percent of total additional employment in services and sixty-one percent in industry and industrially related urban services occurred in Santiago. A subtle change has occurred since 1960, however, as the governments of Alessandri and Frei have emphasized further substitution and the use of national resources through the development of petroleum and its refined products, steel and steel products, chemicals, beet sugar, and pulp and paper. Interestingly, the location of all of these activities are strongly determined by the economics of location near ports or, in the case of pulp, paper, and beet sugar, near the source of the prime material as in the case of nineteenth-century industrialization. This new industrial growth has not led directly to the urban expansion of Santiago, but, indirectly, it has through the growth of management, bureaucracy, and services to these industries in the center.

Meanwhile, the expansion of the industrial output of final consumer products and of construction and services in Santiago continued to provide it with the economic base for urban growth. Between 1961 and 1965, for example, the metropolitan zone accounted for sixty percent of the total national gross product increase in industry, seventy-eight percent of that in construction, and fifty-two percent of that in services, yet it contained, in 1960, just thirty-three percent of the total national population (Chile, B, 1968a, b). There was a tendency towards even more concentration in urban economic activitiy in Santiago between 1965 and 1966, in the second year of the Frei government as shown by provisional figures.

While this government had promised greater attention to regional development, and this was occurring, it was becoming obvious that the gap between the center and the periphery was widening, rather than narrowing, as measured by increases in regional gross product in the urban sector. Between 1965 and 1966, for example, the metropolitan zone accounted for seventy-three percent of the increase in total gross national product in the industrial sector. While the gross regional product in construction in the periphery (outside the metropolitan zone) actually declined eleven percent in 1966 from the previous year, regional product in the construction sector increased by eight percent in the Santiago province. The change in the services sector was even more startling since it showed a two-percent decline in gross regional product outside the metropolitan zone, but a forty-eight-percent increase at the center! Under these circumstances, it is to be questioned whether the first political party to make regional development a major political issue and the first government to make it an administrative policy have yet found the measures needed to bring off the announced objectives.

This can be questioned even further based on government investment in the urban sector (as measured by industry, electricity, gas, water, and housing) during the period 1965-1967. During these years the national government investment in Santiago was forty-seven percent of total government investment in these activities. It can be seen that the promotion by the government of a regional development policy of industrialization, minerals exploitation, and agricultural improvements, all of which have implications for urban growth, can still be thwarted (in terms of an urban policy directed towards greater equilibrium in urban growth) by the expansion at the center of private industry (whose capital for expansion is largely controlled by the government) and by the urban infrastructural investments of the central government. The neglect of these two latter areas, both within the control of the national government, is an indication that present measures are still not sufficient to prevent the center-periphery gap from widening.

While the particular circumstances of urban growth in Chile in terms of: stage of industrialization; promotion of given industrial subsectors; degree of centralization; saturation of population in rural areas; size and location of urban infrastructural investments; allocation of government capital to the private sector; existing distortions in the relative size and function of cities, and so on may not be typical of all Latin American countries, the factors influencing the process of urban growth *are* typical. The tendency, direction, and distribution of urban growth differ in the degree that each of these factors differ internally and among themselves as reinforcing or counteracting. And it can be seen that a serious national urban policy will have to consider each of the factors and the means to influence them towards the objectives of that policy. A clear and valued policy and the will and power to enforce it are primordially essential as components of any transformation in present urban growth paths.

Changes in the relative strength of economic sectors in the Mexican case, too, became much more noticeable after 1940. According to Keesing (B, 1969), major nonagricultural sectors barely grew, and sometimes shrank, relative to agriculture in the years leading up to the thirties. This was, he asserts, due to large jumps in productivity and structural transformation within each sector which threw many traditional specialists out of work. Since that date, the composition of services, as well as that of manufacturing and transportation, have changed enormously, creating in the process a whole new shape in the urban economy, especially for those cities in the 100,000 inhabitants or more category. This appears to be clearly reflected in the rate of population growth in the larger cities. In the decades 1930-1940 and 1940-1950, population doubled, for example, each decade for the class of cities of 100,000 +, while those in the class of 20-100,000 increased by less than fifty percent each decade. Somewhat similar trends were evidenced in Puerto Rico between 1930 and 1960. In the early period (1930-1940) population growth in both classes was almost equal, but from 1940 to 1960 population in the class of large cities (100,000+) more than tripled, while it shrank by half in the class of 20-100,000 (one town in this class passed over to the larger class). No new towns under 20,000 were added, however, to the 20-100,000 class during the entire twenty-year period.

Similarly, in Chile, the population in cities over 100,000 grew by 110% between 1940 and 1960 and by less than 60% in those 20-100,000. This period (1940-1960) of growing industrialization in Mexico, Puerto Rico, and Chile appeared to favor, unquestionably, the urban growth of the larger urban centers and, in fact, the middle-sized towns and cities apparently grew almost exclusively by natural increase, rather than by immigration.

Other countries, such as Venezuela and Brazil, experienced a different pattern in which both classes grew almost equally (420% for the class 100,000+ and 470% for the class 20-100,000 in Venezuela, and 200 and 250% respectively in the case of Brazil). Since industrial growth did not keep up with this growth in the urbanization process, the trend towards overurbanization in both classes for these countries was reinforced.

The Regional Framework for Urban Growth

If one examines the political and economic reasons for the rise of the primate centers as they developed in Latin America during the nineteenth and early twentieth century as expressions of "nation," one may conclude that there are growing reasons to believe a shift in orientation about the meaning of nation is occurring. In many senses Latin American governments and peoples are only now becoming aware of the interior of the continent and the peripheral regions as part of nation in the sense of their being integral elements of the more complex sociopolitical and economic structures existing at the center. This is a change away from nation as metropolis with an orientation toward external national systems and the use of the interior and peripheries as mines whose resources can be bartered on the outside. It is a change which is both subtle in the way in which it has occurred and dramatic in the implications it has for the future. In the next quarter-century it is likely to produce some remarkable changes in the distribution of population and activities, in the development of urban networks, and in the social links between towns and cities in these networks.

At the same time, development *hacia afuera* to European and North American markets is being gradually complemented by economic integration among the Latin American countries. Part of this is still, by necessity, oriented toward port cities which, at times, are also the primate cities. Yet, improved means of transportation toward the interior and connections by land with other countries are bringing about an awareness of the proximity of other nations via land routes. Such awareness is sure to cause a change in the concept of importance and use of the interior and the existing or new urban centers there. They may no longer represent simple transfer points for primary products to the capital. Given their occasional proximity to other markets or prime materials across boundaries, they may, as well, begin to function as linked production and service centers for populations beyond national boundaries. Twin international cities such as Los Andes in Chile and Mendoza in Argentina could progress, for example, through the binational integration of the automotive industries in these two nations. Future complementarities have also been suggested for the Rio Negro area of Argentina, and Valdivia and its region in Chile. A major irrigation and fruit-growing region similar in size and potential to the Central Valley of California has been proposed for the Rio Negro region. Its development would be crucially aided by the supply of forestry products for packing boxes and lumber from Chile, possibly farm labor from there, and the use of ports on the Pacific for shipment of Argentine agricultural products to foreign markets.

Similar possibilities have also been suggested for the Colombian-Venezuelan and Colombian-Ecuadorean frontier zones. (Inter-American Development Bank, 2: D, 1964, 1966). The development of a Hong Kong-type, in-bond, semimanufacturing plant complex along the Mexican-United States border in Mexico by mutual arrangement between these countries is an example of what is politically possible in the border regions. More than one hundred U.S. plants have been set up during the past five years to make high labor-intensive items in Tijuana, Mexicali, and Nuevo Laredo. Here the geographic proximity to the American market and the adaptability of Mexican labor have provided mutual advantages. While it is one example which would be difficult to repeat between Latin American countries because of the particular economic conditions, it does serve as a model of political cooperation between nations.

It may be significant that the geographic integration of national space and of the urban net within it as it has developed will grow in importance as a social and political objective as a result of the compatibility of this objective with the tendency of national economic policy toward economic development *hacia adentro,* and with neighboring countries through common market and international projects. Both objectives are mutually reinforcing and are also strengthened by the multitude of economic decisions deriving from the ethic of opportunism in the private sector as the dormant economic potential in the periphery gradually comes to be recognized in its new forms. It is quite probable that this "potential recognition" has been delayed, in fact, by the growth of the primate center where most economic production tends to revolve primarily around the provision of products and services for the metropole. The peripheral economy is more of the colonial type—the provision of primary materials to fuel the economy at the center. On the other hand, some industrial product-filtering does occur out to the periphery but typically and in good colonial fashion at a considerable increase in final consumer price over purchase at its source. The situation may become so acute, as in Chile, that it is often cheaper to travel up to five hundred miles or more to purchase electrical appliances such as refrigerators (including the costs of travel and lodging overnight for a family) than it is to purchase the same refrigerator in the provinces.

It may be possible to say, however, that the existence of an attitude of internal colonialism may be a necessary condition in certain countries with respect to peripheral development. Certainly, it is not always possible to say how much the exploitation of natural resources and the location of industry and the provision of urban infrastructure in such regions as the Venezuelan Guayana is primarily related to a desire to develop a remote region and to improve the lot of the people who live there. Objectives, it may be said, are not infrequently centrally oriented in scope, and the economic benefits of such development may not infrequently be greater in the national capital than they are in the region itself. To expect an idealistic approach to regional development, then, is to be out of touch with sociopolitical reality. If regional development doesn't positively favor the economic position of the capital somehow, there is a lessened opportunity that a serious policy of regional development will be encouraged. Cuba represents one exception, perhaps, to this, since regional development there is apparently not intended to positively aid the growth of the capital, and many measures appear to be negatively related.

The political sensitiveness about national boundaries which still exists in Latin America cannot be ignored either as influential in the setting of urban and regional policies. As thrusts of development extend to the interior or peripheral areas of certain countries or as population densities build up and, in some cases, overlap national boundaries, the tendency is to promote counter policies as a means of protection of the national space from the subtle infiltration of adjacent nationals. Thus the migration of an estimated 200,000 Chileans into the Patagonia of Argentina has triggered an Argentine policy of increased attention to the regions affected both in terms of regional economic development and regional and urban infrastructural investments.

The difficulty in the application of this policy is that Argentina has reached such a high level of urbanization generally that development in the Patagonia, because of its remoteness from the center and its less attractive environment, offers almost no incentive to the "urbanized" cosmopolite or, even, to the recent immigrant to Buenos Aires. The government, then, is caught in the bind of artificially populating the region with military forces and their families, both in-service and retired, in a manner reminiscent of Eastern Bolivian military colonization efforts or the efforts of the Romans under Caesar in Spain which were aimed at populating or stabilizing frontier areas and establishing a colonial system (Bouchier, H, 1914). Alternatively, the government is faced with the fact that continued development of the area may have to depend continually upon a foreign labor force, namely from Chile. On the opposite side of the border the reverse situation prevails; there, there is an excess of population at the present stage of development.

Since it is a particularly sensitive political issue, it seems almost inconceivable, but not impossible, that an agreement between two mutually agreeable governments of the two nations could be reached which would collaterally serve the interests of both. Effectively, the economy of the Patagonia would suffer serious reverses if the Chileans were repatriated. This became evident when the Ongania government attempted to require all foreign nationals without visa documents to declare their intent to be naturalized or to leave the country. When only a handful responded positively in terms of remaining, the issue was quietly dropped. If common population policies could be successfully formulated in such cases, the actual growth of both the Chilean and the Argentine Patagonias would be favored. Here is one clear example of an area in which a large rural (Chilean) population could be successfully incorporated into a mixed rural-agricultural, minerals, and small urban centers economy on a regional basis in such a fashion as to reduce, at the same time, the tendency towards further hyperurbanization in Chile generally and the aggravation of an overpopulated (at this stage of development) rural region specifically. Urban primacy in Argentina would now appear to prevent the colonization of this area and dramatically demonstrates the negative impact of the primacy syndrome in a nation which has not yet fully developed all its regions in such a way that continuous development of them is assured.

It might be stated that the urban growth of a regional development pole is of limited help to the region if its development is not somehow tied up in terms of primary linkages to the modernization of the region itself as well. This is a development strategy which the Incas understood quite well, but one which has been frequently forgotten in Latin America since the Spanish conquest, which brought the narrower Hispanic emphasis upon the urban development phenomenon. The procedure by which the Incas proceeded to establish urban places (in their civil-political, religious, and preindustrial economic sense) and to "modernize" the rural areas has been described by Hardoy.[7] As new territories were conquered, studies were made of the human resources and the potential of the natural resources, and the people were slowly integrated into the larger common effort. Public works and regulations multiplied; new canals, granaries, roads and cities, new laws and administrative measures were geared towards assuring better production among the incorporated people, a more efficient distribution of more numerous goods, greater security, and order. Some have even asserted that the Indians of the Andean altiplano actually had a superior standard of living under this socioreligious-political system than their descendants have today. In part this is true because the postconquest emphasis on urban development has largely ignored the important issues of rural development, and many of the technologies, much of the infrastructure, and practically all the institutional framework of the Incas has disappeared and been replaced by institutions not always based upon the welfare of the Indian.

According to Hardoy, the Incas achieved, in certain aspects of territorial planning, unequaled levels in both indigenous and colonial America and their planning could even be compared favorably with prior and contemporary civilizations in Europe and Asia. Part of their success can be attributed to an uncanny sense of what the deficiencies were in the social structures of the conquered territories and a knowledge of how to overcome these with a new political and socioeconomic structure, a happy coincidence of events which appears much more difficult to achieve in contemporary Latin America. The end was always the same: the better utilization of all resources with the intent of not losing the equilibrium between production and consumption.

A number of national programs for the development of lagging or frontier regions have been put into operation in Latin America in the last couple of decades. Since many of these "peripheral" regions have experienced a low level of urbanization, there have been complementary programs to influence the urban pattern by focused investment on certain urban centers. In these programs there have been occasional economic inefficiencies and distortions in "showcase" investments on certain types of infrastructure. But, even if such investment patterns are highly questionable, this still does not obviate the purpose for which new or strengthened urban centers are proposed in such regions.

As evidence of the growing interest in regional development in Latin America, two seminars have taken place in the past few years. The First Inter-American Seminar on the Definition of Regions for Development Planning took place in Canada in 1967 under the auspices of the Regional Geography Committee of the Commission of Geography of the Pan American Institute of Geography and History. The Second Seminar on the Regionalization of Development Policy occurred in Santiago de Chile in 1969 with the joint collaboration of the Pan American Institute, the Economic Commission for Latin America (CEPAL) of the U.N., the Chilean Planning Society (PLANDES), the Latin American Institute of Economic and Social Planning (ILPES), and the National Planning Office of Chile (ODEPLAN). The Seminar in Santiago concentrated on the regionalization of national plans, methods for formulating integrated regional plans, the elaboration of methods for harmonizing plans of development and of multinational integration with the plans of the different countries for their own national development, and the mechanism of implementation of regional development policies.

Indicative of the growing concern about the social aspects of regional development, centering inevitably upon urban places as foci and centers of social betterment diffusion, was the United Nations Economic Commission for Latin America Seminar on Social Aspects of Regional Development held at Santiago, Chile, November 3-14, 1969. In this seminar three principal areas were handled:

(1) a general presentation of the context and scope of the social aspects of regional development and their implications;

(2) a review and analysis of the Latin American experience in the management of social problems and policy in regional development programs; and

(3) the identification of the essential elements of social policy and strategy for regional development, particularly with respect to Latin America.

This seminar grew out of a growing concern that programs of community development require an intermediate level of policy and program activity between the local community and central government.

A stage of awareness of the more complex implications of regional development including the role of urban places and social, as well as economic, policy is more and more evident as the new decade begins. Such awareness is part of the new environment, the new urban era, which has altered this cultural area in the last twenty-five years. It is an indication that all future national and international policies will, increasingly, tend to reflect this change which links the national urban system with regional development and a new sense of nation.

Systems of Cities

In 1940 there were only eight cities in Latin America with more than a half-million population, all of which together contained some twelve million persons. Twenty years later, in 1960, there were twenty cities of this size with some thirty-one million, or fifteen percent of the total population of the region. Yet, in this latter year, the population that lived in cities of more than 500,000 was increasing at an annual rate of more than one million, and half of this was due to immigration. Among the cities between 250,000 and 500,000 growth had arrived at a rate of 1,300,000 persons per year (Elizaga, 1: D, n.d.). In this continuing expansion of major and lesser urban centers, it is significant that the rate of natural demographic growth in urban places is only slightly inferior to that of the rural areas due, no doubt, to a carryover to the towns and cities from the rural medium of family social values which are predisposed towards elevated fecundity.

The effect that a dynamic demographic growth rate has had on towns and cities greater than 20,000 in the Latin portion of the Western hemisphere is that their populations are now doubling each

20-25 years. This same doubling effect during the great industrial expansion in the United States and England required 35-45 years.

In sixteen Latin American countries, the population of the principal urban center exceeds by at least four times that of the second largest city. This high "primacy" pattern, one author has asserted, is due largely to the centralization of administration and political power in the capital city. It is not sufficient to say, however, that all such cities are disproportionately out of size, "megacephalic," and "parasitic" as some have maintained. The economy of Uruguay, for example, based as it is on extensive cattle- and sheep-raising, would not seem to require an urban hierarchy and network more in line with nations with complex economies requiring the spatial distributions of large numbers of people at point locations. Further, the country is small enough so that, with adequate transport and communications services, the advantages of a major metropolitan area are not too far from practically all the national population. To suggest that the total urban population of Uruguay should have been distributed according to the rank-size rule in the past might well have meant that such a distribution and the necessary dimunition in the size of Montevideo would have had negative consequences for the overall development of that country. The policy questions may become, in such cases, how to plan the metropolitan area efficiently with satellite metropolitan centers, for example, rather than the continued expansion of a single center. Montevideo in 1960 contained 1,160,000 people, which is not large by world metropolitan standards even though it contains over one-third of the total national population. There is a policy question and an opportunity now, however, which calls for action before it is several times larger and more unmanageable. Given present circumstances and the economic critera for industrial production location it is likely that most future urban growth will continue to occur along the Río La Plata and estuary. Exactly where and how this growth will occur is much simpler a problem than that posed by urban growth in Brazil, but being simpler it is no less important, because the end result will constitute what will be most of urban Uruguay in the near future.[8]

The promotion of satellite cities (with or without an urban field) as one possible policy could help avoid what Francis Violich termed a tendency toward "centralization within centralization," or the overcentralization of services in the one and only commercial center of the metropolitan area, a condition which creates competition for space, requires increasingly expensive public investments in transport, and, otherwise, produces social and economic costs which the

TABLE 4.2
Latin America: Cities Estimated to Contain One Million or
More Persons in 1980 (thousands)

Country	City	1960		1980[a]	
Argentina	Greater				
	Buenos Aires	6,739		9,815	
	Córdoba	586		1,189	
			7,325		11,004
Brazil	Rio de Janeiro	3,223		6,290	
	São Paulo	3,164		7,780	
	Recife	788		1,866	
	Belo Horizonte	643		2,308	
	Salvador	631		1,642	
	Porto Alegre	618		1,671	
	Fortaleza	355		1,055	
	Curitiba	345		1,466	
			9,767		24,078
Colombia	Bogotá	1,662		5,208	
	Medellín	718		1,879	
	Cali	618		1,965	
	Barranquilla	493		1,012	
			3,491		10,064
Chile	Santiago	1,896	1,896	4,400	4,400
Ecuador	Guayaquil	511	511	1,409	1,409
Guatemala	Guatemala City	577	577	1,298	1,298
Mexico	Mexico City	2,832		4,550	
	Guadalajara	737		2,799	
	Monterrey	597		1,914	
	Ciudad Juarez	262		1,113	
			4,428		10,376
Panama	Panama City	273	273	1,160	1,160
Peru	Lima	1,436	1,436	3,563	3,563
Dominican Republic	Santo Domingo	370	370	1,542	1,542
Uruguay	Montevideo	1,159	1,159	1,583	1,583
Venezuela	Caracas	1,336		4,115	
	Maracaibo	442		1,146	
			1,758		5,261
Total in all cities in 1960 and 1980			32,991		75,738

a. The projections were calculated by extrapolating the rate of growth of the last intercensal period. When this rate exceeded 7.5%, this figure was applied as a maximum.

SOURCE: Population Reference Bureau, Inc. Programas Internacionales de Población (1969) Desarrollo Urbano en América Latina. Bogotá: The PRB. Based on the Annual Report of the Social Progress Trust Fund of the Inter-American Development Bank for 1968.

public, rather than the private, sector must pay. Santiago, for example, has just embarked on the initial stage of an extensive subway system whose cost might have been avoided or delayed a decade or more if national policy had encouraged the development of other urban centers earlier. Quite rightly, most critics of such policies say that measures to reduce the rate of urban growth or its concentration in primate cities have been marginal in terms of effect. Among these measures have been rural development, decentralization of administration, and the establishment of social institutions and industry in the periphery. Results depend upon a degree of commitment and follow-up, however, and both of these can be effective through the power or controls that most governments presently wield. But, as many developed countries are now learning, any urban crisis must be of the first order before it becomes a serious policy question leading to serious measures of correction.

A study of the Inter-American Development Bank (1: B, 1968) predicts that between 1965 and 1980 Latin American cities will increase in population by 100 million. It is calculated that 27 cities will have a population greater than 1 million and that 8 of these 27 will present characteristics associated with a megalopolis with the correlated multiplication of critical conditions already existing (see Table 4.2). Some have even predicted that greater São Paulo will be the world's largest metropolis by 1980 and that by 1990 as many as 20 million people will be jammed into it. It is now eighth in size in the world and the other seven have slowed down in growth.

The year 1980 can be viewed as a crucial time from the point of view of the urban crisis in Latin America. Whether the accelerated urbanization can or cannot be braked is almost irrelevant in terms of institutional response, but it does suggest much greater attention should be given to national urban policies and planning than is currently evidenced. (See Figure 4.1 for size and distribution of cities in 1970.)

One may wonder if there are not political, as well as economic and national spatial integration, reasons for the development of a more balanced urban system of cities including new settlements. Is there a political fear of a too highly concentrated urban center containing too many "marginal" people much like the fear which impelled the Romans to build many new towns and develop lesser population centers through enforced or sponsored emigration (Hackett, H, 1950)? Politically, the socially uneasy metropolitan city is to be feared for reasons of stability or change by easy stages. As social tensions rise relatively and absolutely, pressures are engendered to make material and service concessions to the urban rabble and

size of
cities

● 2.5 million +

* 1 - 2.5 million

* 250,000 -
  million

SOURCE: Davis (A: 1969), Table E.

FIGURE 4.1
Distribution of Metropolitan and Medium-Size Cities in
Latin America, 1970

programs to prevent the further building of pressure in the center by diversion to urban places in the periphery become imperative. Efforts are made to channel the marginal population back into newly colonized areas, into the metropolitan hinterland, into the suburbs. Such efforts occurred in Rome; they are occurring in Great Britain and the United States; and they have occurred in Latin America.

The Rise of Modern Urban Networks

Morse suggests in his comments on John Friedmann's essay in this book that "the most useful indicators of rank order for colonial Spanish American towns seem attached to functions determined or approved by politico-administrative decisions of the metropolis." In essence, this hierarchical plan of assigning metropolitan Spain's power in the New World was not intended so much to aid the *ciudad*, *villa*, and *pueblo* to function for local purposes as it was a political plan to create new colonial states and forge control over the vast new territories. During the colonial epoch the urban network was weakly developed and a lack of commercial reciprocity among the cities, accentuated by Iberian mercantilist policies, effectively insulated them from each other and linked them in firm economic bonds with Lisbon and Seville (Morse, A, 1962b).

The case of the Department of Norte de Santander in Colombia up to the nineteenth century is indicative of this lack of internal communication between the three principal towns of the region—Pamploma, Salazar, and Ocaña. Although there was no settlement net by which they were united, they had had from the beginning ready access to foreign markets. By most economic rationale there was, of course, probably little reason that these and many other centers required contact. They produced similar agricultural products and had little to exchange. Lack of industrial activity, even at modest levels, and possibilities of industrial specialization did not exist which would have created mutual interest in trade.

At the urban power apex in given territories during the Hispanic American colonial period were founded or imposed on existing indigenous urban structures the cities of Mexico, Bogotá, Lima, Sucre, and Santiago de Chile. Political power over the economic wealth of the regions was the primary basis for the past aura of the capital, a situation which has changed little in the present. In the face of the intended and accepted political personality of the national center, unquestioning acceptance may be said to prevail among lower-order urban centers of the immutable location and centralized character of political power. In other words, political power has always been centralized and recent events show little, if any, diminishing of this trait.

Economic development and growth has come to be valued locally but, as this flows from the grace of central political and administrative power, there is little opportunity to guide local destinies along surer economic paths. And any serious move to wrench important segments of political strength away from the patrimonial urban center seems foredoomed to failure, or so it seems to those weaned on the prerogatives of the center. The exceptions, as Morse has pointed out, have overcome these deterrents to greater autonomy by their tenacity and ability to subsume within local government institutions a sufficient degree of power that has permitted them to make investments in urban infrastructure at a level sufficient to attract productive activities.

By guidance and conscious design or by the evolving process of development there is growing indication that the stage of incipient industrialization characterized by a metropolitan region does give way in certain circumstances to a network of complementary cities in the stage of growing industrial maturity. John Friedmann postulated this in the case of Venezuela[9] and Fernando Travieso (C, 1968) has presented data to lend greater credence to this idea. Initially the metropolitan center functions in the midst of a national backward region, but this center-periphery phenomenon is gradually replaced by a dynamic national center complemented by secondary cities strategically located in such a way that the periphery is eventually incorporated into the modernization process and the former backward regions shrink little by little. Travieso has identified in the Venezuelan case, for example, some six national growth centers which are contributing in important ways to the national leading economic sectors. The experience of such a linked network forms, unquestionably, a significant aspect of the new urban era in Latin America.

National Urban Policies and Strategies

National development and economic growth in Latin America implies, as one principal ingredient, the presence of a dynamic and viable urban growth and the allocation policy decisions of the national governments affect for better or worse the total urban system and each individual urban center in this respect. Since so many local economies are changed or can be changed by the control of central governments over public and private finances and what sector or project to promote or not to promote (whether policy is intended or not, whether it is implicit or explicit), national urban policies do exist as a result of the normal momentum of government decisions.

In certain specific cases (Chile, for example), there have been policies for first-stage decentralization (or better said, deconcentration) attempts at strengthening a few selected cities in an effort to move away from growing gigantism in the primate city. Other less conscious examples indicate a shotgun approach of dispersed investment in a large number of urban places. Still others tend to ignore in terms of serious intent anything much outside the capital and its port city. Both these latter approaches, however, are policy alternatives which are actually losing ground as governments have become more responsive to rising levels of more-sophisticated regional interests and as regional development has gradually come to be viewed as a necessary accompaniment to and one of the mechanisms for aiding national development in the long run.

The choice of any one urban strategy, implicitly or explicitly, involves its adherents and opponents. There is good reason to believe, however, that each country actually requires a strategy containing a weighted aggregate of options that includes both economic and sociopolitical reasons, as well as a consideration of the level of urbanization, the existing urban system, and the general stage of development—economic and otherwise. One crucial question becomes: can the particular strategy (or decisions which create an implicit strategy in the face of the lack of an explicit one) keep abreast of the urbanization process as it occurs differentially in space? And, where intended, does the strategy have the positive effects intended on the process?

One of the most challenging conclusions of a series of studies, conducted by the Institute of Public Administration and the United Nations, of thirteen major international metropolitan areas, including Lima, is that national-level policies, as expressed in national plans, have important developmental implications for urban centers which need careful appraisal. Additionally, explicit national urban policies have actually proven ineffective in achieving certain urban goals such as those of improved metropolitan administration.

The societal pressures in Latin America tending towards continous and rapid urban growth are considerable, so that stimulation on a national scale, at least, hardly seems necessary. National policies on the location of urban growth are needed increasingly, however. Even though the stimulation of urban growth is not necessary nationally, stimuli for growth in given locations and policies aimed at slowing down or channelling the growth of given urban centers are relevant, however. There are those who maintain that this is not possible, but this view seems to deny the willingness rather than the capability of changing the seemingly inexorable trends or urban development. But trends depend upon the summation of a multitude of decisions, some of which are within the control of government and many of which can produce countereffects to past patterns. It is the willingness to decide that trends must be altered which is a key framer of the future and capability, itself, is strongly dependent upon willingness to act.

In a dramatic sense, not necessarily to be emulated, the governments of Brazil and Venezuela have made decisions to alter the urbanization (spatial) pattern of their respective countries. Each of them has embarked on major and expensive new city projects, projects which have as their primary purpose the development of potentially developable hinterlands. They both also represent clear efforts to break the overpowering economic or political dominance of a single center. In one sense, however, they are opposite in approach. Brazilia represents the establishment of a major urban center, the new national capital, as a catalyst for growth in the great heartland of Brazil. Other than the government sector, no single important sectoral project justified its initial establishment. Ciudad de Guayana in Venezuela, in contrast, was built as a service facility for sectoral projects aimed at exploiting energy and mineral resources in that region of such a scale that a major new city was justified.

Less spectacular but equally important policies of stimulated local growth for existing centers and the spatial channelling of national population growth is also evident in Chile. There Antofagasta, Valparaiso-Viña del Mar and Concepcion have been singled out as second-order centers after Santiago, the capital, and development attention is being devoted to them for the purpose both of building up regional economies and of building up major urban centers capable of absorbing population flow as alternatives to Santiago.

The promotion of policies aimed at a more equitable and, certainly, a less concentrated-centralized distribution of population is growing then in Latin America. As Powelson and Solow (D, 1965) have suggested, these policies constitute:

(1) strengthening of the small and medium-sized urban areas;

(2) concentration of public investment only on selected urban centers;

(3) establishment of new towns related to natural resource development.

Actually, urban policy in Latin America in this sense is becoming even more detailed and sophisticated, and two additional policies can now be identified:

(4) the build-up of economic activities and infrastructure of provincial capitals or medium-sized cities which are "satellites" of the primate city and close enough to draw on the dynamism of the center with easy access for necessary services; and

(5) more implicit than explicit in the case of Chile, the promotion of an "urban field" (see note 11) itself within a one- to two-hour trip of Santiago through the location of urban economic activities in what has been normally viewed as a basically rural environment.

The idea of the urban field (Friedmann and Miller, C, 1965) has been advanced in the case of the United States to indicate the use of the growth-pole hinterland for urban purposes, not merely the modernization and economic growth of the agricultural sector as it has been conceptualized until recently.

In the case of Santiago, major automobile assembly plants and intermediate products firms have been "encouraged" to locate within an hour or so from the capital in the open countryside. The development of a similar urban field is apparently also occurring in São Paulo but not by direct policy of the government (Saia, C, 1963). In this case the market system is forcing a dispersion of industry beyond the city and its outskirts as a result of inadequate urban services and profiteering in urban real estate. Urban "push" factors for private industrial location are creating a dispersal pattern that is eroding the urban-rural polarity. In other words, there is a coalescence of urban and rural activities and land uses into an urban field which is more notable for the dynamics of urban forces than those of agrarian sector complementarity to the center.

Although the economist Benjamin Higgins (A, 1967a) indicates that it is not known whether economic development requires increased concentration in large cities and suggests more research, it is becoming more evident that governments, in fact, are diverting industries from large to medium or small cities without conclusive proof. In some cases, certain projects have clear comparative advantage for location outside the center and, therefore, they serve national economic development. In other cases, social and political considerations are at the core of the location decisions.

Yet the general weakness in the economy of the small towns suffers an even greater and growing degree of disparity when compared with the great urban foci as a result of industrial modernization and the trend to a more complete centralization in one place for economic and technical reasons (location of market, transport, work force, and so on). These apparent economic reasons are often in part a result of national government policy and investment programs which create an unfavorable comparison between the center and the periphery in an analysis of cost-benefit in the location of the private and government-supported firm. In fact, the continued emphasis on social project location by central governments in the metropoli, often completely out of balance with investments in lesser centers as measured by such simple devices as expenditures per capita, can only continue to have the effect of making the center the almost indefinite preference of the private sector. The infrastructure in the capital often precedes the actual demand for it (as contrasted with other urban places) and, therefore, is located where it is in the center because government policy has put it there, not necessarily because the free market mechanism determined it should be there.

While some critics quite rightly insist that egalitarian regionalism should not be undertaken for its own sake, the argument here is that an egalitarian approach would, undoubtedly, in most cases, if not all, have adverse effects on general development. On the other hand, it is equally dangerous to assert that the indefinite and uncontrolled growth of one or a few among many urban centers is necessarily (in the broad sense) advantageous socially for the entire nation after a certain population level has been reached in the primary center. In the initial stages of urbanization, growth which concentrates principally on one or a few large cities with the postponement of major urban growth in other areas may be absolutely essential so that the rich mix of institutional structures, ideas, technology, and new values of modernization can build up to a level that makes their diffusion throughout the entire national space possible. But, as Andrade[10] has observed, "after a while, investment can be diverted in a different direction. The government will have to direct this through a program of industrial development for cities that do not now have capital investment."

Even so, some cities like Santiago have not been the locus of government-financed major industries in the past nor at the present. In fact the government has often done what "it could to hold back Santiago," as one author (Keller, D, 1958) states. The crucial variable in the growth of Santiago, as with other capitals, is the growth of the service sector, both public and private, and small and middle-sized industries. These activities are the ones which are generating most new urban employment opportunities directly and bringing about the expansion of the primate cities in spite of the lack of new "major" industries. Location policies with regard to this part of the economy are much weaker or nonexistent, and while a government may point with pride to its decentralization policies with respect to heavier production facilities of steel plants and refineries, it is these latter types of production units which are capital-intensive and do little with respect to providing employment, as contrasted with the service sector and small and middle-sized industrial plants. This is clearly demonstrated in the case of the service sector employment growth in Chile between 1952 and 1960. Although Santiago province contained just 33.1% of the total national population in 1960, it attracted to it 65% of all service sector growth in the eight-year period 1952-1960 (Chile, B, 1968b). In the industrial sector, the situation was even more pronounced. While industrial jobs increased by 20,149 during this period in all of Chile, Santiago province gained 23,122; or, in other words, there was a total loss of 2,973 industrial jobs from the rest of the country to this province—at the same time that there was expansion in the steel industry, petroleum resource development, and the like outside the metropolitan province. The period 1961-1965 was a continuation of this pattern.

Present policy to permit and encourage the relocation of the automobile industry from the north of Chile to the central valley near, but not in, Santiago represents a further progression of the past tendency. Even though final assembly (the major industry) will not be in the capital city, practically all of the related, intermediate, small- and middle-scale auto products and service functions will probably settle in the metropolitan zone over time, and it is these, not the assembly of autos, which will be the principal employers. It is their location which will determine most of the urban growth related to the automobile industry—unless a firm policy is taken with regard to them as well. Unless this is done, location policy will not constitute a decentralization policy at all and, in fact, may be positively reinforcing as a centralization measure in contrast with the former policy of location in the north—even though automobile assembly will occur outside the center but within one hour's drive of Santiago.

In fact, urbanization policy as it appears to be developing in Chile seems to be aimed, in part, towards the creation of a wide-region metropolitan area including the two port cities of Valparaiso and San Antonio, the "satellite" cities of Rancagua and Los Andes, and the urban use of rural lands in the interstices such as Casa Blanca, where automobile assembly will take place. It constitutes, in fact, the Latin

American equivalent of the urban field phenomenon[11] observed by Friedmann and Miller (C, 1965) in the United States. While the urban field has arisen in the United States as a basically free market response to increased family income, leisure time, population growth, technological change, and the like, it is occurring in the case of Chile through government direction and guidance. Another distinction is that the phenomenon is occurring in the United States in many regions centering on SMSA's of 300,000 or more while in Chile it is evident around only one center. Judgment should not be passed a priori in this new development, however, as it may, in fact, represent one practical and possible alternative inside a broader urban policy for the nation which aims at diminishing the overload of population and functions in one city, while permitting new development to take advantage of products and services within reasonable proximity. The preparation of detailed research and policy recommendations for this macro-zone, or urban field, centering on Santiago is part of current national planning effort in Chile.

An important economic question remains in the case of Chile, however. Will the additional costs (capitalization and maintenance) of the transport and communications net for a Chilean urban field outweigh the economic benefits of regional proximity, or would the same expenditures in a more distant region and urban center produce a better return? And such a policy begs other social and political questions which will probably be ignored if it is implemented on a long-term basis.

It is clearly evident in any case that such a strategy, should it prove beneficial to the general development of the country at the same time that continued-point centralization is avoided to a given degree in Santiago, is not necessarily appropriate to the urban structure and economy of a country like Colombia where an already more balanced rank size distribution of cities exists with three cities over a half-million and a capital city with 1,600,000 (1960), or of a country like Paraguay which could quite easily continue to concentrate development on Asunción. It might be quite appropriate to Montevideo, however, in another decade, or to São Paulo now, as it seems to be happening anyway through nonguided forces. In any event, these differences demonstrate that national urban policies must be formed for each country based upon the conditions peculiar to each country.

It may be argued that the growth of the large metropolitan city, while it may have deterred the general growth of all other cities and other regions outside its own, may have been a necessary stage in the development from basically agricultural, nonindustrial societies to the new urban era. Such a stage, as was stated before, may have been essential for the creation of the base for the types of institutions essential in the diffusion of modernization and change at later stages. It seems less likely, for example, that ten cities in a predominantly primary production economy of 100,000 could generate the necessary innovative level for nationally directed change that one city of 1,000,000 could. What would Uruguay be if Montevideo were replaced by a neat, rank-size hierarchy of cities containing the present population of the capital and other major cities? Less exciting culturally; probably considerably less dynamic.

The more pertinent question may revolve around the continued necessity for the exaggerated growth of a city of two million or more in contrast to the slower growth of second-order and lesser cities. The growth of primate cities is construed through modernization-efficiency criteria as essential, but once they reach a given size, different perhaps for each nation, the alternative growth of lesser-order cities may not be prejudicial. One author (Browning, A, 1967) has stated, for example, that "over the long run, under such conditions, high primacy becomes increasingly a negative factor for several reasons. For one thing, the centralization it represents may serve to handicap the development of other regions of the country. And the development of skilled personnel and facilities in the primate city may actually reach the point of excess supply, while at the same time serious deficiencies continue to exist in other areas." In revolutionary Cuba it would appear that a decision has been made that Havana has already reached or surpassed this critical "given" size. A policy has been initiated, for example, favoring the growth of other centers, and it is a policy whose intent it is, apparently, to let the level of services and facilities decline in Havana so as to make living in other centers more attractive.

Basically, the policy question becomes one of serious and determined decentralization of new activities and, occasionally, of some older activities, including those of the central government, rather than the initiation of policy measures taken to directly prevent the arrival of people at the center or to hold them in rural areas. As Benjamin Higgins has observed, large-scale industries do not necessarily require large cities. Any country wishing to do so could probably achieve some decentralization by moving industry and related services from large cities like Rio and Melbourne to middle-sized cities.

The role of urban centers as foci of rural development should not be ignored, either. There are approximately 29 persons per square mile of land in Latin America, a density that compares favorably with East Asia's 185 persons and Europe's 231 persons per square mile. Well over half of all Latin Americans live actually on about 5% of the region's land area. In a number of cases, the location of major urban centers does not always favor the development of intensive agricultural production close by, due to soil, climate, or terrain; agricultural colonization efforts are frequently located so far from the market that production remains at the subsistence level because there are no urban centers of sufficient size close by to promote commercial crops, and the transportation network does not favor their delivery at great distances. Policies for urban deconcentration and agricultural development are, then, clearly related and, necessarily, should be made for optimal "fit."

Urbanization policy might be better guided if more concrete knowledge were available about the optimal economic size of cities in different countries. This is a quite complex area of research, but certain questions can be posed and are beginning to be posed which will help untangle this Gordian knot. In the area of transportation alone, one can ask: is it more economic to move a half-million people in a metropolitan area by subway than it would be to move 50,000 people in each of ten lesser cities by more conventional methods? Is it more or less expensive to provide water and sewerage facilities for the same number of people in one urban center or in ten when both construction and maintenance costs are included? What are the additional costs to households and firms for use of land in a city of two-and-a-half million or more over what such costs would be in cities one-tenth this size? These are costs which somehow must be borne. When the costs of great urban agglomerations become excessive, it is usual for the central government to subsidize them by one means or another. When these subsidies become large, can they be justified socially when other regions and urban places may be seriously lacking in various of the services expected at the center? All such questions related to the total costs of population growth by both the public and private sectors must be adequately answered before it can be glibly asserted that "economic factors favor continued concentration on the central city." These factors do frequently favor such concentration, of course, when one ignores necessary public expenditures and alternative investment patterns and when one considers only the private costs and benefits deriving from central location.

The argument that special incentives have to be provided for industry to entice it to settle outside the major urban complex is made as if this were somehow "uneconomic" to begin with and as if only special measures would ever achieve this goal. This argument, however, ignores the fact that the central governments frequently provide powerful incentives and indirect subsidies for the location of industry and services at the center. Adequate energy sources and improved transportation modes focusing on and within the primate city, public housing programs, medical and educational services superior to those elsewhere, ease of access to bureaucratic routines important to the firm, and the use of the politically important top-level bureaucrat in key decision areas who is also a potential associate in private business enterprises are all significantly important as incentives for industrial location. Survival elsewhere for the firm may depend less (in making comparative location analyses) on traditional costing procedures for labor, capital, materials, land, and transportation costs than on some of these noncostable social and political variables. In many senses, it is the government which is responsible for the particular mix of social and political advantages of the capital. In fact, purely economic incentives may not be sufficiently powerful, given free choice, to attract production and services away from the center unless these incentives are overwhelmingly favorable to the producer. Certainly it is becoming more evident that subsidies making up, presumably, the difference of the economic advantage of the center over the periphery alone do not tip the balance in favor of the periphery. Organized industrial parks technical training schools, improved hospitals, middle-income housing, as well as moderate income housing, recreational facilities, access to the central government bureaucracy at the regional level with power over certain crucial decision areas, and so forth, must be provided in the periphery as they are in the center—a fact which some socialist countries early recognized in certain respects as an essential for attracting people and providing a reasonable level of varied services.

The danger in the development of new policy with respect to such issues as increased incentives for decentralization is to be so diffuse with such a policy that the effective growth of second-order cities (where they are economically weak) is deterred by decentralization to too many urban centers. A considered policy of deconcentration to a few intermediate-level cities would have, quite clearly, a greater impact on modernizing and industrializing them and in reducing the possible uninterrupted growth of the primary metropolis than a policy of broadcast development. It may be inferred, in fact, that a staged policy for the growth of the national urban system would be one oriented towards bringing second-order-level cities to a level of activity and a size where a more viable and complex economy could be sustained within the total national economy. A shift in a second stage of development following this, then, could focus more attention on third-order cities. Obviously such a policy could not rationally ignore lower-order cities which are clearly and definitely favored by location and other factors for the placement of new economic activities—such as resource extraction and processing and favored transportation siting for transshipment of products and people. What the policy would do would be to avoid an artificial emphasis on those centers that do not qualify as second-order centers or have clear locational advantage for given activities in comparison with other centers.

Another danger in the sudden and concerned focus of central government on the urban centers in the periphery is that central government planners too often do not have an economic sense of what is appropriate in the level of quality and quantity in the provision of community physical infrastructural facilities when called upon to design and construct public projects in the provinces. One can travel throughout Latin America and see public buildings built of materials and of a size out of proportion to local needs. The total effect is that some communities have facilities of a quality and size twice that necessary, and other communities have a grossly inadequate physical infrastructure of social services. As has been shown to be true in at least one country—and it can be assumed to be evidence of a general value—local communities would have preferred twice as many houses of lesser quality instead of what the government actually built in its attempt to reproduce, in appearance if not in fact, replicas of middle-income housing. However, when the centralization of the political structure and administration prevents these types of values from finding an expression in action, then the need for political decentralization becomes concretely apparent. From a health and, indirectly, an economic standpoint deriving from the first, the provision of a satisfactorily healthy housing environment for all the population may be thought to be more important than the housing of half of the population quite well and the other half hardly at all.

It should be pointed out that location policy is most frequently phrased in terms of economic comparative advantage or, occasionally, in terms of social equity and political necessity. This framework of analysis leaves aside location decisions based in part at least on a comparative analysis of the levels of modernization attitudes among different communities, or what Friedmann has referred to as their potential as social development poles. These are the social equivalents of those centers which have been referred to as growth poles, based upon their economic potential. Some studies, such as that of

Manuel Avila (A, 1969) indicate that foci containing substantial elements of change willingness and potential exist even among what too frequently is glossed over as the backward, traditional rural village. In fact, it should only be too clear by now that the tendency to make general statements about certain aspects of any society are only too often contradicted by the exceptions, and it is these exceptions which, when they are favorably disposed towards development, should be seized upon as opportunities and levers for change when an otherwise general condition would tend to support an attitude of pessimism. Avila has shown conclusively that, contrary to common belief, the rural village of Mexico is not necessarily mired in a condition of stagnation, and that some may even possess a "unique dynamism and potential for social and economic growth." He asserts that this is not necessarily attributable to the infusion of Mexican federal aid to these areas, but rather to the "special qualities, characteristics, and habits of the villagers themselves." There is every reason to suspect that the basis for modernization and a latent change-ferment are also present in many other towns and villages throughout Latin America, but that, on the basis of purely economic criteria, they are being overlooked. For the value that they contain in modernizing outmoded traditional attitudes within the society, greater efforts of comparative research among urban places with the purpose of understanding their social preparation for change and for locating the most favored communities is probably justified—at least under a strategy of optimizing input and resources through the selection of pilot areas.

According to John Herbert (Herbert and Van Huyck, D, 1968) many factors suggest the importance of focusing a large part of the immediate development effort on existing major urban centers, although it may also be important to focus some effort on the creation of new industrial and urban centers. It might be suggested, however, that this viewpoint should be tempered by differences in the national economic and urban systems profiles. And the policy question is not only one of urban development; it is also one of regional development. What may be true for Paraguay where there is little industrialization and hardly any urban system, for example, is not likely to be true for Brazil where there is evidence that some new industrial centers or concentration on lesser urban centers could be justified as São Paulo swells by its own voracious appetite and gluttony.

Among the factors which suggest the importance of focusing a large part of the immediate development effort on existing urban centers, according to Herbert, are:

(a) The major concentration of the productive capacity through which the economic condition of the nation can be improved relatively rapidly, at least in the short run. (But, by the same rationality, development would never occur elsewhere if policy is to be based on this.)

(b) The metropolis, institutionally, usually houses the central administrative functions of the nation or the region, and offers the most specialized services in such areas as education and health. It houses the centralized elements of the nation's modern monetary institutions. It is a major communications center and a modern generator of development-oriented attitudes and ideas. (While this may be true, it is not necessarily and wholly a positive characteristic when this centralization is maintained beyond the stage where these characteristics might well be shared with the rest of the nation. Without strength of purpose and definite policy to the contrary, the forces of centripetal attraction will not only maintain themselves, they will grow in strength. What is overlooked in this argument is that the central administrative functions of the nation often contain elements of decision-making which might better be transferred to the region or municipalities as a matter of pure efficiency. Detailed decision overload on local matters at the center typically delays action and prevents more serious consideration of broader policy and program preparation.)

(c) The administrative functions of the metropolis, national and regional, as well as local, make it vital as a center of administrative action. It is often the origin of development ideas and policies. (And it should be. It is also, as any place can be, the defender of negative traditional values. Where would the conservative military dictatorship be, for instance, without the capital as a base? Both elements are forever present. On the other hand, development ideas and policies related to regional and local matters are frequently found at those levels, too, and an optimal system of development is one which permits entry of ideas which advance the society at all levels. Further, power attracts those with ideas. If there is little effective power in the periphery there will be little effective idea formation there; and the ideas needed for local-regional problems may or may not flow back to the periphery once the brain power has settled at the center. This parallels the diminished change influence of the Peruvian *cholo* in Lima over regional problems versus the influence the same cholo is likely to exert if he remains in the region. See the following section, "Innovation Diffusion Through the Urban System.")

(d) The metropolis is a center for both formal and informal political activity. (Since centralization makes it so, it is likely that it will continue to serve in this function. But wider national development would, undoubtedly, be served in the long run by the growth of a finer and stronger network of political activity found throughout the nation which could be channelled into the solution of local and regional problems.)

(e) The provision of a physical base for urban activity is, of course, one of the major functions of the metropolis (as it is for every other urban center).

One is still left with the question of where growth should be encouraged and on what scale. There is a conflict between the allocation of limited capital and skills available for development as between the giant cities (where there is a pressing necessity to do something) and the periphery where there are pressures to create investment opportunities, to exploit the national resources better, and to establish new growth points as reception areas for the continual flow of migrants from the rural areas. Lagging regions in the developing countries, unlike most of those in the developed countries, are dominant and nationally important elements, partly because there are generally recognized growth potentials remaining which have not been thoroughly explored.

Innovation Diffusion Through the Urban System

Change mechanisms of diffusion-spillover out of national centers to regional towns have been altering traditional social patterns throughout Latin America for generations. As a process there is nothing particularly modern about this fascinating social movement of ideas, attitudes, and social structures down or through the urban hierarchy from the principal urbe to provincial outposts. At certain stages of development, these ideas, attitudes, and so forth touch only a small minority of the population and usually in those value areas which do not seriously threaten existing social structures. This is especially true of rural provincial centers where the town-territory relationship has been based upon a truly parasitic bond in which the town survives almost exclusively due to the surplus of its territory. This represents a static symbiosis in which the principal exchange is one of goods, and these primarily in the direction and to the benefit of the rural center.

Actually, as Pedersen (E, 1969) has shown, an innovation-diffusion process is favored by proximity to original point of innovation, a high rate of population participation (willingness and ability), a necessary number of innovators, low threshold levels (low level of economic-technical limitations) in the locality, and rapid urban growth. Diffusion tends, he suggests, to follow two systems. In the early stages of economic development, spatial proximity (or closely linked economic functions such as those of port and capital cities) favors diffusion, but, as development proceeds, diffusion paths tend to shift to a system which follows the nonspatial linearity of the urban hierarchy.

New forms of behavior, new patterns of organization and activity, and new nets of relationships are most frequently posited in terms of the provincial center as a micro-copy of the distant great metropolis. While this penetration of the structural and functional evidence of modernization to the periphery does represent "change" for the more exclusively rural-based center, that penetration can be said to be potentially deeper and more important for continous development where there is a marginal group, such as the cholos in Peru, who aid in bringing about change in the rural territory, as well as in the urban center. Foster (E, 1962: 77) has, for example, indicated that cultural incongruities generally encourage social change. This is, perhaps, one of the important variables in the denomination of a social growth pole, as distinguished from an economic growth pole. Larson and Bergman (B, 1969: 70) believe that the social change function of the marginal (positive sense) population is strengthened when migration centers on a provincial city, as in Huancayo, instead of on the national capital where the migrant is incorporated into the metropolitan structure without contact or opportunity for altering social patterns in the provinces that delay and prevent total societal development. If this is true, perhaps too much emphasis has been placed in the literature on the exclusive role of the major metropolis in change, and more attention needs to be given to the role of regional socioeconomic growth poles—not alone for regional change, but for national change, as well.

In effect, the local elite of the regional center makes use of the distant and more modern cultural artifacts and ideas as long as social structural forms are not altered unfavorably for them, with the result that nothing occurs beyond that single dead-end transmission. Eventually, however, the pursuit of opportunities for personal and familial economic gain through more contemporary urban-, less rural-oriented pastimes, occurs, and there is a penetration of new forms of behavior, new patterns of organization and activity, and new nets of relationships. These involve the community and the outside, both in terms of other centers, especially the principal one, and its own hinterland. In fact, the continued growth and prosperity of the new urban activities may eventually bring about a rearrangement of social structures in the rural territory so as to favor the continual expansion of these activities. Or, they may provide alternatives, such as in employment, which weaken the dependence on the hacienda structure and challenge the ideological hegemony of the older elites. Within this milieu, individuals may arise who are marginal to both traditional, rural-based structures and the older social elite, but who are crucially important for conveying and transmitting innovation and change. Larson and Bergman (B, 1969) have reported on just such a metamorphosis of the regional center of Huancayo in Peru. Among the salient characteristics of the new center is the fact that the local elite is no longer that of a land-based and powerful interest group. Rather, an entire new group has arisen tied neither to any one urban place or to any rural fiefdom. These are the cholos, people who are Indian racially but not culturally, who belong neither to the past nor to the accepted urban social structure deriving from the past. They are best characterized, according to these authors, by geographic mobility, social uprootedness, and intermediate role-playing between development and tradition. In other words, they are the catalytic role agents responsible in part for transformations which are occurring. When such individuals come to form an important minority in a region, the process of "cholification" is said to have occurred. This development is both an effect of the penetration of economic development and, at the same time, a positive aid in its further transmission. It is also likely, because of its rural origins and lack of ties with any recognized and established social structure, that it may even bring with it the seeds of important structural changes in both the rural and urban sectors. It represents in the positive sense of the word social marginality favoring progressive change. Cotler (B, 1967) and Quijano (B, 1965) also adhere to the belief that the cholos will be instrumental in producing social change by mobilizing the rural masses and turning them against the entire system of domination.

This, then, on the social side, is a challenging and exciting area of investigation from which useful policy guidance could come that contrasts sharply in its content with the basis for much of present and suggested urban policy dealing with the economic and physical development of urban Latin America. Clearly channelling urban growth in Latin America over the next decade or two will be a fascinating experiment in how to deal with the realities of major new social thrusts and expressions of change. It also presents a rich complex of policy decision areas to complement those which have engaged the attention of governments in this hemisphere during the sixties.

NOTES

1. Willems (B, 1970) has reported that there was scarce participation in the existing money economy among ten regional towns in the *capitania* of São Paulo during the early nineteenth century. This conclusion is based on census data of the period. Houses were built without a single nail, screw, hinge, or anything that had to be purchased. Spinning, weaving, and pottery-making were all local cottage crafts. In many localities this same type of subsistence barter economy remained virtually unchanged until the third decade of the present century.

2. This esteem often added new words to the local parlance. *Siútico,* a term still in use in Chile, derives from the use of the elegant imported English "suit" by the young dandies of the epoch. In use it refers to the modishly dressed young blades themselves. Other evidences in current language from this golden era of importation include "smoking," "troly," "living" (living room), and "WC."

3. The flow of gold not only enriched the coffers of Lisbon—it left little for colonial government. Official directives, so research by Alden (A, 1968) has indicated, specified that no part of the royal fifth of mining output could ever be diverted to local needs even in the case of extreme necessity since, ran the orders, "they have indispensible application to this court [Lisbon]." In 1773 some 1,200,000 milreis were dutifully exported to Lisbon on royal account, yet the local administration could raise for extraordinary military and naval operations in the south only 95,670 milreis, of which 86,922 were a "voluntary subsidy."

4. This position has also been taken by James R. Scobie who indicates that the city has had little relation to the rest of the country, has expressed the values of dominant minority groups and not those of an integrated society. "Political considerations and motivations," he writes, "rather than economic or social, have historically controlled urbanization in Latin America. The city has, therefore, often emerged as an imposition, an appendage, tacked onto a relatively underdeveloped agricultural countryside . . ." (quoted in Beyer, A, 1967: 63). While this may be debated in the sense that the political may be largely determined by economic motives, it is still nonetheless quite obvious that political (government) determinations are frequently largely responsible for the attraction of economic activities to the major centers and that by not providing a physical and services infrastructure of equal level in other lesser cities, these same cities have had a decreased level of attraction for new production.

5. Sheep and cattle are the basic economic pillars of Uruguay, and Montevideo uses them for the construction of its own economy of industry and commerce. Not only is the shape of Uruguay's global economy determined by agriculture, the form and strength of Montevideo's urban economy hinges upon and is determined by the economic production of the *campo.*

6. As early as 1914, the São Paulo State Department of Labor was defining the condition as "pernicious urbanism" resulting from the attraction of a "plethora" of workers from underprivileged rural areas. Even though employment might eventually be found, the worker was "almost always superfluous, parasitic, tolerated" (quoted in Morse, 9: L, 1951).

7. Jorge Hardoy (1968) Urban Planning in Pre-Columbian America. New York: George Braziller.

8. Montevideo has grown to its present size due to two basic facts. Agriculture is, overall, an extensive type of production in Uruguay requiring few urban centers of any size, a fact which has left the capital in an overwhelmingly predominant position. At the same time, the agricultural sector has been unable to absorb its increasing population; migration, therefore, has been principally to Montevideo, leaving the small rural towns relatively behind and creating large expansions of underutilized land (Brannon, 4: B, 1968).

9. John R. P. Friedmann (1966) Regional Policy for Developing Areas: A Case Study of Venezuela. Cambridge, Mass.: M.I.T. and Harvard University Joint Center for Urban Studies. See also Friedmann (D, 1969) "The future of urbanization in Latin America."

10. Quoted in Beyer (A, 1967: 166).

11. "The urban field may be viewed as an enlargement of the space for urban living that extends far beyond the boundaries of existing metropolitan areas–defined primarily in terms of commuting to a central city of "metropolitan" size–into the open landscape of the periphery. This change to a larger scale of urban life is already underway, encouraged by changes in technology, economics, and preferred social behavior. Eventually the urban field may even come to be acknowledged as a community of *shared* interests, although these interests may be more strongly oriented to specific functions than to area. They will be shared because to a large extent they will overlap and complement each other within a specific locational matrix. Because urban fields will be large, with populations of upwards of one million, their social and cultural life will form a rich and varied pattern capable of satisfying most human aspirations within a local setting.

The idea of an urban field is . . . based on the criterion of interdependency. It represents a fusion of metropolitan spaces and non-metropolitan peripheral spaces centered upon core areas (SMSA's) of at least 300,000 people and extending outwards from these core areas for a distance equivalent to two hours' driving over modern throughway systems (approximately 100 miles with present technology). This represents not only an approximate geographic limit for commuting to a job, but also the limit of intensive weekend and seasonal use (by ground transportation) of the present periphery for recreation" [Friedmann and Miller, C, 1965].

REFERENCES

A. The Role of the City in Latin America
(See also Chapter 9: Reference Section L, Urban History in Latin America.)

ABELLA TRIAS, J. C. (1960) Montevideo: la ciudad en que vivimos, su desarrollo, su evolución y sus planes. Montevideo: Editorial Alfa.

ALDEN, DAURIL (1968) Royal Government in Colonial Brazil: With Special Reference to the Administration of the Marquis of Lavradio, Viceroy, 1769-1779. Berkeley: Univ. of California Press.

ANDERSON, NELS (1962) "The urban way of life." International J. of Comparative Sociology 3 (December): 175-188.

AVILA, MANUEL (1969) Tradition and Growth: A Study of Four Mexican Villages. Chicago: Univ. of Chicago Press.

BAER, WERNER (1970) The Development of the Brazilian Steel Industry. Nashville, Tenn.: Vanderbilt Univ. Press.

BAZANT, JAN (1964) "Evolution of the textile industry of Puebla: 1544-1845." Comparative Studies in Society and History 7: 56-69.

BEYER, GLENN H. (1967) "The role of the city in historical perspective: editor's summary and elaboration." Pp. 56-70 in Glenn H. Beyer (ed.) The Urban Explosion in Latin America. Ithaca, N.Y.: Cornell Univ. Press.

BIRD, RICHARD (1963) "The economy of the Mexican Federal District." Inter-American Economic Affairs 17 (Autumn): 50-51.

BOTERO, GIOVANNI (1956) "The greatness of cities." Robert Peterson (trans.) in Giovanni Botero, The Reason of State and the Greatness of Cities. London: Routledge & Kegan Paul.

BROWNING, HARLEY L. (1967) "Urbanization and modernization in Latin America: the demographic perspective." Pp. 71-92 in Glenn H. Beyer (ed.) The Urban Explosion in Latin America. Ithaca, N.Y.: Cornell Univ. Press. (See also "Editor's summary and elaboration," pp. 92-116.)

CAPLOW, THEODORE (1952) "The modern Latin American city." In Sol Tax (ed.) Acculturation in the Americas. Chicago: Univ. of Chicago Press.

CARDOSA, FERNANDO HENRIQUE (1965) The Structure and Evolution of Industry in São Paulo: 1930-1960. Studies in Comparative International Development 005. Beverly Hills: Sage Publications.

CASIMIR, JEAN and BERTA LERNER SIGAL (1969) "La estructura de dominación ciudad-campo." Revista Mexicana de Sociología 31, 1.

COBB, GWENDOLIN B. (1945) "Potosí, a South American mining frontier." Pp. 39-58 in Adele Ogden and Engel Sluiter (eds.) Greater America. Berkeley: Univ. of California Press.

DAVIS, KINGSLEY (1962) "Las causas y efectos del fenómeno de primacía urbana con referencia especial a América Latina." México, D.F.: Instituto de Investigaciones Sociales.

——— (1960) "Colonial expansion and urban diffusion in the Americas." International J. of Comparative Sociology 1: 43-66.

DEBRIEY, P. (1966) "Urban agglomerations and the modernization of developing states." Civilisations 16: 1-25.

DICKINSON, ROBERT E. (1964) City and Region: A Geographical Interpretation. London: Routledge & Kegan Paul; New York: Humanities Press.

Dominguez y Company (1951) "Funciones económicas del cabildo colonial hispano-americano." Pp. 166 ff. in Contribuciones a la historia municipal de América. México, D.F.

FRIEDMANN, JOHN R. P. (1961-1962) "Cities in social transformation." Comparative Studies in Society and History 4: 86-103.

GERMANI, GINO (1967) "The city as an integrating mechanism." Pp. 175-214 in Glenn H. Beyer (ed.) The Urban Explosion in Latin America. Ithaca, N.Y.: Cornell Univ. Press. (Also as "La ciudad como mecanismo integrador" in Revista Mexicana de Sociolgía 29, 3.

GIL, MUNILLA (1955) "La ciudad de Hispanoamerica." Estudios Americanos 10 (September).

HAAR, CHARLES M. (1963) "Latin America's troubled cities." Foreign Affairs 41 (April).

HARDOY, JORGE E. (1966) "El rol de la ciudad en la modernización de América Latina." Cuadernos del Centro de Estudios Urbanos y Regionales (Buenos Aires) no. 6.

HARRIS, MARVIN (1956) Town and Country in Brazil. New York: Columbia Univ. Press.

HIGGINS, BENJAMIN (1967a) "The city and economic development." Pp. 117-174 in Glenn H. Beyer (ed.) The Urban Explosion in Latin America. Ithaca, N.Y.: Cornell Univ. Press.

——— (1967b) "Urban growth, regional development and their relation to national economic development." Presented to Canadian Economic Association, Toronto, June.

HOSELITZ, BERT F. (1953) "The role of cities in the economic growth of underdeveloped countries." J. of Political Economy 61 (June): 195-208.

HOSELITZ, BERT F. (1955a) "The city, the factory, and economic growth." Amer. Economic Rev. 45 (May): 166-84. (Indicates some ways in which "urbanism" responds to various cultural traditions and modes of economic organization.)

——— (1955b) "Generative and parasitic cities." Economic Development and Cultural Change 3 (April): 278-294.

JACOBS, JANE (1969) The Economy of Cities. New York: Random House.

KOLB, WILLIAM L. (1954) "The social structure and function of cities." Economic Development and Cultural Change 3 (October): 30-46.

LAMPARD, ERIC S. (1955) "The history of cities in the economically advanced areas." Economic Development and Cultural Change 3 (January): 81-136.

MACLEAN Y ESTENOS, R. (1951) "Sociología de la ciudad en el Nuevo Mundo." Proceedings of the Fourteenth International Congress of Sociology (August 30-September 3) 2.

MAZA ZAVALA, D. F. (1966) Condiciones generales del área metropolitana de Caracas para su industrialización. Caracas: Ediciones del Cuatricentenario de Caracas.

McGINN, NOEL F. and RUSSELL G. DAVIS (1969) Build a Mill, Build a City, Build a School: Industrialization, Urbanization, and Education in Ciudad Guayana. Cambridge, Mass.: MIT Press.

MORSE, RICHARD M. (1962a) "Latin American cities: Aspects of function and structure." Comparative Studies in Society and History 55 (July): 473-493.

——— (1962b) "Some characteristics of Latin American urban history." Amer. Historical Rev. 67 (January): 317-338.

NETO, DELORENZO A. (1959) "O aglomerado urbano de São Paulo." Revista Brasileira de Estudos Políticos 3 (July): 121-127.

NUCETE-SARDI, JOSE (1967) La ciudad y sus tiempos. Caracas: Ediciones del Cuatricentenario de Caracas.

OTS CAPDEQUI, JOSE MARIA (1946) El régimen de la tierra en la América Española durante el périodo colonial. Ciudad Trujillo.

PEREZ VALENZUELA, P. (1960) Ciudad vieja. Guatemala: Universidad de San Carlos.

REDFIELD, ROBERT and MILTON B. SINGER (1954) "The cultural role of cities." Economic Development and Cultural Change 3 (October): 53-73. (Sets forth a framework for research on the function of cities in development.)

RIOS, JOSE ARTHUR (1951) "The cities of Brazil." In T. Lynn Smith and Alexander Marchant (eds.) Brazil: Portrait of Half a Continent. New York: Dryden Press.

ROCHEFORT, M. (1966) "Le rôle régional de Rio-de-Janeiro." Civilisations 16: 365-375.

SANTOS, MILTON (1958) "Zones de influência comercial no Estado da Bahia." Pp. 29 ff. in Estudos de Georgrafia da Bahia. Salvador: Univ. of Bahia.

SANTOS, MILTON (1965) A cidade nos países subdesenvolvidos. Rio de Janeiro: Editora Civilizaçao Brasileira.

,SMITH, T. LYNN (1968) "The changing functions of Latin American cities." Americas 25 (July): 70-83. (Reprinted in T. Lynn Smith [1970] Studies of Latin American Societies. Garden City, N.Y.: Doubleday.

——— (1951) "The functions of American cities." Pp. 97-103 in T. Lynn Smith and C. A. McMahan, The Sociology of Urban Life. New York: Dryden Press.

SMOLENSKY , EUGENE and DAVID RATAJCZAK (1965) "The conception of cities." Explorations in Entrepreneurial History. Second series 2 (Winter): 90-131.

SNYDER, DAVID F. (1963) "Ciudad Guayana: a planned metropolis on the Orinoco." J. of Inter-American Studies 5 (July): 405-412.

THERNSTROM, STEPHEN and RICHARD SENNETT [eds.] (1970) Nineteenth-Century Cities: Essays in the New Urban History. New Haven, Conn.: Yale Univ. Press. (Nineteenth-century cities in America, Canada, England, France, and Colombia are examined in an attempt to define the "new urban history.")

THRUPP, SYLVIA L. (1961-1962) "The creativity of cities." Comparative Studies in Society and History 4: 53-64.

TURNER, RALPH E. (1940) "The industrial city: center of cultural change." Pp. 228-42 in Caroline Ware (ed.) The Cultural Approach to History. New York: Columbia Univ. Press.

VIDART, D. D. (1960) Las sociedades campesinas del área ríoplatense: su formación histórica, sus caracteres estructurales, sus vínculos con la economía urbana. Montevideo: Ministerio de Ganadería y Agricultura, Departamento de Sociología Rural.

VIOLICH, FRANCIS (1944) Cities of Latin America. New York: Reinhold.

WEBER,, ADNA FERRIN (1899) The Growth of Cities. Columbia University Studies in History, Economics and Public Law 11. New York.

B. The Regional Framework for Urban Growth

ABDEL-RAHMAN, IBRAHIN HILIMI (1963) "Relations between urban and national planning." In Monroe Berger (ed.) The New Metropolis in the Arab World. New Delhi: Allied Publishers for the Congress for Cultural Freedom.

ALONSO, WILLIAM (1968) "Urban and regional imbalance in economic development." Economic Development and Cultural Change 17 (October): 1-14.

ARCHER, R. W. (1969) "From new towns to metrotowns and regional cities." Amer. J. of Economics and Sociology (October).

BAER, WERNER (1964) "Regional inequality and economic growth in Brazil." Economic Development and Cultural Change 13 (April): 268-285.

BATAILLON, CLAUDE (1967) Les Régions Géographiques au Mexique. Paris: Institut des Hautes Etudes de l'Amérique latine. (An important chapter terminates the first part with a description of the development of urban activities favored by a general policy of diffusion and of polarization, internal transportation, reseau bancaire, industrial location, economic steps, and so on. Good bibliography.)

BERRY, BRIAN J. L. and DUANE F. MARBLE [eds.] (1968) Spatial Analysis. Englewood Cliffs, N.J.: Prentice-Hall.

BRANNON, RUSSELL H. (1968) The Agricultural Development of Uruguay: Problems of Government Policy. New York: Frederick A. Praeger.

Brazil. Ministerio do Planejamento e Coordenação Econômica, Escritório de Pesquisa Econômica Aplicada (EPEA) (1967) Desenvolvimento Regional e Urbano, vol. 7. Plano Decenal de Desenvolvimento Econômico e Social. Rio de Janeiro.

Centre National de la Recherche Scientifique (1968) Regionalisation et Développement. Paris: Editions du C.N.R.S.

CHAPMAN, MURRAY (1969) "Geography and the study of development." J. of Developing Areas 3 (April): 319-338.

Chile. Oficina de Planificación Nacional. Sub-Dirección Regional (1968a) Efectos Regionales del Crecimiento Económico: Período 1961-1965. Santiago.

——— (1968b) Kardex de Estadísticas Regionales. Santiago.

——— (1968c) Política de Desarrollo Regional. Santiago.

COTLER, JULIO (1967) "La mecánica de la dominación interna y del cambio social en el Perú." Lima: Instituto de Estudios Peruanos. (mimeo)

DAEMON, DALTON F. (1969) "Le développement amazonien, défi à l' imagination." Civilisations (Brussels) 19, 3: 347-358.

DEHEM, ROGER (1968) Planification Economique et Federalisme. Quebec: Laval Univ. Press.

DENIS, PAUL YVES (1966) "Régions 'sous-développées' et régions 'déprimées' en Amérique: Intervention et aménagement." Revista Geográfica 65 (December): 109-125.

DIEGUES, MANUEL (1960) Regiões culturais do Brasil. Rio de Janeiro: Centro Brasileiro de Pesquisas Educacionais, Ministério da Educação e Cultura.

FABOS, JULIUS GY (1969) An Interdisciplinary Approach to Regional Planning. Exchange Bibliography 74-75. Monticello, Ill.: Council of Planning Librarians.

FAURA CAIG, GUILLERMO (1966) Los ríos de la amazona peruana: estudio histórico-geográfico, político y militar de la Amazona Peruana y de su porvenir en el desarrollo socio-económico del Peru. Callao: Imprenta Colegio Militar Leoncio Prado.

FREYRE, GILBERTO (1951) Sobrados e mucambos. 3 vols. Rio de Janeiro.

FRIEDMANN, JOHN R. P. (1966) "The urban-regional frame for national development." International Development Rev. 8 (September): 9-15.

FURTADO, CELSO (1963) The Economic Growth of Brazil. Berkeley: Univ. of California Press. (Brazilian edition: Formação Econômica do Brazil. Rio de Janeiro: Editôra Fundo de Cultura, 1959.)

GALMARINI, ALFREDO G. and JOSE M. RAFFO DEL CAMPO (1966) Clasificación geográfica regional de la República Argentina. Buenos Aires: Consejo Nacional de Desarrollo.

GARRISON, W. L. and D. F. MARBLE [eds.] (1967) Quantitative Geography. Part 1: Economic and Cultural Topics; Part 2: Physical and Cartographic Topics. Northwestern University Studies in Geography 13 and 14. Evanston, Ill.: Northwestern University, Department of Geography.

GONSALEZ CASANOVA, PABLO (1965) Internal Colonialism and National Development. Studies in Comparative International Development 004. Beverly Hills: Sage Publications.

GRAHAM, DOUGLAS H. (1970) "Divergent and convergent regional economic growth and internal migration in Brazil–1940-1960." Economic Development and Cultural Change 18, (April): 362-382.

GREENHUT, M. L. (1967) "Location theory, industrial location surveys and regional economic development." Artha-Vikas 3 (January).

HALBWACHS, M. (1939) Morphologie Sociale. Paris: Armand Colin. (Makes distinction between economic space, political space, and religious space.)

HILLMAN, JIMMYE S. (1956) "Economic development and the Brazilian Northeast." Inter-American Economic Affairs 10 (Summer): 79-96.

HOY, DON R. (1968a) "Geography's role in development planning in Guatemala." Professional Geographer 20 (September): 333-336.

––– (1968b) "Industrial location policies in developing countries." Ekistics 25 (March): 155.

KARASKA, GERALD J. and DAVID F. BRAMHALL [eds.] (1969) Locational Analysis for Manufacturing: A Selection of Readings. The Regional Science Series. Cambridge, Mass.: MIT Press.

KEESING, D. B. (1969) "Structural change early in development: Mexico's changing industrial and occupational structure from 1895 to 1950." J. of Economic History 29 (December): 716-738.

LAMARTINE YATES, PAUL (1961) El desarrollo regional de Mexico. México: Banco de México.

LAMBERT, JACQUES (1968) Latin America: Social Structures and Political Institutions. Helen Katel (trans.) Berkeley: Univ. of California Press.

LARSON, MAGALI SARFATTI and ARLENE EISEN BERGMAN (1969) Social Stratification in Peru. Politics of Modernization Series 5. Berkeley: University of California, Institute of International Studies. (An excellent study of the development of relations between a national center-periphery structure, spatially considered.)

LLOSAS, H. P. (1969) "La política de promocion industrial y de desarrollo regional en la Argentina, 1959-1966." Económica 15 (January-April): 39-91.

MALISZ, B. (1969) "Implications of threshold theory for urban and regional planning." J. of Town Planning Institute 55 (March): 108-110.

MENDERSHAUSEN, HORST (1953) "Economic and fiscal problems of a Colombian Department." Inter-American Affairs 6 (Spring): 49-89.

MENDOZA-BERRUETO, ELISEO (1968) "Regional implications of Mexico's economic growth." Weltwirtschaftliches Archiv (Kiel) 101, 1: 87-123.

MENNES, L. B. M., JAN TINBERGEN, and J. GEORGE WAARDENBURG (1969) The Element of Space in Development Planning. Rotterdam: Netherlands Economic Institute–North-Holland Publishing Company.

MORENO TOSCANO, ALEJANDRO (1968) Geografía economica de México (Siglo xvi). New Series 2. Mexico: El Colegio de Mexico, Centro de Estudios Historicos.

NAVARRO ANDRADE, ULPIANO (1965-1966) Geografía Economica del Ecuador. 2 vols. Quito.

NORTH, DOUGLASS C. (1955) "Location theory and regional economic growth." J. of Political Economy 63 (June). (Reprinted in 1964 in John Friedmann and William Alonso [eds.] Regional Development and Planning. Cambridge, Mass.: MIT Press.

Organisation for Economic Co-operation and Development. Development Centre (1969) Multidisciplinary Aspects of Regional Development. Paris.

PAN AMERICAN UNION (1961) Informe sobre la integracion economica y social del Peru central. Washington, D.C.

PERLOFF, HARVEY S., EDGAR S. DUNN, Jr., ERIC E. LAMPARD, and RICHARD F. MUTH (1960) Regions, Resources and Economic Growth. Baltimore: Johns Hopkins Press.

POGGIE, JOHN J., Jr. and FRANK C. MILLER (1969) "Contact, change and industrialization in a network of Mexican villages." Human Organization (Fall).

PRESCOTT, J. R. V. (1969) The Geography of State Policies. Chicago: Aldine.

QUIJANO, OBREGON (1965) "El movimiento campesino del Peru y sus líderes." América Latina 8 (October-December): 43-65.

Resources for the Future (1966) Design for a Worldwide Study of Regional Development: A Report to the United Nations on a Proposed Research-Training Program. Baltimore: Johns Hopkins Press.

RIEGELHAUPT, JOYCE F. and SHEPARD FORMAN (1970) "Bodo was never Brazilian: economic integration and rural development among a contemporary peasantry." J. of Economic History 30 (March): 100-116.

ROBACK, STEFAN H. (1966) "Estrategia del desarrollo económico regional." Trimestre Económico 33 (July-September): 451-467.

RODRIGUEZ TRUJILLO, MANUEL and SIMON RAMOS FARIAS (n.d.) Geografía económica de Venezuela. Caracas.

RODWIN, LLOYD (1963) "Choosing regions for development." Pp. 145-152 in C. J. Friedrich and S. E. Harris (eds.) Public Policy. Cambridge, Mass.: Harvard University, Graduate School of Public Administration.

SMITH, T. LYNN and ALEXANDER MARCHANT [eds.] (1951) Brazil: Portrait of Half a Continent. New York.

STERN, CLAUDIO (1967) "Un análisis regional de México." Demografía y Economía (México) 1, 1.

United Nations. ECLA (1963) Geographic Distribution of the Population of Latin America and Regional Development Priorities. New York.

VINING, RUTLEDGE (1955) "A description of certain spatial aspects of an economic system." Economic Development and Cultural Change 3 (January): 147-195. (Considers the concept of a spatial structure of urbanization, its development over time, and its analytic explanation.)

VON BOVENTER, EDWIN (1964) "Spatial organization theory as a basis for regional planning." J. of American Institute of Planners 30 (May): 90-99.

WILLEMS, EMILIO (1970) "Social differentiation in colonial Brazil." Comparative Studies in Society and History 12 (January): 31-49.

WINGO, LOWDON (1964) "Regional planning in a federal system." J. of American Institute of Planners 30 (May).

WINIARSKI, B. (1969) "Le processus spatial de croissance économique." Economies et Societies 3 (January): 125-165.

WITTHUHN, BURTON O. (n.d.) Place, Process and Theory in National Integration. Discussion papers 7. Columbus: Ohio State University, Department of Geography.

YOUNG, FRANK W. (1964) "Location and reputation in a Mexican intervillage network." Human Organization 21: 36-41.

――― and RUTH C. YOUNG (1966) "Individual commitment to industrialization in rural Mexico." Amer. J. of Sociology 31: 373-383.

――― (1960a) "Social integration and change in twenty-four Mexican villages." Economic Development and Cultural Change 8: 366-377.

――― (1960b) "Two determinants of community reaction to industrialization in rural Mexico." Economic Development and Cultural Change 8: 257-264.

YOUNG, RUTH C. (1970) "The plantation economy and industrial development in Latin America." Economic Development and Cultural Change 18 (April): 342-361.

YUJNOVSKY, OSCAR (1962) Planning regions in Argentina. Ph.D. dissertation. Harvard University.

C. Systems of Cities and Growth Poles

BECKMANN, MARTIN J. (1968) Location Theory. New York: Random House.

――― (1958) "City hierarchies and the distribution of city size." Economic Development and Cultural Change 6 (April): 243-248.

— — — and JOHN C. McPHERSON (1970) "City size distribution in a central place hierarchy: an alternative approach." J. of Regional Sci. 10 (April): 25-33.

BERRY, BRIAN J. L. (1961) "City size distributions and economic development." Economic Development and Cultural Change 9, Part I (July): 573-588.

— — — and WILLIAM L. GARRISON (1958) "Alternative explanations of urban rank-size relationships." Annals of Association of Amer. Geographers 48 (March): 83-91.

BERRY, BRIAN J. L. and ELAINE NEILS (1969) "Location, size, and shape of cities as influenced by environmental factors: the urban environment writ large." Pp. 257-304 in Harvey S. Perloff (ed.) The Quality of the Urban Environment. Baltimore: Johns Hopkins Press.

BERRY, BRIAN J. L. and ALLEN PRED (1965) Central Place Studies: A Bibliography of Theory and Applications Including Supplement Through 1964. Philadelphia: Regional Science Research Institute.

CINTA G., RICARDO (1968) "Un enfoque socio-económico de la urbanización." Demografía y Economía (México, D.F.) 2, 1: 63-80. (Analyzes data from the study of the structure and dynamics of the commercial middle class of small and medium-sized cities of Mexico. Reports on analysis of variance in city size and socioeconomic characteristics and on the definition of an index of the urban phenomenon based on these relationships.)

DACEY, M. F. (1966) "Population of places in a central place hierarchy." J. of Regional Sci. 6: 27-33.

DARWENT, DAVID F. (1968) Growth Pole and Growth Center Concepts: A Review, Evaluation, and Bibliography. Working Paper 89. Berkeley: University of California, Institute of Urban and Regional Development, Center for Planning and Development Research.

FRIEDMANN, John (1969a) "La estrategia de los polos de crecimiento como instrumento de la política de desarrollo." Revista de la Sociedad Interamericana de Planificación 3 (March-June): 16-26.

— — — (1969b) "A general theory of polarized development." (Forthcoming in a volume edited by Niles Hansen, Free Press.

— — — and JOHN MILLER (1965) "The urban field." J. of Amer. Institute of Planners 31 (November): 312-320.

GEIGER, PEDRO PINCHAS (1957) "Exemplos de hierarquia de cidades no Brazil." Boletim Carioca de Geografia (Rio de Janeiro) 10, 3-4: 5-15.

GIBBS, JACK P. and HARLEY L. BROWNING (1961) "Systems of cities." Pp. 436-461 in Jack P. Gibbs (ed.) Urban Research Methods. Princeton, N.J.: Van Nostrand.

GRAVES, THEODORE, NANCY B. GRAVES, and MICHAEL J. KOBRIN (1969) "Historial inferences from Guttmann scales: the return of age-area magic" Current Anthropology 10 (October): 317-338. (Critique of Guttmann scale versus Graves-Kobrin scale in forty Mexican communities with conclusion that actual processes occurring resemble more closely a "multilinear" or a "systems" model of development growth than the unilinear model which Guttman scales are sometimes thought to imply.)

HANSEN, NILES M. (1967) "Development pole theory in a regional context." Kyklos 20, 3.

HAYNER, NORMAN (1966) New Patterns in Old Mexico: A Study of Town and Metropolis. New Haven: College & University Press.

HOOVER, EDGAR M. (1955) "The concept of a system of cities." Economic Development and Cultural Change 3 (January): 196-198.

KORNER, H. (1967) "Industrial 'development poles' as instruments of regional development." Kyklos 20.

KUKLINSKI, A. R. (1969) Growth Poles and Growth Centres in Regional Policies and Planning. Geneva: United Nations Research Institute for Social Development.

LAMPARD, ERIC (1968) "The evolving system of cities in the United States: urbanization and economic development." In Harvey Perloff and Lowdon Wingo (eds.) Issues in Urban Economics. Baltimore: Johns Hopkins Press.

LASUEN, J. R. (1969a) "On growth poles." Urban Studies 6 (June): 137-161.
——— (1969b) "Urbanization hypotheses and Spain's cities system evolution." Journal of the Institute of Social Studies (The Hague.)
NEWLING, BRUCE E. (1966) "Urban growth and spatial structure: mathematical models and empirical evidence." Geographical Rev. 56 (April): 213-225.
NICHOLS, VIDA (1969) Growth Poles: An Investigation of Potential as a Tool for Regional Economic Development. Discussion Paper 30. Philadelphia: Regional Science Research Institute.
OLIVEIRA, BENEVAL DE (1966) Pesado na Balança: um Estudo das Estruturas Rurais e Urbanas do Brasil para Fins de Planejamento Econômico. Rio de Janeiro.
PAELINCK, J. (n.d.) "Systématisation de la Théorie du développement régional polarisé." Synthesis A. Cahiers de l'I.S.E.A. Series L, no. 15.
PARR, JOHN B. (1969) "City hierarchies and the distribution of city size–a reconsideration of Beckmann's contribution." J. of Regional Sci. (August): 239-253.
PERROUX, F. (1961) Théorie et Politique de l'Expansion Régionale. Brussels.
PINCHAS GEIGER, PEDRO (1963) Evolução da Rêde Urbana Brasileira. Rio de Janeiro: Instituto Nacional de Estudos Pedagógicos, Ministerio da Educação e Cultura.
PITTS, FOREST B. [ed.] (1962) Urban Systems and Economic Development: Papers and Proceedings. Eugene, Oregon: University of Oregon, School of Business Administration.
POSADA, REINALDO (1968) "Los polos de desarrollo urbano en Colombia." Revista de la Sociedad Interamericana de Planificación 2 (September): 28-34.
RIOS, JOSE ARTHUR (1951) "The cities of Brazil." Pp. 188-208 in T. Lynn Smith and Alexander Marchant (eds.) Brazil: Portrait of Half a Continent. New York: Dryden Press.
RODWIN, LLOYD et al. (1968) Planning Urban Growth and Regional Development: The Experience of the Guayana Program of Venezuela. Cambridge, Mass.: MIT Press.
SAIA, LUIS (1963) "Notas para a teorização de São Paulo." Acrópole 25 (June): 209-222.
TRAVIESO, FERNANDO (1968) "Sistema de ciudades en Venezuela." Revista de la Sociedad Interamericana de Planificación 2 (September): 25-28.
——— (1967) "Venezuela 1967: polos de desarrollo." Revista de la Sociedad de Planificación 1 (June): 19-23.
VAPNARSKY, CESAR A. (1969) "On rank-size distributions of cities: an ecological approach." Economic Development and Cultural Change 17 (July): 584-595. (The Argentine case.)

D. National Urban Policy and Strategies

CURTIN, T. (1969) "The economics of population growth and control in developing countries." Rev. of Social Economy 27 (September): 139-153.
DYCKMAN, JOHN W. (1966) "The public and private rationale for a national urban policy." Pp. 23-42 in Sam Bass Warner, Jr. (ed.) Planning for a Nation of Cities, Vol. II. Cambridge, Mass.: MIT Press.
EDER, GEORGE JACKSON (1965) "Urban concentration, agriculture, and agrarian reform." Annals of Amer. Academy of Pol. and Social Sci. 360 (July): 27-47.
ELDREDGE, H. WENTWORTH (1969) "Toward a national policy for planning the environment." In Ernest Erber (ed.) Urban Planning in Transition. New York: Grossman Press.
FRIEDMANN, JOHN (1969) "The future of urbanization in Latin America: some observations on the role of the periphery." Regional Sci. Association Papers 23: 161-174.
GEISSE GROVE, GUILLERMO (1965) "Información básica de una política de desarrollo urbano-regional." Cuadernos de Economía (Santiago) 2 (May-August): 41-71.
HANSEN, NILES M. (1970) Rural Poverty and the Urban Crisis: A Strategy for Regional Development. Bloomington: Indiana Univ. Press. (Proposes that development assistance be focused on "intermediate centers"–cities of 200,000 to 500,000 with good records of growth.)

HARDOY, JORGE E. (1967) "The goals of urbanization." Pp. 274-301 in Glenn H. Beyer (ed.) The Urban Explosion in Latin America. Ithaca, N.Y.: Cornell Univ. Press.

HARRIS, C. C., Jr. and M. C. McGUIRE (1969) "Planning techniques for regional development." J. of Human Resources 4 (Fall). (The results of the analysis, where 1975 was used as a planning horizon, indicate the importance of a national migration policy as a complement to and possibly a substitute for industrial location policies as tools for directing the regional pattern of economic growth. Second, the analysis shows that the urban centers of the U.S. have a potential for unacceptably high unemployment rates by the year 1975.)

HERBERT, JOHN D. and ALFRED P. VAN HUYCK [eds.] (1968) Urban Planning in the Developing Countries. New York: Frederick A. Praeger. (Assesses the relevance of present concepts and methods of urban planning to the needs of the developing countries. See, especially, John Herbert, "An approach to metropolitan planning in the developing countries.")

KELLER R., CARLOS (1958) "Seminario del Gran Santiago." Boletín Informativo (University of Chile) 8 (October): 197-198.

LEES, NORMAN D. (1965) Localización de industrias en México. México, D.F.: Banco de México, Departamento de Investigaciones Industriales.

LITTLE, ARTHUR D., Inc. (1961) A Program for the Industrial and Regional Development of Peru. Cambridge, Mass.

LOPEZ MALO, E. (1960) Ensayo sobre localización de la industria en México. México: Universidad Nacional Autónoma.

NEUTZE, G. M. (1965) Economic Policy and the Size of Cities. Canberra: Australian National University.

PONSIOEN, J. A. (1968) National Development: A Sociological Contribution. The Hague: Mouton.

POWELSON, JOHN P. and ANATOLE A. SOLOW (1965) "Urban and rural development in Latin America." Annals of the Amer. Academy of Pol. and Social Sci. 360 (July).

RODWIN, LLOYD (1970) Nations and Cities. Boston: Houghton-Mifflin.

——— (1969) Urban Growth Strategies of Nations: A Comparative Analysis. Exchange Bibliography 105. Monticello, Ill. Council of Planning Librarians.

——— (1957) "National urban policy for developing countries." Papers and Proceedings of the Regional Science Association 3.

STOHR, WALTER (1967) "La definición de regiones en relación con el desarrollo nacional y regional en América Latina." Revista de la Sociedad Interamericana de Planificación 1 (December).

THIESENHUSEN, W. C. (1969) "Population growth and agricultural employment in Latin America with some U.S. comparisons." Amer. J. of Agricultural Economy 51 (November): 735-752. (Policy makers usually assume that the industrial sector will expeditiously absorb the growth of the labor force. But urbanization in Latin America is so far ahead of industrialization that continued advocacy of the type of agricultural modernization that encourages speeding off-farm migration may merely add to urban unrest. An agrarian reform policy of "contrived dualism" is briefly outlined; it may be the most inexpensive manner to provide employment and increase effective demand, thus "buying time" for the industrial sector to catch up.)

United Nations (1968) Urbanization: Development Policies and Planning. New York.

——— Bureau of Social Affairs (1961) "Some policy implications of urbanization." Pp. 295-296 in Philip M. Hauser (ed.) Urbanization in Latin America. New York: International Documents Service.

United Nations, Secretary General (1969) Housing, Building and Planning in the Second Development Decade. New York.

——— (n.d.) Special Report of the Secretary General of the United Nations for the Economic and Social Council's Committee on Housing, Building, and Planning. New York.

La Urbanización y la Planificación Urbana en América Latina: Special Issue (1968) Revista de la Sociedad Interamericana de Planificación 2 (March-June). (Especially: Luis Unikel, "El caso de México"; Luis F. Negrón García and José J. Villamil, "El caso de Puerto

Rico"; Fernando Travieso, "El caso de Venezuela"; Guillemo Geisse, "El caso de Chile"; Jorge Hardoy et al., "El caso de Argentina"; Luis Vera, "Aspectos regionales"; and Pedro Pablo Morcillo, "Política de desarrollo urbano.")

E. Innovation Diffusion Through the Urban System

BENET, FRANCISCO (1963) "Sociology uncertain: the ideology of the rural-urban continuum." Comparative Studies in Society and History 6: 1-23.

BERRY, BRIAN J. L. (1969) "Hierarchical diffusion: the basis of filtering and spread." Prepared for Growth Center Colloquium sponsored by the Center for Economic Development, The University of Texas, Austin, November 20-22.

BROWN, L. A. (1969) "Diffusion of innovation: a microview." Economic Development and Cultural Change 17 (January): 189-211.

——— (1968) Diffusion Processes and Location: A Conceptual Framework and Bibliography. Bibliography Series 4. Philadelphia: Regional Science Research Institute.

DEUTSCHMANN, PAUL J., HUBER ELLINGSWORTH, and JOHN T. McNELLY (1968) Communication and Social Change in Latin America. New York: Frederick A. Praeger. (The communication of new ideas and proposals for the most effective use in the social and economic development of Latin America form the core of this pioneering work.)

FOSTER, GEORGE (1962) Traditional Cultures and the Impact of Technological Change. New York: Harper & Row.

FRIEDMANN, JOHN R. P. (1968) "An information model of urbanization." Urban Affairs Quarterly (December).

HAGESTRAND, T. (1967) Innovation Diffusion as a Spatial Process. Chicago: Univ. of Chicago Press.

HALLER, ARCHIBALD O. (1967) "Urban economic growth and changes in rural stratification: Rio de Janeiro 1953-1962." América Latina 10 (October-December): 48-67.

HUTCHINSON, H. W. (1968) "Value orientations and Northeast Brazilian agro-industrial modernization." Inter-American Economic Affairs 21 (Spring): 73-88.

LEJTER KISNER, ELSA (1966) Una Revolución Silenciosa: Impacto de la Industrialización: El Tocuyo, Estado Lara, Venezuela. Caracas: Senda-Avila.

NASH, MANNING (1967) Machine Age Maya: The Industrialization of a Guatemalan Community. Chicago: Univ. of Chicago Press. (Study of the effects of a textile mill on a Guatemalan village. Conclusion: the effects have been surprisingly few.)

PEDERSEN, POUL OVE (1969) Innovation Diffusion Within and Between National Urban Centers. Copenhagen: Technical University of Denmark. (mimeo)

RAPAPORT, A. (1956) "The diffusion problem in mass behaviour." In General Systems Yearbook. Ann Arbor: Society for General Systems Research.

F. Transportation Networks

"Brazil: federal transport and communications programmes." (1968) B.O.L.S.A. Rev. 2 (September): 495-504.

CORREA GALVAO, MARIA DO CARMO (1966) "Características da geografia dos transportes no Brasil." Revista Geográfica 65 (December): 69-92.

"Monumental programa de carreteras en Brasil." (1969) Progreso (November-December): 49-54.

ROFMAN, ALEJANDRO and OSCAR YUJNOVSKY (1966) "Impacto del transporte en la regionalización." Cuadernos del Centro de Estudios Urbanos y Regionales (Buenos Aires) no. 3.

SOBERMAN, RICHARD M. (1966) Transport Technology for Developing Regions: A Study of Road Transportation in Venezuela. Cambridge, Mass.: MIT Press.

G. Population Movement: Diffusion (Colonization)
(See also Chapter 1: Reference Section D, Population Movement: Concentration.)

Argentina. Consejo Agrario Nacional (1966) Régimen legal de la colonización nacional: textos legales y reglamentarios. Buenos Aires.

ARNOLD, ADLAI (1966) "Reforma agraria y colonización en el Paraguay." Revista Paraguay de Sociología 3 (May-August).

BERINGUIER, CHRISTIAN (1969) Colonisation et développement régional–Le Plan de Badajoz. Paris: Presses Universitaires de France. (Description of city and regional planning in one of the most backward regions of Spain.)

BUTLAND, GILBERT J. (1966) "Frontiers of settlement in Latin America." Revista Georgráfica 65 (December): 93-108.

DOZIER, CRAIG L. (1969) Land Development and Colonization in Latin America: Case Studies of Peru, Bolivia, and Mexico. New York: Frederick A. Praeger.

EDELMAN, ALEXANDER T. (1967) "Colonization in Bolivia: progress and prospects." Inter-American Economic Affairs 20 (Spring): 39-54.

FAULK, ODIE B. (1968) "Projected military colonies for the borderlands, 1848." J. of Arizona History (Spring).

HICKMAN, JOHN M. (1968) "Colonización y movilidad social en Bolivia." América Indígena 28 (April): 389-403.

SALMON, E. T. (1969) Roman Colonization under the Republic. Ithaca, N.Y.: Cornell Univ. Press.

SIEMENS, ALFRED H. (1966) "New agricultural settlements along Mexico's Candelaria River: implications of commitment to planning and *ejido*." Inter-American Economic Affairs 20 (Summer): 23-39.

SIMMONS, MARC (1969) "Settlement patterns and village plans in colonial New Mexico." J. of the West (January).

SMITH, T. LYNN (1969) "Studies of colonization and settlement." Latin American Research Rev. 4 (Spring): 93-123.

STEWART, NORMAN R. (1968) "Some problems in the development of agricultural colonization in the Andean Oriente." Professional Geographer 20 (January): 33-38.

WINSBERG, MORTON D. (1968-1969) "Jewish agricultural colonization in Entre Rios, Argentina." Amer. J. of Economics and Sociology 27, 3 and 4; 28, 1. (Economic problems of resettled townsmen.)

H. General

BOUCHIER, E. S. (1914) Spain Under the Roman Empire. Oxford.

BOULDING, KENNETH E. (1970) "Fun and games with the gross national product–the role of misleading indicators in social policy." Pp. 157-170 in Harold W. Helfrich, Jr. (ed.) The Environmental Crisis. New Haven: Yale Univ. Press.

CHAPMAN, CHARLES EDWARD (1933) Colonial Hispanic America. New York: Macmillan.

HACKETT, BRIAN (1950) Man, Society and Environment. London: Percival Marshall.

MELIDA Y ALINARI, JOSE RAMON (1925) Monumentos Romanos de España. Madrid: Comisaría Regia del Turismo y Cultura Artística.

MOSES, BERNARD (1908) South America on the Eve of Emancipation. New York: Putnam's.

PINTO SANTA CRIZ, ANIBAL (1962) Chile: Un Caso de Desarrollo Frustrado. Santiago: Editorial Universitaria.

VELIZ, CLAUDIO [ed.] (1965) Obstacles to Change in Latin America. London: Oxford Univ. Press.

VICENS VIVES, JAIME (1969) An Economic History of Spain. Frances M. López-Morillas (trans.) Princeton, N.J.: Princeton Univ. Press.

WILLEY, G. R. [ed.] (1956) Prehistoric Settlement Patterns in the New World. New York: Johnson Reprint.

The Role of
Cities in National Development

JOHN FRIEDMANN

The Meaning of National Development

The idea of national development is tantalizingly ambiguous; perhaps precisely for this reason, it has become one of the germinal ideas of the age. Its ambiguity arises from a value judgment: development is always looked on with approval. But the onlookers— the students of development—may be of different minds when they are pressed for closer definitions. Each will envelop the term in an aura of ideological thinking, and among them they are likely to agree on only one thing, that development is in itself desirable and ought to be achieved.

One approach to an understanding of this complex idea is to search for its meaning among the goals and aspirations of national societies, signifying a direction of desired change. To be developing is good; stagnation is bad; indifference is inadmissible. There can be little doubt that national development today displays this and many other features of a genuine social movement. It is taken for granted that national societies have a historical commitment to the idea of continuous and cumulative change.

However, this assumption is not quite exact. All national societies, it is true, may harbor elites that would wish to enter such commitments, but effective power often rests with conservative authorities that see only a threat to privilege and power in development. If this were not enough, many societies are national in little more than name, lacking a genuine sovereignty, brutally torn apart by antagonistic interests, and having yet to achieve a measure of territorial integration. Development as a social movement may thus extend to something less than the whole world. But even nations that reject development must face prevailing international opinion that acts as if a moral obligation were attached to the idea.

This ethical imperative is not invoked for any set of specific policy prescriptions. It is agreed that nations differ in their historical conditions, and that every nation has a right autonomously to determine its own future.[1] Yet even granting this, no nation can entirely escape the moral stricture to "develop" and to continuously transform itself according to a plan. These clashing views are somehow merged. The historically concrete is wedded to a universal expectation.[2]

There is, moreover, a growing conviction that the individual destinies of national societies are converging on a common path, and that the ultimate level of integration is a global one.[3] This belief has given rise to the well-known distinction between underdeveloped (U) and developed (D) societies. The language suggests that the latter are passing through a phase in their historical unfolding that has not yet been reached by the former. Both societies may be "developing," but, as late arrivals, the underdeveloped are obliged to follow in the footsteps of the "developed" nations.

The argument is subtle and can be properly understood only if we introduce two levels of abstraction. On the first, U-countries must, it is believed, acquire certain traits that are common to D-countries in order to survive in a developing world system. On a second, more specific level, each country must itself invent the concrete social forms and institutions corresponding to its actual condition.[4]

To give a simple illustration: all developing societies are faced with the necessity of steadily increasing the productivity of labor and of altering the composition of industrial employment. But it is left for each country to decide not only the pace at which these changes will be introduced, but also the rate at which different industrial sectors will increase their share of employment, the division of the means of production between public and private ownership, and the forms and methods of distributing the national product.

The bifurcation of the world into U- and D-countries is rudimentary. Nonetheless, it suggests that U-countries will hold in common certain comprehensive aims that, at an earlier period, were typical for the presently "developed" nations. These aims include:

(1) *an increase in the autonomy of national society,* by gaining effective political sovereignty, increasing its military strength, enlarging the number and range of available choices, and acquiring a sense of national dignity;

(2) *an increase in the levels of living of the population,* by increasing production at faster rates than population growth, maintaining monetary stability, redistributing income in favor of the poorer segments of the population, and granting the rights of the people to certain basic claims of creature security;

(3) *an increase in social integration,* by promoting a wider and more effective participation of all the adult population in the decision processes of society;

(4) *an increase in modernization,* by creating an institutional framework adapted to the requirements of generating and adjusting to continuous change and promoting those activities, especially in science and artistic creation, which will permit the country to share more fully in an emerging universal culture;

(5) *an increase in spatial integration,* by articulating the development process across the entire settled space of the nation through an internally balanced system of cities.

Although these aims are sufficiently general so that they will, to some extent, be present also in the developed nations, the idea of national development is not confined to them. After a critical point is reached in the evolution of a national society, the erstwhile aims may lose their urgency, while other social goals will rise to take their place. Contemporary D-countries appear to have shifted their attention to the uses of wealth and leisure, the problems of mass culture, the progress of science, and the conquest of space. These new aims of development appear to be so remote from the perceived realities of the U-countries, that they are thought to have but little relevance for them. The idea of development thus undergoes a radical change in content as we pass on to D-countries. The historical meaning is new; what remains is the driving ethical imperative.

Aims, however, are the governing criteria, and the performance of societies is judged in terms of them. Where it is satisfactory, no unusual measures need be taken. But implicit in the idea of development is the preparedness of a society to take responsibility for its performance and to intervene in the normal processes of change where the results expected from them fail to be produced.

Development has the connotation of an *intended* good: it is a process endowed with moral purpose for which developing societies assume responsibility, and almost always this involves attempts at guided change or planning.[5]

The Settlement System

The main task of this essay is to show, by way of introduction, the various modes of interaction between cities and national development.

As a form of human settlement, the city is a social system that is located in geographic space and occupies a precise position in a system of interconnected settlements, extending from hamlet to megalopolis.[6] National development occurs within this social interaction network stretched out over the landscape. But its occurrence in the spatial system is neither uniform nor simultaneous. Impulses for development originate at certain localities and are relayed through existing channels to other localities in a definite sequence. The pattern of settlements creates a structure of potentials for development that will eventually be registered in indices of regional performance and will condition the evolving character of the society.

Since the goals of national development differ between U- and D-countries, each set of countries must be separately studied. In both, the spatial pattern of settlement will bear a close relation to the key events of national development, but the specific role of cities will be radically different in each.

These summary observations may be better understood if we look at a few salient features of the settlement system.

(1) The system of settlements is differentiated according to the functions performed by every subsystem (or unit) within it.

(2) Each subsystem stands at the node of a communications network that originates, absorbs, and transmits impulses of change to the subsystems.

(3) Each subsystem stands at the node of a field of forces that acts upon and influences the location of activities and population.

(4) Each subsystem serves as an agent of change for areas dependent upon it.

(5) The development options of each subsystem are limited partly by its position within a complex system of dependency relations.

(6) The development options of each subsytem are partly determined by its internal capacity to respond to exogenous impulses for change.

(7) A change in the relative position of one of the subsystems in the hierarchy of dependency relations signifies a change in the structure of the system as a whole.

(8) A change in the relative position of one of the subsystems in the hierarchy of dependency relations can result from a disproportionate increase (or decrease) in subsystem size, from changes in its social and political organization, or from a change in its functions for the system as a whole.

If, as is claimed, the pattern of spatial dependency relations is a controlling one for national development, it is reasonable to focus attention on those subsystems that display a greater than average capacity for autonomous transformation and consequently for sustained innovation. The development capacity of the system as a whole will, therefore, come directly to depend on the performance of these centers or *core regions*. For each core region, one or more dependent *peripheral regions* may be defined, bearing in mind that lower-order cores may fall within the periphery of, and be dependent on, one or several higher-ranking cores. Core regions can thus be arranged into a hierarchy according to their relative autonomy in development decisions. Peripheral areas, on the other hand, may be divided into upward- and downward-transitional regions in keeping with their estimated potentials for development. Finally, on the peripheries of core regions, new settlement areas or *resource frontiers* may come into being.

The entire settlement space of the nation will thus be spanned by an array of regions that is articulated through a system of nodes and connecting channels of communication.

This polarized space will display systematic variances in the capacity for development of given areas. Later comment will make the reasons for these differences more explicit. Here it is necessary only to point out that core regions possess the means for limiting and controlling the development of their peripheries and for extracting from them the resources that will contribute to their own accelerated growth. This imbalance of power between core and periphery, which displays a strong tendency to increase over substantial segments of the development path, will naturally lead to social and political tensions. Where these tensions cannot be depressed to tolerable levels, they eventually undermine the stability of the system and its ability to generate further development.

Many appropriate examples come to mind. A striking account of the dangers inherent in this conflict between cores and their peripheries is given by Eric Wolfe (1962: 168-169) in his description of the collapse of Theocratic society in Mesoamerica during the seventh and eighth centuries of our era.

> The web of Theocratic society contained another fatal flaw: a built-in imbalance between holy town and hinterland, between city and provinces. Ultimately, the towns grew wealthy and splendid, because the countryside labored and produced. Not that some of the centers did not flow back into the rural area. Some benefits must be returned to the ruled in any complex society. Undoubtedly the Theocratic society forged its own chain of command with the final links in the villages and hamlets; some men in the countryside must have acted as messengers of the gods and received rewards commensurate with utility of their services. The growing gap between center and hinterland was not based on an absolute enrichment of the center while the countryside remained absolutely impoverished. Both grew in their involvement with each other; but the centers grew more quickly, more opulently, and—more obviously.
>
> Such disparity in growth may produce more conflicts than the absolute exploitation of one community by another. For a measure of prosperity which is yet confronted with the image of an ever more opulent prosperity in its midst breeds not only envy but also the desire to lay hands on the surplus for one's own purposes. Revolt occurs not when men's faces are ground into the dust; rather, it explodes during a period of rising hope, at the point of sudden realization that only the traditional controls of the social order stand between men and the achievement of still greater hopes. In complex societies, this confrontation of hope with the denial of hope pits rulers against ruled, rich against poor, and hinterland and periphery against core area and center. The periphery suffers by comparison while the center grows bloated with wealth and power. Yet it is also at the periphery that the controls of government and religion tend to be at their weakest; it is here that the forces of dissatisfaction can easily gain both strength and organization. Here the pull of the center and its ability to compel people to its will are at a minimum. Theocratic society witnessed this rebellion of the periphery against the center. The fissures opened up in three major regions; along the western margin of the Petén; along the southern border of the central highland; and in the northern marches that held the frontier against the hunters and gatherers beyond.

Spatial integration—which appears as a major development objective for U-countries—thus requires action that will increase the autonomy of peripheral regions with respect to their controlling cores, diminish one of the important sources of conflict between them, and assure the stability of the system during its transition.

Urbanization and the Development Process
in U-Countries

City growth appears as an irrepressible accompaniment of modern development experience in U-countries. The statistical evidence leaves little question on this score.[7] The data for nearly all of the developing U-countries also show that large cities tend to grow at faster rates than smaller ones and that the national capital complex is particularly favored. But statistical associations constitute no proof of a causal relation. It is to this question of causality that we shall therefore turn by examining three fundamental forces in the process of development: the passage from tradition to innovation, from a limited culture to one of constantly expanding opportunities, and from an elitist to a mass political system striving for national integration.

Innovation and urbanization. Invention must be distinguished from innovation. The former consists in the creation of something new out of a rearrangement of already existing elements, while the latter may be viewed as the transformation of inventions into historical fact. Both terms may be applied to tangible and intangible objects. Thus, Gonzalo Aguirre Beltrán (1964: 4-5):

> The term "invention" for anthropology does not mean only the deliberate creation of a machine, of any type of mechanism, or of any other material achievement of a culture, an achievement in the nature of a radical innovation, but also new ideas, new concepts or patterns in social, political or religious organization, as well as new economic systems which play such an important role in the entire historical evolution. Man's inventive mind and the cultural process which ensues from it do not act exclusively upon elements of culture that are in some way tangible, but certainly also upon its universal life.

Accepting this broad interpretation, we may say that a comprehensive development occurs when single innovations—large and small—are linked into innovative clusters and systems. Since innovations arise out of an established traditional matrix, their integration into larger systems occurs as an asynchronic process, pitting new forces against an already established order.

We can now assert a first hypothesis: *the frequency of inventions is positively correlated with a high potential for interaction, that is, a high probability of information exchange or communication.* The probabilities of communication over a given surface can be plotted on a map so as to yield a landscape of communication potentials or communication field (Friedmann, 1968). Cities, especially large cities, appear as peaks in this landscape. It is the large city where the frequency of new idea combinations is generally greatest.[8]

A second and related hypothesis will say: first, *that urbanization will positively vary with the probability of communication at any given locality*—city growth is related to increases in potential communication; second, *as cities are joined into systems*—as the channels for transmitting information expand among cities—*the probability of information exchange among them will increase.* The growth of a single subsystem and expansion of intercity linkages are, to a large degree, substitutes for one other.

When we pass from invention to innovation, a third hypothesis may be stated: *the frequency of innovation in a given locality is a function of its internal structure of social power.* A tightly controlled, rigid, hierarchical (bureaucratic) system of power will be less permissive of innovations than an open, horizontal, nonbureaucratic system of dispersed power. We should expect to find significant variations in the structure of social power among cities. But speaking generally, it is possible to assert that increasing size creates conditions that will bring the city's power structure into greater conformity with our second model.[9]

We are now in a position to ask whether a high probability for information exchange is causally related to certain forms of social and political organization. The answer, presumably, would be affirmative. If so, a fourth hypothesis may be stated: *increases in the level of urbanization will lead to an increasing openness of the system of social power and hence to an increase in the frequency of innovation.* This, then, may be regarded as the first positive contribution of urbanization to national development. It will transform traditional society into an innovative system.

Opportunity and urbanization. George M. Foster (1965) describes peasant societies in terms of what he calls "an image of the limited good."[10] In such societies, the interests of one person can be advanced only, it is believed, by depriving someone else of the coveted benefits. The result is a brutally egocentric, defensive society whose members behave in accordance with this rule: "Maximize the material, short-run advantage of the nuclear family; assume that all others will do likewise."[11]

The image of the limited good—a kind of zero-sum game—tends to be associated with isolated peasant societies. But contemporary urbanization is based on the opposite image, that of constantly expanding opportunities.[12] Cities undergoing development tend to transform the bitter little zero-sum games of traditional peasant society into competitive non-zero-sum games. We should expect this image of the "unlimited" good to vary a good deal both with the rate of increase in employment and with city size. Both variables will increase economic choice and multiply the upward channels of mobility available to individuals.

Of course, image and experience do not always coincide. Expectations are not always bartered for the real thing. The older residents of the city, having pressed against the very real obstacles to opportunity that do exist, may think society a fraud. Their political behavior will reflect a growing frustration with the social order. It is the recent migrant to the city—comparing his present condition to a dismal rural past—who looks upon his new environment with hope.[13] Return migration to the countryside is rare (Lambert, 1961: 135-136).

What we may call the culture of the "unlimited" good is, on the whole, less tooth-and-claw, more given to accommodation, than societies organized around the opposite cultural image. Urban, in contrast to rural, society in U-countries tends to be more tolerant and generous towards the other and it reinforces the achievement impulses of large numbers of people. Continuous expansion of the urban system will tend to lower the level of interpersonal friction that might otherwise be expected.[14] The modern notion that development involves unceasing, positively valued change has grown out of urban experience. This, then, is the second contribution of urban to national development: *the city has not only invented the concept of unlimited opportunity, but also made it possible and finally internalized it as the basis for its own unique form of culture.*

Political transformations and urbanization. Industrialization and urbanization are not always parallel phenomena. Migration to cities in U-countries generally takes place at faster rates than the absorption of new labor force into employment of high productivity. Accelerated urbanization in this sense will inevitably lead to the formation of a massive urban proletariat whose members, lacking special skills, are only partially within the labor market, if at all, and for this reason are excluded from most of the material—and spiritual—benefits of the developing, participant society. The political significance of this situation derives from a heightened visibility of the city proletariat that, being looked at by and looking at the world from which it is excluded in any but the strictest functional sense, may acquire a keen sense of its own "marginal" condition and become potentially available as a potent political force to whatever leadership is capable of capturing its confidence.

The second result for political development is the emergence in cities of innovative groups that pose a challenge to the established powers in their attempt to legitimize new claims and create a social climate favorable to further innovation, insofar, at least, as this would be consistent with their own schedule of values. In this endeavor, innovative counter-elites may seek alliances among successively larger, more inclusive sectors of the population: the upper-middle class, the lower-middle stratum, the workers, the urban proletariat, and eventually also the excluded rural proletariat on the periphery. As their base for political action expands and the masses become politicized, the politics of innovation first turn populist, and later intergrationist, on a national scale (Di Tella, 1965; Silvert, 1963). Strongly doctrinaire and ideological during the struggle for power with the established elites, innovative groups will tend to become open to compromise once they have risen to power (Friedmann, 1965; Levy, 1967). Political parties may consequently become transformed into giant bartering systems striving to aggregate ever widening circles of multiple and overlapping interests.

This outcome is not inevitable; it is merely possible. We may, therefore, wish to test the following hypothesis: *the resistance of the "established" powers to innovative counter-elites diminishes with the acceleration of the urbanization process.* This may be regarded as the third main contribution of the city to national development: *accelerated urbanization hastens the coming of a national mass politics based on bargaining and compromise among competing interest groups.*[15]

Summary. We have tried to suggest that the three basic processes of national development—innovation, social transformation and political transformation—are closely linked to yet another process, that of urbanization, which tends to reinforce the latent predispositions to developmental change through increasing communication potential and a change in the pattern of social organization from Euclidean hierarchies to Einsteinian systems existing in time. We have further tried to show that large cities are more effective in promoting these changes than small cities, and that the linkage of cities into urban systems has an effect analogous to increasing city size. It is also probably true that these variables—urbanization, city size, and expanding urban systems—are positively correlated with conflict. Urban society is a conflict society, but this conflict is only the external and highly visible accompaniment of more creative processes beneath the surface. Where conflict is absent, we can be certain that development does not occur.[16]

The Development Process and Changes in Spatial Organization

In the preceding sections, we have described the development process as if it extended uniformly across a nation, except for a sharp intensification –and acceleration—at a small number of core regions. Superimposed upon a uniform development "surface," core regions polarize surrounding space and set up fields of tensions between themselves and their peripheries. If we now examine this surface more closely, we discover that it is finely articulated by a system of settlements which, subject to change itself, ends by completely transforming the structure of spatial relations in the social economy. The form in which this spatial transformation occurs exerts a decisive effect on the ability of a nation to achieve a satisfactory development of its internal resources.

Two pervasive forces underlie a change in spatial organization. The first is a steady improvement in the overall accessibility of the system that comes as a direct consequence of the five universal characteristics of modern development:

(1) a progressive expansion of transport and communication capacity over larger areas,

(2) an increase in the number of possible interconnections within the system,

(3) a reduction in the unit cost of transportation and communication,

(4) a rise in real incomes per capita,

(5) an increase in the speed and efficiency of the transport and communication system.

Changes in the location propensities of firms and households is the second force determining the path of spatial transformation. The tendencies will differ with the experience of each country, but among the more significant changes in the location propensities of industrial and commercial firms—as development proceeds—will be shifts from a predominant resource to market orientation, from single to multiple firm corporations, from an emphasis on the presence of economic to social infrastructure, from small to large firms (in employment), and from isolated firms to clusters of related enterprise.

During the early and intermediate phases of development, the location of households tends to be determined by the geographic pattern of emerging economic opportunities, but gradually this grim determinism will be relaxed as the classic formula of "labor follows industry" is reversed, and the natural, social amenities of different community environments exert a growing influence on where people decide to settle.

The relation between these changes in accessibility and location propensity, on the one hand, and spatial organization, on the other, is not a linear one, however, and must be studied by tracing the process along a series of feedback loops. Every change introduced into the spatial system will accordingly modify the conditions determining location decisions, and, in a second round, produce further changes in the system. With this important qualification in mind, it is now possible to describe—in the form of a model—the four types of transformation in the spatial organization of society that the development process engenders. It should be added—though it may seem obvious—that a model, which is a guide for research, can never be a substitute for it. Empirical departures from the model throw up questions inviting further and more detailed study.

Transformation from simple to complex structures.[17] The spatial structure of U-countries is, by comparison to later periods, a very simple one. Regional economies show relatively little specialization since most of the population obtains its living from agriculture. Farming activities may be grouped into broad ecological or production zones, but the cities that organize the national economy show only minor functional distinctions. One or two of them, however, will eventually stand out from the rest, evolving to the point where they can be unambiguously identified as core regions that will reduce the rest of the country's economy to peripheries dependent on them. As core-region development proceeds, this simple structure is gradually filled out: territorial specialization occurs and urban functional hierarchies—following a modified Christaller pattern for all but the largest centers—become established. The new system will be coordinated—it would be wrong to speak here of direction— through spatial aggregates at the top of the hierarchy whose internal complexity is so great that new terms have had to be invented to describe them: metropolis, urban field, development corridor, megalopolis. Development comes to be concentrated in these potent spatial forms through which the former national peripheries are reorganized into elaborate patterns of interdependencies. As larger and larger areas are brought into the core regions' structures, the national periphery is trimmed to a vestigial status. Most of the population comes eventually to live within these new foci of development.

Transformation from imbalanced to balanced structures. The initial spatial imbalance may be observed not only in the pronounced core-periphery structure of U-countries, but also in the relationship of population size to rank of cities in the system. According to a widely accepted rule, the size of each city in a fully developed system is determined by its rank, so that by dividing the size of the largest city by the rank of any city, we obtain its population size (Berry, 1964). There is a second rule that connects the sizes and functions of cities with regional income. This states that the number of central functions of a city will increase with regional per capita income—holding size constant—but will also increase with an increase in city size and constant income (Lasuén, 1967). Combining these two rules with what has been said about growing functional specialization in the preceding paragraph, it may be asserted that, whatever the initial structure, continued development will be accompanied by an increase in the rank-size ordering of cities (Lasuén et al., 1967). If we now extend the posited relationship horizontally across the settled space of a nation, the result of a process of increasing rank size will be a fully developed, hierarchically ordered spatial system, in which all places have approximately equal access to similar urban functions (Berry, 1967: 76-79). The system minimizes distances and is a stable one in its overall configuration, even though it may continue to evolve internally. Thus, lower-order functions may be recombined in larger centers, thereby eliminating the smaller places in the hierarchy, while, at the top, entirely new urban forms come into being.

Transformation from narrow impact of urban life-styles to total immersion in urbanism. The spread of urban life-styles is not coincident with the pattern of cities, though it is strongly influenced by it. Initially, the gradients of urban influence are very sharp: urbanism is typically a large-city phenomenon, but the population affected by it will tend to live in very close proximity and constant interaction with the center (Ellefsen, 1961). Development, however, acting through the forces of equalizing access and location propensities, will work to reduce these gradients and to introduce elements of urban life-styles into the remotest corners of the nation. Vast zones of an engulfing urbanism thus appear as the large city penetrates smaller towns and even the countryside with mass information media and modern forms of large-scale organization (e.g., commercialization of agriculture, unionization of farm labor, industrial decentralization). Since urban life-styles may set up expectations that cannot always be fulfilled in situ, massive population readjustments occur as migrant streams move from peripheral areas lightly touched by urbanism to the more thoroughly urbanized development regions of the country (Quijano, 1967a).

Transformation from partial to complete regional integration. Each of the preceding three transformations of spatial systems —functional specialization of areas, increasing urban balance, and incorporation of most of the population into the culture of urbanism—contributes to the full regional integration of the nation. They do so not only by forging multiple and stronger linkages among all parts of the country, but also by encouraging greater geographical mobility of labor, capital, and commodities in expanding national and regional markets. At this point, the classic economic law of equal factor remuneration comes into full force, allocating resources in an efficient way according to the returns expected in each case.[18]

But regional integration has an even more basic meaning. It suggests the transformation of an entire nation into an innovative system with great capacity for self-renewal, the integration of most of the population into a social realm of constantly expanding opportunities, and the creation of a truly national polity whose individual members have roughly equal access to decision-making centers. These results will also tend to lead to less authoritarian patterns of social organization and to a society held together by the force of innumerable strands of crisscrossing communications, producing a "new man."[19]

The system of cities thus appears as a dynamic agent of development, not only generating but also mediating development impulses—an agent subject to change no less than changing, whose structural elements may be arranged in optimal ways to facilitate the process of national transformation.

Notes on Urbanization and National Development in D-Countries

Sometime during the course of the spatial transformation just described, a country will pass, quietly and unnoticed, from U to D, from a condition of underdevelopment to one of development. The exact timing of this changeover is somewhat arbitrary, for the process of transition is a relatively smooth one, and precisely where one elects to place the magical barrier that divides these different worlds is a matter on which experts may differ. Moreover, admission to the select company of D-countries signifies neither that all internal phenomena will automatically be consistent with each other—the oxcart coexists with the jet engine—nor that the process of development will increase. On the contrary, election of D-status means that a country has pushed forward into a period of self-reinforcing and continuous change, based, as in the past, on invention and innovation. Inevitably, therefore, discrepancies arise among the elements of which developing societies are made. Development appears as an asynchronic process.[20]

Nevertheless, in taking stock of the changes that have occurred, students of development will discover that the general situation of a D-country differs radically from earlier periods. For our purposes, the most important change to have occurred is the substitution of time for place. Expressed in different language, this means:

(1) increased freedom from economic constraints in location decisions,

(2) increased geographic mobility of population and productive resources,

(3) larger networks of social interchange,

(4) larger numbers of decision-making centers,

(5) easier communication among centers.

The substitution of time for place also means a substantial reduction in the so-called friction of distance that will enlarge the options for locational choice and make the real time of reaching other places in the system a more decisive fact than out-of-pocket costs of movement. Eventually, even time may cease to be important. As the time for covering a certain distance shrinks, a situation of approximately equal access is eventually approached.

This will extend to the entire space of the nation the salient traits of a core region.

Modern development tends to push these changes farther in the same direction. This does not mean, however, that location decisions will henceforward be treated with whimsey. For even in post-industrial societies, the past bears heavily upon the present. Old centers persist in having strong attractive power, roughly in the same proportions as over past decades, though activities may spill out into urban fields, enlarging the concept of city and constituting a new unit of spatial integration (Friedmann and Miller, 1965). On the other hand, the reconcentration of communication-oriented services and industries into broad zones will tend to influence the location choices of those firms that still perceive an advantage in being physically near to the means of interchange.

If the substitution of time for place reduces economic constraints on location decisions, the city ceases to be a propulsive force of development. Spatial patterns of development were primordial national concerns of an underdeveloped society seeking greater autonomy, higher living levels, more social integration, greater world participation, and a more complete integration of its territory. They cease to be so for countries that are rapidly slipping into post-industrial systems (Bell, 1967). The new salient interests in leisure, mass consumption, and science are no longer dependent on an urban focus—they may be called transurban. Nor is the city any longer an important instrument for their fulfillment.

This is not to claim total irrelevance of the settlement pattern for development in these societies. Problems of transition will continue to command the attention of policy-makers (U.S. Department of Commerce, 1965). Pockets of peripheral poverty remain, dramatic changes in the internal ecology of meta-urban units call for difficult adjustments; the poor are too handicapped to take advantage of the new location freedom; massive transportation problems demand urgent solutions. In addition, the policy of linking national economies into supranational systems, such as a common market, will pose problems of spatial reintegration similar to those familiar to U-countries and amenable to a similar treatment. In both cases, the urban pattern will play a major role.

The problem of urban form, however, remains an open one where the dominant social concerns fall more into the realm of culture than of politics or economics. For locational freedom imposes a special kind of responsibility: freedom for what? The forms of urban settlement are therefore not indifferent to postindustrial societies.

Which patterns are optimal for this new phase of development? In attempting to answer this question, we trespass on terra incognita. U-countries, after all, have the example of the more developed societies as a guide, and we are able to study the regularities and phases of succession in spatial organization. But on what model may D-countries pattern *their* development? We are only now beginning to know postindustrial society and are still missing a full vision of its potentialities.

The Question for Policy

Given the open-ended nature of urban development in D-countries, and without denying a need for urban policies to guide the evolution of their complex spatial systems, it is primarily for U-countries that a scientific basis for policy may be devised. The present study is intended as a modest contribution to this effort.

But to what kinds of questions is urban policy in U-countries to be addressed? Without attempting to be complete in listing them, nor deciding whether urban development policy had not better be called regional, we may pose six leading issues that need to be considered in any serious thinking on the subject.[21] The questions are:[22]

(1) What is the optimal rural-urban balance for successive phases in a process of national development?[23]

(2) What is the optimal rate of urbanization at successive phases of the development process?

(3) What are the optimal patterns of spatial organization at successive phases in the development process?

(4) What are the optimal transformation paths in shifting from one type of spatial organization to another?[24]

(5) What should be the criteria to determine the proper timing in shifts from one kind of urban development strategy to another?

(6) What criteria may be applied to determine the optimal balance between centralization and decentralization in administrative and political decisions for urban development?

Along with these specific issues of urban development policy, more general questions that apply to any attempt in guiding system change ought to be considered.[25]

(1) What are the key points of intervention in a system?

(2) How can system-wide balances be maintained during the transition period while making maximum use of imbalance for promoting change?

(3) How can the asynchronic elements of a system undergoing transformation be reintegrated around emerging focal points of innovative change?

The study of urban development has never been approached in quite this way. Our perspective is normative; the ultimate aim is prescription. The analysis appropriate to this objective is cast in terms of a dynamic systems model in which the relevant aspects of economics, sociology, political science, and geography are brought together. Combined with this is an unfamiliar emphasis on the spatial aspects of development. We are therefore conscious of making a first reconnaissance in difficult terrain.

NOTES

1. This is the ideal. In practice, large-scale intervention is often found, spheres of influence are carved out by contending powers, and national options are limited by the criteria governing international assistance.

2. This probably explains why many American observers admire Communist China's staggering effort to lead 700 million into the twentieth century (despite their disagreement with the methods applied), and why they hold right-wing (but pro-American) dictatorships, from Portugal to Paraguay, in contempt for failing to do likewise. Moral imperatives are stronger than political philosophy.

3. According to Gideon Sjoberg (1965: 249-250)

. . . industrial cities over the world are becoming alike in many aspects of their social structure. . . . Implicit in our analysis is another hypothesis: as technology becomes increasingly complex, a significant number of structural imperatives become more narrowly defined. . . . Cultural values induce stylistic differences among industrial cities that cannot be ignored. However, a value system cannot modify structural arrangements in an infinite variety of ways. Industrial cities share certain values because of their dependence on scientific method and modern technology. Overemphasis of cultural values as an independent variable leads to historicism and a denial of the possibility of making cross-cultural generalizations.

To the extent that development implies the spread of industrial culture, the thesis of cultural convergence may be maintained with certain logic.

4. See Bendix (1967) for a subtle development of this argument.

5. The literature on developmental planning has grown impressively during the past seven or eight years. (For a good summary, see Waterston, 1965.)

6. Differences in urban social systems do not concern us here for the moment. Later, when we return to consider this question, it will be shown that only a few features are important for national development.

7. A good recent summary of data is found in Gerald Breese (1966). See also Lowden Wingo (1967) for a sophisticated comparative analysis of urban population trends in one of the world's major underdeveloped regions.

8. A still excellent reference on the study of innovation is H. G. Barnett (1953). Barnett lists nine conditions favoring the initiation of innovation. Even superficial analysis, however, will show that the large city tends to present the optimal combination of these conditions: the accumulation of ideas, the concentration of ideas, the collaboration of effort, the conjunction of differences, the expectation of change, the lack of dependence on authority, the competition of rivals, the deprivation of essentials, and the modification of a dominant correlate (chain reactions, as change in dominant elements sets up a propitious, and even compelling, condition for change in other elements).

9. The two alternatives describe extreme situations. Optimal innovative systems may result from some combination of authoritarian and democratic power structures. As ideal types, however, the two polar models of social organization may still be useful as a heuristic device. (See Burns and Stahler, 1962: 119-125.)

10. I am indebted to Carlos Delgado for this reference.

11. Banfield and Banfield (1958: 85). Oscar Lewis (1965: 498) confirms this finding. He writes:

. . . recent comparative analysis of the quality of interpersonal relations in small peasant societies, based on anthropological monographs, shows that they are characterized by distrust, suspicion, envy, violence, reserve, and withdrawal. . . . In some villages, peasants can live out their lives without any deep knowledge or understanding of the people whom they "know" in face-to-face relationships. By contrast, in modern Western cities, there may be more give and take about one's private, intimate life at a single "sophisticated" cocktail party than would occur in years in a peasant village. I suspect that there are deeper, more mature relationships among sympathetic, highly educated, cosmopolitan individuals who have chosen each other in friendship, than are possible among sorcery-ridden, superstitious, ignorant peasants, who are daily thrown together because of kinship or residential proximity.

12. This is illustrated by abundant data in Centro de Estudios del Desarrollo, Universidad Central de Venezuela (1965: vols 1-3). The Venezuelan survey shows a surprisingly high incidence of hope among urban population samples. In this connection, it is worth noting that Oscar Lewis (1965: 499) considers the wide "range of alternatives for individuals in most aspects of life . . . one of the most distinctive characteristics of cities, whether industrial or pre-industrial." It is therefore those population sectors that fail to gain access to some or all of these alternatives for improving their condition that are "marginal."

This definition may be useful for reinterpreting the frequently cited fact that large numbers of urban dwellers in U-countries partake of village culture. (See, for instance, the essays by Richard D. Lambert and Bert F. Hoselitz in R. Turner, ed., 1961). These "urban villagers" are, in fact, "marginated" from the dominant urban culture, that is, they may be usefully regarded as being oriented towards, but excluded from, the urban world of constantly expanding opportunities. Their persistance in village folkways is therefore not especially surprising.

13. Weiner (1967). Weiner's facts of voting behavior in Calcutta may be interpreted differently, however, in terms of the theory of "marginality" mentioned in note 12 above. The recent rural migrant to the city is frequently absorbed at first into the "marginal" population sector where he can follow his customary life-style with only minimal adjustments. But for rural population, this style includes a profoundly conservative outlook. It is therefore not especially surprising to discover that the voting behavior of recent migrants is also conservative. It is only as the migrant gains a substantial foothold in the dominant urban society, breaks through the barrier of marginality in at least some respects and thus becomes a "resident"—for instance, a minor bureaucrat in public service—that his political behavior may tend to switch to a more radical position. As Weiner and others have pointed out, urban areas tend to be more "progressive" in their politics than rural areas and peasant farming districts in particular.

14. This, of course, is still a relatively unorthodox view. More commonly, rural arcadia is contrasted with urban violence and anomie. There are no definitive studies on the subject, but the evidence on *rural* violence is steadily accumulating. Irving Louis Horowitz (1967:

Table 7), for instance, cites data on the positive rank correlation of deaths from group violence and numbers of people in farming. At the same time, he notes an inverse correlation between the urbanization process and these causes of death. There are, however, significant exceptions at very high levels of urbanization. This suggests that one should perhaps distinguish between two forms of violent conflict: the urban form, tending to be goal-oriented and limited in time and purpose (e.g., a strike, a street demonstration), even though the frequency of such incidents in the total population may be high; the rural variety, on the other hand, geared to a culture of the "limited good," is characterized by "bitterness and hostility between factions." According to G. M. Foster (1962: 102), "the lengths to which people will go to humiliate their rivals [in small peasant societies] is difficult to believe." Because of environmental circumstances, then, rural conflict tends to be endemic and generational. More recently, however, urban-type violence has taken root also in rural areas. (Specifically on this point, see Quijano, 1967b.) Revolutionary guerrilla activity in the countryside is an urban invention.

15. Rabinovitz (1967). For a more specific country study, see Friedmann and Lackington (1967). An opposite interpretation of the same set of facts is found in Shanti Tangri (1961). The reason for this radical difference in interpretation is given by the implicit belief, held by Tangri, that economic development can be successfully pursued without major structural change in the political system. Our own and contrary position is that conservative, rural-based political structures are incapable of bringing development about and must be changed to achieve development objectives in U-countries. In this connection, it may be observed that rural societies tend to be more prone to totalitarian appeals than highly urbanized societies, though the evidence on this point is admittedly still inconclusive (see Lipset, 1963).

16. The problem of controlling urban conflict is how to guide it towards constructive ends while keeping rapidly changing social systems from disintegration (see Coser, 1956 and note 14 above).

17. The following paragraph is based on Brian J. L. Berry (1967), John Friedmann and John Miller (1965), and J. R. Lasuén (1967).

18. In calculating investment returns, social considerations may, of course, lead one to assign values that are different from those of individual enterprise operating in a freely competitive market.

19. Karl Mannheim (1950: part 3, "New Man–New Values") was among the first to realize the importance of psychological adaptation to the new conditions of an industrializing society. David Reisman's concern with other-directed personality types is a more recent example.

20. The following analysis of Japan's development is to the point: "The attempt to evaluate Japan's place in the scale of economic development reveals a paradox. In terms of a set of variables for which data have been presented by Ginsburg, Japan is in many respects among the most developed countries in the world. On the other hand, in terms of the criteria of backwardness described by Leibenstein, Japan may be classified as a backward country. Especially, Japan is backward as measured by the criterion of per capita national income." (Hollerman, 1964: 139.)

21. Issues of urban development policy have been previously discussed by John Friedmann (1966a).

22. These questions were first posed—though with considerably less precision—in the course of an international conference on India's urbanization about ten years ago. (See the contributions by Chandhuri, Bredo, Harris, Wurster, and Meier, as well as the Editor's Postscript, in Roy Turner [ed.] 1961.) In general, the American contributors to this symposium were more urban-oriented than their Indian colleagues.

23. This issue has been pointedly posed by Gideon Sjoberg (1966).

24. For an earlier discussion of this problem, see Friedmann (1966b).

25. For an elaboration of these questions, see Friedmann (1967).

REFERENCES

BANFIELD, EDWARD C. and LAURA PASANO BANFIELD (1958) The Moral Basis of Backward Society. Glencoe, Ill.: Free Press.

BARNETT, H. G. (1953) Innovation: The Basis of Cultural Change. New York: McGraw-Hill.

BELL, DANIEL (1967) "Notes on the post-industrial society, I and II." Public Interest 6 (Winter): 24-35, and 7 (Spring): 102-118.

BELTRAN, GONZALO AGUIRRE (1964) "Confluence of culture in anthropology." Diogenes 47 (Fall).

BENDIX, REINHARD (1967) "Tradition and modernity reconsidered." Comparative Studies in Society and History 9 (April): 292-346.

BERRY, BRIAN J. L. (1967) Geography of Market Centers and Retail Contribution. Englewood Cliffs, N.J.: Prentice-Hall.

——— (1964) "City size distributions and economic development." In John Friedmann and William Alonso (eds.) Regional Development and Planning: A Reader. Cambridge, Mass.: MIT Press.

BREESE, GERALD (1966) Urbanization in Newly Developing Countries. Englewood Cliffs, N.J.: Prentice-Hall.

BURNS, T. and G. M. STAHLER (1962) The Management of Innovation. Chicago: Quadrangle Books.

Centro de Estudios del Desarrollo, Universidad Central de Venezuela (1965) Estudio de Conflicto y Consenso: Serie de Resultados Parciales. Caracas.

COSER, LEWIS (1956) The Functions of Social Conflict. New York: Free Press.

DI TELLA, TORCUATO (1965) "Populism and reform in Latin America." Pp. 47-74 in Claudio Veliz (ed.) Obstacles to Change in Latin America. New York: Oxford Univ. Press.

ELLEFSEN, RICHARD A. (1961) "City-hinterland relations in India." Chap. 5 in Roy Turner (ed.) India's Urban Future. Berkeley: Univ. of California Press.

FOSTER, GEORGE M. (1965) "Peasant society and the image of limited good." American Anthropologist 67 (April): 293-315.

——— (1962) Traditional Cultures: And the Impact of Technological Change. New York: Harper.

FRIEDMANN, JOHN (1968) "A strategy of deliberate urbanization." Journal of the American Institute of Planners 34 (November): 364-373.

——— (1967) "A conceptual model for the analysis of planning behavior." Administrative Sciences Quarterly 12 (September): 225-252.

——— (1966a) "The urban-regional frame for national development." International Development Review 8 (September): 9-14.

——— (1966b) Regional Development Strategy: A Case Study of Venezuela. Cambridge, Mass.: MIT Press.

——— (1965) Venezuela: From Doctrine to Dialogue. Syracuse: Syracuse Univ. Press.

——— and THOMAS LACKINGTON (1967) "Hyperurbanization and national development in Chile." Urban Affairs Quarterly 2 (June): 3-29.

——— and JOHN MILLER (1965) "The urban field." Journal of the American Institute of Planners 31 (November): 312-320.

HOLLERMAN, LEON (1964) "Japan's place in the scale of economic development." Economic Development and Cultural Change 12 (January).

HOROWITZ, IRVING LOUIS (1967) "Electoral politics, urbanization, and social development in Latin America." Urban Affairs Quarterly 2 (March): 3-35.

LAMBERT, RICHARD D. (1961) "The impact of urban society upon village life." In Roy Turner (ed.) India's Urban Future. Berkeley: Univ. of California Press.

LASUEN, J. R. (1967) "Urbanization hypotheses and Spain's cities system evolution." Paper presented at the Workshop on Regional Development, Institute of Social Studies, October, The Hague (mimeo).

——— et al. (1967) "City size distribution and economic growth: Spain." Ekistics 24 (August): 221-226.

LEVY, FRED D., JR. (1967) "Economic planning in Venezuela." Yale Economic Essays 7 (Spring): 273-321.

LEWIS, OSCAR (1965) "Further observations on the folk-urban continuum and urbanization with special reference to Mexico City." In Philip M. Hauser and Leo F. Schnore (eds.) The Study of Urbanization. New York: John Wiley.

LIPSET, SEYMOUR MARTIN (1963) Political Man. Garden City, N.Y.: Doubleday.

MANNHEIM, KARL (1950) Freedom, Power and Democratic Planning. New York: Oxford Univ. Press.

QUIJANO, ANIBAL (1967a) La Urbanización de la Sociedad en Latinoamérica. Santiago: United Nations, Economic Commission for Latin America, Division of Social Affairs (mimeo).

——— (1967b) "Contemporary peasant movements." Chap. 9 in Seymour Martin Lipset and Aldo Solari (eds.) Elites in Latin America. New York: Oxford Univ. Press.

RABINOVITZ, FRANCINE F. (1967) Urban Development and Political Development in Latin America (Occasional Paper). Bloomington, Ill.: Comparative Administration Group.

SILVERT, KALMAN H. [ed.] (1963) Expectant Peoples: Nationalism and Development. New York: Random House.

SJOBERG, GIDEON (1966) "Rural-urban balance and models of economic development." In Neil J. Smelser and Seymour Martin Lipset (eds.) Social Structure and Mobility in Economic Development. Chicago: Aldine.

——— (1965) "Cities in developing and industrial societies: a cross-cultural analysis." In Philip M. Hauser and Leo F. Schnore (eds.) The Study of Urbanization. New York: Wiley.

TANGRI, SHANTI (1961) "Urbanization, political stability, and economic growth." Chap. 10 in Roy Turner (ed.) India's Urban Future. Berkeley: Univ. of California Press.

TURNER, ROY [ed.] (1961) India's Urban Future. Berkeley: Univ. of California Press.

U.S. Department of Commerce, Area Redevelopment Administration (1965) Area Redevelopmental Policies in Britain and the Countries of the Common Market. Washington, D.C.: Government Printing Office.

WATERSTON, ALBERT (1965) Development Planning: Lessons of Experience. Baltimore: Johns Hopkins Press.

WEINER, MYRON (1967) "Urbanization and political protest." Civilizations 17 (no. 1-2): 44-52.

WINGO, LOWDEN, JR. (1967) "Recent patterns of urbanization among Latin American countries." Urban Affairs Quarterly 2 (March): 81-109.

WOLFE, ERIC (1962) Sons of the Shaking Earth: The People of Mexico and Guatemala: Their Land, History and Culture. Chicago: Univ. of Chicago Press.

Planning, History, Politics

Reflections on John Friedmann's "The Role of Cities in National Development"

RICHARD M. MORSE

John Friedmann's broad and suggestive paper serves in many ways to stretch our thinking about the phenomenon of urban growth in contemporary Latin America. He properly warns us against hermetic preoccupation with single cities or parts of cities as "things in themselves"—and thus against excessive dedication to the case study or community study approach which so largely characterized anthropological research on rural Latin America in the 1940s. He asks that we think of urban clusters not as beads scattered as from a broken necklace but as coalescing into densely populated, spatially extended core regions which pose powerful challenges to the technological and sociological imagination. Moreover, he directs attention to economic as well as physical and social implications of urbanization, and shows that what he has called "hyperurbanization" intimately affects the phasing and imperatives of economic development.

The reflections that follow are not intended as a denial of Dr. Friedmann's promising perspective. Rather, they aim to show that this perspective might be deepened, modulated, and rendered culturally more adaptable by contributions from historical study. In contrast to the social scientist and social engineer, the historian is concerned more with morphology than with theory, more with cross-cultural comparison than with cross-cultural generalization, more with the enduring recurrences and ironies of the human condition than with its ultimate purification. This commentary, then, is offered as lens correction, not as refutation.

Spatial Aspects of Development

Let us begin with Friedmann's emphasis upon spatial aspects of development. He perceives the historical ecology of Latin America as evolving in a unidirectional process from nucleated to interconnected settlement, from aggregations to systems of cities. Now undoubtedly the contemporary urban scene in Latin America is in many ways unprecedented. This should not be taken to mean, however, that it culminates five centuries of uninterrupted development from scattered town nuclei, or that the notion of spatially extended urban systems is wholly new in Latin America.

Among his "universal characteristics of modern development" Friedmann lists "progressive expansion of transport and communication capacity over larger areas" and an increase of interconnections within the system. Precisely these points are made by Caio Prado, Jr., when he analyzes the knitting together of the principal regions of Brazil in the eighteenth century by mule trails and river navigation. In this case, however, the sequel was that: (a) the opening of Brazilian ports to trade restored precedence to coastal urbanization at the expense of spatially extended internal communications; (b) the advent of the steamship restored primacy to the early colonial axis of maritime communication.

> This was a return to the original system of the colony: sea routes were the backbone of the country's communication system, with lines of penetration running in from the coast and entirely cut off from each other. . . . [The] task of integrating the country, the task of the long colonial past, was interrupted [Prado, 1967].

If the historian needs this caution against unilinearism, so too may the prophet.[1]

Far from being a present-day novelty, spatially extended urban systems were a paramount feature of early Spanish colonization. Governor Nicolás de Ovando's strategy (1504-1505) for establishing fifteen towns throughout the island of Española was nothing less than a regional development plan that linked the ports to the mining, farming, and ranching areas, and these latter to the Indian labor supply in the West. A brief moment of prosperity was followed by the precipitous decline of the Indian labor force, by economic crisis, and by fragmentation of Ovando's islandwide master plan.

> In the final analysis, the north-south axis established by Columbus, though it was not part of a premeditated plan for the island, prevailed permanently over the east-west orientation that resulted from the complementary work of Ovando. This was a factor of serious consequences for the island's history, fatally preparing the way for the later seizure of the western part by the French [Palm, 1955].

Comparable to Ovando's scheme was Governor Diego Valázquez' seven-city master plan for Cuba (1512-1515) to promote "the development of the most important regions of the Island."

The conquistadors, far from concentrating in a single locality, were distributed in seven, so advantageously situated that all the Indians were placed under control and the richest zones placed in production. The link established between the first settlers and the land . . . was so firm and the sites chosen with such keen judgment that the original seven Spanish settlements have survived all the economic and political crises of the history of Cuba [Guerra y Sanchez, 1921].

In the Valley of Mexico, which contained dense concentrations of sedentary Indians, the Spaniards simply appropriated an existing urban system. Or more accurately, they interpreted Aztec society as a "mosaic of towns," in Charles Gibson's phrase, rather than a system of tribes. Upon this mosaic, the Spaniards imposed the hierarchical urban nomenclature of Castile *(ciudad, villa, pueblo)*. This honorific hierarchy coexisted with another that was politically and economically more functional, descending from the *cabecera* to the *sujeto* to the urban *barrio* or rural *estancia*. In selecting cabeceras, the Spaniards were guided neither by urban size nor by the prior imperial design of the Aztecs. Instead they erected their classification at a "sub-imperial or pre-imperial level within Indian society," with the cabecera becoming identified as the capital town of a local Indian ruler *(tlatoani)* (Gibson, 1964). What promised to be a system of ecological equilibrium, however, was upset after the mid-sixteenth century by the heavy mortality rate of the Indian population. A severe shortage of rural labor ensued, causing an urban exodus as the hacienda came to offer town dwellers the only alternative to starvation (Gibson, 1955).

Other cases of colonial urban systems can be cited (Buarque de Holanda, 1966; Comardán, 1962; Guarda, 1957, 1967; Marciales, 1948), but the examples of the Antilles and Mexico are enough to suggest that: (a) the use of systems of cities for regional development in Latin America is not unprecedented; (b) such systems have not necessarily evolved in unilinear fashion toward greater complexity and integration.

The process of regional development in colonial times becomes still clearer when we examine it through a single node of an urban network. The study of Tunja by Cortés Alonso (1965) affords a convenient example. In 1623, Tunja had 476 buildings and a population of 3,300 adult Spanish males and an indeterminate number of Indians, Negroes, and mixed bloods. It was second only to Bogotá in regional importance. Two aspects of the city's regional projection deserve attention here: commercial and administrative. Tunja's fifteen leading merchants, commanding a capital of 10,000-80,000 pesos each, were directly engaged in overseas trade with the metropolis; they were also active in regional trade along routes that traversed much of present-day Colombia; finally, the city was a center for traditional semiweekly *tiangues* where the Indians exchanged produce of the immediate area.

Tunja's politico-administrative involvements corresponded roughly to these three levels of commercial activity. First, it was a point of precarious equilibrium between the claims and favors of the far-flung patrimonial Spanish empire on one hand and, on the other, the separatist force of the local *encomenderos,* many of whom were descended from the mutinous soldiers of Pizarro. In the 1590s, Tunja's was the only town council of the region to organize effective resistance to the royal sales tax. Second, Tunja was the administrative capital for the Spanish towns in a surrounding area of 30 to 100 miles in radius. Their allegiance to Tunja was secured not simply by administrative fiat but also by ties of sentiment toward the mother city which had colonized the area. Third, Tunja was the control center for 161 encomiendas (as of 1610) which, as well as being units of agricultural production, represented tributary villages of 80 to 2,000 Indians apiece. In short, the city's laddered administrative functions (outpost of empire, satellite towns, tributary Indian villages) paralleled its commercial ones (metropolitan trade, regional markets, indigenous tiangues).

Precedents From Colonial Urban Systems

Far from being of mere antiquarian interest, colonial urban systems offer many precedents to the modern planner. Cities served as instruments of economic and agricultural development. They were arranged in well formed hierarchies, economic and administrative. Colonial urban systems provide numerous instances of spatially extensive urban-rural equilibrium. Urban form and urban processes were adapted to complex bi- or even multi-cultural situations.

We may go even further. Along with its historical precedents, Friedmann's proposal that we construe national development as an exercise in urban development has perfectly decent credentials in Spanish neo-Thomist thought. In 1647, Juan de Solórzano cited St. Thomas and the ancients to substantiate his view that

> this World, which is like a great City where all men live, is divided into smaller ones. [Aristotle and Cicero] define the City as a perfect Congregation of men who were once scattered in huts through the forest and woods and who then joined together. Thus they acquired the many praiseworthy benefits deriving from this social and political life, which is surely far superior to the solitary one . . . for the solitary man must be either beast or God [de Solórzano, 1736-1739].

Friedmann explicitly warns against cultural determinism, and he points us toward universal or transcultural imperatives as those which significantly control and shape national development. My own reflections lead in the forbidden direction. Early Spanish American urbanization was culturally determined to an important degree. One is struck by the considerable correspondence among actual colonizing practice, royal colonizing ordinances, and the philosophy of colonization as articulated by Solórzano and others. Spanish American cities—in their urban form and social structure, in their relation to hinterlands, in their subordination to royal power—reflected the hierarchical, patrimonial order of the larger society.[2]

Partial confirmation for this view is found in the recent attempts of Jorge Hardoy (1966, 1967) to determine a rank order for colonial cities. He found that the omission of economic functions from his weighted scale of urban functions produced no significant distortion of his conclusions. That is, the most useful indicators of rank order for colonial Spanish American towns seem attached to functions determined or approved by politico-administrative decisions of the metropolis. This is almost the reverse of the case for the cities of late-medieval Europe, or for those of colonial or nineteenth-century United States.

Historical considerations such as these yield at least two important guidelines to the contemporary Latin American planner who shares Friedmann's concerns. First, when we raise the question of interurban integration (that is, creation or cultivation of systems of cities), we are led to two contrasting historical archetypes. In fifteenth-century Spain municipal brotherhoods were organized into the Santa Hermandad, presided over by the Bishop of Cartagena as the direct representative of the crown and for consolidation of the central power. A New World corollary was the *junta de procuradores,* an intermunicipal body which brought petitions and grievances before royal authorities, reflecting the principle that "the total representation of the vassals of the kingdom consisted in the sum of urban representations" (Meza Villalobos, 1958). The patrimonial dependency and regional inclusiveness of this type of organization clearly differentiated it from the Hanse of northern Europe, a league of autonomous cities allied in furtherance of their respective commercial interests.

A second point is that the calculated use of the patrimonial capital city as an instrument of development is well rooted in Iberian tradition. A classic example is the proposal of a royal magistrate in 1699 to transfer the capital of Santo Domingo to a central inland site, to assemble in it the scattered populations of a score of villages, and to make it the seat of all the royal bureaucracies, the university, and the colleges.[3] "The Court is the image of the heart," he wrote, "and like it should be located virtually in the center so that justice and assistance may be rendered with the greatest uniformity and dispatch." Territories are ineffectively administered, he continued, by capitals situated peripherally as ports, garrisons or borderland outposts. With a central location, on the other hand,

> the Church, Tribunals and Communities draw everything with them. Merchants, students and claimants throng the highways; their trips increase the welfare of many; neighboring places benefit from the consumption of their produce, and the Royal Treasury profits from the numerous inns and markets [de Haro Monterroso, 1942] .

One is struck by the similarity of this argument to that advanced for the creation in our time of Brasilia. And one is led to contemplate the difference between speaking loosely of the role of cities in the development of hinterlands (or the role of commercial cities, as in the nineteenth-century United States) and speaking of the role of capital cities in this process.

Roles of the Patrimonial Urban Center

Friedmann's analysis suffers, then, from intentional neglect of the historical and cultural role of the patrimonial urban center in Latin America. He writes as though transformation paths and optimal patterns of spatial organization are to be determined by economic and technological factors; as though the decentralization of urban functions and the strengthening of communication systems are to take place in quarantine from political influence; as though the Boston-to-Washington megalopolis or metropolitan corridor is soon to be replicated in several areas of Latin America, posing identical problems for planners. With regard to the last point, it should be remembered that the metropolitan corridor of the United States eastern seaboard developed along the axis of the historic colonial commercial port cities (Boston, New York, Philadelphia, Baltimore). The capitals (Albany and Harrisburg) of the two most important states of the region and even the national capital are peripherally located. In fact, in United States urban experience it is not at all prescriptive that a politico-administrative center should become a foyer for commercial and industrial development.

In Latin America, it seems important that a city be a patrimonial center if it is to serve as a growth pole for economic development. Brasilia is already the classic case for a modern frontier zone. Or, if a capital is not actually transferred to a frontier, the central power may spin off an outlying city under its direct support and tutelage, as in the case of Ciudad Guayana. Without denying the regional economic and ecological justifications for this city, it is probably accurate to say that its ultimate legitimation derives from a process of patrimonial schizogenesis. Or again, if planners speak of decentralizing economic functions from a central corridor not to a frontier but to existing peripheral cities, it is usually implied that provincial capitals will be the beneficiaries. Thus it is no accident that the flourishing second-echelon growth centers (Monterrey, Guadalajara, Cali, Medellín, Córdoba, Pôrto Alegre, Curitiba) are so frequently regional political capitals. When this is not the case, as with Chimbote, Peru, the city may face enormous obstacles in developing urban infrastructure for economic activity because of its weak political leverage.

The continuing importance of major Latin American cities as combined patrimonial centers and economic growth poles throws into question Friedmann's insistence that urban societies translate the zero-sum games of peasant societies into competitive nonzero-sum games, and his Wirthian statement that the city in Latin America, as elsewhere, has internalized the concept of unlimited opportunity as the basis for its unique form of culture. This view contrasts sharply with the following generalization about Latin American urban society:

Considerable social mobility has therefore continued to occur. But if one examines the occupational careers of a few individuals at the middle levels, one forms the impression that they have kept on taking advantage of a system of semiclosed relationships—a true prebendary distribution of opportunities—which has resulted in the creation of extremely unequal opportunities for the various middle groups of society. In other words the values of *competition, merit* and technical *efficiency,* as principles of social organization, seem to have been unable to play the role that they did in the more advanced industrial societies [CEPAL, 1963] .

This conclusion is supported by considerable research on Latin American entrepreneurship, education, and social mobility, and forms of urban association (such as Leeds' study [1965] of the Brazilian *panelinha*) by the fact that major cities are generally unable to provide steady, predictable employment for the increasing numbers of rural migrants, and by the fact that the Durkheimian concept of anomie (if taken as meaning a pathological reaction in the face of unlimited opportunity) does not seem generally relevant to the Latin American urban scene. One might go so far as to say that the real challenge facing the urban planner in Latin America is to achieve a creative and appealing vision of the city as a limited good. Because it would correspond to the finite condition of man, such a vision might even have implications for the world at large as a corrective to the Faustian spirit run amok.

Transcultural Requirements

Essentially, Friedmann casts his analysis in the terms of classic nineteenth-century sociology. His distinction between peasant and urban worlds seems like Tönnies stood on his head; his transformation from simple to complex structures smacks of Spencer's homogeneous-to-heterogeneous; and his description of the urbanization process fits neatly into Durkheim's paradigm for the organic solidarity which results from division of labor. What is lacking under the last heading is the acknowledgment that Durkheim's sociological requirements for division of labor are transcultural. When they conflict with recalcitrant historical or cultural situations, they produce abnormal forms of division of labor, which Durkheim (1933) carefully identified and two of which (forced division of labor, malcoordination of functions) seem especially pertinent to Latin America.

The fact that the transcultural requirements for organic solidarity harmonized more or less effectively with cultural imperatives in the cases of the United States, Germany, Russia, or Japan causes confusion for observers of the Latin American scene, where such harmony is much less in evidence. Scholars therefore tend to polarize into hostile camps of economic-stage theorists and cultural determinists. North Americans are almost inevitably among the former, and they invariably provoke reactions such as the following from Otávio Ianni (1967):

> The problems posed on the basis of the outlook of industrialized nations are not always restated in the light of the different approach suggested by the peculiarities of underdeveloped nations. Here, more than anywhere else, the lesson taught by C. Wright Mills has been forgot. There is research concentrated on formation of attitudes favorable to innovation, or the formation of managerial elites, but it fails to take account of the historical context and the overall social structure which is indispensable to the initiation and execution of creative social policies and relationships.

Innovation

This criticism applies to Friedmann's treatment of innovation. In part, perhaps, because he confuses the Latin American city's obvious role in transmitting innovation from abroad with its capacity to generate innovation, he establishes a positive correlation between level of urbanization and frequency of innovation. This proposition is hard to square with the view of Guillén Martínez (1968) who, while acknowledging the contributions of industrial capitalism to the growth of Mexico, São Paulo and Buenos Aires, asserts that none of these cities "shows a visible tendency toward political democratization or a lessening of social injustice. On the contrary, the old problems of authoritarianism, social inertia and violent struggle for Power are more evident here than they were and still are in the old rural zone."

Now some sorts of innovation emanate by definition from urban environments: stock markets, high-rise architecture, use of mass media, yearly fashions in clothing, and the like. If our concern, however, is not with artifacts, techniques, styles, and outward forms of urbanization, but with the psychic energies that produce innovation, then the correlation is much less secure. It may be significant that when Friedmann adopts the conventional sequence of city to metropolis to megalopolis, he optimistically omits the customary final stage of necropolis, an urban possibility that is daily present in the twentieth century. When Western Europe did experience this stage in the fourth century A.D., an outstanding feature of the period was the transfer of innovative forces from urban to rural settings. Yet even if we discount such Spenglerian possibilities, there is no shortage of instances where innovation, or innovative attitudes, can be linked with the rural or small-town milieu. In sixteenth- and seventeenth-century Brazil, for instance, the rural zones were a much more important theater for innovation (cultural, linguistic, sociological, technological) than the urban centers.

Examples more relevant to the case at hand can be drawn from Western countries in the industrial era. Page Smith has shown that the extraordinary dynamism of the nineteenth-century United States derived not so much from its cities as from its small towns, where the simpler, more rigorous faith of seventeenth-century Puritanism remained kindled.

> Here was the paradox: the covenanted community, remarkably stable and unshakably conservative produced outwardly propelled, inner-directed individuals capable of the most startling innovation and the most revolutionary change, carried through the name of the ancient values of the town (Smith, 1966).

Sociological studies since the 1920s show that the small towns of the nineteenth-century United States contributed a disproportionate amount of leadership at the big-city and national levels, particularly in education, the sciences, the ministry and the professions, though less so in business and the fine arts.

Louis Chevalier's study (Chevalier, 1950) of the growth of Paris in the nineteenth-century shows that the megalocephalic capital recruited trained workers in such numbers from the departments that it scarcely needed to provide apprentice training. In many ways, the ethos of Paris was relatively undifferentiated from that of the towns supplying migrants. Chevalier even suggests that the revolutionary political programs of 1830 and 1848 were inspired by migrants from the eastern and northern regions of France; they emanated from but were not in the strict sense generated by the capital.

The point to be made with respect to contemporary Latin America is that innovation cannot be thought of as linked exclusively to facilities for education, communication and technological experimentation. It depends for its vitality upon social protest and a sense of outrage, which makes identification of its source a problem in sociology, as well as in human geography.

Friedmann brings classic Western sociological assumptions to Latin America. In the industrial nations, innovation became associated with urban middle classes who acquired influence by a process long ago designated as the "circulation of elites." Studies of Latin America seem to be reaching the conclusion that its aristocracies or elites have been coopting middle groups while maintaining a degree of innovative capacity sufficient for year-to-year survival. This view is implicit in the now generalized use of the term counterelite, which suggests that one cannot look to upward-circulating elites for structural innovation but only to potential or disaffected elites who feel themselves marginal to the social process. For such groups, the immediate goal is not economic and educational improvement but seizure of central power in league with popular sectors which may be rural or urban, as circumstances dictate. Guillén Martínez (1968) puts this interpretation in historical context:

> Free creation and individual disposition of wealth allowed the European bourgeois to win freedom as a human being and social power within the community. The Iberian man, on the other hand, came to enjoy and freely dispose of material wealth *by having previously acquired social power*. In both cases the collective ethos is closely linked to the historical process of personal liberation. Bourgeois wealth was the means to attain power in Europe. In medieval Spain social power was the only path toward control of wealth.

In his study of social classes in Uruguay, Carlos Rama (1960) includes a chapter ("Power as a Factor of Social Stratification") which supports the view that power, at least in this particular Latin American society, is a weightier determinant of social level than education, occupation, prestige, tradition, or style of life.

In short, the outlook of the neo-Mumfordian megalopolitan planner in Latin America needs desperately to be complemented by that of the political sociologist. Urban planning in the conventional sense is in fact totally subordinate to the prospects for political change.[4] At the moment, Cuba seems the only country which offers a political climate favorable to planning of the scope which Friedmann envisions. Hardoy's recent survey of planning agencies in the South American countries suggests that under prevailing political conditions the urban or regional planner may well despair of achieving bold and generous results in the foreseeable future.

> Strictly speaking, one cannot say that any of the countries of South America possesses an effective national organization for planning. It would appear that the urbanization process . . . interests none of the national and regional planning organisms, and that the social, economic and political role which human masses are playing, and will play with greater intensity in the future, has no influence on the economic and social development of the countries of the area [Hardoy, 1967].

Friedmann's vision of the innovative potential of metropolitan centers and his generous appraisal of possibilities for the spatial organization of communities must be deepened—though not necessarily effaced—by an image of the large Latin American city as a bastion of privilege and conservatism whose wealth and opportunities are denied to increasing numbers of its poor. A counterpart to the Friedmann thesis, then, would be the *Estrategia de la guerrilla urbana* of Abraham Guillén (1966) who, with an eye at least as clinical as Friedmann's, outlines a program of unrelenting, pervasive, small-group insurrection of Latin American urban workers and peasants. Whenever the urban population predominates in a country, the center of gravity of the struggle must move to the large cities, those "enormous cement forests where all the techniques of guerrilla warfare can be correctly employed."[5]

I have cited Guillén not to substantiate a prediction of generalized urban violence but to make the points that: (a) there are those who see Latin American cities as citadels of privilege whose walls might be reinforced rather than eroded by mere planning, in the North American sense; and (b) at the very moment when Latin America seems on the way to becoming massified and megalopolitanized, humble, unaided single men and their families—squatters, for example, more importantly than *guerrilleros*—are suddenly visible as the most significant architects (in the literal and extended meanings) of the changing societies. If we could but learn the lesson, it is the squatter community which will teach us how the culture of poverty can become livable, just as the guerrilla band has taught us the impotence of nuclear power. But then Ralph Waldo Emerson foresaw our own megalopolis a century ago and, in a brilliantly prophetic passage, made precisely this point.[6]

Development

Friedmann's distinction between developed and underdeveloped countries requires a final word. He suggests that development creates a shift of attention to the uses of leisure, the progress of science, and the conquest of space. If this is the case, and if age-old, universal moral concerns have no paramountcy, he is describing a descent into the puerilism of idiocy. And if, as he claims, underdeveloped countries can be guided by developed ones while the latter are bereft of any model, how can one account for the impact of the overseas Peace Corps experience on our domestic poverty programs? Or understand the interest of Berkeley students of the 1960s in the Córdoba reform of 1918? Or explain why a North American living in a black urban ghetto learns dignity and self-confidence from the example of a West Indian or a tribal African? It is high time that the cultural relativism of the old bushwhacking anthropologists was refurbished for the cultures of cities and nations.

NOTES

1. Another of Friedmann's universal development characteristics is "a rise in real incomes per capita." Again, Brazil seems a gigantic exception if there is any truth to the admittedly controversial assertion of Celso Furtado that his country has never again attained the level of real per capita income that prevailed for the population of European origin at the turn of the sixteenth century. For nineteenth-century Mexico, also, William Paul McGreevey claims a decline in per capita income. (See Celso Furtado, 1963; McGreevey, 1968).

2. I use the term "patrimonial" as explicated by Max Weber; for the application to Latin America, see Morse (1964).

3. More than a century and a half later, the Dominican Constitution of 1858 provided for the inland transfer of the capital for similar reasons.

4. This is somewhat less true in precisely the countries Friedmann knows best and from which he perhaps generalizes: Venezuela and Chile.

5. Guillén is a Spaniard who writes of Latin American guerrillas against the historic episodes of Paris (1870-1871), Petrograd (1917), and Madrid (1936). He is more sanguine about the uses of urban guerrilla movements than was Che Guevara, who recognized their importance but wrote in his "Suburban Warfare" that "a suburban guerrilla band can never spring up of its own accord" and must be "under the direct orders of chiefs located in another zone." Guevara's analysis is therefore less favorable than Guillén's to the Friedmann thesis of urban innovation! (See Guevara, 1968).

6. "I see the immense material prosperity—towns on towns, states on states, and wealth piled in the massive architecture of cities: California quartz-mountains dumped down in New York to be repiled architecturally alongshore from Canada to Cuba, and thence westward to California again. But it is not New York streets, though stretching out towards Philadelphia until they touch it, and northward until they touch New Haven, Hartford, Springfield, Worcester, and Boston—not these that make the real estimation. But when I look over this constellation of cities which animate and illustrate the land, and see how little the government has to do with their daily life, how self-helped and self-directed all families are . . . I see what cubic values America has, and in these a better certificate of civilization than great cities or enormous wealth" [Michael H. Cowan, 1967: 53].

REFERENCES

BUARQUE DE HOLANDA, SERGIO (1966) "Movimentos da populacão em São Paulo no século XVII." Revista de Instituto de Estudos Brasileiros 1: 55-111.

CEPAL [Comisión Económica para América Latina] (1963) El Desarrollo Social de América Latina en la Post-guerra. Buenos Aires: Solar/Hachette.

CHEVALIER, LOUIS (1950) La Formation de la Population Parisienne au XIXe Siècle. Paris: Presses Universitaires de France.

COMADRAN RUIA, JORGE (1962) "Nacimiento y desarrollo de los núcleos urbanos y del poblamiento de la campaña des país de Cuyo duranto la época hispana (1551-1810)." Anuario de Estudios Americanos 19: 145-226.

CORTES ALONSO, VICENTA (1965) "Tunja y sus vecinos." Revista de Indias 25 (January-June): 155-207.

COWAN, MICHAEL H. (1967) City of the West: Emerson, America, and Urban Metaphor. New Haven and London: Yale Univ. Press.

DE HARO MONTERROSO, FERNANDO JOSEPH (1942) "Medios propuestos para poblar sin costo alguno de la Real Hacienda la Isla de Santo Domingo," pp. 345-359 in E. Rodríguez Demorizi (ed.) Relaciones Históricas de Santo Domingo. Cuidad Trujillo: Editora Montalvo.

DE SOLORZANO, JUAN (1736-1739) Política Indiana. Madrid.

DURKHEIM, EMILE (1933) Division of Labor in Society. New York: Macmillan.

FRIEDMANN, JOHN and TOMAS LACKINGTON (1967) "Hyperurbanization and national development in Chile." Urban Affairs Q. 2 (June): 3-29.

FURTADO, CELSO (1963) The Economic Growth of Brazil. Berkeley: Univ. of California Press.

GIBSON, CHARLES (1964) The Aztecs Under Spanish Rule. Stanford: Stanford Univ. Press.

——— (1955) "The transformation of the Indian community in New Spain, 1500-1810." Cahiers d'Histoire Mondiale 2, 3: 581-607.

GUARDA, GABRIEL (1967) Influencia Militar en las Cuidades del Reino de Chile. Santiago: Academia Chilena de la Historia.

——— (1956) "El urbanismo imperial y las primitivas ciudades de Chile." Finis Terrae 4, 15: 48-69.

GUERRA Y SANCHEZ, RAMIRO (1921) Historia de Cuba. Havana: Imprenta "El Siglo XX."

GUEVARA, CHE (1968) Guerrilla Warfare. New York: Vintage.

GUILLEN, ABRAHAM (1966) Estrategia de la guerrilla urbana. Montevideo: Manuales del Pueblo.

GUILLEN MARTINEZ, FERNANDO (1968) "Los Estados Unidos y América Latina." Aportes 7 (January).

HARDOY, JORGE (1967) Typescript Report on Planning Agencies in South America.

——— (1966) "Escalas y funciones urbanas de América Hispánica hacia 1600, un ensayo metodológico." Presented to the Thirty-Seventh Congress of Americanists, Mar del Plata, September 4-10.

——— and CARMEN ARANOVICH (1967) "Cuadro comparativo de los centros de colonización española existentes en 1580 y 1630." Desarrollo Económico 7 (October-December): 349-360.

IANNI, OTAVIO (1967) "Sociology in Latin America," in M. Diégues, Jr. and B. Wood (eds.) Social Science in Latin America. New York: Columbia Univ. Press.

LEEDS, ANTHONY (1965) "Brazilian careers and social structure: a case history and model," pp. 379-404 in D. B. Heath and R. N. Adams (eds.) Contemporary Cultures and Societies of Latin America. New York: Random House.

McGREEVEY, WILLIAM PAUL (1968) "Recent research on the economic history of Latin America." Latin Amer. Research Rev. 3 (Spring): 89-117.

MARCIALES, MIGUEL [ed.] (1948) Geografía Histórica y Económica del Norte de Santander. Bogotá: Editorial Santafé.

MEZA VILLALOBOS, NESTOR (1958) La Conciencia Política Chilena Durante la Monarquía. Santiago: Editorial Universitaria.

MORSE, RICHARD M. (1964) "The heritage of Latin America," pp. 123-177 in L. Hartz et al. (eds.) The Founding of New Societies. New York: Harcourt, Brace & World.

RAMA, CARLOS M. (1960) Las Clases Sociales en el Uruguay. Montevideo: Ediciones Nuestro Tiempo.

SMITH, PAGE (1966) As a City Upon a Hill: The Town in American History. New York: Alfred A. Knopf.

A Theory of Urbanization?

Rejoinder to Richard M. Morse

JOHN FRIEDMANN

No one has written more incisively about the history of urbanization in Latin America than Professor Morse. I am therefore particularly grateful to him for having devoted an entire essay to the questions posed in my paper. I have learned from it and learned also to be humble in face of knowledge that I do not have. But Professor Morse goes beyond the customary scholastic comment. Everything he says is permeated by a fundamental doubt concerning the nature of our knowledge. At issue is the possibility of a theory of urbanization.

To set the stage for the debate, let me say that we begin from dialectically opposed positions: I think a theory of urbanization is possible; Professor Morse inclines to the view that it is not. "In contrast to the social scientist and social engineer," he writes, "the historian is concerned more with morphology than with theory, more with cross-cultural comparison than with cross-cultural generalization, more with the enduring recurrences and ironies of the human condition than with its ultimate purification." He offers his comments not as a refutation, however, but as a "lens correction." Neither of us wishes to put in doubt the relevance of the other's discipline for the study of urbanization, but an airing of the issues may lead to clarification of the possibilities and limits of both social science and history. It is in this spirit that I shall venture these brief comments.

I shall have relatively little to say about urbanization as such. It is a subject that has attracted numerous social scientists—from geographers to political scientists—as an infinitely complex and therefore doubly challenging phenomenon for study. Both Professor Morse and I would agree, I think, that the term refers to both ecological shifts in the population and economic activities (and specifically their aggregation into large settlement clusters) and a cultural process by which a specifically urban culture evolves in a given place and spreads from there to other populations. The study of urbanization is concerned with these meanings, as well as with the relationship of urbanization to other societal processes and structures.

The problem of a theory of urbanization does not lie so much in its subject matter as, more generally, in the social sciences. Social scientists defend the view that theory, in common with physical science, is ahistorical and predictive. But if Professor Morse is right that the pursuit of this is a chimera, then social science would appear as nothing more than a subspecialty of history concerned with recent events; it would become an ideographic science.

Stated in this form, the two positions seem irreconcilable, and the argument would have to cease at this point. In fact, the contradiction is more apparent than real, though some differences will always remain; the problem resides in elucidating the meanings of ahistoricity and prediction. If these are properly understood, historian and social scientist should be able to live amicably side by side, rather than meet in deadly confrontations.

Prediction and Prophecy

In my essay "The Role of Cities in National Development," I advanced a series of hypotheses that were intended to have predictive value. Prediction, of course, refers to a future state of affairs, and this may suggest that social scientists have mastered special techniques for telling what will happen, for predicting history. Whatever else they may claim to be, social scientists are not prophets, and prediction is different from prophecy insofar as it is restrained by a precise statement of the conditions under which the prediction is expected to hold true. In experimental science, a statement of these conditions permits the replication of the experiment. In social science—where experiments are usually not capable of replication under identical conditions—the statement of conditions refers to a multitude of historical variables that are subsumed under the famous *ceteris paribus* clause: the prediction is claimed to be true only to the extent that the relevant conditions are held constant.

A second distinguishing characteristic is that predictions are quasi-statistical in form: they are expected to be subject to a certain margin of error; only an *average* state of affairs can be predicted.

The prediction of what will happen is therefore conditioned by the variables that are held constant. What the social scientist cannot know is how the predicted state of affairs may change if the restraining conditions are relaxed. The scientist who ventures statements predictive of history is either speculating or prophesying. Since the future cannot be known in any accepted sense of the term, the present is the stage for action, and the past can only be reconstructed in an exercise of disciplined speculation, what *really* is, or was, or will be, can never be found out.

Professor Morse delights in producing certain historical evidence that appears to be in conflict with the hypotheses proposed in my paper. What should the social scientist do under these conditions? Three alternatives would seem to be open to him. He can argue that the evidence is really not in conflict because it falls within the expected margin of error of the prediction. Or he can say that the contradictory evidence occurred under conditions for which the prediction would not be expected to hold. Finally, he can choose the alternative of extending, reformulating, or abandoning his initial hypotheses. The choice among these paths is not an arbitrary one, though it may be difficult to make and, in the end, may even turn out to have been wrong. The evaluation of evidence is part of the process of scientific work.

The Generality of Hypotheses

The generality of a hypothesis is determined by the number of restraining conditions imposed upon it. Thus, a hypothesis that "social differentiation is greater in urban than in nonurban areas" is a very general one which probably requires no conditional statement other than a definition of urban and nonurban. On the other hand, a hypothesis that "the attainment of increased economic power is a determining motivation for all urban social strata" requires a good deal of qualification. Where the many restrictive conditions that would be necessary to render the hypothesis predictive do not hold, the hypothesis cannot be considered to apply.

Unfortunately for both science and planning, it would seem that the more general the form of a hypothesis, the more likely it is to be self-evident, the less likely is it capable of being rejected by appeal to empirical data, and the less useful will it be as a basis for decision. The inverse of this proposition is also largely valid. The more specific a hypothesis, the more will it tend to reveal hidden relationships, the greater will be its probability of refutation, and the more useful will it be for planning. It is a pity that the art of applying reason to the guidance of society is so fraught with risks of error even in fundamental knowledge.

These considerations are pertinent to the issue of historical relevance on which Professor Morse calls me to task. In contradiction to my hypothesis that the locus of high innovative capacity is in large cities and core regions, he points out, for instance, that there have been periods in the past, and in different parts of the globe, where the innovative locus was rather in small towns and rural settings.

As it happens, both hypothesis and evidence in this case are imprecise, since neither of us proposes an operational definition and measure of innovative capacity. But I will go further and admit that my hypothesis was stated incompletely, since it failed to specify the conditions under which it would be expected to be valid. I am unable at present to do justice to this task with all the necessary rigor. In very general language, however, the conditions would comprise the existence of a modern industrial society. Evidence contradicting the hypothesis should, therefore, be found in any society that, at the time of observation, exhibited a degree of industrialism, from the beginnings of industrialization in the eighteenth century up to, but not including, postindustrial society in the United States in the 1960s.

This conditional statement prevents me from retrojecting the hypothesis into the fourth century A.D. While Professor Morse's observation on the shift of innovative activity from urban to rural settings is therefore interesting and historically important, it is irrelevant as evidence for or against my thesis.

More to the point is his observation—following Page Smith—that "the extraordinary dynamism of nineteenth century United States derived not so much from its cities as from small towns, where the simpler, more rigorous faith of seventeenth century Puritanism remained kindled." But whatever the formative influences of national leadership, it took the big city to provide it with an appropriate stage for its actions.[1] And the same, I would hold, is true for the Latin American city, despite its comparatively low level of innovative activity.[2] Regardless of who the innovators are and whether innovations are self-generated or imitated, it is the metropolis which makes them possible on a large scale. And this function is best explained, I believe, by the concept of communications potential as suggested in my paper.

Conclusion

I have argued that theory in the social sciences is ahistorical, in the sense that its validity is always circumscribed by a number of explicitly formulated assumptions. What is to be predicted is not future history but the behavior of certain variables under conditions that are held constant. It is only in this sense that a theory of urbanization appears possible.

The historian, on the other hand, is constrained from holding constant anything at all; palpable reality reappears in his vision, and with this he regains for us a sense of the tragic or, in the more favored American phrase, of the ironic condition of man. It is in spite of this knowledge and in its very face that we seek to impose a measure of reason on the course of history with such vague assurances as we are able to shore up.

NOTES

1. See, for instance, Pred (1966).
2. Frank Bonilla (1967) presents a rather dismal picture of self-generated innovation in Latin America.

REFERENCES

BONILLA, FRANK (1967) "Cultural elites," in S. M. Lipset and A. Solari (eds.) Elites in Latin America. New York: Oxford Univ. Press.
PRED, ALLAN (1966) The Spatial Dynamics of U.S. Urban-Industrial Growth, 1800-1914. Cambridge, Mass.: MIT Press.

Participants' Comments

Jorge Hardoy

In the final part of his work, John Friedmann presents a list of interrogatives relevant to the elaboration of urban development policies. The list is wide and covers the essential aspects which should be considered in an analysis of urban development and its regional implications. Nevertheless, there are three points that are particularly significant and that have scarcely been mentioned or have been omitted.

The urban system of a nation and the regional subsystems that have been formed spontaneously in that country, as well as the internal hierarchy of each of those systems, reflect the orientation of the national economy and of the cultural characteristics of the nation throughout the respective phases of its development. The spatial distribution of urban centers and the particular pattern of the urban hierarchy in a country with a minerals and agricultural export economy is considerably different from those of an industrial nation whose economy is based on regional integration. Different economic models require and result in different urban systems. Therefore, in order to determine the role that cities will play in national development, it is necessary to take into account the orientation of the government of that nation (the model of development that it adopts) and to undertake an interpretation, until now not realized in developing countries, of the influence that government programs will have in urbanization. Cities respond functionally and physically to the stimuli of government programs and private investment, and the economic, cultural, and political role that the cities fulfill cannot be abstracted merely from the national facts.

The second point that I desire to emphasize is that, even if one could empirically determine the functions that each city should fulfill in national and regional development, we find that the institutions and the necessary mechanisms for implementing urban policy do not exist. We may be able to define the functions and establish the urban system hierarchies, but we are unable to bring them into existence. This is a complex problem that is intimately related to the system of government and each country's stage of development.

Finally, we should remember that the internal structure of the cities in developing countries is totally inappropriate and impedes basic interrelations between urban districts. The rapid growth of cities occurs in chaotic form. The deficit of jobs, housing, and services increases. The deterioration of the city's physical environment is developing in an accelerated form. The public sector does not seem to find the means of creating the necessary employment, and the employment, the disguised unemployment, an exaggerated, unnecessary bureaucracy, and the proliferation of intermediate groups seem to be the habitual characteristics of employment structures in almost every city. On the other hand, the private sector is not interested in the problems of housing and services for low-income groups, and it brings pressures to see that its prerogatives of managing the fixed assets market at its caprice are not suspended or limited. Moreover, housing programs with external credits are not accessible to the low-income groups. In synthesis, the critical problem of how to finance the urbanization that is occurring in developing countries does not now have an answer, nor is there a foreseeable solution.

Friedmann has presented a work full of ideas and suggestions. Without doubt, his questions constitute in themselves lines of research and continuous inquietude for the planners. Perhaps his omission can be synthesized in the three points that have been indicated in the following questions:

(a) What model of development does a country desire to adopt and how will it affect its process of urbanization?

(b) What institutions, in the widest sense of the word, should be created or readapted for producing this model?

(c) How can we improve the structures of the cities in order to condition them technically and environmentally to the necessity of an industrial phase?

My impression is that if we don't achieve a general consensus around these three questions it will be very difficult to find the replies to the interrogatives that Friedmann formulates, especially if we want to convert these interrogatives into research lines that permit us to define the optimum national and regional urban-rural equilibrium for each phase of national development, as well as the most efficient schemes for spatial organization.

Moreover, the harmony that should exist between institutions of a country and their participation in the process of government, in the economic orientation of the nation, and in the promotion of regional balance—as well as the determination of the national urban system and of the role that the principal cities should fulfill in national development—cannot be achieved in many of the developing countries due to the lack of functional cooperation that should characterize relations between different sectors of the population. I believe, then, that the government system, a national economic orientation, and an urban system constitute three interrelated aspects, and that one of the outlets to stagnation or slow growth in developing countries is precisely in the better interrelation of these parts.

As this has not been produced up until now, it should not surprise us that the role of the cities in national development may not have been more efficient in terms of modernization.

Antoni Kuklinski

The paper by Friedmann is one of the few examples of a comprehensive approach in this field. Regional and urban development in Friedmann's interpretation is an integrated process wherein the economic, social, political, and cultural factors create one interrelated set of phenomena. These phenomena are analyzed from the perspective of macro-urbanology, which concentrates attention not only on individual regions and cities but also on systems of regions and cities. Last but not least, Friedmann's paper is not an exercise in ivory tower introspection, but is rather a policy-oriented paper. I hope that these contributions will reinforce the trend of comprehensive macro- and policy-oriented studies which are now most important for the rapid promotion of regional and urban development and planning.

Having in mind these positive aspects of the paper, let me express a note of disagreement concerning the validity of the experience of developed countries for developing countries in the field of regional and urban development. Specifically, here is a statement from the paper which refers to this transference of experience: "U-countries, after all, have the example of the more developed societies as a guide, and we are able to study the regularities and phases of succession in spatial organization."

I have some doubts concerning the "phases of succession in spatial organization," especially if this idea is interpreted to mean it is inevitable that the developing countries have to repeat the errors the developed countries committed in the field of regional and urban development. I am convinced that we should concentrate our efforts in research and planning so as to open new perspectives for the developing countries in regional and urban development, free of the deterministic implications of past experience.

A second note of disagreement concerns the fact that Friedmann uses the usual division of nations into developed and developing countries without qualifications. I am convinced that this division is too crude from the point of view of a realistic typology for regional and urban development policy. We should perhaps recognize that these two groups of countries are not internally homogeneous, but that they are clearly differentiated if we take into account as a minimum such criteria as levels of economic development, political and social systems, size of country, and density of population.

These two problems—the validity of experience of the developed nations for the developing countries, and a realistic typology of regional development policies applied throughout the world in the second half of the twentieth century—are among the topics dealt with in the research program on regional development which was started in 1967 by the United Nations Research Institute for Social Development in Geneva.

Ernest Weissmann

We are witnessing a phenomenon of change in the role of the city from a parasite to the producer in the national economy. This is happening particularly in the developing countries, but we see that the "development" which is producing this change is not actually focused on *national* development. Rather, it is geared to the requirements of international trade and the world economy. As a consequence we find that, in most countries, there are two development processes that are evolving alongside each other, but they are very rarely interconnected. The first is the so-called "national plan," which absorbs most of the resources (one could say practically all the resources); directly, it involves and benefits a very small part of the population. The second process (either spontaneous or planned) involves a real struggle for survival for the majority of the people as the economic or industrial base is gradually created. If development is to reach this part of the population, social benefits deriving from development must be provided.

What John Friedmann points out in his paper is that the city is beginning to create a bridge between these two processes by bringing together masses of people who want to benefit from advancement derived from development in the city, since it is not occurring in the countryside. They have voted, in fact, what the national priorities should be (distributed benefits of development) by coming to the cities and by ultimately creating the political force which will prevail, maintain, or impose this priority on the system. They have made use of the city, in a sense, to extend the benefits of national development to a wider group of people.

Part IV

Political Development Vis-à-Vis Urban Growth

Chapter 6

The Distribution of Political and Government Power in the Context of Urbanization

JOHN MILLER

The distribution of rewards in a society is a function of the distribution of power, not of system needs.

—Gerhard Linski
Power and Privilege. New York: McGraw-Hill, 1966.

Introduction

Political development, according to Karl de Schweinitz, Jr. (A, 1969), is the "creation of attitudes and values and the building of institutions which raise the governmental efficiency, somehow measured, with which rulers transform the inputs of a political system into its outputs." As defined by him, political development involves the socialization of individuals in the society to an acceptance of political bodies with which they have little or no sensory contact and whose governors are remote or even unseen. These individuals must be integrated into an impersonal polity and must believe that it symbolizes their mutuality, interdependence, and uniqueness. They must believe, in essence, that there is a "community whose interests governors may legitimately represent."

De Schweinitz postulates that the creation of "political monuments" by the government may be an instrumental means by which political socialization is furthered. Political monuments are defined as public goods which articulate and reify the state or nation and facilitate the process of political socialization. While these may be sculptural or architectural monuments, they also include industrial factories and output, even if uneconomic by neoclassical criteria, and regional development projects, even when economically marginal from the viewpoint of additions to the gross national product. Even planning may be subsumed under this definition in underdeveloped economies. The question he asks is, how does one measure the payoff in the building of the political community, in political development? Clearly it cannot be measured in the same terms as economic development, but in certain respects it may be crucially important for economic development. Can an organized nation survive, for example, when, economically and politically, the periphery is not sufficiently integrated in its development with the center? Periphery here may be interpreted either in terms of social groups or regions of the country. As long as relationships between the two (center and periphery) predominantly favor the center, and as long as the population of the periphery is relatively small, stability may continue indefinitely. As the periphery increases relatively in size, it becomes more difficult to ignore the question.

The Minister of Housing and Urban Development of Chile raised, during his inaugural address to the Jahuel Seminar, what some might consider an alarmist viewpoint in terms of the proper distribution of national political and administrative power. He asserted that, given the present momentum toward urbanization and

> the predominance of the urban population and the concentration of production in the cities, the administration of the nation will come to be confounded with the government of its cities. If within the cities a social harmony is not achieved and if the marginality of vast sectors [is] not overcome in order to incorporate them into the plenitude of the national community, there will not only be conflicts between regions or states, but the urban territories will be transformed into fields of battle. Yet, if we have the will to achieve a new communitarian organization, a change in the structure of power, and an acceleration of economic growth, the cities will be our principal environmental and territorial instrument and on them the future of our people will be constructed.

Explicit recognition, then, has been given to the awareness that a redistribution of power is an essential ingredient in the avoidance of serious urban strife. The devolution of power not only to the marginal groups but also to the governments representing the cities is seen as a necessary strategy, since it appears questionable that the best interests of nation-governing could be served by the conversion of the national government into one which increasingly "administers" the cities through its central powers. The central administration of a national urban system totaling tens of millions of citizens is a far cry from the concept of the administration of the "city-state" of Greece, which involved a mere 20,000 citizens. Politically and administratively, it has yet to be proven feasible for national government to involve itself intimately in the administrative control of an urban system composed of one or more city-states exceeding the size of those of Greece by 100 to 200 times, as well as in the control of numerous lesser centers.

Latin American cities, as they have been aptly described, are the "crucibles" in which important political action tending toward modernization is brewing.

The reverse may also be true, that is, that the political processes in Latin America could serve as the "crucibles" in which the renaissance of the city and the development of more rational patterns of urbanization could be brought about. As a result of the intimate association between urbanization and politicization and of the disproportionate rate of growth of the cities over rural areas in Latin America, a deep transformation is underway in power relations and power balances. It is quite probable that this is not fully understood or appreciated by most of the political-governmental institutions that are still oriented toward questions of power framed in terms of broad, national class support, rather than in terms of growing urban consciousness.

Horowitz (D, 1967a: 226-228) has suggested, for example, that the large scale shift of population from rural-agricultural to urban-industrial pursuits has restructured basic power loci through six principal means:

(1) Urban politicization makes possible the growth of an electoral party apparatus which displaces direct revolutionary action by absorbing the goals without using the methods of revolutionary movements and which makes it difficult for the traditional land-based power elites to control the rural electoral base.

(2) The traditional classes, now isolated, are faced with the need to engage in coalition politics for the first time and are no longer able to exercise effective, exclusive, political power.

(3) Control of the leading metropolitan area is bringing about the effective political control of the nation.

(4) The city provides a great deal of personal stability in contrast to rural regions for the members of the power structure.

(5) Agrarian upper-class interests are increasingly losing ground and yielding to urban-based interests (or merging with them through commercial activity) as they engage in combat with radical or revolutionary forces deriving basically from urban activities and as they lose their indispensability to the structures of the national economy.

(6) Urbanization enfranchises large numbers of people by bringing them into contact with political organizations.

As Horowitz concludes, however, the redistribution of power is not necessarily more democratic because it is based in cities, but it must be more opportunistic—that is, responsive to the "will of the people"—to survive. Urbanism does not necessarily yield democratic parties either; rather it makes possible the kind of mass participation which is a necessary, if not sufficient, condition for the development of democratic polities.

Nonetheless, he makes a strong argument that, basically, urban politics are simply politics and that the "personal approach" focused on national parties and national issues acts to prevent any meaningful urban reform by the tactic of rigorously avoiding specific issues related to urban life—issues such as slum dwellings, sanitation and sewerage systems, fire-fighting units, garbage disposal trucks, protection against false weights and measures, and so forth.

A strategy of urban development is just as necessary for determining the future course of politics in Latin America as has been the strategy of industrial development. In fact, social science analysis, especially that of economics, may not have given sufficient importance to urbanization vis-à-vis industrialization. Those Latin American nations usually considered most developed (Argentina, Chile, Venezuela, and Brazil) have a level of urbanization twice their level of industrialization, yet those considered to be the least developed (Bolivia, Ecuador, Paraguay, and Peru) have levels of urbanization and industrialization in an almost exact one-to-one ratio.

While it is possible to bemoan, as many do, the negative influence on the municipality of the Spanish heritage of strong centralized authority in Latin America, this tradition may also be thought of as beneficial. With bold, imaginative enterprise and innovative policies, the power that is now concentrated at the center could be turned into a much-needed guiding hand aimed at developing the means, through central institutions, for providing capable and better-trained technicians and professionals who can cope with the complexities of modern urban development. This is especially true when one realizes that the basic complexities are often national in scope and complicated by the necessary consideration of national and regional development objectives in which population and settlement distribution is an essential policy question in the resolution of both national and local problems. It may be stated that central direction is needed in this regard, direction which would with great difficulty, if at all, derive from a loose federation of municipalities. It is a policy question which the Roman Caesars and Queen Isabella understood quite well. The value of a national urban-settlement policy is even beginning to be understood in the United States, after several centuries in which private initiative in the creation of the urban system of cities, their location, and local autonomy and power were considered to be outside the policy area of central government (Downs, C, 1970).

This does not eliminate the question of centralization versus the devolution of power to municipal governments, however. No one can rationally argue that all governmental power should reside at the center or that governmental control over all new functional areas dealing with recent problems of urbanization can or should be acceded to the individual cities.

Centralization and Devolution

A growing and significantly important major focus of concern relevant to a national urban policy is the issue of the centralization or devolution of governmental powers, both over decision areas and over finances. It is an issue which has sufficient adherents on both sides, and the strength of arguments from both positions are frequently convincing. Centralization through central planning and implementation of policy, so its proponents insist, is necessary for bringing about the major structural changes in the economy and society essential for growth. Part of the argument for continued centralization of political-governmental power includes the shortage of technical personnel, the existence of an economy integrated at the national rather than at the urban level, the weakness of local government and other local institutions, and the frequent merging of urban and national politics as one in which most urban political (policy) questions are really phrased in terms of national political (policy) questions.

Arguments of the "devolutionists" include the existence of a self-serving bureaucracy behind its paper curtain at the center (which prevents an effective communication about urban problems); decision-making congestion in the ministries with respect to the multiplying decisions to be taken, if at all, on local matters; desire for local autonomy deriving from a local motivation for socioeconomic change and as a basis for a more extended network of political development; and the continued distortions in the urban growth of the nation. This latter is seen as a consequence of the interlocking relationships of political, economic and social groups in the capital which favor growth there and much less elsewhere.

But, as Robert T. Daland (C, 1969) has pointed out, it is crucially relevant to know what the utility and the consequences of devolution may be. Does it produce political participation and socialization with high costs in developmental efficiency, or is it actually a more efficient political structure for development? Frank P. Sherwood (C, 1969) cuts even more closely to the bone when he suggests that "no organization form is going to solve the truly awesome problems of urbanization, [but] it is fair to suggest tests against which alternative organization strategies might be judged." In effect, government organization strategies should be submitted to tests of function. It is less important, actually, to phrase the question of structure as a centralization-devolution question than it is to recognize that government, including local government, comprises an open system in which roles may be changed according to the most favorable strategic means of carrying out given functions and to recognize that structure should necessarily follow these functional strategies. With due respect for the field of knowledge concerning developmental efficiency, it may be conceded, for lack of proof to the contrary, that governmental structures which permit functional efficiencies in the field of urbanization will be positive contributors to developmental efficiency. In most cases, if not all, this will be a mixed bag in which some functions will clearly be central and others of intermediate or lower-level government.

Probably the most significant fact to keep in mind is that the structural means for achieving functional efficiency, in terms both of values and of concrete results, is bound to be as changeable as any other aspect of society—especially those undergoing broad and rapid social change. In certain functional areas, the change in scale alone may require more centralization given impossibly limited technical resources or given the changing nature of the problem to be resolved, such as environmental control. On the other hand, increasing local competence in political and organization matters, along with a sufficient level of technical input, may suggest that certain functional matters formerly handled at upper structural levels may in fact be devolved. This would tend, thereby, to relieve the congestion on upper levels so that resources at these levels may be devoted to functional areas more efficiently resolved there. If they aren't, unnecessary overload on the upper structure is likely to ensue, and functional efficiency, it may be assumed, will decline.

Certain aspects of development such as function, role, and structure (as they occur along the continuum of the political-governmental axis from central to local government and the neighborhood) have only been casually touched upon as an area of research by the social scientist in any highly developed country, much less in Latin America. This would appear to be a glaring oversight in terms of important development variables when one considers that the centralization of actual function, role and structure as related to urban problems reaches such proportions in Latin America that over half the central governments exert a power over total government finances that exceeds ninety percent (see Table 6.1 in the next section of this chapter). In such cases there are bound to be circumstances in which development disadvantages will occur as a result of the severe financial limitations on the actions of local governments.[1]

A debate between centralist and decentralist proponents is not actually so revealing for development purposes as a serious examination of the social functions of government in terms of social values and the organizational potential for achieving societal objectives. Such an examination would undoubtedly suggest more efficient alternative political-administrative government structures than now exist. Even a simple examination of how the objectives of government are presently attained or sought and at what cost in areas related to urban growth would unquestionably suggest different structural arrangements for government in most cases, and these arrangements would be almost certain to alter the power relationships among levels of government. Efficiency would be promoted, for example, by removing to the control of central government those wide-scale problems which a dispersal of power cannot effectively control or handle—as in the case of communications, transportation, and pollution for more than any one community. It would also be promoted by returning certain problem or functional areas to lower units of government when technical resources are available, when a viable level of political responsibility exists, and where the consequences of carrying out functional roles do not seriously damage the interests of other communities.

Lack of finances at the lower level should not be a deterrent to devolution. In the sense that structural rearrangement requires changed role responsibilities in the polity, it also will require rearrangement in the collection or disbursement of total government funds so that the former is possible. Even within the same functional area, it is not unlikely that certain roles and responsibilities can remain with central authorities while others are decentralized or devolved to local authorities. To speak of housing or education, for example, as an exclusively central responsibility may not, in fact, be efficient for all aspects of such a service function.

The danger of a centralization-decentralization[2] dichotomy is that it ignores the subtleties of responsibility allocation by function among the different levels of government for efficiency purposes. There are few functions related to urbanization which would lie exclusively at either extreme if complete efficiency in terms of the social value system and results expected of government were attempted. In fact, responsibilities within each functional area may often be found along the continuum between the extremes. The structure of the polity should reflect this for development purposes in view of the fact that the problems of accelerated urbanization in Latin America constitute one of the most important current strategy-policy areas. The determination of the most appropriate structure for the total governmental system and the distribution of power (political and economic) among the elements of the system for purposes of urban-growth guidance could yet become one of the major political and constitutional questions of this century in Latin America, if not the most important.

Centralization of the Budget: Municipal Financing

In actual fact, most Latin American countries do not delegate significant authority to local government bodies. A few, like Brazil, provide broad independent authority for municipal government in law, but not in reality. Municipalities have the most meager financial resources in practically every case. The result of this has been a formal city, which has been referred to by Frank Sherwood (7: 1967) as nothing more than an administrative district of the central government. Much of the urban "governing system," he says, may actually consist of elements of state and national institutions.

According to Walter Stöhr (B,1969) there are only three countries in Latin America where municipal governments spend greater than ten percent of all national public expenditures. These are Colombia, Ecuador and Guatemala. The extreme of budgetary centralization, where more than ninety-five percent of total public expenditures are controlled by central government is encountered in Bolivia, Chile, El Salvador, Peru, Costa Rica, and Nicaragua. In each of these countries, all levels of government below the national government have less than five percent of total government financial resources at their disposal (see Table 6.1). In fact, according to a publication of the Organization of American States (Secretaria General de la Organización de los Estados Americanos, Unidad de Finanzas Públicas, D, 1966), the trend is towards even greater concentration in the central government of functions related to towns and cities. This has been accompanied by a slower rate of growth in government income for the municipalities than there has been for central government.

Metropolitan Government Systems

Metropolitan government in Latin America is a problem that a number of countries there have been grappling with recently. The development of theoretical and practical models for a metropolitan system in this cultural context is an area of effort which, increasingly, will require more attention on the part of political scientists and legal experts. Various models of the metropolitan political system which have been devised for the United States appear inappropriate. Victor Jones' model of a metropolitan system similar to

TABLE 6.1
Distribution of Total Government Budgets in Latin American
Nations, Public Expenditures by Administrative Level (percentages)

(a) Nation	(b) Year(s)	(c) Central Govt.*	(d) State, Provincial, Dep'tal. or Territory	(e) Munici- palities	(d)+(e) Govt. Below Central
BRAZIL	1966	57.99	34.01	8.00	42.01
ARGENTINA	1) 1963	68.86	22.98	8.16	31.14
Colombia	1958-60	70.60	17.00	12.60	29.60
MEXICO	1958	90.50	7.10	2.40	19.50
Ecuador	1963	81.00	1.00	18.00	19.00
VENEZUELA	1964-68	87.06	10.46	2.48	12.94
Guatemala	2) 1960-67	89.69	—	10.30	10.30
Honduras	2) 1966-67	90.50	—	9.50	9.50
Nicaragua	1962	95.20	—	4.80	4.80
Costa Rica	1966	95.60	—	4.40	4.40
Peru	2) 1962	95.62	—	4.38	4.38
El Salvador	2) 1967	96.80	—	3.20	3.20
Chile	1966	97.48	—	2.52	2.52
Bolivia	1958	97.80	—	2.20	2.20
Dominican Rep.	1966	88.70	—	—	11.30 3)
United States	1966	57.80	15.20	27.00 4)	42.20

* Includes Autonomous and Decentralized Agencies, Public Utility Companies, and Social Security Institutes.

CAPITALIZED NATIONS have federal systems of government. All others have unitary forms of government.

1) Current expenditures only.

2) Capital expenditures only.

3) Not disaggregated between municipalities and other subnational levels.

4) Includes Municipalities, Special Districts, School Districts, Metropolitan Government, and Counties.

SOURCE: Derived from Walter Stoehr (1969) Regional Development in Latin America: Experience and Prospects. Paper presented at the Seminar on Social Aspects of Regional Development, Santiago, Chile, 3-14 November 1969. United Nations. Economic and Social Council. Data for U.S. is from Advisory Commission on Intergovernmental Relations (1967) Fiscal Balance in the American Federal System. Vol. I, Table 4, p. 56. Washington, D.C.: The Commission.

international politics (in the sense that local governments deal with each other as more or less independent sovereignties) fails for the majority of Latin American municipalities because their effective sovereignty over even minor functional areas is lacking.[3] Another formulation of the metropolitan area as a system analogous to an economic market also seems to fail in great part (Warren, C,1964). This model suggests that each political unit supplies a different combination of services and levels of service from which the individual or firm chooses for purposes of location. In effect, it is the national government which often provides the services so that, effectively, the metropolitan system as composed of municipalities offering services is almost nonexistent in these terms. Differentiation for choice among municipalities does exist, but it is a result of central government intervention or, in the case of lack of service, nonintervention.

It goes without saying that the hydra-like process by which new urban communities are springing up around the major urban centers is creating a time lag between urban growth and formal urban organization, both politically and administratively. Almost no work has been carried out which would attempt to suggest practical means for incorporating these communities into the political process or bringing them adequately into local government's sphere of responsibility. Is the mere extension of political boundaries the appropriate answer or should these communities come within the planned efforts of national government "land-planning corporations" aimed at controlling and planning the type of growth? The question of whether metropolitan-local government can deal with this or whether the central government will have to intervene depends largely on national circumstances. Cases where it is being handled adequately by either are scarce.

The balkanization of government in metropolitan areas is a further political problem which currently begs a solution in a number of countries. While this situation may not have reached the level and complexity of the U.S. experience, it constitutes a growing concern in such Latin American cities as Santiago, where seventeen municipalities make up what is known as Greater Santiago. These local units have little effective power, however, and practically all decisions which alter the metropolitan area through project implementation are made by divisions within the central ministries.

It is a case of centralization without unification, unfortunately, as there is seldom agreement among these divisions, including those within the same ministry, about the shape and direction of growth for the capital city with the result that the projects of different agencies may often be contradictory in their effect on the pattern of development. Further, the objectives of one may act negatively upon the objectives of another. The proposed new rapid transit system, for example, is based on a growth model and plan which no other government group is presently using as a basis for its project decisions.

In 1967, the central government invested 57.6% of its total national capital investment on housing, electricity, gas, water, and education in Santiago Province, principally in Greater Santiago. (The 1967 population of the province as a percentage of total national population was 34.3%.) In other words, the central government was investing almost 60% of the total national budget for urban services in the center at a per capita rate almost double its per capita investment rate in the rest of the country. Obviously for the sheer allocation and political power that these proportions represent, some arrangement for metropolitan administration needs to be worked out within the central government. In fact, some divisions within ministries operate almost as if they were actually the technical arms of "metropolitan" government rather than of central government.

Walsh (1: C,1969) has made the observation that the governmental institutions in various world metropolitan areas appear to fall on a continuum rather than into two discrete groups—central and local. By the sheer weight of economic resources and the power to act, central ministry politics and administration are actually metropolitan politics and administration in the case of Santiago, and proposals to formalize this fact have actually been made (see Gakenheimer, D, 1969).

It may be postulated that the disproportionate share of total urban investments made in Santiago on a per capita basis arises, in part at least, as a result of the political tension generated in the capital city out of proportion to the actual size of the population. If so, modernization, including political modernization, may have politicized the capital resident more profoundly than is true for other urban places with the result that political communication is more intense. This would follow Sherwood's thesis that such tension growing out of politicization and expectation of government performance will encourage government response to the pressure group. If such pressure parallels other political objectives and interests (such as those of elite groups within both the public and the private sectors), then an investment pattern favoring the center is almost certainly assured. In other words, this suggests that there is a raison politique as well as a raison economique behind the accelerated growth patterns of national capitals.

In the case of the Santiago subway system, a "rough" estimate of the initial rapid transit proposal places the "maximum" annual cost of construction and equipment (pro rated equally during the first decade of construction) at close to $15,000,000. What this might have done in terms of sociopolitical alternatives for the use of the fund which will be expended can be illustrated on the basis of unit costs of government programs in housing, education, and health facilities for 1966 (see Gakenheimer et al., D, 1969). With the same expenditure, the government would have been able to build 8,254 more houses annually (it constructed 13,433 in 1966); or 422 new schools (it built 109 in 1966); or 32 new public health units (hospitals, blood banks, clinics, first aid centers, sanitariums, and the like) throughout the country (it built 18 in 1966). Inasmuch as the construction of this system is planned over a 20-year period it can be seen that the provision of one specialized service for limited areas of one city effectively eliminates the use of this investment fund for a quite substantial number of social units throughout the nation. This annual sum is, incidentally, only slightly under the total investment the central government made in electricity, gas, and water projects in the period 1965-1967 (including major dams) in Chile outside of Santiago Province. This, then, is not merely an economic question; it is, potentially, a rather substantial political question.

Clearly a more useful input on the part of social scientists, including economists, in the examination of social costs and benefits, is needed to help provide policy makers with project evaluation data. Few, if any, major policy decisions involving construction costs of this size should be made on the basis of the project evaluation of an engineering firm or single ministry alone. It is most probable that the first estimates are low if one examines the history of major project costs in other countries, and it is also likely that Chile will be strapped to an investment decision from which it will find difficulty in extricating itself.

Community Political Integration

Community political integration, as Daland (C, 1969) has shown, is a rather recent area of study, although the political integration of given territories, social groups (ethnic, tribal, or religious), or urban centers has historically been a political objective for states. The idea of political integration is now beginning to extend down to the neighborhood level. Even efforts at community development may be viewed as scantily clad moves to achieve a higher degree of political integration between the citizens involved (through community development projects) and higher levels of political organization represented by party and government.

It is generally assumed that the political socialization of the immigrant and his integration to urban political life constitute a positive addition to the precondition for problem resolution. This may be either as a participant in cooperative efforts made possible by organization or as an antagonist joined with others in political moves aimed at pressuring the authorities to respond with adequate levels of service and infrastructure.

As Mangin (D, 1968: 400) has stated,

Integration, community solidarity and morale are not always figured into evolutionary or developmental scales used in measuring change. But they are patently significant for the political life of communities and subcommunities, and thus may have a good deal more to do with change, albeit indirectly, than rather static sequential models would suggest.

He then proceeds to explain two approaches to such variables that have gained attention in recent years: Foster's hypothesis of "the image of limited good" (Foster, A, 1965) and Lewis' (9: H, 1961) hypothesis of a "culture of poverty." Foster's hypothesis is that there are broad areas of peasant behavior that are patterned in such a way as to suggest that the peasant views his social, economic, and natural universes—his total environment—as those in which all of the desired things in life such as land, wealth, health, friendship and love, manliness and honor, respect and status, power and influence, security and safety exist in finite quantity and are always in short supply as far as the peasant is concerned. Not only do these and all other "good things" exist in finite and limited quantities, according to Foster, but in addition there is no way directly to increase the available quantities through the use of peasant power. In effect, the system is viewed as a closed system and an individual or family can improve in position only at the expense of others. This leads the peasant, Foster believes, to extreme individualism as opposed to cooperation in the preservation of his security, because cooperation implies leadership and leadership brings with it criticism and sanctions.

Foster concludes that, in view of the light of the limited good, peasant societies are not conservative and backward brakes on national economic progress due to economic irrationality. Neither is the absence of psychological characteristics in adequate quantities a major deterrent. Basically, he feels, they are conservative because individual progress is seen as the supreme threat to community stability. All cultural forms, therefore, must conspire to discourage changes in the status quo.

Mangin concurs with Foster in the sense that he believes the scheme to fit his own experience with migrants from the Peruvian highlands to Lima. He withholds complete acceptance in that he feels that the idea fails to deal sufficiently with the impact of outside forces on the peasant community and the position of peasants in relation to more powerful members of their society (Mangin, D, 1968: 401). Presumably, it seems he is suggesting that certain types of outside force impact and the diminishing influence over the peasant of powerful members of the society could release him from a reticence to engage in cooperative activity, an activity which is so essential to political development and necessary in an increasingly urban society. Urbanization, in fact, leads precisely to a higher potential for outside force impact which it seems should propel the individual into cooperative efforts. This may be stymied, however, for the weaker personality, by the transfer of loyalties for a rural patron to employment, welfare, or political-patron relationships in the urban center.[4] More knowledge is needed about the actual pattern of relationships between individuals, the family, and the broader community prior to migration and urbanization. Differences prior to urbanization in the degree of independent action, as well as recognition of the value of and desire for participation in cooperative efforts, may very well determine the nature and depth of political development for the individual once he has begun to urbanize.

Such speculation can only begin to suggest the actual possible variables impinging on urban political development as the urban process advances with the forces of migration. Mangin (D, 1968: 403) postulates, for example, that, if the local value system is such that the aspirations of most of the members of a community can be realized through local resources and with little threat from the outside, then change does not always appear attractive. Such local value system enclaves may even be transferred to or arise in the urban center under certain conditions.

Certainly, the idea of an "image of limited good" is not sufficient for explaining limited change. External economic and political conditions also appear important. The image, in fact, seems more likely to operate in the nonurban cultures where certain values and modes of thinking have not yet arrived. Such places can be found in both rural and urban places, but the likelihood is that knowledge about the external economic and political conditions will more rapidly penetrate the thinking of the urban resident. This may explain why there is often a period of indoctrination for the rural migrant to the city during which time he is assimilating the new value system, recognizing his ability to act in individually small ways which, when combined in cooperative action with those of others, constitute a form of political power not generally recognized when he first arrives in the urban environment. Whether he does or not could easily depend upon his personality development up to that stage and account for differences of motivation and action among migrants. While it may be assumed that, on the surface, a condition of massive political inertia apparently exists, this does not necessarily hold as the newcomers and their children begin to recognize, through the modernization process, that resignation to their plight is not necessary. For all practical purposes, as Breese (C, 1968: 458) claims, the newly urbanizing man is not *disenfranchised;* he is *unfranchised.* This means that he is not participating. If, as his political consciousness is awakened, he cannot participate positively, he is likely to do so negatively—in terms of the formal ruling system. This represents a major challenge to governments which are the institutional embodiment of political life.

Lewis' (9: H, 1961: xxiv) hypothesis of a "culture of poverty," on the other hand, assumes an equally pessimistic attitude about the psychology of the urban poor, that is, that it is a remarkably stable and persistent way of life, passed down from generation to generation along family lines. In a spirit of resignation and fatalism, children are oriented, according to Lewis, to the present with little capacity to delay gratification or plan for the future. The difficulty of this view of the urban poor in Latin America is that it is based, in large part, on situations in which there may have been few, if any, significant changes in the economic and political matrix within which the urban poor form a part and within which the hopes and motivations leading to greater internal ferment for action might have been aroused. As Mangin states (D, 1968: 407), blocked access to opportunities would seem to account for all of these attitudinal patterns as much as any passing down of a culture of poverty.

The psychology of the individual in the squatter settlement as Mangin, Leeds, and Turner have shown is a contradiction in action to the negative, almost regressive type of psychology which Lewis postulates as present in the individual submerged in the culture of poverty. Studies of the barriadas of Peru and the favelas of Brazil have shown that the settlers are very frequently highly organized and politically sophisticated.

This level of political sophistication is especially demonstrated in the Lima barriadas, where elections for barriada association leaders are held, on the average, once a year under conditions of spirited campaigning and with respect for results. This contrasts with the infrequency with which local municipal elections themselves are held. (Until the administration of President Belaunde Terry, local elections had not been held regularly for years.) Although not officially recognized, the barriada elections have represented probably the most viable evidence of a popular and democratic local government in the metropolitan capital. It appears now that the present military government will launch a policy which will incorporate some of this popular initiative into a more formal relationship with the central government.

A number of authors have noted that strength of organization is strongly related to the defense of the community and to the advocacy of one or more causes with the government. Where barrios have been formed by organized invasion, Mangin (8: C, 1967a) reports, the original organization is strong in the initial stages. Some of these lose their power as the barriada becomes integrated with the city, while others remain important as intermediaries between the community and the government or as organized structures for mutual aid in local projects (see Goldrich et al., 7: 1966). This drive to form a degree of "political" organization outside all formal party channels has also been noted in Panama by Lutz (D, 1966) and in Rio de Janeiro's favelas by Leeds (D, 1966), Hoenack (D, 1966), Wygand (D, 1966), and Morocco (D, 1966).

The internal social force for organized cooperation has been one of the major factors recently permitting and encouraging the Chilean government to formally organize a level of government below that of the municipality. They have been named the *juntas de vecinos,* or neighborhood councils (Chile, Congress, D, 1968). The juntas, according to national legislation, will become territorial community organizations representative of the persons who live within their limits, both urban and rural. As such, they are recognized as "an expression of the solidarity and organization of the people in the territorial ambiance for the permanent defense of members of each community and as collaborators with the State and the municipalities." This new and potentially dynamic form of government has the power to contract or make agreements for the improvement of the neighborhood (construction of houses and urbanization projects). It may also prepare an annual plan of works in which costs and the contributions of the community are set forth in the form of financial, material, and labor contributions, a collaborative mechanism linking them with the municipality and central government.

This direct attempt in Chile to capitalize on the sociopolitical sense of defense, cooperation, and power relationships is a trend away from what has been described as the "paternalistically provided, ready-made housing project," which is not a vehicle for either social or economic development and which too often fuels the vehicles by which opportunistic politicians attempt to stay in power (Mangin and Turner, D, 1968). In every sense, this type of effort is a "development" effort that could reverse what John Herbert (C, 1968) has called the administrative system that belongs to a predevelopment era in the sense that it is organized and operated as a policing system (following earlier colonial patterns) rather than as a development system.

As a policy issue, it seems critically important that the Latin American governments (at whatever level) should encourage the development of urban and regional communities in such a way as to foster activities favoring political participation through organizations that will help resolve urban problems. Such potentially political issues as excessive physical remoteness from work of residential areas and an accompanying lack of transport;[5] financially distorted housing programs which aim at too-high standards and result in high costs per unit, provide shelter for a limited few, but establish mortgage payments so high as to force families out of the market or bring about disrespect for government through nonpayment ot rents; elimination of common-law marriage couples (up to sixty percent in some communities) from housing loan qualifications (Peru); and the withholding of urban services to communities without paved streets and sidewalks (Chile) have in many countries hardly reached the level of serious policy debate and definition at the decision centers. Until they do it is little likely that professional planners will be effective in ameliorating the problems. In this sense political development is a key ingredient for the planning effort, a situation which has not been widely recognized or accepted.

The work of social scientists recently in Peru has been partly responsible for certain government policies attempting to overcome past errors of judgment about the nature of the community at the barrio level. Credit cooperative experiments in low-cost housing loans with technical assistance, combined government services and owner contracting of house construction, and the organization of neighborhoods by the national government for priority and participation setting are stretching housing budgets and sheltering and serving more people.

How do these issues push their way through the detritus of bureaucratic indifference, elite control, lack of political awareness, and other blocks to more open policy debate? Lewis' and Foster's hypotheses of the "limited good" and a "culture of poverty" suggest a presently hopeless base for political development at the barrio level. But Mangin disagrees in part. He suggests that the new settlement inhabitants do, in fact, handle adversity and hostility with remarkably little social breakdown. Yet governments take little advantage of these qualities in any conscious way, although this is beginning to change in isolated cases. It is not easy, of course, for the state to support conflict against itself. In the face of conflict which may become inevitable, it seems more appropriate to foster the emergence of effective community action and the political organization which makes this possible. Government is, after all, the arena in which divergent group interests and values are resolved. If certain groups are inadequately represented, concrete central policies are almost always a condition necessary to bring these groups into full social participation.

Institutional Guidance

"Authentic" development, according to one study (ECLA, B, 1969) on Latin America, should be, among other things, a process of social change with transcendental modifications in the power functions and relations of the different groups in the society. An authentic development, states the ECLA paper, seeks the active and organized participation of all the sectors with the end of counterarresting the marginalization and changing the control and distribution of social public action. Part of this necessary change, some would assert, can be brought about by a program of devolving or deconcentrating power, not only to lower-strata social groups, but also to regions and localities. Imbalance exists not only as a fact of social class distinctions, but also in terms of spatial concentrations of wealth which may well tend to exaggerate the concentration of wealth among certain groups.

The Charter of Punta del Este focused almost exclusive attention on a sectoral-economic approach to national development and directed attention and resources to the preparation and implementation of sectoral plans. Little notice was given to the role of institutions in the development process—either in their creation or strengthening. Practical considerations have altered this, as it became necessary to create industrial and agricultural credit systems, cooperatives, credit unions, and other institutions founded to promote sectoral programs. Yet almost no attention has been given to the creation of more effective local government as an input to social and economic development. Some institutions do exist, however, which are aimed at increasing the competence and strength of local government, but they are few. Among some of the more important are:

(1) **FUNDACOMUN (Venezuela)**, the Municipal and Community Development Foundation, which was founded in 1961 and is intended to aid in the development of the structure and practice of local administration in Venezuela.

(2) **IBAM (Brazil)**, the Institute of Municipal Administration, a nonprofit, nationwide organization created in 1952 and fully organized in 1956. According to Diego Lordello de Mello, Executive Director, "IBAM believes that strong political institutions are an indispensable instrument of political democracy . . .; local communities have particular aspirations that can be satisfied only through local action . . .; the urbanization process is putting an ever-increasing demand on the efficiency of local governments and on their capacity to meet the challenge of rapid urban growth . . .; and a good system of local government requires the effective participation of the people in the governmental process . . ." (reported by Phillips [A, 1969]). In addition to symposia, seminars, meetings, the publication of professional journals; surveys and the development of organizational projects; research; and so on, it is helping intermediate institutions that are involved in assisting urban centers, such as federal-regional bodies, state institutions of municipal administration, and the cities themselves.

(3) **INFOM (Guatemala)**, the Municipal Development Institute, was created in 1957 as one of the pioneer municipal credit institutions in the western hemisphere. It makes loans for municipal public works projects and gives limited technical assistance to municipalities in the design of public works, as well as provides the credit for construction. Its work is based upon a recognition of the quality and quantity of human resources at the local level and on financial resources as the decisive factors in determining progress in municipal governments.

(4) **LIGA (Dominican Republic)**, the Dominican Municipal League, is a league of ninety-seven member municipalities and a quasi-autonomous institution that receives funds from the national government. These, it disburses as loans for local projects where local participation can be generated. It also has a technical assistance program which assists municipalities in preparing budgets, improving administration, preparing investment programs, bettering municipal services, and upgrading personnel.

These programs are attempting to provide what Rouse (D, 1968) has termed the four major requirements for orderly and accelerated urban development:

(a) a rational distribution of legal authority at all levels of government and within a pattern that is compatible with the existing structure of political administration;

(b) institutions which are sound, progressive, stable, and oriented around action programs and project implementation, and which form an administrative channel through which local goals and objectives can be achieved;

(c) human resources competent for accomplishing plans and realizing objectives;

(d) natural and financial resources which provide the material for the execution of plans, programs, and projects.

Too many Latin American countries are sadly lacking in one or more of these requirements, and too little attention is being given to them in terms of national policy.

NOTES

1. The situation is so extreme in Chile that there is a central government agency whose functional charge is the construction of sidewalks throughout cities in the entire 2,500-mile length of that nation.

2. Henry Maddick (A, 1963: 23) has defined these terms in the following manner: decentralization embraces both processes of deconcentration and devolution. Deconcentration is the delegation of authority adequate for the discharge of specified functions to staff of a central department who are situated outside the headquarters (hierarchical within organization but not in terms of levels of government). Devolution is the legal conferring of powers to discharge specified or residual functions upon formally constituted local authority, (nonhierarchical in organization but hierarchical in terms of level of government).

3. See Jones (C, 1957). This is further elaborated in Holden (C, 1964).

4. As demonstrated by some studies, there is often a continued identification with authority figures among the semi-assimilated urban dwellers. See Horowitz (B, 1959).

5. See the report by Wagner et al. (D, 1966) as an example which shows that the Rio satellites are too far away from work, a fact which results in lost job opportunities due to transportation difficulties.

REFERENCES

A. Political Development: General

AGGER, ROBERT G., DANIEL GOLDRICH, and BERT E. SWANSON (1964) The Rulers and the Ruled. New York: John Wiley.

BINDER, L. (1964) "National integration and political development." Amer. Pol. Sci. Rev. 57: 622-631.

DE SCHWEINITZ, KARL, Jr. (1969) "Growth, development, and political monuments." Pp. 209-224 in Muzafer Sherif and Carolyn W. Sherif (eds.) Interdisciplinary Relationships in the Social Sciences. Chicago: Aldine.

DIAMANT, ALFRED (1966) "Political development: approaches to theory and strategy." Pp. 15-47 in John D. Montgomery and William J. Siffin (eds.) Approaches to Development: Politics, Administration and Change. New York: McGraw-Hill.

DREITZEL, HANS PETER [ed.] (n.d.) Recent Sociology No. 1: A Reader in the Social Basis of Politics. New York: Macmillan.

EASTON, DAVID (1968) "The theoretical relevance of political socialization." Canadian J. of Pol. Sci. 1 (June): 125-146.

EULAU, HEINZ (1969) Micro-Macro Political Analysis: Accents of Inquiry. Chicago: Aldine.

FOSTER, GEORGE (1965) "Peasant society and the image of limited good." Amer. Anthropologist 67: 293-315.

FRANK, ELKE (1966) "The role of bureaucracy in transition." J. of Politics 28 (November): 724-753.

JACKSON, W. A. DOUGLAS (1964) Politics and Geographic Relationships: Readings on the Nature of Political Geography. Englewood Cliffs, N.J.: Prentice-Hall.

KATZ, SAUL M. (1966) Guide to Modernizing Administration for National Development. Pittsburgh: Univ. of Pittsburgh Press.

――― (1965) A Systems Approach to Development Administration. Papers in Comparative Administration, Special ·Series 6. Washington, D.C.: American Society of Public Administration, Comparative Administration Group.

KEESING, DONALD B. (1969) "Small population as a political handicap to national development." Pol. Sci. Q. (March).

LA PALOMBARA, JOSEPH [ed.] (1963) Bureaucracy and Political Development. Princeton, N.J.: Princeton Univ. Press.

LIPSET, SEYMOUR M. and ALDO SOLARI [eds.] (1967) Elites in Latin America. New York: Oxford Univ. Press.

MADDICK, HENRY (1963) Democracy, Decentralization and Development. London: Asia Publishing.

MARCH, JAMES G. (1966) "The power of power." Pp. 39-70 in David Easton (ed.) Varieties of Political Theory. Englewood Cliffs, N.J.: Prentice-Hall.

McCRONE, DONALD J. and CHARLES F. CNUDDE (1967) "Toward a communications theory of democratic political development: a causal model." Amer. Pol. Sci. Rev. 61 (March): 72-79.

PHILLIPS, HIRAM S. (1969) Guide for Development: Institution-Building and Reform. New York: Frederick A. Praeger. (The role of interacting social and political forces, administration, and technology in creating institutions in the developing countries.)

PYE, LUCIAN W. (1965) "The concept of political development." Annals of Amer. Academy of Pol. and Social Sci. 358 (March): 1-13.

RUBINGER, MARCOS M. (1968) "Social participation as an instrument for the development and formation of society in Latin America." International Labour Rev. 97 (June): 551-570.

SCHWEINITZ, KARL DE, Jr. (1969) "Growth, development, and political monuments." pp. 209-224 in Muzafer Sherif and Carolyn W. Sherif (eds.) Interdisciplinary Relationships in the Social Sciences. Chicago: Aldine.

TAYLOR, CHARLES LEWIS (1969) "Communications development and political stability." Comparative Pol. Studies (January).

VELIZ, CLAUDIO (1969) Centralism, Nationalism and Integration. Budapest: Center for Afro-Asian Research, Hungarian Academy of Sciences.

WEINER, MYRON (1965) "Political integration and political development." Annals of Amer. Academy of Pol. and Social Sci. 358 (March): 52-64.

WISEMAN, H. V. (1966) Political Systems: Some Sociological Approaches. New York: Frederick A. Praeger.

B. Political Development: Latin America

ADAMS, RICHARD N. (1967) The Second Sowing: Power and Secondary Development in Latin America. San Francisco: Chandler.

ANDERSON, ROBERT W. (1967) "Social science ideology and the politics of national integration." Caribbean Integration: Papers on Social Political and Economic Integration. Rio Piedras: University of Puerto Rico, Institute of Caribbean Studies.

ASTIZ, CARLOS (1969) Pressure Groups and Power Elites in Peruvian Politics. Ithaca, N.Y.: Cornell Univ. Press.

BLANKSTEN, GEORGE I. (1960) "The politics of Latin America." In Gabriel A. Almond and James S. Coleman (eds.) The Politics of the Developing Areas. Princeton, N.J.: Princeton Univ. Press.

BOURRICAUD, FRANCOIS (1966) 'Las élites en América Latina." Aportes (July): 121-151.

CUE CANOVAS, A. (1960) El Federalismo Mexicano. México, D.F.: Libro Mex.

DILLON SOARES, GLAUCIO (1964) "The political sociology of uneven development in Brazil." Pp. 164-195 in Irving L. Horowitz (ed.) Revolution in Brazil: Politics and Society in a Developing Nation. New York: E. P. Dutton.

HERRERA, ALARCON, DANTE F. (1961) Rebeliones que Intentaron Desmembrar el Sur del Perú. Lima.

HOROWITZ, IRVING LOUIS (1959) "Modern Argentina: the politics of power." Pol. Q. 30 (October-December): 400-410.

JAGUARIBE, HELIO (1968) Economic and Political Development: A Theoretical Approach and a Brazilian Case Study. Cambridge, Mass.: Harvard Univ. Press.

KANTOR, HARRY (1969) Patterns of Politics and Political Systems in Latin America. Chicago: Rand McNally.

LAMBERT, JACQUES (1968) Latin America: Social Structure and Political Institutions. Helen Katel (trans.) Berkeley: Univ. of California Press.

LARSON, MAGALI SARFATTI and ARLENE EISEN BERGMAN (1969) Social Stratification in Peru. Politics of Modernization Series 5. Berkeley: University of California, Institute of International Studies.

McDONALD, RONALD H. (1967) "Electoral systems, party representation, and political change in Latin America." Western Pol. Q. 20 (September): 694-708.

MELLO, JOSE LUIZ DE ANHAIA (1960) O Estado Federal e as suas Novas Perspectivas. São Paulo: M. Limonad.

MORAZZANI DE PEREZ ENCISO, GISELA (1966) La Intendencia en España y América. Caracas: Consejo de Desarrollo Científico y Humanístico, Universidad Central de Venezuela.

NEEDLER, MARTIN C. (1968) "Political development and socioeconomic development: the case of Latin America." Amer. Pol. Sci. Rev. 62 (September): 889-897.

Organization of American States (1968) Bibliografía Selectiva de Administración Publica en América Latina. Washington, D.C.: PAU.

RANIS, PETER (1968) "Trends in research on Latin American politics: 1961-1967." Latin American Research Rev. 3 (Summer): 71-78.

SARFATTI, MAGALI (n.d.) Spanish Bureaucratic-Patrimonialism in America. Politics of Modernization Series 1. Berkeley: University of California, Institute of International Studies.

SCOTT, ROBERT E. (1966) "The government bureaucrats and political change in Latin America." J. of International Affairs 20: 289-308.

SEGAL, AARON (1969) Politics and Population in the Caribbean. Rio Piedras: University of Puerto Rico, Institute of Caribbean Studies.

SIRI, EROS NICOLA (1965) San Martín, los Unitarios y Federales, y el Regreso del Libertador al Río de la Plata en 1829. Buenos Aires: A. Peña Lillo.

STEIN, STANLEY J. and BARBARA H. STEIN (1970) The Colonial Heritage of Latin America: Essays on Economic Dependence in Perspective. New York: Oxford Univ. Press.

STEPAN, ALFRED (1966) "Political development theory: the Latin American experience." J. of International Affairs 20: 223-234.

STOHR, WALTER (1969) "Regional development in Latin America: experience and prospects." Presented at the Seminar on Social Aspects of Regional Development, Santiago, November 3-14.

TORRES, J. D. DE OLIVEIRA (1961) A Formação do Federalismo no Brasil. São Paulo: Companhia Editôra Nacional.

United Nations Economic Commission of Latin America (1969) "Tendencias sociales y políticas de desarrollo social en América Latina." Presented at the Special Meeting of UNICEF, Santiago, May 19-20.

VELIZ, CLAUDIO (1968) "Centralism and nationalism in Latin America." Foreign Affairs (October).

C. Urban Government and Political Development: General

ALDERFER, HAROLD F. (1967) "Deconcentration and decentralization." Pp. 53-72 in H. F. Alderfer, Public Administration in Newer Nations. New York: Frederick A. Praeger.

――― (1964) Local Government in Developing Countries. New York: McGraw-Hill.

ALFORD, ROBERT R. (1967) "The comparative study of urban politics." Pp. 263-302 in Leo F. Schnore and Henry Fagin (eds.) Urban Research and Policy Planning. Beverly Hills: Sage Publications.

BECKMAN, N. (1963) "Our federal system and urban development: the adaptation of form to function." J. of Amer. Institute of Planners 29 (August).

BREESE, GERALD (1968) "Some dilemmas in poverty, power, and public policy in cities in underdeveloped areas." In Warner Bloomberg, Jr. and Henry J. Schmandt (eds.) Power, Poverty and Urban Policy. Beverly Hills: Sage Publications.

BURBY, RAYMOND J. (1968) Planning and Politics: Toward a Model of Planning-related Policy Outputs in American Local Government. Chapel Hill: Univ. of North Carolina Press.

CLARK, TERRY N. [ed.] (1968) Community Structure and Decision-Making. Scranton, Pa.: Chandler.

DALAND, ROBERT T. (1969) "Comparative perspectives of urban systems." Pp. 15-59 in Robert T. Daland (ed.) Comparative Urban Research: The Administration and Politics of Cities. Beverly Hills: Sage Publications.

――― (1966) "A strategy for research in comparative urban administration." Bloomington, Ill.: Comparative Administration Group. (mimeo)

DOWNS, ANTHONY (1970) "Alternative forms of future urban growth in the United States." J. of Amer. Institute of Planners 36 (January): 3-11.

HANNA, WILLIAM JOHN (1966) "The cross-cultural study of local politics." Civilisations 16, 1: 81-96.

HAPGOOD, DAVID [ed.] (1969) The Role of Popular Participation in Development. Cambridge, Mass.: MIT Press.

HAWLEY, WILLIS D. and FREDERICK M. WIRT (1968) The Search for Community Power. Englewood Cliffs, N.J.: Prentice-Hall.

HERBERT, JOHN (1968) "An approach to metropolitan planning in the developing countries." In John D. Herbert and Alfred P. Van Huyck (eds.) Urban Planning in the Developing Countries. New York: Frederick A. Praeger.

HICKS, URSULA K. (1961) Development from Below. Oxford: Clarendon Press.

HOLDEN, MATTHEW (1964) "The governance of the metropolis as a problem in diplomacy." J. of Politics 26 (August): 627-647.

HUMES, SAMUEL and EILEEN MARTIN (1961) The Structure of Local Governments Throughout the World. The Hague: Martinus Nijhoff.

JONES, VICTOR (1957) "The organization of a metropolitan region." Univ. of Pennsylvania Law Rev. 105 (February): 538-552.

KOTLER, MILTON (1969) Neighborhood Government. Indianapolis: Bobbs-Merrill.

MADDICK, HENRY (1963) Democracy, Decentralization and Development. London: Asia Publishing.

POLSBY, NELSON W. (1963) Community Power and Political Theory. New Haven: Yale Univ. Press.

PYE, LUCIAN W. (1962) "The political implications of urbanization and the development process." Pp. 84-89 in United Nations Conference on the Application of Science and Technology for the Benefit of the Less Developed Areas, Geneva, 1963, United States Papers. Washington, D.C.: Government Printing Office.

RABINOVITZ, FRANCINE F. (1969) City Politics and Planning. New York: Atherton.
SHERWOOD, FRANK P. (1969) "Devolution as a problem of organization strategy." Pp. 60-87 in Robert T. Daland (ed.) Comparative Urban Research: The Administration and Politics of Cities. Beverly Hills: Sage Publications.
——— (1967) "The correlates of decentralization: interpretation, speculation, strategies." Presented to the Comparative Administration Group Urban Studies Seminar, University of North Carolina, August. (mimeo)
United Nations Technical Assistance Program (1962) Decentralization for National and Local Development. New York.
VIERA, PAULO REIS (1967) "Toward a theory of decentralization: a comparative view of forty-five countries." Ph.D. dissertation. University of California, Los Angeles.
WARREN, ROBERT (1964) "A municipal services market model of metropolitan organization." J. of Institute of Planners 30 (August): 193-204.

D. Urban Government and Political Development: Latin America

ALF TONESS, ODIN (1969) Relaciones de Poder en un Barrio Marginal de Centroamérica. Estudios Centroamericanos 5. Guatemala: Seminario de Integración Social Guatemalteca.
ANDUJAR, GERARDO (1966) "Migración urbano-rural y autoritarismo político." Revista Paraguaya de Sociología 3 (May-August).
AUSTIN, ALLAN (1964) Research Report on Peruvian Local Government. New York: Institute of Public Administration.
BAMBERGER, M. (1968) 'A problem of political integration in Latin America: the barrios of Venezuela." International Affairs 44 (October): 709-719.
BASTIAS ROMO, LIONEL (1966) Responsabilidad en el Régimen Municipal. Santiago: Editorial Jurídica de Chile.
BLASIER, COLE (1966) "Power and social change in Colombia: the Cauca Valley." J. of Interamerican Studies 8 (July).
BULNES RIPAMONTI, CRISTIAN (1967) Relaciones y Conflictos entre los Organos del Poder Estatal. Santiago: Editorial Jurídica de Chile.
Chile, Congress (1968) Ley No. 16,800: Juntas Vecinales y Otras Organizaciones Comunitarias. Santiago: Ed. Gutenberg.
CINTA G., RICARDO (1969) "Desarrollo económico, urbanización y radicalismo político." Revista Mexicana de Sociología 31, 3.
DESAL-CEDEP (1967) Antecedentes y Criterios para una Reforma del Gobierno Municipal. 2 vols. Santiago: Centro para el Desarrollo Económico y Social de América Latina and Centro de Desarrollo Popular.
DONALD, CARR L. (1959) "The politics of local government finance in Brazil." Inter-American Economic Affairs 13 (Summer): 21-37.
Eagleton Institute of Politics (1964) Urban Leadership in Latin America. Brunswick, N.J.: Rutgers University.
EBEL, ROLAND H. (1969) Political Modernization in Three Guatemalan Indian Communities. New Orleans: Tulane University.
EDWARDS, HAROLD T. (1967) "Power structure and its communication behavior in San José, Costa Rica." J. of Inter-American Studies 9 (April): 236-247.
FLINN, WILLIAM and ALVARO CAMACHO (1969) "The correlates of voter participation in a shantytown barrio in Bogotá, Colombia." Inter-American Economic Affairs 22 (Spring): 47-58.
FRANK, ANDREW GUNDER (1966) "The politics of urban reform in Latin America." Studies in Comparative International Development 2, 5.
GABALDON MARQUEZ, JOAQUIN (1961) El Municipio, Raiz de la República. Caracas: Pan American Institute of Geography and History, Comisión de Historia, Comité de Orígenes de la Emancipación.
GAKENHEIMER, RALPH A. (1969) "Metropolitan administration." Policy paper submitted to Chilean government. Santiago. (mimeo)

––– RODOLFO AMENABAR, JUAN ESCUDERO, MARGARITA ONAT, and
FERNANDO SOLER (1969) Evaluación del Estudio del Sistema de Transporte
Metropolitano de Santiago de Chile. Santiago: CIDU.

GUISTI, JORGE (1968) "Rasgos organizativos en el poblador marginal urbano latinoamericano." Revista Mexicana de Sociología 30, 1.

GOLDRICH, DANIEL, RAYMOND B. PRATT and C. R. SCHULLER (1967-1968) Studies
in Comparative International Development 027.

GRANT, C. H. (1967) "Rural local government in Guyana and British Honduras." Social
and Economic Studies 16 (March): 56-57.

HOENACK, JUDITH (1966) "Marketing, supply and their social ties in Rio favelas."
Presented at the Thirty-sixth International Congress of Americanists, September, Mar del
Plata. (mimeo)

HOLDEN, DAVID E. W. (1966) "La estructura del liderazgo y sus características en una
comunidad de Costa Rica." J. of Inter-American Studies 8 (January): 129-141.

HOROWITZ, IRVING LOUIS (1967a) "The city as a crucible for political action: electoral
politics, urbanization, and social development in Latin America." Pp. 215-273 in Glenn
H. Beyer (ed.) The Urban Explosion in Latin America. Ithaca, N.Y.: Cornell Univ. Press.

––– (1967b) "Electoral politics, urbanization, and social development in Latin America."
Urban Affairs Q. 2 (March): 3-35.

JOHNSON, JOHN J. (1951) "The Latin American municipality deteriorates." Inter-
American Economic Affairs 5 (Summer): 24-35.

LEEDS, ANTHONY (forthcoming) "Locality power in relation to supra-local power
institutions." In Aidan Southall and Edward Bruner (eds.) Urban Anthropology.
Chicago: Aldine.

––– (1966) "The investment climate in Rio favelas." Presented at the Thirth-sixth
International Congress of Americanists, September, Mar del Plata. (mimeo)

LLAVE HILL, JOAQUIN DE LA (1960) El Municipio en la Historia y en Nuestra
Constitución. México.

LUTZ, THOMAS (1966) "Some aspects of community organization and activity in the
squatter settlements of Panama City." (mimeo)

MANGIN, WILLIAM (1968) "Poverty and politics in cities of Latin America." In Warner
Bloomberg, Jr., and Henry J. Schmandt (eds.) Power, Poverty, and Urban Policy. Beverly
Hills: Sage Publications.

––– and JOHN TURNER (1968) "The barriada movement." Progressive Architecture
(May).

McDONALD, RONALD H. (1969) "National urban voting behavior: the politics of dissent
in Latin America." Inter-American Economic Affairs 23 (Summer): 3-20.

MOORE, JOHN PRESTON (1966) The Cabildo in Peru under the Bourbons: A Study in the
Decline and Resurgence of Local Government in the Audiencia of Lima, 1700-1824.
Durham, N.C.: Duke Univ. Press.

MOROCCO, DAVID (1966) "Carnaval groups: maintainers and intensifiers of the favela
phenomenon in Rio." Presented at the Thirty-sixth International Congress of Americanists, September, Mar del Plata. (mimeo)

MOUCHET, CARLOS (1961) Tendencias Actuales de las Instituciones Municipales en
América. Buenos Aires: Abeledo-Perrot.

MURILO DE CARVALHO, JOSE (1968-1969) "Estudos de poder local no Brasil." Revista
Brasileira de Estudos Políticos (July-January).

OLIVEIRA FRANCO SOBRINHO, MANOEL DE (1966) Município e Municipalização. Rio
de Janeiro: Seção de Publicações, Serviço de Documentação, D.A.S.P.

OLIVEIRA, I. DE (1960) Curso de Derecho Municipal. Buenos Aires: Abeledo-Perrot.

POWELL, SANDRA (n.d.) "Political participation in the barriadas: a case study."
Comparative Pol. Studies 2.

PHELAN, JOHN LEDDY (1967) The Kingdom of Quito in the Seventeenth Century:
Bureaucratic Politics in the Spanish Empire. Madison: Univ. of Wisconsin Press.

RABINOVITZ, FRANCINE F. (1969) "Urban development and political development in Latin America." Pp. 88-123 in Robert T. Daland (ed.) Comparative Urban Research: The Administration and Politics of Cities. Beverly Hills: Sage Publications.

––– (1968) "Sound and fury signifying nothing? a review of community power research in Latin America." Urban Affairs 3 (March): 111-122.

––– FELICITY M. TRUEBLOOD, and CHARLES J. SAVIO (1967) Political Systems in an Urban Setting: A Preliminary Bibliography. Gainesville: University of Florida, Center for Latin American Studies.

RAY, TALTON F. (1969) The Politics of the Barrios of Venezuela. Berkeley: Univ. of California Press.

RIOS, JOSE ARTHUR (1960) "El pueblo y el político." Política 6 (February).

ROBERTS, BRYAN (1968) "Politics in a neighbourhood of Guatemala City." Sociology 2 (May): 185-203.

ROUSE, LOUIS A. (1968) "The Agency for International Development and the Municipality in Latin America." Presented at the Twelfth Inter-American Municipal Congress, New Orleans, December 11. (mimeo)

SANTA, EDUARDO (1969) "Les communautés locales: origines et état actuel de l'organisation municipale en Amérique Latine." 2 parts. Civilisations (Brussels) 19, 2 and 3: 231-240 and 373-382.

Secretaría General de la Organización de los Estados Americanos, Unidad de Finanzas Públicas (1966) Financiamiento de los Municipalidades. Volume II. Presented at the Reunion sobre Financiamiento Municipal en Latinoamérica. Washington, D.C.: Banco Interamericano de Desarrollo.

SEHWERERT FERRER, ARNALDO (1967) Curso de Derecho Municipal. Maracaibo: Universidad de Zulia, Dirección de Cultura.

SHERWOOD, FRANK (1969) "Brazil's municipalities: a comparative view." Unpublished.

SMITH, T. LYNN (1944) "The locality group structure of Brazil."Amer. Soc. Rev. 9 (February): 41-49. (Reprinted in T. Lynn Smith [1970] Studies of Latin American Societies. Garden City, N.Y.: Doubleday.

TAPIA, FRANCISCO XAVIER (1966) Cabildo Abierto Colonial. Madrid: Ediciones Cultura Hispánica.

USANDIZAGA, ELSA and EUGENE A. HAVENS (1966) Tres Barrios de Invasión: Estudio de Nivel de Vida y Actitudes en Barranquilla. Bogotá: Ediciones Tercer Mundo.

VON POTOBSKY, GERALDO (1967) "Participation by workers' and employers' organisations in planning in Latin America." International Labour Rev. 95 (June): 533-552.

WAGNER, BERNARD, DAVID McVOY, and GORDON EDWARDS (1966) "Guanabara housing and urban development." Program Report and Recommendations by AID Housing and Urban Development Team. (mimeo)

WALSH, ANNMARIE HAUCK (1969) The Urban Challenge to Government: An International Comparison of Thirteen Cities. New York: Frederick A. Praeger.

WHITTEN, NORMAN E., Jr. (1965a) Class, Kinship, and Power in An Ecuadorean Town: The Negroes of San Lorenzo. Stanford: Stanford Univ. Press.

––– (1965b) "Power structure and sociocultural change in Latin American communities." Social Forces 43 (March): 320-329.

WOLF, ERIC R. and EDWARD C. HANSEN (1967) "Caudillo politics: a structural analysis." Comparative Studies in Society and History 9 (January): 168-179.

WYGAND, JAMES (1966) "Water networks: their technology and sociology in Rio favelas." Presented at the Thirty-sixth International Congress of Americanists, September, Mar del Plata. (mimeo)

Chapter 7

Urbanization Policy and Political Development in Latin America

ROBERT T. DALAND

National government policies to plan or control urbanization are, ipso facto, economic development policies. This statement is too generally recognized to require argument here. What is less readily perceived—or if perceived, less readily admitted—is that urbanization policies are, ipso facto, political development policies. This paper is devoted to analyzing this assertion. In practical terms, it is the argument of this paper that policy planners need to consider the political development implications of urban development policies.

There are two reasons why it is important to be concerned with politics when doing urban planning. The first is that the failure to do so may prejudice the achievement of planned goals.[1] The second is the desire to prevent negative effects on political development insofar as the latter is as legitimate a goal as economic, social, or urban development.

Recognizing the relation of political and urban development, John Friedmann (1967) offers a strategy of political development as a context within which planned urbanization and modernization may take place. We may summarize his five requisites as follows: (1) a government resting on an inclusive base of popular support, (2) the political mobilization of the population, especially the formerly excluded parts of both urban and rural sectors, through a network of associational groups extending to the neighborhoods, (3) an interest-aggregating national party with local roots, employing bargaining and compromise strategies in order to maintain a broad base, (4) a chief executive chosen from the party in power to whose policies a high level of partisan loyalty is shown by party leaders, and (5) a strong governmental planning system relying heavily on technical opinion.

This strategy, especially in its first four points, typifies the Western European political systems, especially the Anglo-American system of universal suffrage, high level of mobilization, two-party system, and a party-responsible chief executive. We presume such a system to be both stable and democratic. On the basis of these qualities, an urbanization policy must surely be well grounded. But Friedmann sees such a strategy as instrumental for solving the "crisis of inclusion"—the unmet demand for participation—that is chronic and perhaps increasingly virulent in Latin America. This is a political strategy with urbanization consequences. It should be pointed out that there is also a need to consider the reverse: the extent to which a strategy of urbanization may be functional for the achievement of positive political development. The question of which is strategy and which is goal is dependent on the feasibilities of change in the respective sectors and on the priorities of the observer. If we can obtain a sound urbanization policy, it will help attain democratic political development. If we can obtain political development, a sound urban policy will be feasible.

It is our hope in this paper to keep both of these perspectives in view through the following steps. First, the issues of political development that are raised by urbanization (and by certain urban policies) will be identified. Some of the evidence that social science offers with respect to these issues will be noted. The gaps that remain in the evidence will be presumed to represent some high-priority research needs. Finally, we will attempt to relate existing evidence to two models involving relationships between urbanization and political development as a means of suggesting urban policies consistent with political development goals.

Before proceeding it is necessary to be specific about the meaning of "political development."[2] The concept is an extremely complex one used in varying ways by leading scholars. It includes four dominant elements: participation based on equality, the specialization of political roles, political stability, and the capacity to adapt to changing pressures.

Participation based on equality includes such ideas as the legitimacy of competition, equal access to centers of decision, and universal suffrage; these may or may not appear in combination.[3] The specialization of political roles, including separation of political from nonpolitical roles, as an element of development, is closely related to the necessity of creating coordinating mechanisms that link the newly separated roles.[4]

A third element is political stability. This notion is frequently related to continuity of legitimate regimes, lack of extralegal political behavior, general institutional development and continuity, or regular circulation of persons who govern through procedures stated in the rules. The ambiguity of the stability concept rests in the conflict between the idea of stability as lack of change versus stability as change permitted within certain guiding rules. Moreover, what those rules consist of is crucial to the concept. Indicators of stability have frequently measured lack of change rather than the quality of change processes. As such, then, the variable is ambiguous.

Finally, an increasingly utilized element in the general concept is the capacity to adapt to changing pressures (see Shils, 1964: 7-8; Eisenstadt, 1966: 40-43; Halpern, 1965). This concept varies to include emphasis on the ability of a system to undergo internal change as a reflection of changing exogenous pressures (or, as some would say, for processing environmental demands), through decision-making capacity, to mere survival power.

Each of these four central themes contains potential ambiguities and internal conflicts, not to mention the possibility of conflict among them. To what extent are stability and adaptability in conflict? Does specialization of roles and institutions interfere with adaptability? To what extent do legitimacy of regimes and universality of participation conflict? Does a powerful, centralized bureaucracy contribute to decision-making capacity and stability? If so, does it also contribute to participation? At a later point in this paper such questions will be raised again. We are taking all four of these elements to be aspects of "political development" in the long run.

Urbanization and the Modernization Problem

The literature contains a multitude of assertions that urbanization leads to modernization. Modernization has most often been identified with physical, technological, and economic change, but it is increasingly presumed to include changes in social values, beliefs, and political attitudes and behaviors. The first issue that is raised concerns the viability of the modernization syndrome concept. Is it true that economic, social, and political change in fact reflect a single underlying process, "modernization"?

Using data aggregated at the national level, it is possible to show that urbanization does in fact correlate with indicators of each of these three changes.[5] It is equally easy to show that economic development can be achieved at the expense of social and political development. In fact, the very persons who plead the necessity of economic development, in order to serve the general purposes of modernization within any Latin American country, are likely to be the first to assert that the affluence (development) of urbanized metropolitan powers, such as the United States, is based in part on the exploitation of peripheral rural economies in Latin America. To investigate this argument, one is forced to look for negative developmental effects in "backward" regions of a country in exchange for positive developmental effects in the major national urban centers.

Other kinds of evidence show that urbanization does not necessarily lead directly to modernization in a simple cause-and-effect relationship. Were this true, surely urbanization would correlate very highly with industrialization, as it does, for example, in the states of the United States. However, a variety of findings report distinct differences between the relation of urbanization and industrialization. This fact is the basis for the widely observed phenomenon which Friedmann and Lackington (1967) call "hyper-urbanization."[6]

It is necessary, therefore, to abandon the notion of a modernization system or to modify it for determining under what circumstances, if any, it uniformly appears. In order to do this it is necessary to consider its separate parts, and so we now turn to a consideration of the political aspect of urbanization.

The Issue of Participation

Political development includes the notion of greater participation of people in political decisions. Does urbanization contribute to broadened participation? The usual hypothesis holds that it does. Setting aside the question of evidence on this point for the moment, what is the rationale for such a hypothesis? There are chiefly two. The first is the middle-class or middle-sector rationale.[7] It is asserted that the functions of the urban center demand the fulfillment of specialized roles that require people with appropriate expertise. Historically, these roles were originally associated with the administrative needs of the governing center. Later commercial functions and corresponding roles were required to handle trade. Eventually industry required additional specialized roles. Increasing economic complexity led to increasing governmental bureaucratization for controlling or guiding development. With each functional increment, the tertiary sector grew. The result of these additions to urban function was an expansion of the number of people who were neither members of the ruling elite oligarchy nor of the politically inert masses. These new middle sectors (1) were associated with the seat of power by virtue of location in the city from which political power was exercised, and (2) possessed the potential resource of political skill by virtue of serving those who exercised power.

Having these potential political advantages, the middle sectors acquired political strength of their own in proportion to their increase in numbers, but more particularly because they sought organized labor, other urban groups, and, less frequently, rural-based groups as political allies.[8] There were basically two strategies for utilizing this new strength. The first involved the advocacy of policies favorable to labor (policies administered by members of the middle class, of course) through governmental agencies established for this purpose. With the growing power of the middle class, achieved through control of the expanded governmental machinery and incorporated into the power structure, the middle class established a base of power independent of labor and swung ideologically to the right, identifying now with the ruling elite that the rising middle sectors aspired to join. The second method has been referred to as the "national-popular revolution," and it is characterized by authoritarianism and the integration of the lower strata, accompanied by an ideological swing to the left. This path to participation is usually preceded by the presence of disaffected groups of both the lower and middle classes.[9]

Thus increasing urbanization not only increases the potential of the middle class for political participation, but prescribes stages through which middle-sector politics can pass.

In contrast to the middle-class rationale is the education-communications rationale expounded by Lerner (1958: 60). He explains the development of political participation as the result of a causal chain in which urbanization occurs first, and urbanization is regarded as virtually identical with industrialization. The processes of industry rely on literacy, which therefore grows as industrialization proceeds. Literacy, then, is the second step in the process. When this stage is well advanced, as industry continues to increase literacy, the mass media begin to appear. This third stage has the effect of rapidly stimulating further growth in literacy, which strengthens the mass media still further. Out of this dynamic interaction between literacy and media growth arise the techniques that make mass political participation possible, expressed through electoral campaigns and voting.

These two rationales are not inconsistent with each other, since both causal chains could be in process at the same time and might even be mutually reinforcing. However, they should not be confused with each other, as is often done. The middle-class rationale is based on the notion of access to power and the development of political leadership skills. The education-communications rationale relies on the idea of information as a lever in obtaining power and suggests a broader base than the middle sectors alone. Whether the distinction is more apparent than real is an empirical question. Since the education-communications rationale relies on industrialization and since the middle class, as a response to a functional need, relies partly on the growth of technical activities associated with industry, the two may be difficult to separate. However, in the real world we know that some urbanization is not industry-based. If, in those countries where urbanization is not industry-based, the urbanite is a participant, as in industrialized countries, the middle-class rationale would seem to represent a distinct process. In terms of empirical evidence we are confronted with our first research gap.[10]

In addition to industrialization, there are some clues as to other intervening variables in the relationship between urbanization and participation. The most frequently found idea is that governmental structures in fact condition participation. I do not refer primarily to the administrative organization chart, but rather to the amount of power in the hands of urban government officials. Where little power is devolved, participation may be low.[11]

A second variable which clearly has a different impact in different urban situations is the behavioral characteristic of governmental authorities associated with formal or informal practices of meting out sanctions or rewards on participation. For example, to what extent do they impose sanctions on participation? Are sanctions imposed differentially on different groups in the community? Daniel Goldrich et al. (1967) have illustrated the functioning of this variable in Chile and Peru, and they have found that participative activity of rural migrant communities in cities is affected by sanctions in such a fashion that the most "urbanized" settlements are not necessarily the most popularly participative. Moreover, Goldrich found that sanctions may reflect previous participative activity on the part of the settlement, and, when applied, they have the effect of reducing subsequent participation of the community in question. Participation once begun does not necessarily continue.

Finally, it is frequently remarked that, in Latin America, political control of the largest city is tantamount to political control of the nation (see Horowitz, 1967: 13). Where it applies, what effect does this situation have on political development? In one sense it increases urban influence in the national arena, but in another sense it presumably leaves lesser cities outside the ring of power. An important research question would then seem to be: "Where are the urban nodes of political power and what are their relative weights?" The answer to this question would provide leads to further factors that add to or detract from urban participation in national governance.[1 2]

If we carefully inspect the historical writings related to the middle-class thesis, it is evident that many reservations have been expressed. Speaking of Brazil, Celso Furtado (1965: 152-153) asserts that urbanization has not produced political changes of significance. The name most closely associated with the middle-sector approach is that of John Johnson. However, his extensive analysis of this question contains no encompassing statement of what was described above as the middle-class thesis. In fact, he shows how variations in the economic structure produced middle-class political dominance in Uruguay, Chile, and Mexico, while it did not do so in more highly urbanized and industrialized Argentina. He notes, in addition, that the differing groups with whom the military were allied in each of the countries contributed to the difference of outcome among these countries (Johnson, 1958: 95).

With this type of evidence before us, let us return to the general question: does urbanization, ipso facto, tend to increase political participation? The generalization is a common one (Horowitz, 1967; Solari, 1965; Ríos, 1960). When tested statistically with aggregate data, it seems to be confirmed for Latin America when voting is measured in terms of the total adult population. However, when it is measured in terms of *eligible* (literate) voters, urbanization has no effect.[1 3]

This suggests that literacy and social-mobilization variables are the crucial ones, and it remains for research to establish the relation between urbanization and these variables, in the face of such known phenomena as urban illiteracy pockets and low mobilization indexes in some urban areas.

If anything on the proposition can be said with assurance, it is that participation, mobilization, education, and communication are facilitated within concentrated populations, so that urban conditions are at least conducive, and possibly necessary, for increasing participation; but these conditions are by no means sufficient.

The Issue of Stability

The phrase "stable democracy" suggests an ideal situation in the abstract. It is when we are somewhat dissatisfied with certain conditions related to what is basically regarded as a democracy that we begin to advocate change. When does the intensity, frequency, or process of such change render the system itself "unstable"? Paradoxically, it is the excessive stability which flows from rigidity of structures, institutions, and policies that produces radical change. In Latin America the usual assumption is that political systems are weighted on the unstable side of the stability-change equilibrium.[14] If this is so, then the typical political instability presumably has negative effects on economic development in addition to being intrinsically bad from a political democracy point of view.

What does urbanization have to do with political stability, then? Two general positions are marked out. One asserts that urbanization breaks down the social fabric and juxtaposes different interests, thereby producing conflict. This is the familiar Jeffersonian position. The more prevalent contemporary position is that urbanization involves certain integrative and social learning processes that provide the skills and incentives for resolving small differences before they become large ones. In the long run, this produces stability in political processes and institutions. These skills and incentives are transferable from the urban to the regional and national political levels.[15]

More specifically, if urbanization does produce integration and stability, what are the relevant processes? It is asserted, in the first place, that class conflict between the urban classes and the rural masses is reduced through urbanization—that is, through the rural-to-urban migration process. The premise is that in countries like Brazil, Mexico, and Peru the immigrants to the cities are able to relieve their discontent by bettering their condition (see, for example, Horowitz, 1967: 6-7). They become upwardly mobile in the cities and less disposed to making political demands. In Brazil and Mexico it was confirmed that rural migrants were more content with their lives than long-time residents (Kahl, 1965: 28). On the other hand, rural migration to cities may provide a base for conflict, as it did in Argentina, where rural migrants formed part of a revolutionary base for Peronism. Similarly, in Italy, rural migrants were successfully organized for political actions by the Communists, especially in the cities of north Italy. Anomic movements in the cities increased, as did sectional hostility between north and south Italy (see Fried, 1967).

Clearly, what happens to the migrant in the city in relation to his previous status is the crucial variable. In Italy the urban migrants were virtually pariahs because of the antiurbanist policy of the government. This conclusion is somewhat disturbing in view of the fact that sanctions against the mass of migrants stimulated political activity, while, in the Goldrich study, sanctions dampened politicization. Possibly the existence of the organized Communists in Italy accounts for the difference. It is possible, then, that the research gap respecting migration and conflict may be concerned particularly with the leadership roles and their interrelationships as they exist in the city to which migrants go. If the probability of sanctions is high and preexisting opposition leadership is weak, conflict will be minimal. What happens with other combinations of these two variables deserves further investigation.

There is increasing evidence that linkage roles represent a crucial element in integration and, presumably, in stability. These linkages occur (at least potentially) both vertically and horizontally. A good example of a horizontal linkage is represented by the phenomenon of the mobile ruralite who migrates to the city, but who continues to circulate back to his original home on occasion, thereby maintaining ties. As this process continues, rural values are imported to the metropolis, and urban values are exported to the village.[16]

Another type of horizontal political linkage is that described by William and Judith Hanna in the African milieu. Here in the person of one type of leader was a bridging of the gap between the urban, ethnic enclave, in which a certain tribal group lived, and the large tribal community still living in the hinterland of the central city. This leader not only integrated the political activity of urban and nonurban elements of the ethnic group, but he also acted in concert with his counterparts from other ethnic enclaves to form a layer of urban influentials among whom bargaining over decisions could take place. In addition to this, the same leader was instrumental in a vertical linkage with political leaders at the center of the national government (see Hanna and Hanna, 1967).

The question of the urban politician's horizontal linkage roles requires investigation in Latin America, particularly in terms of the establishment of relationships between urban power structures and rural migrant settlements. Probably more significant in Latin America is the vertical linkage role. The vertical linkage is not entirely distinct from the geographical element of the horizontal linkage due to the effect of the hierarchy of cities. Consider, for example, the comments of Robert Scott (1959) on Mexico. He describes the urban center as the political center and indicates that the secondary urban metropoli serve as transmission channels of Western ideas to smaller centers, and these in turn to the countryside. Viewed in reverse, political leaders ascend the same hierarchy, from smaller to larger urban places, until (if successful) they arrive at

Mexico City. Thus a political integration of the country is achieved through the hierarchy of urban places. Scott notes, however, that political influence is not evenly spread through this network, but that it is preponderantly located at the center—which is why so much effort is placed on rising to higher positions in politics.[17]

Perhaps the most dramatic description of the vertical linkage structure is that of Anthony Leeds (1964) in his description of Brazil. The form is consistent with Scott's comments on Mexico, but more detailed. Leeds describes the *panelinha* as an informal mutual support group that does not even meet for purposes of decision-making, but that is, nevertheless, strongly tied together in a web of cooperative relationships. A typical panelinha would include a customs official, an insurance man, a lawyer, a businessman, an accountant, one or more legislators, and a banker. These structures exist at municipal, state, and national levels. Those at lower levels establish ties with "the juridical political hierarchy," which reaches up to the president of Brazil himself. These ties are of various kinds, but include the *cabide,* or collector of several positions or roles, and each tie has its own reciprocal set of relationships. The milieu in which the panelinha forms is necessarily urban, and in fact Leeds notes that its incidence increases with the size and urbanity of the city. Normally these relationships channel from the *municipio* to the state capital to Rio de Janeiro and Brasilia. Research that would map the panelinha structure and its equivalent in other countries, but, more particularly, study the ways in which such structures condition elite circulation and help to overcome the discontinuity between sharp changes from one formal political regime to the next, would probably demonstrate more systemic continuity and stability than at first seems apparent.

In considering linkage roles as we have done, we must not disregard the possibility that they represent the functional means for adjusting older, rural, and traditional ways to the tremendously dynamic new situation created by rapid urbanization. Whether such roles slow political development or enhance it is an open question. They do rely heavily on personalistic ties. It has been noted that urbanization tends to discourage personalism in politics. This traditional mode of politics, then, must be replaced, so that rationale goes, and what replaces it is policy, interest, or ideology. Urbanization appears not only to heighten the role of ideology as an integrating factor in politics, but also to produce a shift to the left in the predominant ideology (Sherwood, 1967: 26-28). This is a testable proposition. As ideology and policy increasingly dominate politics, political leadership necessarily will be measured more in achievement than in personalistic terms. Are urban political leaders in fact more achievement oriented? This is another crucial gap in our data.[18]

It is difficult to suggest what policies are positively associated with political stability. Presumably a simple policy of urbanization is not enough. Deliberate policies may be needed to minimize personalistic reward to urban leaders and to maximize rewards for achievement of the manifest goals of urban governments, such as the provision of urban services. This raises the question of the role of tension in political development. Sherwood (1967: 76-77) has argued persuasively that a certain tension (dissatisfaction) level is probably necessary in the developed urban political system in order to establish a mechanism for relating expectations to performance of the system. Without such a mechanism, stability itself may be endangered. In terms of political development in general, it seems apparent that the gap between expectations and performance is greatest in urban areas, where the visual evidence of affluence is most universal. Sherwood's point is that expectations from the municipal government are very low in Brazil. A distinction should be made between this and the expectation of return from the social system as a whole. The affluent, for example, may have low expectations of municipal service as such, while being quite content with their general position. What kind of gap in expectations contributes to, and what kind detracts from, political stability? Friedmann argues strongly that politics in Chile have been stabilized by hyperurbanization. The rationale is that as migration to cities becomes more rapid than industrial growth, the migrants are held at marginal existence levels; but as they become aware of the affluence around them, they make political demands that feed the moderate political leftist movement and strengthen the hand of the middle class as a force between the polarized radical left and radical right, thus stabilizing Chilean politics.[19]

To sum up these complex considerations, it appears that urbanization does potentially produce a setting in which tensions develop. These may be channeled into behaviors positive for political development and for stimulating change. On the other hand, such positive effects are by no means automatic (Pye, n.d.). They depend on the presence of integrating forces, such as political parties and labor unions as well as effective government agencies, which exercise some degree of control over the new pressures while not suppressing them through severe sanctions, as do some military-dominated regimes.

The data we have on the correlation of urbanization with political stability, measured by years of constitutional government and by the levels of deaths from group violence, show that urbanization as such has not insured political stability. The two do not correlate (Rabinovitz, 1967: 43). On the other hand, since constitutional government in Latin America may represent oligarchical rigidity rather than political stability, it is hard to interpret this finding. This is particularly emphasized since indicators of "urbanism," as measured by the number of dwellings with water and sewer connections, *does* correlate positively with political stability. It would appear that where higher urban service levels exist, either there is, in fact, an underlying political stability, or oligarchies provide more effectively for cities than do other regimes. A plausible rationale for either of these conclusions is not difficult to erect, so further research is immediately suggested. The remaining possibility is that the findings cited are an artifact of aggregate data methods of research. Comparative case studies are needed to check out this possibility.

Specialization and Change Capacity

The remaining two elements of our political development concept, though quite distinct, seem to be affected by the same set of factors, and we shall discuss them together. These are specialization of political institutions and political leadership roles, and the capacity of the system to respond to changes in the internal and external demand pattern.

In its simple form, the usual proposition is that urbanization produces devolution of political authority. This multiplication of decision centers, and thus of centers of potential innovation, provides a system that adapts to changed demands more quickly than would a more centralized system. This process is closely related to specialization of roles and institutions at the periphery. As real power moves to the urban communities, the planners, technicians, legislators, interest groups, and administrators must exercise their roles there rather than exclusively at the center, keeping in mind that the continuing preponderance of the primate-capital city in much of Latin America means a concentration of power in one relatively small locality, although it may be devolved from the national government. Because of regional differences the interests that can now gain access at the center cannot do so at the periphery in areas where their interest is strong.

This does not mean merely that specialization moves from the center to the periphery.[20] The requirements of national integration, and particularly of central, national, economic-development planning, produce a considerable specialization at the center even when the same process is going on at the periphery. Probably each process stimulates the other. In Brazil, for example, the creation of regional authorities for Amazonia, the Northeast, the South, and the Southwest resulted in the creation of a new ministry to coordinate regional efforts. In addition, a Ministry of Planning was established, which began to spin off other entities (such as the Service for Housing and Urban Development, SERFHAU) intended to carry on relationships with state and local governments.

The number of observers who have concluded that decentralization is positive for development—usually economic development—is impressive.[21] Therefore, when we look at the correlation between urbanization and devolution of authority to local units of government we hope to find that the two are related. This does not, however, appear to be the case (Vieira, 1967). Where devolution is judged by the proportion of governmental expenditures made at the local level, urbanization does not correlate significantly with devolution. There are, however, significant variables with which it does correlate. These include status as an industrial nation, gross national product, and the degree of development of communications in the country. So we may infer that while nonindustrial urbanization is not conducive to devolution (and thus to political development) as such, industrial urbanization is. This again underlines the kinds of policy considerations that are related to the matter of stimulating urbanization. Tying urbanization to industrialization appears to be the basis for decentralized political development, rather than urbanization alone, which seems to uphold Lerner's education-communication framework discussed earlier.

Yet we are now forced back to the original proposition. Does urbanization enhance the adaptability of the political system to changing conditions? From the perspective of the total system we may take it for granted that, insofar as adaptation occurs, the urban centers and at least some of the urban elite groups are the channels and leaders of change. If we can accept this, then it is a question of greater as against lesser potential for adaptation. Some of the dysfunctional urban conditions may be noted. Lerner (1958: 65-66, 218) shows that increase in population density without countervailing urbanization has negative effects on education, Egypt being the case in point in contrast to Turkey and Lebanon, which have deliberate urbanization policies. We presume education is the most critical political modernizing force. Variable education policies should then produce variable degrees of political development.

Urbanization without an increase in educational opportunity may then produce negative political development. Simply increasing the educational opportunity for the poor in urban areas, however, is not a certain road to the goal sought, nor is increasing the adaptive capacity of the political system. Social planning and planning for amenities in the cities increase the pull factor and can lead to a spiraling rate of urban immigration with more problems than solutions (see Hauser, 1961: 62-63).

Shifting our ground, what evidence do we have that urban groups share modernist and, therefore, presumably adaptive values? In a study reported by Kalman Silvert (1963), the national identification attitudes of a variety of urban groups in Brazil, Argentina, Chile, and Mexico were compared. If it is reasonable to assume national identification is modernist rather than traditional, the results show greatly varying degrees of modernization both within and among such groups as managers, students, teachers, and members of Congress. The percentages rated "high" on national identification varied from 15 to 62 among such groups. The difference between "high" and "low" varied from 3 to 57 when comparing levels of national identification within individual groups. Brazilian slum dwellers included 17 percent "high" on national identification and 38 percent "low." For skilled workers the figures were about the same, 20 and 39 percent respectively. But Chilean Catholic University professors and Mexican members of Congress showed a rather similar pattern of 15 and 53 percent in each case: almost as many national identifiers and a few more with low identification scores than in the larger sample.

Such data suggest not only that urbanization as a modernizing and adapting force should be accepted with great caution, but also that there is a great need for further research on values of urban groups.

Little is known about how to measure "capacity for adaptation" as compared to participation, stability, or specialization. Is mere survival of a system indicative? Perhaps so, but this test can best be applied to past regimes. Predicting survival capacity is another matter. Internal satisfaction with the system would seem a useful indicator, but an additional indicator of ability to adjust to the external, international environment is important. Perhaps some index of aid-getting ability corrected for need would be a rough indicator. The writer has not seen either of these kinds of data for Latin American countries. In their five-nation study, Almond and Verba found marked differences between nations in the levels of pride in the political system.[22] In Mexico, 30 percent of the respondents (in an urban sample) mentioned governmental institutions with pride, as contrasted with 7 and 3 percent in Germany and Italy respectively, and with 46 and 85 percent in Britain and the United States respectively.

If satisfaction and pride in governmental and political institutions can in fact be linked with system adaptability, then capacity to adapt would be linked in turn with the whole identity of "politically modern man"—judging by research, applicable to the United States.[23] A final question is whether role specialization correlates with capacity to absorb change. It may be relevant then to correlate satisfaction with the political system and the degrees of role specialization.[24]

Suggested Models

We have attempted to indicate some of the effects of urbanization on political development as suggested by social science research. In the process we have found that the research gaps are rather broader than the areas of firm information. Since it is never useful merely to end with a plea for more research before tackling the problem at hand, however, we will attempt to focus more clearly on alternative policies toward urbanization, and their possible effects on political development, keeping a special lookout for unanticipated and dysfunctional elements from the political point of view. We shall do this through describing in general terms some policies which are presumed to be conducive to some specified political outcomes. This procedure should improve on the previous discussion, which was unreal to the extent that individual variables were examined more or less independently of others to which they are in fact related.

The policies can be presented in paradigms describing situations in which urbanization produces positive political development con-sequences. It is not assumed that these paradigms (Figures 7.1, 7.2) are the only road to political development. The two paradigms are combinations of policies, policy consequences, and the relationships among them which appear consistent with the evidence presented in the preceding portion of the paper. The arrows in these highly simplified paradigms indicate causal relationships. Most of the causal relationships are portrayed as unidirectional, except for three that are central to the paradigm. Feedback loops are not indicated, though a change toward pluralistic democratic politics would surely have consequences for the entire system, presumably reinforcing the elements. Finally, no effort has been made to indicate the relative efficacy of each of the four policies vis-à-vis the different parts of the proposed outcome—it is possible to visualize *one* policy as the key

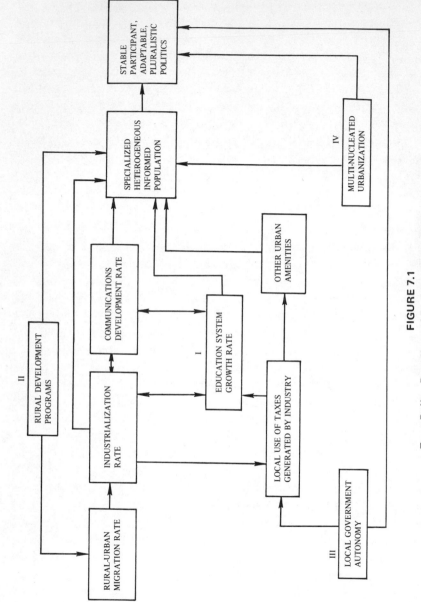

FIGURE 7.1

Four-Policy Paradigm of Positive Political Development

250

rather than four, or that all the policies might in fact be strengthening one aspect of the end results more than the others.

In the first paradigm, four policies are represented. The first policy (Figure 7.1, I) is the central requisite to which the other elements are keyed. It is the presumption here that from the point of view of political development it is optimal that the rate of industrialization, the rate of growth of the communication system, and the rate of growth of the educational system be kept congruent.[25] The definitions of these need only brief comment. Industrialization as measured by traditional indices of the economist appears to correlate highly with education and communication indicators, which is why the term is used here. It might be that commercial and bureaucratic expansion should be included. We leave this possibility open. By "the communication system" is meant the movement of ideas through media development, and movement of people and things through transport systems. The system of education refers to both lower and higher education. "Growth" of this system refers in particular to the expansion of educational opportunity for groups to which it has not traditionally been available. These three growth variables are seen as mutually reinforcing, which is the first reason they must be tied together. The second reason is that each of the three makes a contribution to creating the politically modern population, which is specialized, heterogeneous and informed.

The argument is that, optimally, governmental planning should keep these three growth rates parallel. We cannot now say in operational terms what exact rates represent parallelism. One factor would be the relative positions of each factor at the start of the planning period. But even assuming we could make the rates exactly parallel, we cannot now recognize when we would have achieved this condition. On this problem, all that can be said now is that it is necessary to avoid making the assumption that the proper mix of educational, industrial, and communications development should be the same for less developed nations as it is for the United States. Probably that would *not* be the optimal mix, since the whole problem is a matter of achieving a political end-condition that is not necessarily the same political system as now obtained in the United States. Moreover, even if the United States' political system were the objective, the requisite mix en route is presumably different from the mix on arrival. Thus the establishment of what the congruent rates actually should be depends on extracting inferences from desired "end-conditions" which may be found in subsystems of the system in question. One might, for example, study the mix in cities or states perceived as stable, participant, adaptable, and pluralistic.

From what we already know, the establishment of education policy is easier said than done, chiefly because of the paradox that when we improve education, build radio stations, build roads, and establish industry, these developments act as a magnet for a mass immigration that can leave the basic condition worse than it was before. Progress per capita may be negative. Something is needed to attack this problem (Figure 7.1, policy II). We have represented this policy as "rural development programs." From the systems point of view, which is now permeating professional planning, "urbanization policy" is not necessarily something that occurs in cities. Its heart may be in the countryside. An example is the rural development program of Malaya (see Guyot, 1968). There the policy is not (as in India) a policy deriving from a basically urban elite that is trying to stem the tide moving toward the cities through community development, but rather it is a policy stemming from a rural elite that is attempting to develop the countryside through colonization programs that will provide a counter-magnet to the cities. Incidentally, the planning problem of the cities is eased. Guyot's analysis indicates that the countryside is being politically developed in the process.

In our paradigm, then, rural development is intended to stem the tide of migration to the cities, not through sanctions against those who migrate, as in Italy, Peru, or Chile, but through removing the "push" factor. The second contribution of rural development would be to contribute to a more informed and, possibly, a somewhat more specialized population which any of the kinds of rural or community development programs now extant is likely to do. The famous case of Vicos, Peru, is the best case in point. Thus rural development has two effects on political development, one direct and the other indirect.

The third key policy of the paradigm is that urban governments should be awarded a relatively high degree of autonomy by the central government. That is, they need to perform functions that are valued by the local inhabitants, as well as the financial resources with which to perform them. Several relationships are involved here. We have indicated in the paradigm that the urban government is empowered to draw taxes from industry. (An alternative, but less politically effective, source would be federal grants-in-aid.) With a local income source, the urban government would develop the competence to establish policies and to manage the programs on which the money is spent. From the political development point of view the most useful expenditure would be public education, though other urban amenities would presumably receive a share. The point is, national expenditures for the very same purpose would strengthen support for central politico-administrative institutions rather than for local government institutions. This would deprive the local political system of any share in innovation, experience in governance, and representation regarding the particular needs of the locality as viewed at home. There would be no occasion locally for development of specialized political roles, political education, or diverse points of view. Only at the center of the society would these characteristics appear. To sum up, devolution of real power to urban governments would indirectly produce the kind of population we have described as the required base for political development, as well as providing direct practice in politics through the need to manage the local government system.

The final requirement (Figure 7.1, policy IV), as stated in the paradigm, is a policy of multinucleated urbanization. This policy addresses itself to the difficulties associated with the primate city and its preeminent role in national politics. The sort of excessive centralization that is at worst a breeding ground for dictatorship and at best a highly bureaucratized decision-bottleneck, appears to be dysfunctional to political development, not only in large countries but in small ones as well. Switzerland, the Netherlands, and Denmark, to cite three cases, are examples of multinucleated small countries. It is difficult to state either the number or the population needed in the ideal distribution of urban political systems. The number is presumably not related to the size of country, but rather to the necessity for sufficient autonomous subsystems of the national system so that no two or three centers can, through alliance, permanently dominate national politics. An even distribution over a dozen cities would seem to assure a virile interest-aggregation process through some form of bargaining and shifting of alignments.

City size cannot be reduced to a standard from the political point of view, but rather is related to the proportion of the total population and of the total urban population. A greater, rather than lesser, number of cities would be desirable up to the point where the number of distinct economic interests in the country could be represented. The extent to which economic interests are focused in particular cities, in contrast to being spread evenly among them, is relevant as well. While different patterns immediately come to mind, the least that can be said is that it would be useful to have a major city in each region of distinctive agricultural, extractive, or industrial activity—these, in fact, are frequently distributed regionally by reason of climate and topography. Conceivably, industrial pluralism

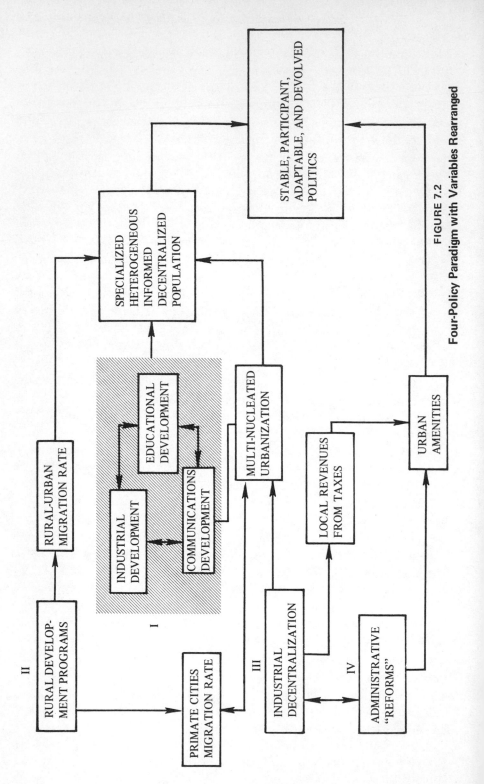

FIGURE 7.2
Four-Policy Paradigm with Variables Rearranged

254

could even be planned on a regional basis, though the sticky political questions this would raise suggest that we not rely heavily on this possibility. Multinucleated urbanization in terms of a series of major cities (rather than a myriad of small communities) seems to satisfy the requirements of specialization, heterogeneity, and information that are related to sizeable urban centers, while at the same time insuring the pluralistic characteristic already specified as necessary for political development.

The second paradigm is similar to the first in many respects. It makes the same basic assumptions about the desirability of parallel growth through national planning in education, industrialization, and communications—all of which are referred to collectively as policy I (Figure 7.2). Further, it uses the same basic arguments for a policy of rural development, referred to as policy II (Figure 7.2). As stated earlier, the paradigms may be oversimplified in that most of the causal-relationship arrows are unidirectional. This second paradigm rearranges some of the variables and, in effect, changes the direction of some of the causal relationships proposed in the first paradigm.

While there are national differences within the area known as Latin America, there is, to some extent, a distinct Latin American political culture. The second paradigm seeks to incorporate some of this and to present a framework more specifically geared to this cultural area.

One aspect of the political culture of Latin America is the identification of politically active people with national rather than local political orientations. Tannenbaum (1960) has written of the "dilemma" in Latin American politics, the seeming contradiction between the definition of "democracy" and the overriding power of the presidency.[26] The assertion has been made recently that this situation may be changing as a result of the urban development process, but it is also noted, in referring to local power structures, that the national political reality continues to play a major role (Rabinovitz, 1968: 122, 116, 119).

This aspect of the political culture, plus the relative scarcity of competent administrators, has helped shape the reality of political centralization in Latin America. On this topic, one study (Vieira, 1967: 16-162; table, 161) shows that only two Latin American nations rank above the median in a decentralization index comparing a stratified grouping of forty-five nations from all regions of the world. Brazil is often considered to have the least centralized system in Latin America, but at least two authors (Donald, 1960; De Mello, 1961) point out that the Brazilian system is essentially centralized, constitutional provisions notwithstanding. The political reality of

Latin America is still one of centralization of power in the national government and, within the national government, in the presidency.

National integration, or the lack of it, is another problem confronting much of Latin America. In some nations, significant ethnic or other groups are not integrated politically or economically. Integration as a national goal militates against the desirability of significant devolution of power.

These considerations bring us to the first major differences between the two paradigms. Here, local government autonomy as a national policy is not seen as a practical cause of political development in Latin America, whatever its theoretical value in developmental frameworks in general. Rather, it is seen as a result of development, if only because the reality of Latin American politics suggests that devolution will not take place until a higher level of political development is attained.

An alternative can be suggested, one that, hopefully, would help spur the developmental process and bring about more quickly the devolution of political power by creating the conditions that lead to such devolution. This would be a policy of decentralization of industry away from the primate city, policy III (Figure 7.2) in the paradigm. This alternative can be based on two premises. The first, expressed by Fred Riggs (1960: 390), is that local government will become stronger and contribute more to overall development when there is both *local demand* for local government and *local capacity* to support it. Riggs (1960: 417-418) suggests: (1) that local economic development will result from local industrialization, (2) that this must be accompanied by improvements in administration, and (3) that these two policies can best be carried out by the centralized power in the national capital.

These improvements in public administration might consist of a deconcentration (without devolution) of administration away from the national capital and of reforms to improve communications within and among agencies of a government. Both of these changes, presumably, would make the process of local economic development through industrialization a smoother one. These changes are referred to in the paradigm as policy IV (Figure 7.2).

The second premise on which to base this alternative policy of decentralized industrialization is that the various processes, known collectively as "urbanization," will follow from industrialization, whereas we know from Latin America that the converse is not necessarily true. Whereas in the first paradigm, multinucleated urbanization was listed as the fourth national policy, this second paradigm conceives of multinucleated urbanization as a result of a combination of other policies, namely, multinucleated industrialization, communications development, and rural development. The statistical reality of Latin America is that the highest migration rates are to the national capital-primate and largest cities rather than to the middle-range cities. A combination of the three policies mentioned, it is believed, would alleviate not only the rural-urban migration rate, but also the proportion of the migrants going to the primate cities, which would result in multinucleated urbanization.

It should be borne in mind with respect to both paradigms that we have not attempted to specify the variables except in the broadest terms. In so doing we run the danger of missing some even more crucial variables. Conceivably it is the character of the rural development program, between psychological reorientation of the small farmer versus purely economic and technical approaches, that is crucial. Industrialization may fall into our scheme only if it is labor-intensive as compared to capital-intensive industrialization that is stimulated. Education may support our case only if a break is made away from traditional Latin American education. We grant that such refinements and several others are probably of high importance. We do not refine the paradigm in detail, however, due to limitations of space as well as to the danger that the broad policy directions would be thereby obscured.

It remains to comment on the relevance of heterogeneity and information as causes of political development. Much of what needs to be said has already been stated or implied, so we shall merely summarize at this point.

Heterogeneity is related, not only to the mix of specialties, but also to the mix of social characteristics such as ethnic, religious, regional, or national groups. The very presence of a variety of different groups may be a pluralistic factor in politics, but it has been noted that achievement orientation is higher among heterogeneous populations, presumably because of intergroup competition. This orientation is widely heralded as a key element of the politically modern man, in contrast to ascriptive orientations, which are viewed as politically dysfunctional. It is hardly necessary to comment on the correlation of information levels with political participation, since the empirical evidence is so conclusive.

The final link in the paradigm, from the characteristics of the population to the political behaviors of the system they compose, is a rather big leap. The more highly informed participate more actively. The heterogeneity of the population provides at least a condition for pluralism, even if it does not ensure it. The specialization of skill presumably increases adaptability, and the specialization of role fits the notion of pluralistic politics. Beyond the seeming reasonableness of these relationships, reinforcement of certain characteristics comes directly from other elements of the paradigm. Multinucleation should promote pluralism. Local autonomy is usually associated with participation and with adaptability in the sense of training for higher level roles. The weakest element of the final syndrome may be stability. Does this outcome really reflect elements of the paradigm? Bypassing the definitional problems involved with the term itself (which are serious) it appears that political stability may be so strongly affected by exogenous factors that the entire matter is academic. But in purely internal terms, we have not built in any assurance of a neutral military, for example. The high degree of role specialization and the high educational level of the military leaderships does not appear to ensure nonintervention in politics, nor does the region-based characteristic of some military forces produce such a result. The observed types of military intervention range drastically from a simple moderating role to unadulterated dictatorship. It may be only a hope that our paradigm provides for the former (for the purposes of reinforcing stability and freedom or communication processes) rather than for the latter.

In addition to problems of this order is the broader question of the role of stability in development in general, which is very much an open question. Two general positions exist here. One is that stability is a necessary prerequisite to development (including political development). The rationale is that development depends on the creation of a high level of consensus in the society as to goals, rational planning processes that indicate appropriate means of reaching them, and implementation that follows the path of scientific management. However, some are sharply critical of this procedure on the grounds that development is innately an unstable process. Consensus is a sign of elite dominance, and the real problem is how to attain development amid dissensus.

These critics employ a different rationale. This is to institutionalize planning as a part of the political system itself (the case of Venezuela being suggestive), to focus developmental efforts on "islands of development," and to decentralize implementation. We would argue that the process performed in the context of stability creates economic development at the expense of political development, while the feeling that dissension is required could encourage both political stability and economic development on the basis of that political stability.

One final comment, on a matter not raised in this paper, seems appropriate. It is very possible that the stage of social welfare is an important political development variable associated with urbanization. In all likelihood, the static paradigm suggested above would vary according to the degree of modernization in the country. The next logical question then, would be: What is the optimum paradigm during the stages of "primitive unification," "industrialization," "national welfare," or "abundance," to use Organski's (1965) stages? Our paradigm fits the stage of "industrialization" rather better than the other stages. Can we range any of the classifications of political systems along a time continuum? For example, do developing nations pass through mobilization, modernizing autocratic, neo-mercantilist, and reconciliation stages, following Apter's (1965) categories? Should it appear that they do, our paradigm is useless, since it is based on the idea of continuous progress toward a defined political development goal, rather than on the strategy of an authoritarian tutelary interlude that produces "modernization," after which democracy can be installed in the now modernized base that has been constructed by the Platonic planners. The second paradigm, however, comes closer to such an interlude than the first, at least to the extent that it depends on the strong central governments that exist in most of Latin America, to implement major policies that might have negative short-run political consequences for those in the primate cities that favor the status quo.[27] While we readily grant that the paradigm may change as modernization occurs, we are not ready to defer political development until all the other elements of modernity have been achieved.

A less cosmic problem not taken into account by our data is the question of generational differences in political behavior. If the first-generation urban migrant is relatively satisfied and tied to his original family system, what of the third generation? Perhaps that is where the radical revolutionist is born. By now he may have forgotten the improvement of life chances that the urban condition seemed to offer his grandfather, and family solidarity may dissolve surely, though slowly, in the specialized and achievement-oriented urban place. This kind of possibility requires close attention to the presumption that our paradigm is of general applicability—in this instance that one outcome will be a desired degree of political stability in the long run.

What we *can* conclude, with some assurance, is what we set out to contend, that development policies do have political implications as deserving of study by planners as economic or social implications.

NOTES

1. Political compatibility with plans is a recurring theme that may be found in such writings as Hirschman (1963), Robock (1963), Friedmann (1966 and 1965), Shafer (1966), Daland (1967), and Levy (1968).

2. Compare the discussion of this by Pye (1965).

3. The democratic concept of political development is discussed in Lipset (1959).

4. This view of political development is developed by Cutright (1963).

5. This subject is discussed with reference to Latin America in Rabinovitz (1967: 11-22).

6. On the general point, see also Sherwood (1967: 17-21), Hoselitz (1960: 161), and Dorselaer and Gregory (1962: 21-22).

7. The two terms will be used interchangeably here. A distinction is made by those who prefer to regard the people between the politicized elite and the nonparticipant mass as a single class with important common characteristics, as compared to those who prefer to stress the lack of homogeneity among the people in the middle.

8. Di Tella (1965 and 1964) illustrates this process of political alliance and resulting political movements in Latin America.

9. See Germani and Silvert (1961: 71), Di Tella (1964), and particularly on Cuba, Goldenberg (1965: part 2).

10. Sherwood (1967: 22-30) discusses this problem with respect to Brazil.

11. This has been suggested by Klapp and Padgett (1960). Sherwood (1967) has suggested the same thing as a major theme. See also Steiner (1965: 468-470) and Maddick (1963: 24, 54, and 225).

12. Sherwood (1967: 25) reports that in Brazil the giant cities of Rio de Janeiro and São Paulo participate electorally above the level expected, based on their registered electors, and that the same is true of the political capitals of the states.

13. These findings appear in Rabinovitz (1967: 42).

14. For one exception to this assumption, see Anderson (1964). This is not intended as a subtle discussion of the relation between stability and change, which is of intrinsic interest on its own account. To pursue the matter we would inquire about the problems encountered in the conflict between changes toward stability as compared to changes away from stability, as well as in the problems of consensus on ultimate social goals, on which the concept of political stability must necessarily rest. Change in regime may be unstable, while change in the structure of the system itself remains minimal.

15. On the general question of the middle-class urbanite as an integrating force, see Scott (1959: 80-82) and Johnson (1958).

16. Compare Weiner's description (1960: 173-174) of this process in India, where it seems to undercut unionization of the urban workers because of their transient nature and rural ties. The same type of linkage in Mexico is described by Lewis (1952: 39) and is frequently encountered elsewhere in Latin America.

17. See Scott (1959: 47-53) and, for a comparison of Brazil and the U.S. in this regard, see Sherwood (1967: 72-73). In Brazil, urban politics is a key stop on the road to higher office but this is not the predominant pattern in the United States.

18. A scrap of evidence from India (Saikia, 1963) shows that as a population becomes more heterogeneous it also becomes more achievement oriented.

19. See Friedmann and Lackington (1967: especially 29). The Chilean institutional expression of this effect is the Christian Democratic Party. See also Johnson (1964).

20. Eisenstadt (1966) develops the idea of center and periphery in considerable detail.

21. See Tinker (1954: 334-335), Sherwood (1967: 163), and Hicks (1961: 1-9). It should be noted, however, that some writers (Dotson and Dotson, 1956: 49; Isomura, 1958; Lewis, 1958; Maddick, 1963) view decentralization as the *effect* of economic development.

22. See Almond and Verba (1963: 102). In the case of Mexico, Padgett (1966: 8-9, 46) attributes this national "pride" to the nationalistic subject matter of the educational system's historical approach.

23. See the thorough investigation of the concept of "politically modern man" in Sherrill (1967).

24. Alford and Scoble (1969) have pioneered in this research area in their study of mobilization and bureaucratization in cities of the United States. It should be noted that considerable progress has been made in studies of "institution-building" of the processes of adaptive capacity. These studies, however, are case studies of particular institutions rather than political systems or urban subsystems. Nevertheless, their findings are suggestive.

25. No effort has been made to consider whether the paradigm presented here does or does not conform with sound economic theory. Just as economists are prone to exclude political constraints from their theory, we here exclude economic theory. The first assumption of the paradigm is that the three rates must be kept tied together, and this sounds like notions of balanced economic growth. However, the writer believes that "unbalanced" economic growth (Hirschman et al.) fits more appropriately with political constraints than the balanced theories, and that the present paradigm is more consistent with the "unbalanced" economic theories than the balanced ones. This matter would be worth exploring at the point at which the paradigm might be supported with more empirical data than presently exists.

26. Many other writers (Pierson and Gil, 1957; Gomez, 1961; Stokes, 1967) refer to this centralization of power in the presidency. For a more specific example see Payne (1965).

27. "Here strong centralization appears to be not only a symptom of under-development, but also perhaps an essential precondition for starting local developmental processes" (Riggs, 1960: 390).

REFERENCES

ALFORD, ROBERT R. and HARRY M. SCOBLE (1969) Bureaucracy and Participation: Political Cultures in Four Wisconsin Cities. Chicago: Rand McNally.

ALMOND, GABRIEL and SIDNEY VERBA (1963) The Civic Culture: Political Attitudes and Democracy in Five Nations. Princeton: Princeton Univ. Press.

ANDERSON, CHARLES W. (1964) "Toward a theory of Latin American politics." Nashville: Vanderbilt Univ., Graduate Center for Latin American Studies (Occasional Paper No. 2).

APTER, DAVID E. (1965) The Politics of Modernization. Chicago: Univ. of Chicago Press.

CUTRIGHT, PHILLIPS (1963) "National political development." Pp. 569-582 in Nelson Polsby et al., Politics and Social Life. Boston: Houghton Mifflin.

DALAND, ROBERT T. (1967) Brazilian Planning: Development Politics and Administration. Chapel Hill: Univ. of North Carolina Press.

DE MELLO, DIOGO LORDELLO (1961) "A descentralizaçao administrativa é á realidade municipal brasileria." Revista Brasileira de Estudios Políticos 11 (June): 109-130.

DI TELLA, TORCUATO (1965) "Populism and reform in Latin America." Pp. 47-74 in Claudio Veliz (ed.) Obstacles to Change in Latin America. New York: Oxford Univ. Press.

——— (1964) "Monolithic ideologies in competitive party system: the Latin American case." Pp. 181-190 in vol. 3 of Transactions of the Fifth World Congress of Sociology. Belgium: International Sociological Assn.

DONALD, CARR L. (1960) "Brazilian local self-government: myth or reality?" Western Political Quarterly 13 (December): 1043-1055.

DORSELAER, JAIME and ALFONSO GREGORY (1962) La Urbanización en América Latina. Bogotá: Feres.

DOTSON, FLOYD and LILLIAN OTA DOTSON (1956) "Urban centralization and decentralization in Mexico." Rural Sociology 21 (March).

EISENSTADT, S. N. (1966) Modernization: Protest and Change. Englewood Cliffs, N.J.: Prentice-Hall.

FRIED, ROBERT C. (1967) "Urbanization and Italian politics." Journal of Politics 29 (August): 505-534.

FRIEDMANN, JOHN (1968) "The strategy of deliberate urbanization." Journal of the American Institute of Planners 34 (November).

——— (1966) Regional Development Strategy: A Case Study of Venezuela. Cambridge, Mass.: MIT Press.

——— (1965) Venezuela: From Doctrine to Dialogue. Syracuse: Syracuse Univ. Press.

——— and THOMAS LACKINGTON (1967) "Hyperurbanization and national development in Chile: some hypotheses." Urban Affairs Quarterly 2 (June): 3-29.

FURTADO, CELSO (1965) "Political obstacles to economic growth in Brazil." In Claudio Veliz (ed.) Obstacles to Change in Latin America. New York: Oxford Univ. Press.

GERMANI, GINO and KALMAN SILVERT (1961) "Politics, social structure and military intervention in Latin America." Archives Européenes de Sociologie, no. 1.

GOLDENBERG, BORIS (1965) The Cuban Revolution and Latin America. New York: Frederick A. Praeger.

GOLDRICH, DANIEL et al. (1967) "The political integration of lower-class urban settlements in Chile and Peru." St. Louis: Washington Univ., Social Science Institute.

GOMEZ, ROSENDO A. (1961) "Latin American executives: essence and variations." Journal of Inter-American Studies 3 (January): 81-96.

GUYOT, JAMES (1968) Creeping Urbanism and Political Development in Malaysia. Bloomington, Ill.: Comparative Administration Group.

HALPERN, MANFRED (1965) "The rate and costs of political development." The Annals 308 (March).

HANNA, WILLIAM JOHN and JUDITH LYNNE HANNA (1967) "The political structure of urban-centered African communities." Pp. 154-174 in Horace Miner (ed.) The City in Modern Africa. London: Pall Mall Press.

HAUSER, PHILIP M. [ed.] (1961) Urbanization in Latin America. New York: UNESCO.

HICKS, URSULA (1961) Development from Below. Oxford: Clarendon Press.

HIRSCHMAN, ALBERT (1963) Journeys Toward Progress. New York: Twentieth Century Fund.

HOROWITZ, IRVING (1967) "Electoral politics, urbanization, and social development in Latin America." Urban Affairs Quarterly 2 (March).

HOSELITZ, BERT F. (1960) Sociological Aspects of Economic Growth. Glencoe, Ill.: Free Press.

ISOMURA, EIICHI (1958) "The problem of the city in Japan." Confluence 7 (Summer): 153-155.

JOHNSON, JOHN (1958) Political Change in Latin America: The Emergence of the Middle Sectors. Stanford: Stanford Univ. Press.

JOHNSON, KENNETH F. (1964) "Causal factors in Latin American political instability." Western Political Quarterly 17 (June): 432-436.

KAHL, JOSEPH A. (1965) "Social stratification in metropoli and provinces: Brazil and Mexico." América Latina 8 (January-March).

KLAPP, ORRIN E. and L. VINCENT PADGETT (1960) "Power structure and decision-making in a Mexican border city." American Journal of Sociology 65 (January): 400-406.

LEEDS, ANTHONY (1964) "Brazilian careers and social structure: an evolutionary model and case history." American Anthropologist 66 (December): 1321-1346.

LERNER, DANIEL (1958) The Passing of Traditional Society. Glencoe, Ill.: Free Press.

LEVY, FRED D., JR. (1968) Economic Planning in Venezuela. New York: Frederick A. Praeger.

LEWIS, A. B. (1958) "Local self-government: a key to national economic development and political stability." Philippine Journal of Public Administration 2 (no. 1): 54-57.

LEWIS, OSCAR (1952) "Urbanization without breakdown: a case study." Scientific Monthly (July).

LIPSET, SEYMOUR M. (1959) "Some social requisites of democracy." American Political Science Review 53 (March): 69-105.

MADDICK, HENRY (1963) Democracy, Decentralization, and Development. London: Asia.

ORGANSKI, A. F. K. (1965) The Stages of Political Development. New York: Alfred A. Knopf.

PADGETT, L. VINCENT (1966) The Mexican Political System. Boston: Houghton Mifflin.

PAYNE, JAMES L. (1965) Labor and Politics in Peru. New Haven: Yale Univ. Press.

PIERSON, WILLIAM and FREDERICO GIL (1957) Governments of Latin America. New York: McGraw-Hill.

PYE, LUCIAN W. (1965) "The concept of political development." The Annals 358 (March): 1-13.

––– (n.d.) "The political implications of urbanization and the development process: social problems of development and urbanization." In vol. 7 of Science, Technology and Development. Washington, D.C.: Government Printing Office.

RABINOVITZ, FRANCINE (1968) "Sound and fury signifying nothing?" Urban Affairs Quarterly 3 (March).

––– (1967) Urban Development and Political Development in Latin America. (Occasional Paper) Bloomington, Ill.: Comparative Administration Group.

RIGGS, FRED W. (1960) "Circular causation in development and local government: the Philippines as a test case." Economic Development and Cultural Change 8 (July).

RIOS, JOSE ARTHUR (1960) "El pueblo y el político." Política 6 (February): 12-36.

ROBOCK, STEFAN H. (1963) Brazil's Developing Northeast: A Study of Regional Planning and Foreign Aid. Washington, D.C.: Brookings Institution.

SAIKIA, P. D. (1963) "Village leadership in north-east India." Man in India 43 (April-June): 92-99.

SCOTT, ROBERT (1959) Mexican Government in Transition. Urbana: Univ. of Illinois Press.

SHAFER, ROBERT J. (1966) Mexico: Mutual Adjustment Planning. Syracuse: Syracuse Univ. Press.

SHERILL, KENNETH S. (1967) Political Modernization and the United States. Ph.D. dissertation, Univ. of North Carolina.

SHERWOOD, FRANK (1967) Institutionalizing the Grass Roots in Brazil: A Study in Comparative Local Government. San Francisco: Chandler.

SHILS, EDWARD (1964) Political Development in the New States. New York: Humanities Press.

SILVERT, KALMAN H. (1963) "National values, development, and leaders and followers." International Social Science Journal, no. 4: 560-570.

SOLARI, ALDO (1965) "Impacto político de las diferencias internas de los países en los grados e indicios de modernización y desarrollo económico." América Latina 7 (January-March): 5-22.

STEINER, KURT (1965) Local Government in Japan. Stanford: Stanford Univ. Press.

STOKES, WILLIAM S. (1967) "Latin American federalism." Pp. 158-173 in Peter G. Snow (ed.) Government and Politics in Latin America. New York: Holt, Rinehart & Winston.

TANNENBAUM, FRANK (1960) "The political dilemma in Latin America." Foreign Affairs 38 (April): 497-515.

TINKER, HUGH (1954) The Foundations of Local Self-Government in India, Pakistan, and Burma. London: Atherton Press.

VIEIRA, PAULO REIS (1967) Toward a Theory of Decentralization: A Comparative View of Forty-Five Countries. Ph.D. dissertation, Univ. of Southern California.

WEINER, MYRON (1960) "The politics of South Asia." In Gabriel Almond and James Coleman (eds.) The Politics of Developing Areas. Princeton: Princeton Univ. Press.

Participants' Comments

José A. Silva Michelena

There appear to be two important defects in the model presented by Daland. The first is that communication and, especially, education have effects that are not immediate. We have found that approximately ten years are necessary before education can produce significant changes in the level of modernization of the population. Only after having received ten years of education have people begun to manifest some of the characteristics associated with being more or less modern. Now that means, of course, that the education that is being given does not serve well and that it is necessary to change it qualitatively. The problem, therefore, is not to provide more education but the question of what type of education to provide. An alternative, for example, that society itself has come up with is political participation. This is partially true because people like the *campesinos,* who have an average of one year of education, or union members, who have an average of three years, have been found to have developed more modern attitudes through political participation than executives of manufacturing firms who have had between seven and ten years of education.

The other criticism is that the model (Figure 7.2), which appears to be the final product that Daland presents us of a pluralistic, adaptable, participant, and stable policy (produced by an informed, hetereogeneous, and specialized population), brings more and not less conflict. This conclusion appears to be plausible in that the growth of the middle class, as he calls it at times, also brings more and not less tension in Latin America. Therefore it is necessary to insist that the problems of political development in Latin America should lead to the planning of alternative political systems and not to the inside changing of the actual political system, as one may conclude from the proposal set forth by Daland.

Gideon Sjoberg

One problem implicit in Daland's paper—i.e. the relationship between education and political development—deserves attention. If we are to understand and analyze political development, we should distinguish between two types of education: (1) that which stresses the transmission of established knowledge, values, and beliefs in the realm of politics, economics, or whatever; and (2) that which emphasizes resocialization and the remaking of people's attitudes, values, and normative system.

The distinction I have drawn seems to be especially important if we are to understand the rapid social change which has taken place in at least some of the developing nations. For it is difficult, if not impossible, to remake men's world views and action patterns within the context of formal—notably highly bureaucratized—structures. Jerome Frank, for one, has noted the similarities in structure among religious sects, political cadres, and therapeutic groups—all of which emphasize the resocialization process rather than the transmission of traditional wisdom.

Therapeutic-like groups facilitate the rapid resocialization of the participants for a number of reasons. Within these, it is possible for persons to expose their attitudes and values and to subject these to self-criticism and to the criticism of others. The criticism process is facilitated by the deemphasis upon status barriers among the participants. And we should recognize that this criticism is a necessary step in the resocialization process inasmuch as it destroys faith and legitimacy in the traditional patterns and makes it possible for persons to adopt new values and modes of conduct. Moreover, these kinds of groups also provide their members with the social reinforcement which is necessary if new value and action patterns are to be sustained. Overall, then, this type of educational system differs markedly from the more widely understood form—in both structure and function—and plays a critical role in building a bridge between modes of conduct in traditional orders and participation in the emerging industrial-urban system.

Part V

Metropolitan Policy for Squatter Settlements

Three Proposals Regarding Accelerated Urbanization Problems in Metropolitan Areas

The Lima Case

EDITOR'S INTRODUCTION

Until recently the social nature of the Latin American rural peasant was conceptualized in simplistic terms as a neutral ingredient in the culture. While still living in the isolated rural areas, the agricultural people were pictured as resisting development in all forms, as having an invariant life style as methodical as the severe climates and topography from which they made their living, and as having energies toward purposive change that could be unleashed only explosively by the likes of a Che Guevarra. The image followed closely the perspective of Oswald Spengler, perhaps an understandable view on the part of aggressive urban people during a time of rapid urbanization. When emigrating to the city the peasants were seen as undergoing devastating trauma upon collision with the cosmopolitan life style and complex economy of such a different world.

269

Carlos Delgado's paper is a contribution to the current efforts of the social sciences to replace this unsatisfactory, perilous, simplistic image with a more adequate portrait of the varied conditions of low income Latin American urban and rural dwellers and the kinds of positive initiatives they display. The effort is an exciting one because it is revealing important development dynamics in these long-misunderstood populations. It is a crucially important one because policies that do not take advantage of these dynamics are destined only to fail.

Recent studies in the rural areas have suggested the existence of interesting capacities for initiative in bettering the quality of rural life (see, for example, Doughty, 1968, and Whyte, 1969). With respect to the urban areas, there has been even more activity toward dispelling the old myths. It has been assumed that rural immigrants were very dissatisfied and that the only constructive policies were those that would help them improve their lot in the countryside, but recent surveys have disclosed that they often consider themselves much better off in the city, and that, indeed, they are. It was assumed that at least they went through a period of intense dissatisfaction, but surveys have suggested that the most recent immigrants are in some cases the most satisfied. It was assumed that they were unable to get jobs, but apparently some do get them and display a good measure of social mobility by them (Herrick, 1966: 94-95). It was assumed that they suffer high levels of mental illness and other disturbances, but studies have not revealed these in expected proportions (Mangin and Cohen, 1965). Finally, it was assumed that they were at the base of radical movements reflecting, thereby, their desperation, but the evidence on this point is very mixed (as a good compendium on this and related points, see Nelson, 1969).

As a logical consequence of these earlier attitudes toward the urban life of rural immigrants, the pervasive squatter settlements of the large Latin American cities were considered uniformly malignant environments toward which public policy could only aim construc-tively by planning their eradication and replacement. Then a series of studies, led especially by John Turner and William Mangin, began to perceive powerful dynamic impulses within these communities. It was discovered that in many cases the squatter community provided a constructive solution to the housing problem which was not approached in any sense by public policy, notwithstanding the small investment in solutions. They found, further, that these communities in some cases had the capacity for development into reasonably satisfactory living environments by any standard, and that by providing the opportunity for the inhabitants to add elements one by one to their environment, as their means permitted, the squatter communities offered a usefully flexible pattern of development both in social and physical terms.

This leaves a key problem to be solved by social science methods as a crucial basis for public policy. Which are the squatter communities that should be aided by public policy on the basis of their capacity for constructive development, and which are those which are moribund for social and/or physical reasons such that an entirely different policy orientation must be taken? In this paper, Delgado makes an effort to unravel the complex social and physical circumstances that characterize squatter settlements in Lima, one by one, in order to develop a typology of squatter settlements, a basic need in this important task.

R.G.

REFERENCES

DOUGHTY, PAUL (1968) Huaylas: An Andean District in Search of Progress. Ithaca, N.Y.: Cornell Univ. Press.
HERRICK, BRUCE (1966) Urban Migration and Economic Development in Chile. Cambridge, Mass.: MIT Press.
MANGIN, WILLIAM and JEROME COHEN (1965) "Culture and psychological characteristics of mountain migrants to Lima." Sociologus 14, 1: 81-88.
NELSON, JOAN M. (1969) "Migrants, urban poverty, and instability in developing nations." Occasional Papers on International Affairs 22. Cambridge, Mass.: Harvard Univ. Press.
WHYTE, WILLIAM F. (1969) "Rural Peru—peasants as activists," Trans-action 7 (November): 37-56.

Three Proposals Regarding Accelerated Urbanization Problems in Metropolitan Areas

The Lima Case

CARLOS DELGADO

Theoretical aspects of urbanization in general are not discussed in this essay, nor does the essay offer a theory of urbanization. Rather, two important characteristics of metropolitan underdevelopment are analyzed, and a descriptive scheme is proposed, which includes these characteristics as parts of the same phenomenon.

The first of these two problems concerns the misnamed "marginal settlements," or *barrios marginales*. This study rejects the traditional method of viewing these settlements and the terminology which has been used to qualify and describe them. They are treated here as urban phenomena that are highly heterogeneous and that have marked differences among themselves as far as their possibilities for development are concerned, as phenomena inherent to an accelerated process of urbanization, as positive ingredients in the development of cities, as factors inseparable from other expressions of metropolitan underdevelopment and the process of internal national migratory currents, and, finally, as elements of foremost significance with reference to future policies for metropolitan development. The discussion of the barrios marginales ends with the presentation of an operational typology of underdeveloped urban settlements. The typology establishes the different positions of the various kinds of marginal settlements on an axis of urban underdevelopment-development, and recognizes the gradation in intensity of concrete problems. Thus the typology suggests an order of priorities that can be used as a guide for differentially conceived urban development policies and programs taking into consideration fundamental differences that, then, could in fact, clearly separate the diverse types of underdeveloped settlements.

The typology is primarily based on the use of criteria of density, center-periphery location, and state or urban development in terms of consolidation, both of area and dwellings. These are not, as one could assume, purely spatial or "urbanistic" criteria. On the contrary, they are criteria which strongly reflect social characteristics. Density, for example, in measuring population concentration, consequently is a concept that is clearly social in nature. Center-periphery location reveals the problem of accessibility which, in its broadest sense, is also a social issue. Finally, the consolidation of area and dwellings has diverse and important social implications.

The lack of social research as such in Lima makes it impossible, for the time being, to have use of more specifically social information for analytical purposes. This situation will prevail until the results of a comparative social investigation now in progress in the underdeveloped districts of the Peruvian capital are known. This investigation is being completed by the Office of Metropolitan Development Plan, based on the typology presented in this essay.

The second topic of concern is the slum problem, which is understood here as overcrowding in insubstantial housing. Slums, or *tugurios*, as they are called in Peru, are the greatest single social problem in the urbanization process. This characterizes various types of settlements mentioned in the typology, but they are mostly found in old and deteriorated zones in the central urban nucleus. In spite of the crucial importance of this problem, very little is known about it, and its treatment in literature has been sporadic and superficial. It has by no means been considered the main characteristic of urban underdevelopment, nor has there been an attempt to explain its origin, which might establish a basis for devising preventive measures against its growth in the future. With this objective in mind, this essay proposes a hypothesis aimed an an explanation of the existence and growth of slums. The hypothesis may be useful as a guide for the work of urban planners who are interested in solving the problem of overcrowding in large areas of the metropolitan center and periphery.

Finally, based on a consideration of slums and marginal settlements as phenomena that are inseparable within the same problem, this essay proposes an overall scheme of urban underdevelopment which will allow for focusing on these phenomena as a unit; until now they have been treated as separate and independent subjects. This scheme will permit a wider and more coherent vision of metropolitan underdevelopment and render it easier to interpret as a whole.

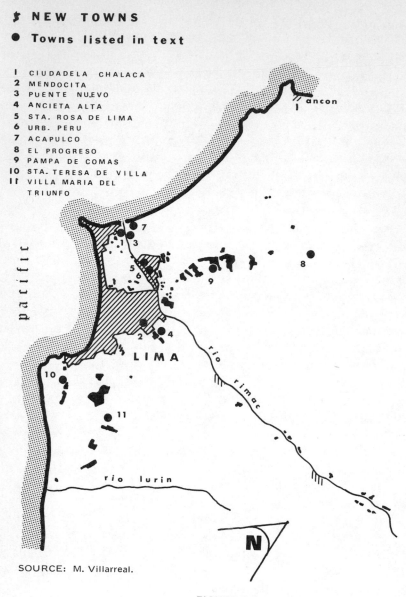

𝄢 NEW TOWNS

● Towns listed in text

1   CIUDADELA   CHALACA
2   MENDOCITA
3   PUENTE   NUEVO
4   ANCIETA   ALTA
5   STA. ROSA DE LIMA
6   URB. PERU
7   ACAPULCO
8   EL PROGRESO
9   PAMPA DE COMAS
10 STA. TERESA DE VILLA
11 VILLA MARIA DEL
    TRIUNFO

SOURCE: M. Villarreal.

FIGURE 8.1
"New Towns" (Towns in Formation) in Metropolitan Lima

General Considerations

The principal purpose of this essay is to suggest criteria of a descriptive and analytical nature which will permit the beginning of a systematic ordering of certain problems derived from the accelerated rhythm of urbanization problems that one can observe in metropolitan centers such as Lima. While it is not theoretical, it is intended to supply certain empirical facts around which theories may be formulated with greater scientific rigor. The essay is entirely based on investigations made in one metropolitan center, Lima, but it could have wider application in other Latin American metropolitan areas.

The urban growth of metropolitan Lima has been surprising, although it is not exceptional in Latin America. Between 1940 and 1961 the capital of Peru nearly tripled in population,[1] and current 1980 projections for metropolitan Lima point to a population of 5,800,000 (Oficina Nacional de Planeamiento y Urbanismo, 1967: 161). This will mean a concentration of nearly 33 percent of the total population of Peru within the geographic area of the national metropolis. This process of accentuated demographic growth generates varied and intense problems that bring into sharper focus the disequilibrium between Lima and the rest of the nation and the matter of what Lima has meant and what it now means within the entire Peruvian culture. Throughout Peru's republican history the process of preferential differentiation has increased between the coast and the interior, on one hand, and between urban and rural zones[2] on the other. The resulting disequilibrium assumes greater intensity when one passes from the coast to the Andean zone, and from the cities to the country, reaching its maximum intensity in the rural interior areas.[3]

Within the context of this internal national imbalance Lima has always occupied a privileged position, not without being subject to a crucial ambivalence—on one hand, its dominating position with respect to the interior and, on the other hand, the position of dependency and subordination with respect to the "international system."

In recent decades the duality of these roles appears to have increased, and Lima is, more than ever, the center of the economic, financial, administrative, political, social, and cultural life of the country.[4]

This phenomenon of growing concentration in all aspects of national power in Lima has been accompanied by a rapid increase in the metropolitan population. This latter, however, should be seen within the context of significant changes from the traditional composition of the Peruvian population; between 1940 and 1961, for example, the urban population in Peru increased from 35.4 to 47.4 percent according to the census definitions of urban.[5]

The urban expansion of Lima, consequently, must be seen within the framework of alterations in the nature of the country's urban-rural demographic composition, the continuing concentration of vital national functions in Lima, and the marked duality of the role that Lima performs as a metropolitan center—dominant internally and dependent externally.

Beyond the brief introduction to structural changes underway in the contemporary Peruvian society, a more detailed analysis falls outside the narrower range of this essay.

Metropolitan Expansion and the "Marginal Settlements" (Barriadas)

The demographic increase of the metropolitan area during the last few years derives fundamentally from the impact of national internal migratory currents that have converged progressively and with increasing intensity on Peru's capital city. Lima has had an increase in population and an expansion in its urban perimenter basically as a result of inmigration that has increased without interruption during the last twenty-five years.[6] The marginal settlements have arisen in partial response to this inmigration.

In general, there are two noticeable currents of opinion which may be observed with respect to problems related to the marginal settlements, or barriadas. One, surely the less sophisticated, the most traditional, and possibly the most generalized, considers these residential settlements, implicitly and explicitly, as a sort of eradicable social cancer. The same current of opinion also considers that these barriadas constitute a phenomenon lacking social dynamics or any significant relationship to the process of global urban development. The other current of opinion tends to consider them as positive factors of urban growth and as essential aspects of ecological-social transformations that take place in metropolitan centers such as Lima and in countries such as Peru. The writings of William Mangin and John Turner belong to this tendency (see especially Mangin, 1967; also Turner, 1967, 1966a, 1966b, 1966c; and Turner and Goethe).

Briefly, the barriadas may be characterized as follows:

(1) The phenomenon of the *barriada* forms part of the accelerated urbanization process that Peru has been experiencing for approximately two decades.

(2) This process is making a significant contribution to changes in the image and nature of the traditional Peruvian society.

(3) As a consequence, the *barriada* phenomenon may be viewed as a significant element of processes that are related to internal changes in the contemporary society of Peru.

(4) The rapidly expanded cities, largely a result of *barriada* growth, constitute ecological environments within which a profound process of resocialization takes place. This process affects a considerable number of people who are experiencing urban and metropolitan life for the first time.

(5) Like all historical processes of great significance, that of rapid urbanization on a national scale constitutes an irreversible process. For this reason, the phenomenon of the *barriada*—which constitutes the main part of this urbanization process—must be considered as a new and perhaps permanent feature of the social life of the urban population in Peru today.

(6) The aforementioned involves accepting the fact that the *barriadas*, as a social phenomenon, will not disappear rapidly from the urban scene in Peru. Consequently, the acceptance of this fact has to be a principal part of any focus that is given to the country's urban social problems.

(7) The *barriadas* account for a large part of the urban growth of the metropolitan area and for the increase in size of Peruvian cities in general. With reference to the case of the Lima metropolitan area, approximately 25 percent of the population inhabits the barriadas.[7] Approximately 100,000 dwellings have been built, primarily through the effort of the settlers and without economic or technical assistance from the nation. It should be stressed that the input from the settlers of the *barriadas* towards solving the housing problem has been comparatively much greater than the organized input provided by society through the government.[8]

(8) As a consequence, far from being a kind of eradicable social cancer, the *barriadas* are a positive force in the urbanization process and a more or less permanent ingredient of Peru's new social reality. It is considered here, therefore, that the *barriadas* represent an element of great potential significance in Peru's urban development.

(9) The existence of *barriadas* is intimately linked with other equally inevitable social phenomena reflected in the migratory currents which contribute decisively to the growth of Peruvian cities. The displacement from the country to the city, and from the suburban and semiurban centers to the actual urban nucleus, will almost inevitably continue in the future. These migrations constitute a principal factor in the process of accelerated urbanization through which the country is now passing and though which it will undoubtedly continue to pass in the future. Urbanization, migration, and *barriadas* thus represent, in fact, inevitable social phenomena within the general change orocess which Peru is currently experiencing. Consequently, if the urbanization process cannot be stopped and migration cannot be prevented, the *barriadas* cannot be eradicated.

(10) Therefore, if the *barriadas* are an inevitable part of an urbanization process that cannot be avoided, if the migratory currents that contribute to their formation are also inevitable, if they are an integral part of the global changes of a society that is modernizing, if they are a permanent factor in the new social reality of a Peru that is changing towards new forms of socioeconomic life, and if, finally, they are ineradicable, then a policy of urban development cannot afford to ignore them. Neither can future policies consider them, as has been traditional, a social cancer of the cities. Future policies should be based on the supposition that they are endowed with an appreciable potential for development, which has not yet been used, but which is of crucial importance for facing the difficult problems resulting from the emergence of an increasingly larger urban nucleus.

(11) From what has just been said, we can surmise that the social problem of the *barriadas* should be focused in such a way as to recognize two perspectives of analysis and programming. The first one refers to the underdeveloped settlements that currently exist, while the second refers to the need of a future-oriented policy aimed at guiding and channeling the creation of future marginal settlements within the metropolitan area. Any scheme of action with regard to the *barriadas* should consider this important dual perspective.

(12) In the underdeveloped settlements, social investigation and possible programs related to urban development must begin by establishing a valid typology of the marginal settlement phenomenon that is capable of regulating, from the point of view of urban development, the great variety of settlements that form part of the social universe of the *barriadas*; in

effect, they are far from being homogeneous and are characterized by great morphological complexities with a wide range of differential possibilities for development.

A global perspective of this type raises the question of whether the terminology used up to now for focusing on the problem of the *barrios marginales* is adequate for analysis and description. The principal objections to the traditional terminology and to the concepts that it implies are the following: (1) The qualification of a residential area as barriada inevitably carries the implications of inferiority. This inevitable derogatory conceptualization predetermines negative psychosocial implications that influence the attitudes of those who view the marginal settlements from the outside as well as of the inhabitants themselves. (2) Under the name of barriadas or barrios marginales, residential areas of very different natures and that they constitute an ecological and social universe of great disparity have been included. This means that the generic vocabulary used previously is totally inadequate for classifying and describing a reality which is basically heterogeneous. (3) The reduction of a fundamentally heterogeneous situation to an inaccurate homogeneous concept makes it impossible to obtain a realistic view of the problem and to identify, in terms of a policy of urban development, the different stages of evolution among the marginal areas with their accompanying differences in characteristics and potential for advancement.

The first task is essentially that of recognizing the multiple urban differences alluded to by the term barriada. As this has not been considered in the past, the problem of definition, essential in all scientific planning, has virtually ended in a dead-end street. Descriptive definitions have tried to incorporate the formal characteristics that all the manifestations of the phenomenon are seen to show, the things that all these manifestations seem to have in common.[9] This kind of definition is that used by Turner (1966a) who classifies this urban penomenon as "nonregulated settlement." Some Peruvian city planners define barriadas as the "urban developments produced on the urban periphery, or within defined urban limits, and which have as their common characteristics physical and legal disorder, and insubstantial construction" (Oficina de Planificacion, 1967: 4).

These generic definitions necessarily consider only some of the central characteristics which are apparently most universal and are not, therefore, sufficient.[10] They do not permit a differentiation of various important types among barriadas. Furthermore, neither nonregulation, physical and legal disorder, nor insubstantial construction are, strictly speaking, actually universal among them. The only thing actually universal to the barriadas is their participation, to a greater or lesser degree, in the global context of urban underdevelopment. Consequently, it is impossible within the pretense of universal validity to go further than considering these residential settlements as underdeveloped urban formations, some of which are in the act of advancement within the dynamic process of metropolitan creation. Through this method of viewing the barriada, the inevitable limitation of former definitions can be more easily overcome. One may also use this concept of the barriada as dynamic process as an instrument of classification suitable to applied development policies.

Operational Typology

We now propose an operational typology that reflects the different locations of the settlements along an axis of urban underdevelopment-development.[12] As a result, the typology attempts to serve a specific objective: orientation in the design of urban development policies. Its usefulness can only be evaluated in relation to the ends it intends to serve. In consequence, the operational typology does not pretend to have universal or permanent application. On the contrary, it is classifying instrument that can be modified—always subject to the distribution adjustments that derive from the rapidity or slowness with which the different urban settlements are capable of altering their own status within the classification scale.

The operational typology includes eight categories and has been basically created by utilizing the following criteria: density, location in terms of the center-periphery spatial relation, and stage or urban development in terms of consolidation. The interrelation of these fundamental criteria determines the location of the different settlements in the typological scale, and this scale, in reflecting the differential levels of urban development, demonstrates an order or priorities that could assist in guiding concrete policies of urban development for these types of residential communities.

Furthermore, accepting the prior implications for the term *barriada*, the proposed typology reserves this term for the residential areas that can be considered as actually decadent or regressive settlements within the urban context.[13]

The proposed typology is the following:[14]

(1) High-Density Internal *Barriadas* (Slums)

(2) High-Density Peripheral *Barriadas* (Slums)

(3) Internal Settlements in Incipient Consolidation

(4) Internal Settlements in Advanced Consolidation

(5) Recent Peripheral Settlements

(6) Peripheral Settlements in Incipient Consolidation

(7) Peripheral Settlements in Advanced Consolidation

(8) Peripheral Settlements in Rural Areas

Categories (1) and (2) consist of the Internal and Peripheral *Barriadas* (Slums), meaning those where the phenomenon of over-crowding in unsafe dwellings is found in an intense and predominant form. The High-Density Internal *Barriadas* (Slums) are found in many districts of the metropolitan area and, in general, correspond to those vaguely referred to in the classification, according to geographical groups adopted by the Junta Nacional de la Vivienda, as "Others in Metropolitan Lima." This classification deals with residential formations encrusted as true enclaves of underdevelopment inside the urban context, generally characterized by mani-festations of decadence.

Their dimensions and population vary considerably, but in all cases the densities fluctuate between 500 and 2,000 inhabitants per hectare. The dwellings, very small, are of perishable materials (wood, tin, cardboard, sometimes adobe) and, with some outstanding exceptions, are distributed along canyons and narrow passages or pedestrian trails in chaotic elements that cross through larger settlements in different directions. The degree of congestion is impressive; the absence of hygienic services is generalized; the hygienic conditions are extremely precarious; the organization of the inhabitants with respect to local centers is very weak or nonexistent; tenancy is by rent and, more frequently, by illegal possession; localization is next to working centers and nuclear zones within the urban area; and the possibilities of local development are virtually nil. Typical cases of Internal Slums in Lima are, for example, Huerta Perdida and Chacra Rĭos (in El Cercado), Concentración Ruggia and Ciudadela Chalaca (in Callao), Leoncio Prado and Jardĭn Britania (in Rĭmac), Mendocita and San Cosme (in La Victoria), and so forth. Actually about sixty Internal Slums exist in metropolitan Lima, and they represent approximately 15 percent of the total population of the underdeveloped settlements referred to by the operational typology.

The High-Density Peripheral *Barriadas* (Slums) have, generally speaking, the same characteristics as the High-Density Internal *Barriadas*, but their location is outside the urban zone, they are fewer, and the size of population included is much smaller. Typical cases of this kind of settlement are found, for example, in Puente Nuevo (Callao) and Flor de Amancaes (Rímac). Most of the time the Peripheral Slums are formed by relatively small sections without any precise spatial delimitation within the context of what could be referred to as "towns in formation." One finds them at different points of the metropolitan perimeter where slum development is conditioned by the extreme spatial limitations imposed on housing by topographical conditions of the settlement (e.g., steep slopes of the hills). The inhabitants, furthermore, are migrants from the interior, especially from the *sierra*, who have arrived late in the formation of the settlement, of which the immediate area of the dwellings forms a part. Thus, they occupy, as one might say, the periphery of the periphery. Here, as in the previous case, the possibilities of local development are virtually nil.

Categories (3) and (4) comprise the nonslum urban settlements that are developing within the urban nucleus. In the Internal Settlements in Incipient Consolidation the process of replacement of the dwellings by more substantial ones is found in the initial stages and, in general, is characterized by its slowness. In terms of the urban area, the renewal of these settlements starts after a previous and indispensable clarification of the legal situation of the tenancy. In fact, the replacement of the original and temporary dwelling and the process of consolidation only occur when the legal status of tenancy has been cleared by a grant from the municipal authorities or the Junta de la Vivienda or, at least, a formal promise for the legalization of the occupied property. This period of legalization of tenancy is usually very long in the cases of older settlements and quicker with more recent ones.

In this type of metropolitan settlement the densities tend to remain under 400 inhabitants per hectare, and the transition towards forms of definite urban consolidation is clearly perceptible. The cases of Mirones (in El Cercado), Huascarán (in Rímac), Villa Victoria (in Surquillo), Ancieta Alta (in El Agustino), and Santa Rosa de Lima (in San Martín de Porres) illustrates this group in the Peruvian capital.

The process of replacing temporary dwellings and the transformation of the urban area within the Internal Settlements in Advanced Consolidation is not in its last stages. Density levels consistently tend to remain under 350 inhabitants per hectare, and, consequently, slums due to congestion are nonexistent. Residential planning is manifest throughout by wide streets, although they have not yet been paved, and the establishment of a basic urban infrastructure is generalized. The large settlement known as Urbanización Perú (in San Martín de Porres) is a typical example of this type of metropolitan settlement.

Here, as in categories to which reference will be made later, the degree of consolidation is related to two basic criteria: state of the area in terms of a greater or lesser amount of urban infrastructure of services, and the condition of dwellings in terms of the quality of the material used in their construction. Matting, wood, tin, and the like, are considered perishable materials, while brick, cement, and, to a lesser degree adobe, are considered permanent materials.

Categories (5), (6), and (7) include the urban peripheral settlements that show a type of lineal development (improvement) and can be generically considered "towns in formation," a term which has been established by some of the leaders of the existing local organizations. These settlements, as in the Internal Settlements in Advanced Consolidation, demonstrate a noticeable level of operational sophistication. By Recent Peripheral Settlements, we mean those urban settlements not more than three years old, while Peripheral Settlements in Incipient Consolidation and Peripheral Settlements in Advanced Consolidation can be considered those metropolitan communities in which the consolidation of areas and the replacement of provisional dwellings can aptly be described as, respectively, just initiated or in an advanced stage of development.

A typical case among the Recent Peripheral Settlements is that of Año Nuevo, a peripheral urban formation created by the invasion of family groups at the end of 1967. More than 1,000 families established themselves in provisional shelters during the course of a few weeks on lands that were claimed as the private property of a powerful family of landowners. The formation of Año Nuevo was made easier by the aid and support that the invaders received from municipal authorities belonging to the Comas District and from some political leaders.[15]

There are very few cases which can be cited as examples of Peripheral Settlements in Incipient Consolidation (El Progreso in Carabayllo, or Acapulco in Callao), but the occurrence of these peripheral settlements is generalized in terms of definite settlements currently experiencing consolidation. Finally, the Peripheral Settlements in Advanced Consolidation consist of settlements which have, up to this date, been observed with considerable interest by social scientists and others dedicated to the study of this subject.

Settlements of this kind may be found in districts such as Chorrillos, Comas, and Villa María del Triunfo, that is, in districts located on the perimeter of the metropolitan nucleus in areas of access to main roads, which communicate with the interior of Peru and have large areas of empty terrain with respect to which there are no serious conflicts as far as ownership is concerned.[16] The density in these settlements tends to remain under 300 inhabitants per hectare, and the settlements consist of a total population that easily surpasses 100,000 inhabitants. Typical cases of such peripheral settlements are found, for example, at El Altillo (Rímac), Nueva Esperanza (Villa María del Triunfo), Pampa de Comas (Comas), and Santa Teresa de Villa (Chorrillos).[17]

The so-called towns in formation illustrate a clearly defined development process. They start as residential settlements formed by temporary dwellings, which are built with matting. Afterwards, and based on the distribution of lots, which clearly establishes the property rights of the settlers, a rapid process of replacement of the temporary shelters is initiated. This is entirely financed by local resources. This cycle usually takes from two to eight years. Towards the end of that period, the total morphology of the area goes through a radical change and the settlement acquires the semblance of a stable, striving, and progressive residential area. There is a world of difference, no matter how viewed, between the towns in formation and the slum areas. It is thus obvious that policies with respect to urban development of the marginal settlements have to admit a differential basis in matters of purposes, orientation, and content when they face the problems pertaining to one kind of settlement or another.

Finally, the last typological category must be considered differently from all the others.[18] The Peripheral Settlements in Rural Areas are different by nature from and, in many ways, similar to the small populated centers that appear along the coastal roads in rural areas. Among the few cases of this kind of settlement are El Carmen de Monterrico and Matazango in the Ate district near Lima. These settlements have a peculiar morphology. They have emerged through the lineal juxtaposition of individual dwellings aligned along old farm roads and built on the narrow stretch of land that separates the road from the irrigation ditches. When one becomes familiar with this type of settlement the radical difference between it and any other settlement referred to in the operational typology stands out quite clearly. Despite this distinction, and this goes without saying, these and the other urban formations briefly described here, have all been indiscriminately called "settlements."

Conceived in this manner, the operational typology consists of all the underdeveloped settlements in the metropolitan area, stresses their crucial differences, and permits a classification along the urban underdevelopment-development axis.

It is quite clear that the potential for self-help varies considerably in relation to each one of the categories of residential settlements included in the typology. Under certain favorable conditions, those which have here been called towns in formation go through a process of gradual movement through time with noticeable stages, ranging from an initial insubstantial situation characterized by the rudimentary quality of the dwellings, the minimum amount of urban equipment, and the virtual lack of basic infrastructural services, to a situation in which the differences distinguishing the peripheral developing settlement from the rest of the city tend to disappear, or at least to diminish, in a noticeably significant way.

From another point of view, the elements that stimulate or hinder the aforementioned gradual development through time appear to be related to locations (nearness to centers and levels of access to urban activities), space limitation (topography and possibility of physical expansion), ownership of the land (greater or lesser permanency in the legal uncertainty of the occupied lots), and, perhaps to a lesser degree, the political situation at the time the urban settlement is being founded and during its growth.[19]

The extreme situation of urban underdevelopment is found in those residential areas in which the aforementioned factors operate in a negative fashion, especially with reference to the first three categories. Extreme underdevelopment involves the formation of slum areas, which may be understood as overpopulation in insubstantial dwellings. Slums are not exclusive to those in town areas that have been known as slum areas until now, but also appear among residential areas, which up to now have been described as marginal settlements. Thus, the orderly presentation of marginal settlement characteristics requires a consideration of the slum-growth phenomenon as another feature of urban underdevelopment in metropolitan areas. And it is in relation to this aspect that this essay proposes a "hypothesis of slum growth (*tugurización*)" in order to explain the origin of the phenomenon, which is here considered as the most important social problem in relation to metropolitan underdevelopment. Should the hypothesis prove valid, it would suggest policies to stem the future growth of slums.

Hypothesis of Slum Growth (Tugurización)

It is surprising to find that, in contrast to the relatively abundant literary output in relation to the misnamed barriadas, or marginal settlements, there are very few studies with respect to metropolitan slums (tururios).[20] This is especially surprising when one considers that the preliminary work of the Oficina del Plan de Desarrollo Metropolitano, Lima-Callao, allows us to estimate that the minimum population affected by overpopulation in the slums is in the order of 500,000 persons. (Slums are operationally defined as insubstantial dwellings with high population densities.)

The field studies carried out by the Oficina del Plan de Desarrollo Metropolitano, Lima-Callao, make it possible to establish a first classification of Lima's metropolitan slums. There are five main categories: alley slums, courtyard slums, rooftop slums, subdivided houses, and deteriorated compact urban housing projects.[21] These diverse types of slums have to be located in different parts of the metropolitan area. Subdivided houses, for example, tend to concentrate in the oldest sector of the city, the alley slums in various points of the central urban nucleus, and the courtyard slums, in peripheral areas or in zones which, up until a short time ago, were considered to be far from the urban nucleus. They all have high densities of population.

The lack of interest so far shown in the social significance of life in the Lima slums enables us to know very little about the nature and significance of this phenomenon. But investigations such as that of Rotondo in Lima fully confirm the impression derived from the field of observations: that in the slums the problems of social disorganization, family crisis, criminality, juvenile delinquency, and ill health are greater than in the underdeveloped peripheral settlements. Until we have the results of the comparative investigation started a short time ago by PLANDEMET on the significance of our two basic features of urban underdevelopment within the Lima-Callao area, it is impossible to give a precise idea of the social problems derived from the growth of slums. But what is now known about this phenomenon allows us to assert that, fundamentally, slum growth constitutes the most important social problem related to the conditions of urban underdevelopment.

Among what have been called the barriadas or marginal settlements, and the metropolitan slums (tugurios), there are, in the case of Peru, some important common characteristics. In the first place, it is in both of these types of residential settlements that the largest number of immigrants have settled and continue to settle, especially those of low income. This means that both central elements (barriadas and slums) of metropolitan underdevelopment are intimately related to the phenomenon of migratory currents, a fact which in turn means that the same considerations that lead us to consider the existence of marginal settlements inevitable, and, in a sense, permanent, must also lead us to consider the existence of metropolitan slums inevitable and permanent. In fact, as long as the accelerated demographic increase of a low-income population creates an acute demand for dwellings, the presence of "substandard" residential areas appears to be, to a certain degree, unavoidable due to the lack of a clear social policy on the part of the government.

Secondly, the population that occupies the underdeveloped residential areas belongs to the so-called dominated sectors of the metropolitan society.[22] They are low-income social groups in which underemployed,[23] laborers, and very low-paid employees are characteristics. This population is also composed of social groups whose members have a definite place in what may be referred to as the "range of ethnic color." Practically all the members are mesitzos, Indians, *cholos* (European and Indian), blacks, and mulattos. The "white" population is conspicuously absent in the underdeveloped residential zones.

Thirdly, the precarious conditions of buildings is a generalized factor (but not universal) in both types of urban underdevelopment. But while slum housing is characterized by a virtual absence of possibilities for overcoming given conditions, housing in nonslum settlements, which are in the underdeveloped category established by the operational typology, have the distinct probability of improvement through a definite consolidation in terms of area and type of permanent construction.

From another point of view, the phenomenon of slum growth affects not only the individual slum as such, but also the previously defined type of underdeveloped marginal settlements called High-Density Internal Settlements and High-Density Peripheral Settlements. It was the confirmation that high density is a common characteristic, not only of slums, but also of the High-Density Internal Settlements and High-Density Peripheral Settlements, which led to the necessity of formulating a hypothesis that would permit an explanation of the phenomenon of slum growth. And this hypothesis, first elaborated in order to explain the occurrence of high density in a specific type of underdeveloped settlement, after modifications suggested by field work, was converted into an instrument for interpreting all cases in which slum growth is present as a relevant feature of urban underdevelopment.

As mentioned more briefly before, the social phenomenon related to the formation of slums, understood as overpopulation in precarious dwellings, is mainly due to three central factors:

(1) spatial limitation;

(2) lack of property rights over the land;

(3) proximity to highly diversified working centers that have a great capacity for absorbing unskilled labor, and location in relatively compact zones of the city where there is a mixed and intensive use of labor.

Slum growth appears in places where these three factors converge and does not exist where they are not found.

Spatial limitation refers to the virtual impossibility for the spatial extension of the inhabited area. This can be a result of the encirclement of the slum dwellings by others with equally limited space or because of topographical circumstances.

Nonownership of the land takes one of two forms: the lack of a legal status in the occupation, or occupation by rental. Field studies carried out in Lima confirm fully the crucial aspect of the land ownership factor stressed formerly by Turner (1966a, and Turner and Goethe). There is, in fact, a direct relationship between security to ownership and the process of replacement of temporary dwellings. Concrete cases of developed urban settlements that occupy similar and contiguous areas, and were formed at about the same time, and which inhabited by populations with comparable social and employment level, yet have a different location within the scale of development established by the operational typology, can only be explained if one accepts the fundamental importance of ownership of the land.

A classic example of this situation may be found in three settlements, which are located within a very limited area of the right margin of the Rimac river and are called Castilla Alta, Huascarán, and Castilla Baja. The first of these settlements is a slum of the High-Density Internal Settlement type; the second is an example of the High-Density Internal Settlement that is beginning to consolidate; and the third is a clear case of a High-Density Internal Settlement that is in an advanced stage of consolidation. These three settlements have everything in common except the ownership of the land. Nobody has legal title to property in Castilla Alta. In the case of Huascarán definition of the settler's legal status has begun. In the case of Castilla Baja, the settlers' ownership of land received legal sanction a number of years ago. In the first case the process of replacement of temporary housing and consolidation is nonexistent. In the second case, both processes have been initiated, and in the third, urban consolidation of the area and replacement of temporary housing is now reaching its final stages.

The final factor of proximity to work centers refers to the conditions of accessibility to work in terms of spatial proximity and time, obviously related to the existing type and methods of transport. Viewed differently, the hypothesis qualifies the nature of the work centers whose location and characteristics tend to stimulate the formation of slums. In fact, the work centers related to the phenomenon of slum formation have, in accordance with the hypothesis presented here, the following characteristics:

(a) diversification of their economic functions with a predominance of service activities and jobs related to underemployment;

(b) a high capacity for absorbing generally unskilled manual labor;

(c) location in relatively compact areas within the urban nucleus; and

(d) intensive use of the land.

There are, of course, other features concomitant to the formation of slums, but which do not explain it. For example, factors which refer to the socioeconomic characteristics of the slum population can exist and, in fact, do exist in nonslum areas of the city.

Consequently, the evidence gathered in field investigations appears to show that the formation of slums, as a massive social phenomenon, only presents itself in places where there is a concurrence of the factors indicated in the hypothesis. In fact, we find that all the metropolitan areas in which there exists a noticeable concentration of slums have, as a common characteristic, spatial limitations, nonownership of the land, and poor proximity to work centers, as described in the hypothesis. This is certainly true of the slums belonging to the most populated districts of the metropolitan area, such as El Cercado, Rímac, La Victoria, Surquillo, and Callao. It is also true where there is a concentration of slums in districts of less abundant incidence of the slum formation phenomenon. Furthermore, the conditions set forth in the hypothesis are clearly and unquestionably fulfilled in the case of the High-Density Internal and Peripheral Settlements.

There are, nevertheless, cases which, at first sight, could be taken as an exception to the rule. These are areas in which individual slums have concentrated on the periphery of the metropolitan area bordering on agricultural zones that are being submitted to rapid and intensive conversion to urban uses. Such areas are located in the urban periphery of districts such as Surquillo, Barranco, and Magdalena del Mar, where we find the proliferation of individual slums concentrated within the context of a surprisingly similar urban growth.

These areas have the following common characteristics: (a) recent agricultural use of the land, (b) rural properties that are being subdivided due to inheritance or other reasons, (c) substitution of an agricultural area for residential use by two principal means, both of which are characterized by land speculation: either conversion of extensive zones to urban uses with quality housing (large private companies) or the construction of precarious and high-density dwellings for speculative purposes (alley and courtyard slums), which provide the owners with high incomes and constitute barriers to better organized urban development, and (d) proximity of the slum zone to major interdistrict avenues of easy accessibility (Avenida Panamá which joins Surquillo with Barranco, and Avenida La Paz which joins Magdalena with Callao).

In these cases slums are formed in circumscribed zones as a phenomenon that is due, basically, to speculative activities. On the other hand, easy transportation accessibility places these zones near a number of work centers (markets, factories, workshops, business centers, and the like), many of which are located on the interdistrict avenues that have already been mentioned. It must also be added that the slum areas of Barranco-Surquillo, as well as those at Magdalena de Mar, border on vast urbanized areas representing an important labor market for nonskilled workers who are, in part, absorbed by the construction industry.

The slum growth hypothesis proposed here presents the urban planner with an instrument for interpretative analysis capable of opening up the possibility of avoiding the future formation of slums. If slum formation is determined by the concurrence of the factors indicated by the hypothesis, the urban planner can guide the creation of residential settlements towards areas, and in such ways, that will avoid the conditions that tend to generate slums.

General Scheme of Underdevelopment

If the arguments that have been briefly presented beforehand can be considered valid, there arises the need to establish an overall descriptive focus that would lay the basis for a unitary analysis of the general phenomena of urban underdevelopment in metropolitan areas. That is to say, there arises the need to elaborate a descriptive instrument for the classification of the different aspects of urban underdevelopment. This instrument would be capable of identifying significant gradations along a scale of development and of reflecting degrees of their importance in terms of the seriousness of the problem, both from the point of view of their intrinsic importance and from the point of view of the size of the population affected by such problems. Scheme 1 derived from the acceptance of this fact.

SCHEME 1
General Scheme of Metropolitan Underdevelopment
Based on a Spatial Distribution

Within the Urban Nucleus	Individual Slums	Alley Slums
		Courtyard Slums
		Rooftop Slums
		Subdivided Houses
		Deteriorated Compact Housing Projects[a]
	Internal Slum Areas	High-Density Internal Settlements
		Concentrated Individual Slums
		"Modern" Slums[24]
	Developing Internal Areas	Settlements in Incipient Consolidation
		Settlements in Advanced Consolidation
On the Periphery	Peripheral Slum Areas	High-Density Peripheral Settlements
		Concentrated Individual Slums
	Towns in Formation	Recent Peripheral Settlements
		Peripheral Settlements in Incipient Consolidation
		Peripheral Settlements in Advanced Consolidation
		Peripheral Settlements in Rural Areas

[a] These are **quintas:** housing projects of unified design which share the same street access.

The basic criteria that have been employed for the elaboration of this general scheme are practically the same as those used for the elaboration of the operational typology presented in the first part of this essay, but the principal basis for classification refers to the spatial location of the settlements. Thus, the order of priorities on which a possible urban development policy could be based would have to accept one of two levels of applicability, one referring either to improvement programs with respect to internal urban settlements or to peripheral urban settlements. Naturally, policy which is, for example, based on an urban renewal program, would primarily involve urban underdevelopment, and consequently would introduce priorities with respect to the two global forms of underdevelopment within the urban nucleus, eliminating first the problem of individual slums.

It is also obvious that the spatial criterion used for setting priorities would be applicable to the two most important aspects of peripheral urban underdevelopment, which are included in the scheme, but applications to the whole of peripheral development would have to express various policies precisely because of the enormous disparity in the conditions that characterize the peripheral slum areas and the towns in formation.

Finally, it is obvious that if one postulates the existence of the two fundamental aspects of urban metropolitan underdevelopment as parts of the same problem, any improvement policy derived from the pragmatic orientation suggested by the scheme would have to accept the inseparability of the programs referring to internal underdeveloped areas on the one hand and to peripheral underdeveloped areas on the other. This means that, in spite of the fact that the actual focus for improvement may be radically different for the different circumstances where they are to be applied, they should always be considered interdependent.

It is then possible to achieve a greater degree of internal unity in the general scheme by reordering its elements to reflect not only their spatial location, but also the impact of slum formation on the underdeveloped social universes. The reordering of the elements in the general scheme results in the delimitation of two principal areas of metropolitan underdevelopment. The first is in terms of a social universe in which the process of slum formation (tugurización) is found, and the second is in terms of a social universe in which slum formation is not found. This focus for the scheme naturally imposes the necessity of reformulating the operational typology in order to incorporate into the first of the social universes mentioned (where the process of slum formation is found) both the High-Density

Internal Settlements and the High-Density Peripheral Settlements. In this way a revised scheme is obtained as indicated in Scheme 2.

Clearly, the policies of urban development that are directed towards one or the other of the social universes of the revised scheme will vary radically, depending on specific objectives and means of implementation. Moreover, these policies will vary perceptibly in their application (through taking as their base the predominance or the absence of slum formation as a social phenomenon) in approaching the chracteristic problems of each one of the subareas that the revised scheme identifies within the two universes defined. For this reason, it is important to reiterate explicitly a distinction

SCHEME 2
**Revised Scheme of Metropolitan Underdevelopment Based
on the Social Problem of Slum Formation**

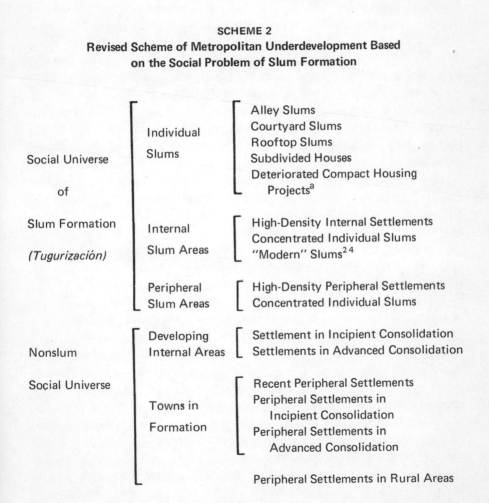

Social Universe

of

Slum Formation

(Tugurización)

    Individual
    Slums

        Alley Slums
        Courtyard Slums
        Rooftop Slums
        Subdivided Houses
        Deteriorated Compact Housing
           Projects[a]

    Internal
    Slum Areas

        High-Density Internal Settlements
        Concentrated Individual Slums
        "Modern" Slums[24]

    Peripheral
    Slum Areas

        High-Density Peripheral Settlements
        Concentrated Individual Slums

Nonslum

Social Universe

    Developing
    Internal Areas

        Settlement in Incipient Consolidation
        Settlements in Advanced Consolidation

    Towns in
    Formation

        Recent Peripheral Settlements
        Peripheral Settlements in
           Incipient Consolidation
        Peripheral Settlements in
           Advanced Consolidation

        Peripheral Settlements in Rural Areas

[a] These are **quintas**: housing projects of unified design which share the same street access.

that reflects the enormous difference between the two social universes that are included in the revised scheme. The first universe (where slum formation predominates) represents a situation of static and stagnant underdevelopment lacking virtually any potential for change. The second universe, on the contrary, represents a situation of great dynamism and high potential for self-development. This difference in the possibilities for inherent change within the two great universes of metropolitan underdevelopment is too acute and evident to be ignored in the formulation and application of concrete policies of urban development.

Naturally, the types of residential settlements indicated in the revised scheme do not include all the manifestations of urban underdevelopment. Besides those specifically mentioned in the scheme there are, for example, the numerous cases of individual dwellings or of dwellings concentrated in small residential groups, both badly "substandard," which are spread throughout the whole metropolitan mosaic. These cases add up to many thousands of residential units, and consequently affect tens of thousands of people. Sometimes they are temporary shelters for caretakers and buildings or residential groups under construction; others are groups of supposedly provisional shelters which are physically joined to factories and industrial establishments, or are huts inhabited by family groups which do agricultural work in the rural pockets that still exist in the periphery of the metropolitan zone.

As a final note, it can be said that a need has been shown not only for approaching the problems of urban underdevelopment in a new and different way, but also for reorienting housing programs by revising the criteria that have served as their basis up until now and by revising the standards that have been used for setting program objectives. Without these imperative revisions any future policy will be doomed to sterility and impotence, which is a current characteristic of efforts made by governments for resolving the problems of housing. This problem, in essence, is neither spatial nor technical. It is mainly a problem that involved social and political policy and is related to the structural characteristics of Peruvian society. Because of this, its total solution cannot be derived from the existing conditions in the country, but, on the contrary, can only succeed within the context of basic changes that affect the meaning and the nature of the economic, political, and social power relationships in Peru.

This, of course, does not mean that nothing can be done until such time as a revolutionary process changes the existing order of things. But it does mean that the phenomenon of urban underdevelopment will not be definitely solved either within the "political vacuum," which expresses the intangibility of the prevailing order, or by a feeling of remoteness from the problems which considers them unrelated to more affluent groups within contemporary Peruvian society.

Speaking only in terms of dwellings, the demand in the metropolitan area for the next twelve years will exceed 500,000 residential units PLANDEMET, 1967: 269-274). Obviously government resources available are insufficient for a scheme of such vast proportions. Consequently, the need arises for a new and different way of examining the problem without awaiting a radical political change that could open the doors to significant alterations in the current order of things. In order to have reasonable chances to succeed, policy of urban development could well be initiated now based on the following minimum requirements: (a) abandonment of the paternalistic notion that the population of underdeveloped and developing settlements are incapable of solving, their housing problems when starting from a determined and definite basis; (b) active government participation to provide two substantive elements to the solution of the problem: adequate residential space, and legal ownership of the land; (c) channelization and orientation of local resources to housing in accordance with guidelines in whose formulation the settlers would be active participants; (d) determination of new standards for housing reflecting the needs, preferences, and possibilities of the future inhabitants; (e) technical assistance that would minimize the difficulties of construction; (f) based on the above, the execution of programs of urban serves to give the new residential areas, before occupation, the basic urban infrastructural services. The cost of these could be met, to a very significant degree, by the local population.

NOTES

1. In 1940 the province of Lima and the province containing the port city of Lima-Callao had a combined population of 645,172, which had increased to 1,845,910 by 1961 (see "Dirección Nacional de Estadísticas y Censos" in *VI Censo Nacional de Población* (subsequently cited as *Censo Nacional*), 1965: vol. I, Cuadro 3, pp. 4-5.

2. See Note 9.

3. Verification of this differentiation was obtained by the author in 1959 as a result of an investigation of national educational problems (see Delgado, 1960).

4. An indication of the power of the metropolitan area with respect to the nation can be illustrated by the following data for Lima: 67 percent of the industrial labor; 44 percent of employment in the service sector; 53 percent of commercial employment; 60 percent of services; 60 percent of the industrial production; 98 percent of the financial operations; 83 percent of imports; 65 percent of the income from the retail business sector, and 73 percent of the income from industries (see Oficina Nacional de Planeamiento y Urbanismo, Plan de

Desarrollo Metropolitano, Lima-Callao (PLANDEMET), *Esquema Director, 1967-80:* 27-33; this document is hereafter referred to as PLANDEMENT, 1967).

5. The census definition of urban population includes the population in all district capitals (regardless of their population size) and all populated centers that are not district capitals but "have urban characteristics of streets, squares, water systems, sewage, street lighting, and in which the number of inhabitants is equal to or greater than that of the capital city of the same district" (*Censo Nacional*, 1965: iii). On the other hand, if every populated center with 2,000 or more inhabitants were to be defined as urban, the percentages would be 25.4 percent for 1940 and 39.4 percent for 1961 (see "Servicio de Empleo y Recursos Humanos, Población del Perú in *Censo Nacional*, 1965: Cuadro 11, p. 25; and Note 9 herein).

6. The volume of migration to the metropolitan area in the five-year period 1956-1961 showed an increase of 300 percent over the number of migrants that arrived in the five-year period 1941-1946. It is estimated that during 1967 there was an influx of approximately 75,000 people to the capital city, an increase equivalent to the total population of such important Peruvian cities as Huancayo (PLANDEMET, 1967: 52).

7. In 1955, José Matos Mar, on the basis of estimates that he himself considers questionable (United Nations, 1955: 19), estimated that the population of the thirty-nine settlements that he identified during that year in Lima and Callao was 119,140 inhabitants. This estimate represents approximately ten percent of the population of the metropolitan area considered as the urban nucleus and its immediate periphery in that year. This work, apparently, served as the basis for another study made by Matos Mar in 1956 in which the existence of fifty-six settlements is mentioned; these have a slightly lower population than that indicated in 1955—119,886 (see Matos Mar, 1962: 181 ff.). In 1959, another investigation identified 154 settlements with a total population of 236,716, which represented 14.7 percent of the metropolitan population estimated for that year (see Fondo Nacional de Salud y Bienestar Social, 1960: 27, table 4). The census of 1961 mentions 150 settlements containing a total population of 318,262, which would have been 17.2 percent of the metropolitan population at that time. In addition to the prior estimate, the Oficina del Plan de Desarrollo Metropolitano (PLANDEMET), working on information issued by the Junta Nacional de la Vivienda with respect to 154 settlements, arrived at the conclusion that the total population of those settlements in 1963 was 335,919 (see Negromonte, 1968). Later, in 1965, a study prepared by the Technical Personnel of the Junta Nacional de la Vivienda mentioned a total of 211 settlements which contained 90,250 families; as the Junta Nacional della Vivenda estimates the average family as 5.3 individuals, this gives those settlements a total population of 478,325, which represented 20.4 percent of the estimated metropolitan population in 1965 (see Oficina de Planificacion, 1966: table 8). Finally, PLANDEMET has been able to provisionally identify fifty-five additional settlements which had not figured in the list prepared by the Junta Nacional de al Vivienda; this would increase the number of settlements that exist in all the metropolitan area (provinces of Lima and Callao) to 266. It is impossible to determine the population of all the underdeveloped settlements, but a conservative estimate would be 600,000 inhabitants, more or less, representing about 25 percent of the total population of the area. Furthermore, PLANDEMET, based on demographic projections, estimates that if the actual tendencies persist without modification, the population of settlements by 1980 would represent more than 40 percent of the total population in the provinces of Lima and Callao.

8. The total number of dwellings built in Lima between 1949 and 1967 by the Corporación Nacional de la Vivienda, the Instituto de la Vivienda, and the Junta Nacional de la Vivienda (which replaced the previous housing institutions) was 26,514 units. This includes those financed and build directly by these organizations such as the Fondo Nacional de Salud y Bienestar Social, Ministerio de Marina, Banco Central Hipotecario, Fondo de Jubilación Obrera, and others. To these we must add 2,768 dwellings, built between the years 1951 and 1967 by the Junta de Obras Públicas y del Callao, plus 1,609 provisional shelters and emergency dwellings, built between the years 1958 and 1967, for a total of only 30,991 dwellings built directly or indirectly by the national government in the

metropolitan area during a period of eighteen years. Some 11,707 dwellings were built in the remainder of the country between 1955 and 1967, thus producing a grand total of 42,698 dwellings built in Peru as a result of direct government intervention. These numbers compare unfavorably with the results of popular initiative in the marginal settlements of the Lima metropolitan area. (Information was supplied by the Oficina de Planificación Sectorial de Vivienda y Equipamiento Urbano.)

9. The most representative definitions of the descriptive type would be the following: (a) "They are settlements formed on invaded land which have not been built according to a preconceived plan or, if built to a plan, it is a very rudimentary one. They lack the most elementary public and social services and are the settlements in which one finds the most deplorable health conditions" (Oficina Nacional de Planeamiento y Urbanismo, 1955: viii, 1); (b) ". . . a marginal settlement . . . is . . . a social conglomeration formed by a group of families that invade empty lands, generally owned by the State and to a lesser degree by agencies of public welfare, municipalities or private parties, lands which are not being used by the proprietors; these lands are located on the periphery of the city" (Matos Mar, 1962: 179); (c) "*Barriada* is a social conglomerate formed by groups of families which invade empty lands which are mostly national government properties and to a lesser degree properties of non-governmental institutions and private owners. This land is usually located on the periphery of the city, and the families proceed to build their dwellings clandestinely, a fact which accounts for their rudimentary construction" (Instituto de Investigaciones Económicas, 1965: 8-9); (d) "A marginal settlement or barriada is considered to be an area of fiscal, municipal, communal or privately owned land that is located within the limits of populated centers (the political-administrative areas of capital cities or their respective suburban areas or outskirts) and that has been invaded in disregard for legal ownership, with or without municipal authority. These lands are divided and distributed without officially approved plans, and groups of dwellings are built with a variety of basic structures. Further, the areas lack one or more of the following services: water, sewage, lighting, sidewalks, roads, etc." (Law No. 1317 on Barrios Marginales, Lima: 1963).

10. In any case, general descriptions have to sacrifice exactitude in order to be applicable, and, by so doing, they tend to lose precise meaning.

11. Matos Mar (1962: 28-30) proposes two classification criteria. One is based on the "urban configuration" of the settlement and the other on the "isolation" and "relationships" of the barriadas among themselves and with the urban zones. Leaving aside the inevitable mutual exclusiveness of these classification criteria—the first considers the settlements as an urban reality and the second implicitly and clearly denies that consideration—the first criteria leads Matos Mar to consider six generic types of settlements: (1) regularly planned gridiron, (2) irregularly planned gridiron, (3) adapted to topography of the hills, (4) with central corridor, (5) in radial form, and (6) other types. The second type is further subclassified as (a) autonomous, (b) settlement complexes, and (c) assimilated to the city.

12. The word "operational" lacks theoretical implications. I wanted to emphasize by the term that the typology has been designed to guide the operational meaning of concrete policies for urban development.

13. Turner (1966a: 8) refers to the "existing polarity between progressive development and regressive degeneration." As an example of the latter and redundant classification, Turner refers to Mendocita, a typical case of what I call an "internal slum settlement." In another place, Turner declares that this settlement is on the road to "regressive degeneration," alluding in this manner to a certain degree of dynamism and changeability. Far from perceiving a characteristic of this in internal slums like Mendocita, I consider that within such internal slum settlements there is a note of definite suspension that predominates and implies nonchangeability.

14. The order in which the typology appears conforms to simple purposes of presentation. According to a strict criteria of priorities in terms of definite policies for urban development, the typological order would surely be the following: (1), (2), (5), (6), (3), (7), (4), (8). It is clear that at the level of the specific cases one can most certainly weight more

heavily the importance of the factors referring to the size of affected population and the intensity in the seriousness of the problems of the urban area considered for purposes of a determined improvement project.

15. The eradication or violent ejection of groups of invaders is becoming increasingly difficult within a climate of political freedom. The need for increasing the margin of popular backing has led the political parties to support the creation of settlements by invasion. The case of Año Nuevo clearly illustrates this situation. There is also a subtle but important change in the attitude of the invaders vis-à-vis the traditional respect towards private property. It appears that the tendency to question the inviolability of property among the dispossessed sectors who strive towards the ownership of a piece of ground on which to build their dwellings is slowly taking root, especially in the case of empty lands.

16. Obviously, the invasion of empty land owned by the government does not present a direct threat to the established order. But when the invasion affects land that is private property it is met with very strong rejection.

17. There are important differences between El Altillo and the other settlements noted here. El Altillo is a relatively older settlement located on steep hillsides. A considerable amount of effort and investment has poured into it during a fifteen-year period. Most of this area is currently consolidated and it presents a very interesting feature because it shows the technical capacity and size of investment in dwellings made as an input by the settlers. A number of cement staircases more than 100 meters long constitute vertical streets that give pedestrian access to brick and cement dwellings, many of which have been built in the live rock. It is obvious that, in this case, the topographical conditions increase the costs of the consolidation of this type of settlement.

18. Peripheral Settlements in Rural Areas involve relatively small populations and this contributes to lessen their priority.

19. The significance of the political situation at the time the settlement is being formed is a matter that has not yet been studied. The invading groups have always tried to obtain the support and patronage of some source of power. The possibility of achieving this objective increases considerably when the political conditions are such that they assure an alliance with important groups or individuals who have access to the mechanisms of power.

20. Apart from some theses presented to the Escuela de Servicio Social, the literary output referring to Lima's metropolitan slums includes only Richard W. Patch (1961), John Turner (1965) and Humberto Rotondo et al. (1963).

21. The first field investigation carried out by PLANDEMET in 1967 ascertained the existence of about 10,000 alleys and yards within the metropolitan area. Briefly, these various types of slums may be described as follows: Alley slums are groups of very small dwellings, usually less than thirty square meters, which have been built on relatively small lots. The dwellings are aligned along a passage perpendicular to the street to which there is a common access. Courtyard slums are larger groups of small dwellings, mostly built with adobe and distributed along differently traced passages, through which the dwellers have indirect access to the street. Rooftop slums are groups of precarious dwellings that are generally built with perishable material on terraces or roofs of multistoried buildings located within a slum area and nearly always close to the commercial centers. This category is normally found in definite zones within the city. Subdivided houses are usually old buildings that originally belonged to one family and have, through the years, become a place of shelter for numerous families. Deteriorated *quintas* constitute run-down versions of a type of collective dwelling, which, in a good state of maintenance, represents an evolutionary and "acceptable" form of the essential model of the traditional courtyard.

22. A more complete development of the ideas related to this type of social group appears in one of my works titled "Hacia un Nuevo Esquema de Composición de la Sociedad en el Perú."

23. The first studies of PLANDEMET (1967: 200 ff.) concerning the utilization of the work force in the metropolitan area make it possible to estimate that approximately 18 percent of the economically employed population is underemployed. Projections place this percentage at approximately 29 percent in 1980.

24. I refer to groups of dwellings of relatively recent construction that have been built with speculative aims and in which maximum rentals have been obtained with a high sacrifice in space. A typical example can be found in the populous suburb of El Porvenir.

REFERENCES

DELGADO, CARLOS (1960) Educación en el Sur del Perú: Problemas y Perspectivas. Lima: Oficina del Plan Regional para el Sur del Perú.

Censo Nacional de Poblacion VI (1965) Lima.

Fondo Nacional de Salud y Bienestar Social (1960) "Barriadas de Lima metropolitana." Lima.

Instituto de Investigaciones Económicas de la Universidad Nacional Mayor de San Marcos (1965) "Estudio socio-económico de la barriada El Hermitaño." Lima.

MANGIN, WILLIAM (1967) "Latin American squatter settlements: a problem and a solution." Latin American Research Review 2 (Summer): 65-98.

MATOS MAR, JOSE (1962) "Migración y urbanización—las barriadas Limeñas: un caso de integración a la vida urbana." In Philip Hauser (ed.) La Urbanización en América Latina. New York: UNESCO.

NEGROMONTE, FABRICIO (1968) "Análisis de la información organizada existente sobre las barriadas de Lima." Lima: Oficina Nacional de Planeamiento y Urbanismo, Plan de Desarrollo Metropolitano, Lima-Callao (mimeographed internal document).

Oficina de Planificación Sectorial de Vivienda y Equipamiento Urbano (1967) Demanda de Tierras para un Plan Estatal de Vivienda en Lima-Callao 1967-1971. Lima: Oficina de Planificación.

——— (1966) Análisis Censal para una Evaluación de la Vivienda. Lima: Oficina de Planificación.

Oficina Nacional de Planeamiento y Urbanismo (1967) Plan de Desarrollo Metropolitano, Lima-Callao (PLANDEMET), Esquema Director, 1967-80. Lima.

——— (1955) "Demarcación de las zonas de carácter uniforme." In Análisis Censal. Lima.

PATCH, RICHARD W. (1961) Life in a Callejon: A Study of Urban Disorganization. West Coast and South American Series 13 (no. 6). American University Field Staff, Inc.

ROTONDO, HUMBERTO et al. (1963) "Studies of social psychology in Peru." Lima: El Sol Editions.

TURNER, JOHN (1967) "Barriers and channels for housing development in modernizing countries." Journal of the American Institute of Planners 33 (May): 167-181.

——— (1966a) "Asentamientos urbanos no regulados." Cuadernos de la Sociedad Venezolana de Planificación 36 (December).

——— (1966b) "A new view of the housing deficit."

——— (1966c) "La marginalidad urbana: ¿calamidad o solución? " Desarrollo Económico 3 (nos. 3-4): 8-14.

——— (1965) "Lima's barriadas and corralones: suburbs versus slums." Ekistics 19 (March).

——— and ROLF GOETHE (n.d.) "Environmental security and housing input."

United Nations (1955) Estudio de las Barriadas Limeñas. (Published in 1967 by the Department of Anthropology of the Universidad San Marcos.)

ADDITIONAL REFERENCES APPENDED BY THE EDITOR

A. Urban Social Ecology
(See also Chapter 9: References G, H, J.)

ABU-LUGHOD, JANET (1968) "The city is dead–long live the city: some thoughts on urbanity."Pp. 154-165 in Sylvia Fleis Fava (ed.) Urbanism in World Perspective. New York: Thomas Y. Crowell.

AMATO, PETER W. (1969) "Population densities, land values, and socioeconomic class in Bogotá, Colombia." Land Economics (February).

CAPLOW, THEODORE (1961) "The social ecology of Guatemala City." Pp. 331-48 in George A. Theodorson (ed.) Studies in Human Ecology. Evanston, Illinois: Row, Peterson. (Summaries of ecological studies made of other Latin American cities are also included in this book; also in Social Forces 28 (December, 1949): 113-33.)

— — — and SAMUEL WALLACE (1965) "Social ecology of the urban area of San Juan." América Latina 8 (no. 3, July-September).

CAPLOW, THEODORE, SHELDON STRYKER and SAMUEL WALLACE (1964) The Urban Ambiance: A Study of San Juan, Puerto Rico. Totowa, N.J.: Bedminster Press.

DOGAN, MATTEI and STEIN ROKKAN [eds.] (1969) Quantitative Ecological Analysis in the Social Sciences. Çambridge, Mass.: MIT Press.

DOTSON, FLOYD and LILLIAN OTA DOTSON (1954) "Ecological trends in the city of Guadalajara, Mexico." Social Forces 32 (March): 367-74.

— — — (1957) "La estructura ecológica de las ciudades mexicanas." Revista Mexicana de Sociología 19 (January-April): 39-66.

HANSEN, ASAEL T. (1934) "The ecology of a Latin American city." Pp. 124-52 in Edward B. Reuter (ed.) Race and Culture Contacts. New York: McGraw-Hill.

HAYNER, NORMAN S. (1966) "Mexico City: its growth and configuration, 1345-1960." Pp. 166-77 in Sylvia Fleis Fava (ed.) Urbanism in World Perspective. New York: Thomas Y. Crowell.

HOMERO FORNI, FLOREAL (1966) "Análisis ecológico de una ciudad media: metodología y aplicación a la ciudad de Rafaela, provincia de Santa Fe." Cuadernos del Centro de Estudios Urbanos y Regionales (Buenos Aires) (no. 4).

MORSE, RICHARD M. (1965) "Review article: the sociology of San Juan: an exegesis of urban mythology." Caribbean Studies 2 (July).

SCHNORE, LEO F. (1965) "On the spatial structure of cities in the two Americas." In Philip M. Hauser and Leo F. Schnore (eds.) The Study of Urbanization. New York: John Wiley.

SMITH, T. LYNN (1963) Brazil: People and Institutions. Baton Rouge: Louisiana Univ. Press.

B: The Urban Migrant and Acculturation

BALAN, JORGE (1969) "Migrant-native socioeconomic differences in Latin American cities: a structural analysis." Latin American Research Rev. 4 (Spring): 3-29.

BAPTISTA GUMUCIO, MARIANO (1967) "La ruralización de las ciudades latinoamericanas." Política 6 (February): 13-24.

BOCK, F. WILBUR and SUGIYAMA IUTAKA (1969) "Rural-urban migration and social mobility–the controversy on Latin America." Rural Sociology (September).

BORRIE, WILFRED D. (1959) The Cultural Integration of Immigrants, A Survey based upon the Papers and Proceedings of the UNESCO Conference on the Cultural Integration of Immigrants held in Havana, Cuba, April 1956. Paris: UNESCO.

BRANDAO LOPES, JUAREZ RUBENS (1961) "Aspect of the adjustment of rural migrants to urban-industrial conditions in Sao Paulo, Brazil." Pp. 234-48 in Philip M. Hauser (ed.) Urbanization in Latin America. New York: International Documents Service, Columbia Univ. Press.

BRYCE-LAPORTE, ROY SIMON (1968) "Family adaptation of relocated slum dwellers in Puerto Rico: implications for urban research and development." J. of Developing Areas 2 (July): 533-40.

BUTTERWORTH, DOUGLAS S. (1962) "A study of the urbanization process among Mixtec migrants from Tilantango in Mexico City." América Indígena 22: 257-74.
COHEN, ERNESTO (1968) Marginality: An Explanatory Essay. Santiago: Catholic University, CIDU.
FLINN, WILLIAM L. (1968) "The process of migration to a shanty town in Bogotá, Colombia." Inter-American Economic Affairs 22 (Autumn): 77-88.
FRANK, ANDREW G. (1966) Urban Poverty in Latin America. Studies in Comparative International Development, No. 019. Beverly Hills: Sage Publications.
GERMANI, GINO (1964) "Migration and acculturation." In Philip M. Hauser (ed.) Handbook for Social Research in Urban Areas. Paris: UNESCO.
HOWTON, F. WILLIAM (1969) "Cities, slums, and acculturative process in the developing countries." Pp. 431-47 in Paul Meadows and Ephraim H. Mizruchi (eds.) Urbanism, Urbanization, and Change: Comparative Perspectives. Reading, Mass.: Addison-Wesley.
HUTCHINSON, BERTRAM (1963) "The migrant population of urban Brazil." América Latina 6 (April-June): 41-72.
NELSON, JOAN M. (1969) Migrants, Urban Poverty, and Instability in Developing Nations. Occasional Papers in International Affairs, No. 22. Cambridge, Mass.: Harvard Univ. Center for International Affairs. (A very useful compendium of issues on these subjects.)
ORTIZ, YOLANDA (1957) "Algunas dificultades de adaptación de las poblaciones rurales al pasar al medio urbano en los países latinoamericanos y especialmente en Colombia." Revista Mexicana de Sociología 19 (January-April): 25-38.
PASTORE, JOSE (1969) Brasília: a cidade e o homen: uma investigaçao sociológica sôbre os processos de migraçao, adaptaçao e planejamento urbano. Biblioteca Universitaria, Série 2: Ciências Sociais.
PETERSON, CLAIRE L. and THOMAS J. SCHEFF (1965) "Theory, method and findings in the study of acculturation: a review." International Rev. of Community Development (13-14): 155-76.
USANDIZAGA, ELSA and A. EUGENE HAVENS (1966) Tres barrios de invasión: estudio de nivel de vida y actitudes en Barranquilla. Bogotá: Ediciones Tercer Mundo.

C. Popular Urban Settlements

CASASIO, JUAN A. (1969) "The social function of the slum in Latin America: some positive aspects." Ekistics 28 (September).
CHOMBART DE LAWE, PAUL HENRY (n.d.) "A perspective on the resettlement of squatters in Brazil." América Latina (Rio de Janeiro).
DIETZ, HENRY (1969) "Urban squatter settlements in Peru." J. of Interamerican Studies 11 (July).
FRANKENHOFF, C. A. (1967) "Elements of an economic model for slums in a developing economy." Economic Development and Cultural Change (October).
MANGIN, WILLIAM (1967a) "Latin American squatter settlements: a problem and a solution." Latin American Research Rev. 2 (Summer): 65-98. (Extensive bibliography.)
――― (1967b) "Squatter settlements." Scientific American (October): 21-29.
――― and JOHN F. C. TURNER (1968) "Barriada movement." Progressive Architecture 49 (May): 154-62.
PINEDA GIRALDO, ROBERTO (1968) "Una política sobre los tugurios." Revista de la Sociedad Interamericana de Planificación 2 (March-June): 70-71.
Programas Internacionales de Población (1969) Urbanización y Marginalidad. Bogotá: The Programas. (Papers given at a seminar in Soyamosa, Colombia, March 28-31, 1968, for purpose of analyzing the different aspects of the urbanization process in relation to the appearance and development of the marginal barrios, of discussing the actual and potential role of educational, industrial and governmental institutions in relation to this phenomenon, and of establishing bases for a plan of action.)
ROGLER, LLOYD H. (1967) "Slum neighborhoods in Latin America." J. of Inter-American Studies 9 (October): 507-28.
SANABRIA, TOMAS JOSE (1966) "Los ranchos—aflicción urbana." Desarrollo Económico (New York) 3 (no. 1): 22-26.
TURNER, JOHN F. C. (1966) "Asentamientos urbanos no-regulados." Cuadernos de la Sociedad Venezolana de Planificación 36 (December).
――― (1968a) "Housing priorities, settlement patterns, and urban development in modernizing countries." J. of the Amer. Institute of Planners (November).

――― (1968b) "Uncontrolled urban settlement: problems and policies." In United Nations, Department of Economic and Social Affairs. Urbanization: Development Policies and Planning. New York: UN.

D. Housing

ABRAMS, CHARLES (1964) Man's Struggle for Shelter in an Urbanizing World. Cambridge, Mass.: MIT Press.

CABELLO, OCTAVIO (1966) "Housing, population growth and economic development." In Mayone Stycos and Jorge Arbas (eds.) Population Dilemma in Latin America. Washington, D.C.: Potomac Books.

CAMINOS, HORACIO, JOHN F. C. TURNER and JOHN A. STEFFIAN (1969) Urban Dwelling Environments: An Elementary Survey of Settlements for the Study of Design Determinants. Cambridge, Mass.: MIT Press.

FRANKENHOFF, CHARLES (1969) "Aspectos económicos de una política popular de vivienda." Pp. 175-202 in John Friedmann (ed.) Contribuciones a las Políticas Urbanas, Regionales y Habitacionales―Chile: La Década del 70. Santiago: Ford Foundation.

FRIEDEN, BERNARD (1965) "The search for housing policy in Mexico City." Town Planning Rev. 36 (July).

MENDONCA, MARIO LARANGEIRA DE (1965) "O plano habitacional e a expansão das áreas urbana." Revista de Administração Municipal (Rio de Janeiro) 11 (May-June): 155-75.

RODWIN, LLOYD (1967) "Measuring housing needs in developing countries." In Wentworth Eldridge (ed.) Taming Megaloplis. Vol. 2. Garden City, N.Y.: Anchor Books.

SOLOW, A. A. (1967) "Housing in Latin America: the problem of the urban low income families." Town Planning Rev. 38 (July): 83-102.

TURNER, JOHN F. C. (1966) "A new view of the housing deficit." In Charles A. Frankenhoff (ed.) Housing Policy for a Developing Nation's Economy. Rio Piedras, Puerto Rico: Univ. of Puerto Rico.

――― (1967) "Barriers and channels for housing development in modernizing countries." J. of the Amer. Institute of Planners 33 (no. 3): 167-81.

UN Centre for Housing, Building and Planning (1969) Social Aspects of Housing and Urban Development: A Bibliography.

VAN FLEET, JAMES A. (1969) "Recursos de vivienda en comunidades marginales." Temas del BID (April): 18-32.

E. Urban Community Development

CABEZA DE GONZALEZ, BETTY and ISMAEL SILVA (n.d.) "La participación popular en el desarrollo y su planificación." Boletín Informativo de PLANDES (Santiago) (no. 30).

COHEN, WILBUR J. (1967) "Social planning and urban development." Pp. 237-45 in Urban Development: Its Implications for Social Welfare. New York: Columbia Univ. Press.

"Concepts and methods of area programming for community development." (1967) Economic Bulletin for Latin America (May).

JHAVERI, DILIP (n.d.) "Aspectos socioculturales en el concepto de la unidad vecinal." Plerus 2, (no. 1.) University of Puerto Rico, Graduate School of Planning

MARTINEZ, GUSTAVO (1969) "El óptimo poblacional de las Juntas de Vecinos." Cuadernos de Desarrollo Urbano Regional (Santiago) (June): 97-120.

PEPPELENBOSCH, P. G. N. (1967) "Community development and human geography." Community Development J. (July): 17-23.

OAS (1968a) Las Cooperativas Como Método de Desarrollo de Regiones y Comunidades. Washington, D.C.: Pan American Union.

――― (1968b) Organización de la Comunidad para el Bienestar Social. Washington, D.C.: Pan American Union.

VIOLICH, FRANCIS (1968) "Desarrollo comunal y planificación urbana en América Latina." Revista de la Sociedad Interamericana de Planificación 2 (December): 18-27.

――― and JUAN B. ASTICA (1968) Community Development and the Urban Planning Process in Latin America. Los Angeles: Univ. of California, Latin American Center.

J. M.

Participants' Comments

José A. Silva Michelena

The typology of subdeveloped urban zones that Delgado offers us is a useful step forward. Delgado subscribes to the thesis of Turner and Mangin with respect to the positive effects of the barriadas. But even if we accept this thesis, which appears to me to be laudable, we should realize that we are only focusing on a small part of the transformations that are occurring in the social order as a consequence of urbanization. As is known, the barriadas, the callampas, the ranchos, or the favelas obtain their greatest concentration in the large cities, but, even so, they do not exceed a third of the population in such national centers as Lima, Santiago, Caracas, or Rio de Janeiro. What occurs in the remainder of the social groups? What are the modernizing effects of urbanization on all groups? We can postulate that if urbanization is in truth modernizing, then the groups that live in the largest cities (a measure of urbanization) should be the most modern.

Fortunately, as a product of research that has been realized in Venezuela at CENDES in collaboration with Frank Bonilla of the Massachusetts Institute of Technology, sufficient data is available for testing this hypothesis.[1] In this study, samples were taken of twenty-eight strategic groups of the population (from disperse campesinos to high functionaries of the government). It is known that rural groups are primarily less modern than urban groups. Accordingly, they were eliminated from that part of the study which dealt with urban groups only. These latter groups were examined according to the size of city in which they lived. The rank correlation obtained between that variable (size of city) and some key indicators of modernism such as social and political participation, degree of national identification, political effectiveness, and degree of sophistication in the style of evaluation demonstrated that there is no relation between size of city and these indicators of modernism (maximum $r_s = 0.35$).[2]

303

This, of course, could be due to the fact that the size of city where one lives is a poor indicator of the impact of urbanization on the individual, since a person may live, for example, in Lima yet be a recently arrived campesino. For overcoming this problem, we selected as a variable what we call the urban experience—the percentage of persons in each group who were born and have lived all their lives in urban zones. On calculating the rank correlation, it was evident that there is a certain correlation with style of evaluation and national identification, but not with political effectiveness and participation. This is indicated in Table 8.1.

One notes then that the results only half confirm the hypothesis about the modernizing effects of urbanization since they fail in what is referred to as the political area. An evaluation of the hypothesis can also be made through seeking other variables that are associated with modernism. We took, therefore, the socioeconomic status (SES), as shown in Table 8.2.

Obviously the correlation is greater. The doubt arises, as a result, if the correlation between urban experience and modernism is not more than a reflection of the greater SES of those that have more urban experience. In effect, if one controls the SES, the correlation between urban experience and the global index of modernism disappears. (The Kendall partial rank correlation coefficient equals -0.20.)

A more detailed examination of the groups considered reveals other salient facts. It is especially important to note that the functional sphere of activity (politics, cultural, economic) is a variable also closely associated with modernism, as shown in Table 8.3.

TABLE 8.1
Urban Experience and Modernism

Indicators of Modernism	Urban Experience	
	r_s (n=20)	p
Style of evaluation	0.50	(0.01)
National identification	0.53	(0.01)
Effectiveness, political	0.37	(0.20)
Participation, political	0.03	—
Global index of modernism	0.46	(0.05)

TABLE 8.2
Socioeconomic Status and Modernism

Modernism	Socioeconomic Status	
	r_s (n=20)	p
Style of evaluation	0.86	(0.01)
National identification	0.75	(0.01)
Effectiveness, political	0.80	(0.01)
Participation, political	0.48	(0.05)
Global index of modernism	0.81	(0.01)

TABLE 8.3
Occupational Sphere and Modernism

Occupational Sphere	High	Modernism Medium	Low
Political-	University professors	Government office staff	
	High government functionaries		
cultural	Government technicians		
	Secondary-school teachers		
	Student leaders		
	Union leaders		
		Small industrialists	Small merchants
		Central region industrial executives	Central region industrial workers
		Western region industrial executives	Western region industrial workers
		Petroleum executives	Inhabitants of ranchos
Economic		Eastern region industrial executives	
		Executives of large commercial houses	
		Office employees of large commercial houses	
		Eastern region industrial workers	
		Petroleum employees	

Furthermore, this data reveals the existence of a curious paradox. If one considers that industrialization, and economic activity generally, are the impulses of modernization, it is evident that in the Venezuelan situation the entrepreneurs, office workers, and laborers are not the most modern. The political-cultural groups are much more in the vanguard. Does this mean that there should be greater inclusion of the political and cultural groups in economic affairs if one wishes to accelerate modernization? We believe that this would be a favorable strategy.

We have more evidence on the same point, but perhaps what has been stated up to now is sufficient for qualifying the proposition that urbanization and modernization always go hand in hand. What can truly be inferred from the data that has been presented is that one needs to examine with much more care the following: (1) identification of key groups, including high-level administrators in charge of defining and implementing the urban policies, and (2) determination of the differential impact of the variables that one may consider most important. This sociological perspective can provide a more refined base on which to **plant** the urban development policy. This policy should be both differentiated and sufficiently adaptable as to be able to change the structure of decision-making in the short- or medium-run.

Part of the task of the planner is that of defining the feasibility of the strategies that he proposes. We can offer some indication of this, although it is given in a somewhat simplified form. It is known that the implementation of a policy of this nature requires, of course, a certain ideological compromise with change. Even if it may be true that the government executives participate in great measure in the development orientation, it is probable that they will remain paralyzed in the face of the necessity to implement such measures as the control of land prices or equitable tax evaluation of property. This indecision—-or incapacity for carrying out measures that may alter the status quo—is a structural-type factor characteristic of liberal democratic and reform-minded governments. The data and knowledge of government indicate that for increasing the effects of industrialization and accelerating modernization one needs another political alternative that is more ideologically defined and committed to change. This seems essential for assuring the sufficient firmness in decision that is required for overcoming the substantial obstacles that the actual structures of power present—including the influence of the United States.

[Notes and references for Dr. Silva Michelena's comments are found at the end of this section.—Ed.]

Gideon Sjoberg

My comments are limited to certain broad theoretical and methodological issues. Although they focus on Delgado's paper, they are also useful in considering certain aspects of John Friedmann's paper.

Both Friedmann and Delgado have raised a number of theoretical issues which need to be objectified. One in particular concerns me. We should recognize that all scholars build into their frame of reference certain assumptions about the nature of man and social reality. These assumptions are especially important if we are to understand present-day research and theory in urban sociology and planning.

Throughout much of the history of urban studies we have witnessed a tension between those scholars who espouse a "deterministic" (or mechanistic) model in contrast to those who advocate a more "voluntaristic" orientation. Within these broad groups, there are various subgroupings and shades of views. Yet, in ideal-type terms the determinists (e.g., the subsocial ecologists in American sociology) posit a highly structured reality which operates outside of human control and direction. Man responds to but does not control the urban environment. The voluntarists, on the contrary, posit the potential maleability of urban social arrangements and assume that man's intervention in the social and ecological order will make a difference.

I think that John Friedmann has mixed these two orientations without explicitly recognizing the consequences of his argument. He seems to assume that there is a deterministic ordering of events which can be rearranged through men's purposive intervention. Delgado, on the other hand, seems to be working within a deterministic, almost subsocial, framework.

Delgado's hidden assumptions about urban reality are not unrelated to the typology on which he places so much emphasis. In developing his typology, he seems to be attempting to delineate subcommunities within the urban center. Surely, any effort to delineate subcommunities could have significant theoretical and practical applications. There are many aspects of urban community or subcommunity life which stand in need of exploration. But I have serious reservations about Delgado's approach.

There have been two main orientations for delineating communities or subcommunities. One stresses the importance of "natural" class, where the scientist takes account of the actor's values and social organization; the other involves "artificial" groupings where the scientist tends to impose his scheme upon reality. Delgado's "artificial" classification scheme is, if I may appear redundant, a little too artificial. The criteria which he employs in constructing his typology seem to have no link with a broader theoretical framework, nor do these criteria appear to have any particular relationship to the broader societal structure or to the "natural" communities, which, I assume, exist in greater or lesser degree.

Again, we need knowledge about the community or subcommunity structure of Latin American cities. This would be a vital first step in helping us to understand the relationship between social groupings in the city and the structure of the broader community and the society.

NOTES

1. This research derives from a study of conflicts and consensus in Venezuela. See Bonilla and Michelena (1968). Gabriela Bronfenmajer and Josefina de Hernández (1968), sociologists of the URVEN study, computed the correlations that are presented here.

2. National identification is measured by capability to make sacrifices for the nation, the loyalty to nation versus other loyalties, and the degree in which the state is considered as a primary social value. Style of evaluation is meant to indicate the degree of secularism, the capacity of innovation, the exposure of oneself to mass-communication media, and the level of information. For a definition of variables and the procedure that was utilized, see Bronfenmajer and Hernández (1968).

REFERENCES

BONILLA, FRANK and JOSE A. SILVA MICHELENA [eds.] (1968) Exploraciones en Análisis y Síntesis. Volume I of Cambio Político en Venezuela. Caracas: Imprenta Universitaria.
BRONFENMAJER, GABRIELA and JOSEFINA DE HERNANDEZ (1968) "Actitudes, participación y urbanización." Part III of Volume IV of Informe General del Estudio URVEN. Caracas: CENDES-UCV. (mimeo)

Part VI

A Future Role for the Social Sciences

Policy and Action

Chapter 9

The Contribution
of the Social Sciences to
Urban Policy Formulation
in Latin America

JOHN MILLER

The Social Sciences and Public Policy

Since so much is said of urban policy in this volume, it is only appropriate that a brief treatment of what is implied by the term be introduced here as a launching statement for an examination of the contribution of the social sciences to urban policy formulation in Latin America. Specifically, public policy is any or all of those guidelines—legislation, administrative regulations, standards, executive decisions, and judicial determinations—which attempt to regulate the allocation of public and private resources (goods, services, monies, infrastructure, and land) for the benefit of social groups. Urban policy simply treats those guidelines and resources where they bear on urbanization, urban processes, and urban problems.

In the typical planning typology, policies stand at the head of the planning process and normally determine what kinds and forms programs and projects will take. Often, of course, policy per se is not explicitly stated, since one can formulate programs and projects on an ad hoc basis and cast them within the frame of what are intuitively felt to be the important policy positions.

For whom the policies are designed is a question of considerable interest, however. They could, for instance, be devised for socioeconomic elites or follow the whims of dictatorial powers. They might be for the benefit of members of given political parties or ideologies. They could be for specific social classes. They might even be for the population of given localities, cities, or regions. Basically, the intention of this volume is that urban policy serve, first of all, all those populations whose welfare is somehow aided by improved urban functions and environments, a qualification which, in effect, includes the entire national

311

population. There is no difficulty in seeing that it should be and is formulated for the urban population itself; there may be greater difficulty in seeing its relevance for the rural community.

Recognition of the role of the urban center in bringing the advantages of the urban culture and services to the rural areas should dispel any initial doubts, however. A largely rural region with a few weak urban centers or none at all, for instance, is not likely to represent a situation conducive to a fuller development of individuals and social groups within that region. As a result, the strengthening and building up of one or more urban centers in the region through national urban policy is clearly a policy important to the rural population. In fact, one may say that in given cases rural policy itself requires a complementary urban policy, although it is more professionally chic to speak of the need of a rural policy (to keep them "down on the farm") as a complementary of urban policy (to reduce the exaggerated growth of urban centers and related investments in infrastructure).

This points up a second and more restrictive "client" category for which urban policy needs to be formulated and on which special social emphasis is placed. This client category is that population which is inadequately served in the private marketplace in the provision of employment positions and opportunities, goods, services, infrastructure, and land. It is an area where, if social goals of equality are to be even partially met, the government will have to intervene. This is quite obviously a normative view of the function of government and the purpose of policy. It is a view which calls for redirection or reversal of public policy for the direct benefit of the poor and minorities.

Appropriately, it is readily apparent how this view of government function may be applicable to policy and planning at the metropolitan-urban level where poor and minority groups are readily located and identified. It is less apparent at the regional, national, and international level where a discussion about planning on behalf of the poor seems one step or more removed from this client category. This is not the case, however, if entire regions and their urban centers have per capita incomes that represent a fraction of those in the capital, if urban services and provisions of public goods are a country cousin version of those in the metropolis, and if the regions and urban centers are effectively prevented from action on these matters by a bureaucratic centralization of power and finances that freezes them institutionally into the permanent status of a colonial role with respect to the center. Greater equity in planning is also relevant to this situation. It requires, as a result, political confrontation and redirected or reversed public policies in urban-regional issues. This is similar in public importance to the need for new policies for the disadvantaged in specific urban communities, that is, policies leading to greater equity in the production and sharing of social product.

Public Policy and the Explicandum
of the Social Sciences

The basic tasks of the social sciences in aiding policy formulation are those tasks basic to social science itself: the discovery and explanation of relationships involving various aspects of human behavior, individually and collectively. The added responsibility of making these tasks useful for policy is in choosing the field of research endeavor in such a way that it is somehow pertinent to the issues around which policy is or should be formed.[1] Fundamentally, what is sought and needed is an explanation of the relationships rampant in the society which somehow prevent or aid the overcoming of problems that must be resolved in order to meet various social needs—what has been referred to elsewhere as "intervention in the sociohistorical field." What should not be overlooked, as is easily done, is that those problems extend even to the area of human behavior within government itself.

As Homans (A, 1967) pointed out, we judge the success of a science by its capacity to explain. It can be added that the ultimate usefulness of social science derives from its capacity to explain relationships in such a way that they guide policies and serve the society. Explanation is used here in the sense of explaining why, under given conditions, a particular phenomenon occurs which social objectives would indicate is desirable and needs to be promoted, or is detrimental and needs to be reduced in its effect. Hopefully, the explanation is sufficiently clear in terms of the more important relationships that it will suggest policy and the details of such policy in terms of programs and specific projects. As Homans concludes, too much of social science, especially sociology and anthropology, appears to have many theories with few explanations. He pleads for less emphasis on a theory search and more on explanation—the *explicandum*, or how social phenomena are to be explained—within which he believes lies the truer and shorter path to theory itself.

This plea by Homans represents a call to the social scientists to give more attention to the opposite end of theory, that is, to selected and interrelated aspects of the empirical world within which some causal or connected relationship is to be ascertained and proven or disproven. Rather than building a great body of theory (hypothetical) out of a set of presumably interrelated axioms, principles, and definitions which are conceptually and neatly organized in a systematic way but not yet verified, his approach has a more modest, but presumably better-grounded, orientation. It is the gradual development of theory through the verification of predictive hypotheses or ex post facto explanation (explanation after research and without benefit of prior hypotheses)—both systems of which, nonetheless, constitute scientific law when widely accepted. In essence, he proposes a process of induction whereby research is used to provide generalizations that will be incorporated into and modify theory rather than the process of deduction whereby intuitively and rationally developed theory provides specific hypotheses for research. Actually, of course, the process of induction in research is aided by prior attempts to form theory and the distinction as to whether the approach is inductive or deductive is often blurred. Policy, too, is often developed on the basis of theoretical assumptions as well as on verified hypotheses or ex post facto explanation. Scientifically, the latter basis would appear to be preferable and, as such, it comprises an additional argument for the use of the explicandum as the basis for policy. Gunnar Myrdal (A, 1969) has referred to the orientation of social science in terms of causes and effects as its "theoretical" orientation and to its orientation in terms of means and ends (i.e., objectives, policies, programs, and projects) as "practical." Actually, of course, knowledge about causes and effects are necessary to guide the means and ends (policies, and so on), not only to construct elegant theory.

In the same book, *Objectivity in Social Research,* he analyzes the nature and causes of distortion in the social sciences and the attitudes and categories that keep research from a creative approach to social problems. He is concerned, too, about values and biases. From the beginning he asserts that the logical means available to the social scientist for protecting himself from biases are:

(1) to raise the valuations which actually determine both theoretical and practical research to full awareness;

(2) to examine them from the point of view of relevance, significance, and feasibility in the society being studied;

(3) to transform them into specific value premises for research; and

(4) to determine an approach and definition of concepts on the basis of value premises which have been explicitly stated.

Myrdal's concern in this area originally grew out of the recognition that economic and other social theory, based upon facts and factual relationships, attempts to advance policy conclusions and to solve practical and political problems with one equation missing, that involving stated value premises. But, as he says, even the ordering of facts and factual relationships out of the chaos of an almost interminable number of such requires the formulation of questions, and these questions themselves are, in the final analysis, valuations. The responsibility of the social scientist is in raising the value premises implicit in his empirical research to the level of explicit statement so that their suitability for use under given conditions may be determined—i.e., do his value premises coincide sufficiently with those of policy makers and those more vague ones of the society itself?[2]

Value Premises in the Research

The use of the social sciences in contributing to policies, urban or otherwise, and problem solution in Latin America raises two rather interesting questions, both of them also related to values. First of all, *which social science knowledge* will be employed? This does not imply which discipline, be it economics, sociology, anthropology, psychology, or political science. It means *which body of social science knowledge resulting from which questions.* Since "scientific" knowledge is based upon which questions are asked and, as Myrdal has emphasized, since questions asked are biased by which set of valuations is taken implicitly or explicitly into account in the research, as well as by which data are included and which ignored, "results" can be different. Scientific knowledge based upon answers to research questions, then, is determined, in part, by the valuations of the social scientist himself and by his cultural makeup. It seems fairly obvious that this has occurred in the past and will continue to occur in the future. It has led, for example, to conflicting research results involving the same research areas and hypotheses. While each investigation appears to be internally organized on sound scientific bases, the fact that conclusions are different suggests that additional elements have altered outcomes.

This issue of cultural valuation became explicit in the Jahuel Seminar with some social scientists, notably the Americanists, claiming that the body of social science knowledge was universal, while others, some of the Latin Americanists, claimed cultural bias and, therefore, distorted answers on the part of the Americanists.[3] What both viewpoints ignore is that in all the weighty judgment on the value and relevance of social science, cultural and other biases nearly always permeate the results, whether by Americanists, Latin Americanists, or others. What makes research results difficult to assess is the hidden nature of the biases when value premises are not exposed. It also tends to prevent a greater social use of results because, as Louis Wirth notes, "without valuations we have no interest, or sense of relevance or of significance, and, consequently, no object." By claiming not to have built-in value premises or biases, the social scientist is creating a research environment in which the relevance, significance, and object of his work comes into question, as well as the theoretical and substantive value of it.[4] The social scientists of Latin America and other developing nations can ill afford to undertake so patently false a neutrality if they expect to make policy-action contributions to their societies. Policy implies some degree of value commitment; action makes such commitment imperative. But those values must, somehow, be reasonably congruent with at least certain substantial sectors of the society, more especially with those which are seriously disadvantaged by the present system.

One is led to recognize, in summation, that it may not always be possible to eliminate value premises which bias results of research but, if they are present, they should be apparent. Scientifically, values are especially useful in identifying the problems and they contribute substantially to the question of what "should" be researched. Ideally, perhaps, the research of the problem itself would be best cast in a situation involving value-neutral commitment. This is easier said than accomplished, however, especially since decisions have to be taken continuously within the research period—about such things as what to ignore among seemingly related aspects of the problem. This again calls up the need for value judgment about what appears to be most important. Further, once results are in, values play a necessary role in appraising the social significance of the research conclusions, in determining what should and should not be emphasized in terms of recommendations, and in setting the degree to which conclusions are so serious as to compel action.

This leads us to the second question: *which social scientists* should or will play a role in setting urban policy as a practical result of their efforts? If events up to the present are guiding in this respect, it couldn't be the typical North American or European social scientist unless a change in research attitude comes about. Why? Because a preponderant amount of Latin American research carried out by the non-Latin American social scientist has as its principal objective the satisfaction of institutional requirements in his own country, i.e., doctoral and postdoctoral research, publications, intellectual curiosity, and personal advancement in his own profession—all subsumed under the general, but not necessarily practical, objective of "knowledge of the area." It would be unfair to say that there aren't exceptions, but, in terms of the total expenditure of external resources in the quaternary sector of research in Latin America, the exceptions are disappointing. Since the institutional requirements of his own country do not require research relevance in terms of practical policy use in Latin America, and since institutional requirements also insist unrealistically upon research based upon questions and answers without value premises, it is, more often than not, difficult to see the utility of a great bulk of the research undertaken in these conditions.

Diegues and Wood (B, 1967) have reported that:

United States specialists, sociologists, anthropologists, and economists study problems or subjects in Latin America which are of particular interest to them, or are connected with their teaching activities or with the university courses which they give, or again because they have received a grant for this purpose from some university or foundation. But these problems or subjects are usually not those of most direct concern to Latin Americans themselves; they are not those which have the most direct bearing on the needs or aspirations of our peoples; nor are they problems or subjects of importance for the regional development process.

A similar point is made by Florestan Fernandes (in Diegues and Wood, B, 1967: 33) in that:

A deeper understanding of the pathos and logos of the communities under study would help the Americanists to plan their activities in a way which would reduce or eliminate the number of failures resulting from selecting projects of little scientific interest and of no dynamic importance for the processes of perception, awareness, and actual intervention in the socio-historical field.

The issue of which social scientist is also complicated by what George Homans (A, 1967) has called the "strong element of historicity." He states that the psychological propositions, which he believes to be the basis of all the social sciences, are conditioned by past history combined with present circumstances, both of which determine behavior, both individual and social. An important question then becomes: who is best prepared to take into account the historicity of behavior in formulating and analyzing the relationships present in the society, the non-Latin American or the Latin American social scientist? Obviously, it requires sensitivity and knowledge on the part of either one, and this may not favor the individual Latin American social scientist, necessarily, although we might expect that, in general, it would. Finally, even if some practical use can be derived from "foreign" research, the published results often do not find their way back to or are not diffused within the Latin American nation in question.

This leads in turn to a consideration of the Latin American social scientist and his role in setting urban policy; the situation is mixed on this score. If he is nurtured too strongly upon the idea of a "valueless" or "unbiased" social science research ethos, he may be little more useful than the foreigner as a contributor to policy input. If a breakthrough, however, can be made to an expression of the value premises upon which his research is based; if these premises are, somehow, parallel and close to those prevailing in the larger society of which he is a part; and if the government itself is sensitive to these values and open to the contributions of social science, then his research efforts will, most likely, be positive aids to societal change and progress through their use in policy formulation. These are large "ifs," but, as preconditions, they are essential to the practical (policy) role of the social scientist in the urbanization process.

It was pointed out at the 1965 Rio de Janeiro Conference on Latin American Studies that

the most promising cooperation among social scientists now would appear to be collaborative field research on applied problems, selected by Latin American scholars, with colleagues from abroad whose interests are compatible. Field research on applied problems would minimize arguments about disciplinary boundaries and focus attention on trying to solve problems which have feasible solutions [Diegues and Wood, B, 1967: 330-331].

One difficulty in this is the frequently distinct philosophical orientation of each discipline at the university level in Latin American education and, in research, the existence of fragmented problem interests. However, to the extent that Latin Americans can define the problems, the uselessness for Latin America of irrelevant research by foreigners would be mitigated. Further, the apparent intrusion of outsiders would be diminished, since their participation would be as members of local institutes. The Foreign Area Fellowship Program now, as a matter of fact, requires an institutional link for scholars going abroad to do their research in order to assure closer fit of interests and better contacts and communication with Latin American professionals.

Adams, in addition to the Latin American scholars, has pointed out the importance of greater concern in the social sciences for focus on problem (action) research along with the use of improved methodology and theory.

It is clearly evident from the direction that the work that the Latins themselves do that the attention to real contemporary problems is the important thing. This is, somehow, separated from the improved techniques that have developed in the U.S. and Europe. *The logical thing, it would seem, would be to encourage the development of methodology and theory on problems of importance* [Adams, B, 1963: 5].

Disciplinary Unity and Disunity

Among social scientists who have been trained in a single discipline, who have successfully broken through the rigid boundaries between the separate categorizations of social science, and who have received the esteem of members of the disparate specializations is Gunnar Myrdal. His own explanation of this metamorphosis is that he has gradually developed a growing recognition of the fact that "in reality there are not economic, sociological or psychological problems, but simply problems, and that as a rule they are complex" (Myrdal, C, 1965; A, 1969).

It is becoming increasingly necessary to master this complexity by whatever tools are at hand. Yet, an overly arbitrary division of knowledge about the social nature of man into distinct fields at the point of problem analysis weighs against the hoped-for moment when the complexity is mastered. There is, perhaps, no clearer demonstration of the need for disciplinary coalescence than in the area of the urban problem, with all of its ramifications. While a primary and endemic interest on the part of the separate disciplines in narrowly defined areas of study has been a positive overall contribution in the past for theoretical and methodological purposes, the urgency of certain problem areas suggests a relaxation of disciplinary boundaries. The complexity of the issues related to environmental decay and racial integration, for example, in the "developed" system of the United States is presently inclining educational institutions and research facilities towards problem focus and interest. At the same time, however, the necessary training of individuals in disciplinary skills continues. Both this need for "problem" focus and the limitation of overall resources in Latin America, including relatively few social scientists, is an impelling argument for the relaxation of exaggerated disciplinary exclusiveness in the approach to societal crises.[5]

The whole question of interdisciplinary knowledge or interrelated multi-disciplinary research necessarily raises some questions as to the nature of the disciplines and the way in which they differ from each other. In large part, the distinctions exist, according to Murray L. Wax (A, 1969), because the pursuit, teaching, and use of knowledge in the social sciences has been at times artificially organized and maintained in separate categories by universities, foundations, and publishing houses, a division whose purpose has been "to structure the social-scientific discipline into a set of mutually exclusive and exhaustive enterprises."

It may also be added that the age-old drive of the human species to specialization (which very early enshrined the medicine man-witch doctor) has always been a means for establishing demand for specialized products, and this desire for specialty has had its imprint on social science. The beginning of sociology is illustrative. As Wax points out, sociology and the "other" sciences that are taken to constitute the social sciences make but little sense from the viewpoint of a systematic and logical division of scientific labor. Sociology before its enshrinement as a separate social discipline formed part of the interests of economists, political scientists, and those in between, the political economists. It arose, however, as a specialization through an initial amalgam of interests in political reform, total societal reorganization, and theoretical science; it was directed towards programs for relieving social conditions, especially those of the urban poor. In other words, its purpose in the moment of birth was that of policy and action for correcting various social ills. As professionalism took over, it and economics, anthropology, and political science moved further apart from these interests and focused increasingly on narrow theoretical and empirical explanations of social phenomena. Each discipline proceeded to stake out its own area of interest within these phenomena and to defend that territory against possible infiltration, as well as to deny, by omission, the importance of social processes outside each narrow disciplinary interest. This strict delineation has been furthered by the gradual development of theories, models, and methods particular to each category—each all too frequently mutually exclusive from the others. The professionals and institutions weren't entirely successful, however, in drawing the lines so that entire joint and overlapping boundary areas were occupied by the social psychologists, the political economists, the ethnopsychologists, the social anthropologists, the psycheconomists,[6] the political sociologists, the social and human geographers, and the economic anthropologists among many such hybrids who grasped the importance of breaking through the bounds of a too narrow examination and intellectual categorization of the social animal and body.

One is still left with the fact, of course, that a general social theory has not been created and that it is helpful to break social processes down into categories that aid in building partial and limited theoretical structures. The scientific misfortune is to assume that these represent the social complexities adequately when in fact they rarely do unless the social scientist has been successful in bridging disciplines and in bringing the most relevant material together from strongly linked "other" disciplines. This condition of exclusion in intellectual interests and applications has shown to be a weakness of some of the best theoretical and model-building economics used in developing countries. There, for instance, the elements leading to unfulfilled goals, have often been seen on hindsight to be "noneconomic" in origin.

The actual arbitrary division of social knowledge is less distressing, perhaps, at the level of purely intellectual activity since categorization does serve useful conceptual purposes. It is at its worst, however, when the new individual being socialized into the profession has little contact with other closely associated disciplines. This gives rise, almost inevitably, to professional "snobbism." It is further accentuated when the education is not oriented towards practical applications, in that one does not have to come to grips with the complexity actually present in the circumstances and continues to deal with the simple abstractions and "neat" theories. When the individual enters the marketplace to sell his skills for problem solution, however, functional distress may become evident, especially in those situations where a broader understanding, as a minimum, is required for effective participation.

Leo Klassen suggested quite rightly at the Jahuel Seminar that interdisciplinary research should not be treated as a fetish. He pointed out that all disciplines are not at the same level of professional development for urban studies and that it is difficult to combine or bridge the gaps between. This does not preclude, however, such integration when improved understanding is assisted in small but important ways.

The economist as an individual and economics as a profession, while they serve functional purposes in national planning, often focus too exclusively on mathematical models which elevate gains in gross national product to the be-all objective and primary concern of policy-making. How often have the national and sectoral plans and resource allocation patterns been examined, however, for their potential effect upon urbanization and the settlement pattern and upon the resultant necessary urban infrastructural investments? Urbanization and the settlement pattern have social, political, and other dimensions, as well as economic, for which policy is needed. Greater awareness of these dimensions on the part of the economist is called for. From a purely economic viewpoint, however, alternative investment patterns might be selected if there were improved knowledge about the economic consequences of urbanization growing out of global and sectoral policies. Even as a basic economic question, so little attention has been given to the optimum economic size for cities that nothing can be truly said to exist which would guide economic policies in an area in which most developing countries are sinking a phenomenal amount of total capital investment.

A growing awareness of the importance of this economic question is evident on several fronts. Some exploratory work along these lines has been done in Poland over the past several years in an attempt to optimize the use of available resources allocated to the urban sector. It was also the topic of the Seminar on the Economics of Urbanization and Urban Overhead Investment in Developing Countries sponsored by Resources for the Future, Inc., in Washington, D.C., on April 16-17, 1969. The International Bank for Reconstruction and Development has even set up a new division within the bank recently on the economics of urbanization, in an attempt to begin to deal with this issue in terms of its own loan programs and advice to participating countries. One of its objectives is to sensitize economic planners in these countries to the implications for urban development of national sectoral planning, primarily since the bank sees the seventies as a decade in which considerable capital investment must be made in urban infrastructure. One can only hope ideally, however, having tossed this rather new and large question into the laps of the economists in these countries as a possible research and information condition for loans, that the urbanization problem will be formulated in terms of broader political, social, legal, and cultural variables as well. If political and legal factors are going to delay, frustrate, or drain off the positive economic effects of chosen urban policy alternatives and subsequent investments, then an analysis of urban problems based upon purely economic variables and economic cost-benefit will continue to be less than satisfactory.

A survey conducted recently by the Centre for Housing, Building and Planning of the United Nations indicates an increasing interest among governments worldwide in development strategies which integrate and promote both physical and economic variables at the urban level into patterns of settlement based on local "cluster" centers or towns—"growth poles." But even so, much research is needed to refine, for instance, the justification for the selection of one center over another. Questions can be raised about the optimum "efficiency" size, under varying conditions, of towns and cities; about cost-benefit (diseconomies as well as the advantages of size); about the functional relationships between different patterns of land use and activities; and about the social and economic criteria for the establishment of new growth poles. These topics, in fact, will form part of the discussion at the 1972 Conference on Human Environment to be held in Sweden under United Nations auspices.[7]

It would be a mistake, however, to posit research on the economics of urbanization as an exclusively economics-of-finances issue. There are also social, psychological, and political economies in the urbanization game. In short, economics, properly speaking, should consider economies outside those of the purely monetary, land, labor, and capital goods nature. This requires a reorientation of economics and the collaboration of other social scientists. As Wax (A, 1969) has stated, the defect of our present division of labor is not too much overlap but too little. He finds that:

> The fault is not that several different disciplines are each studying the same subject matter, while giving different labels to their activities, but that the gaps among our disciplines are much too large.

Since problems are not structured in the real world in terms of gaps in the relationships, this effectively means that each discipline arbitrarily considers only certain limited relationships, with the result that gaping holes develop in research, and problem analysis is only approached partially.

Towards Inter- or Multidisciplinary Effort

Stanley Milgram (A, 1969) has detailed what it means to treat a problem in an interdisciplinary fashion, a treatment which is absolutely essential in the search for reasonable solutions to the problems created by the urbanization process.[8] The way in which it is handled, he says, depends upon the exact point in the process of inquiry at which interdisciplinary thinking is introduced. There are several stages involved.

Formulation: An interdisciplinary effort may begin depending upon how the problem chosen for study is formulated—e.g., if it is conceived in such a way that it lies astride two or more academically defined disciplines. Although it is possible as an exercise in the arbitrary division of knowledge, it is difficult to see how the process and problems of urbanization could be conceived, practically, in terms of a single discipline.

Method of investigation: After the posing of the problem, the researcher must decide what techniques and procedures will be used to study it. As these techniques and procedures are occasionally developed for use in a single discipline, but are applicable to others, an interdisciplinary outlook can be at least mechanically introduced.

Explanation: As any observant researcher has experienced, research efforts not infrequently encounter important unexplainable events that the concepts of one discipline alone do not cover adequately. If the professional is to be honest as a social scientist, he must seek the assistance of neighboring, related fields for the needed explanatory principle. Urban processes, by their complexity, probably could not illustrate this explicandum, or ex post facto explanation, dilemma better.

Application: Finally, findings, insights, or concepts arising even within the subject area of a single discipline may illuminate problems in other subject areas and achieve interdisciplinary breadth.

In order to prevent superficiality, however, one may conclude that an early introduction into the urban research process of all seemingly relevant social sciences is essential. To formulate the urban growth problem purely as an economic one, for example, and to establish the methods of investigation before inviting in the political scientist (who might have suggested its formulation, in part, as a politically influenced problem) will certainly tend to diminish the opportunity for research explanation and application.[9]

George C. Homans (A, 1967) calls for the acceptance of the view that the fundamental proposition of all the social scientists is the same, that this proposition is psychological in origin, and that it derives from the various forms of human behavior. In fact he asserts that the social sciences of psychology, anthropology, sociology, economics, political science, history, and probably linguistics are in fact a single science that share the same subject matter—the behavior of man. Furthermore they employ, without always admitting it, the same body of general explanatory principles. The acceptance of the psychological-behavioralist view, he feels, might mean that "the solution each of the social sciences has reached in dealing with its particular problems could be seen as relevant to, and contributing to the solution of, the problems of the others." It would result in an intellectual unity against which it should be difficult to raise many serious arguments since no individual is likely, for example, to want to be treated in isolation simply and purely as an economic man or a social being or a biological organism with a psychological dimension. There is, therefore, little reason to expect, in our search to understand human behavior in its many "disciplinary" forms, that we will be able to explain it or to find the solution to social problems through the use of the disciplines in isolation. What is called for is a humanist-behavioralist recognition of the common base of human activity, no matter by what name the separate studies of man may be called.

Involvement in Urban Policy

The question of the purpose and use of fundamental social science knowledge dealing with urbanization and urban problems is the one, basically, of the purpose and use of fundamental social science knowledge itself. Should one's focus be on the mere intellectual acquisition of fundamental knowledge about the urban phenomenon in the particular case? Should social science research have, as one of its objectives, the influencing of social change and reform, on one hand, outside the formal social action system of the government? Or should it make an effort to relate research results to the government-political system so as to affect urban policy? For the Americanist there is probably little choice; there is a danger of sorts in "trying" to influence social change and reform from outside the system and, with few exceptions, he is not part of the Latin American system. Yet this does not preclude his formulating research in such a way as to be relevant to significant urban policy issues for Latin American governments or of collaborating with those governments when possible. The Latin Americanist within his own country, however, is not open to criticism as a foreigner and, politically, is entitled to cast his research into a framework aimed at policy for social change. The Latin American social scientist also is more deeply committed to the fundamental problems of urban society in his culture and not merely to topical issues of the passing moment. Part of this commitment derives from the politically involved and committed nature of Latin American universities and their faculties, plus the fact that extensive hard data and financial resources are frequently lacking. This lack effectively prevents any excessive zeal for theoretical empirical work that might lead research away from practical issues.

As a result of the more socially useful orientation suggested here for social science, there is an enlarged opportunity that the behavioral sciences will be able to become involved in experimental research as a secondary characteristic of policy-aiding activities. It must be recognized that, whether there are social science inputs or not, the policy implications and programs of government constitute, in many cases, experiments. Further, many of these experiments lack the proper guidance which could assist the government in the achievement of social objectives. The social scientist then has an opportunity to participate in the experiments and to assist in their evaluation for future guidance.

Institutional managers and policy givers, however, seldom have or take the time to search research findings for policy implications; there is also a lack of operational mechanisms which would permit them to indicate to the social scientist what policy areas they view as critical and what research would aid in policy formulation and implementation. And too often the social scientist who works for the government is reduced to the status of a technician who must accept a narrow definition of his research areas in terms of the emphases of the institution or in terms of the lack of vision in the institution for the more valuable uses of the social sciences beyond the empirical-statistical level of data collection and compounding of social indicators. Political leadership is nearly always present; technical leadership is not.

A real gap is thereby created between what Robert S. Lynd (A, 1939) called the orientation of the scholar and the orientation of the technician. This gap has narrowed in the United States since Lynd first made his observation, but it still exists in Latin America, where many of the social sciences are only now experiencing an expansion of their roles beyond a purely directed technical one in government.

In effect, there has been a communications gap between government and the social science disciplines which could be closed slowly as the social scientists take greater professional responsibility in altering research patterns, in forming research conclusions as policy recommendations, and in bringing these conclusions to the attention of the institutions. The Latin American institutions, on their side, could make better use of the social scientist as an active collaborator in forming policy and the means of implementation.

The continued growth of most urban settlements, the establishment of new communities, and the dramatic increase in the sizes of existing metropolitan complexes represent trends which are seemingly irreversible for the near future. These facts, however, are not those of mere population size and urban physical expansion. They represent, as can be seen from the foregoing chapters, complex forces, interrelated problems, potentials, and challenges to which response would be greatly improved by better knowledge and the increased use of knowledge. Better knowledge represents a cast-down gauntlet to the social sciences; an increased use of knowledge represents a challenge to the policy makers and implementers of the future.

Policy formulation and its implementation depend upon the identification, conceptualization, and evaluation of the problems to be tackled. Policy formulation involves a given set of values and attitudes about the stated problem and some idea of the ends hoped for. Urbanization and concomitant problems in any culture are complex, inadequately understood, difficult to alter under any political system, and fraught with rapid shift and change.

Identification and conceptualization often lag far behind the actual development of urbanwide problems and the necessary creation of new institutions or the restructuring of existing institutions to deal with these problems. Efforts, in large part, depend upon mere alleviation and limited guidance and upon the hope of a continuous self-renewal arising from the organic process which brought about the problems in the first place. In fact, growth policy and programs for guidance may occasionally depend upon the identification of the existing mechanisms by which the population manages to survive, by which self-renewal is brought about, by the means with which roadblocks are circumvented, and so on, under adverse conditions. These mechanisms, in themselves, constitute an important area of research for the social scientist, and the implications for policy guidance are probably only limited by the imagination of the scientist and the receptivity of the government in making use of the results.

An essential in the contribution of the social scientist to policy areas over the next decade is dedication and concern for research areas and theory formulation which aid urban policy development. More effort is needed beyond mere general orientation for policy makers; clearer detailed guides are needed based upon a better appreciation of and concentration on the special characteristics of urban growth within this cultural grouping of nations. Social scientists do have a crucial role in making their specialized intellectual interests and knowledge useful in the resolution of problems growing out of one of the major phenomena of this century.

This professional contribution must also be met by a greater receptivity on the part of government officials and bureaucrats so as to provide access to policy and program aspects of government activity in a way that will make social science contributions possible. Universities must strive to encourage the development of interdisciplinary contact among their faculties, research centers, and students in building a future base for the use of the social sciences in government policy-making—primarily because policy issues almost inevitably involve a matrix of variables which, if properly considered, require an interdisciplinary approach.

The Jahuel Seminar Working Group on Training and Education Programs for Urban and Regional Development in Latin America noted that:

Existing Latin American research and training institutions have developed a tradition of action research programs which are of enormous assistance to governmental agencies—both in clarifying policy issues and implementing and evaluating current efforts in urban and regional development. Government agencies may well assist themselves as well as these existing education centers by using these centers for research and advisory purposes. They may also help these centers by making available, when appropriate, some of their specialized consulting staffs (local and foreign).

The Working Group on Improved Communications in Urban and Regional Development: International, Inter-American, and University-Government[10] also pointed out that one way of

improving communications from the outset is to design research projects so that there are essential links to action and training. Research projects should be undertaken in three basic categories: action, policy and basic research. While no clear cut responsibilities can be defined, it seems advisable to foster basic research in the universities and action oriented research within or in close connection with government and other decision-making agencies. Policy research should best be done with close collaboration between the government and university.

Although improved communication between action, policy-making and research units is generally considered beneficial within the present context of some Latin American countries, it should not be taken at face value. For instance, an excessive dependence of university based research on government may be quite harmful under certain circumstances. Therefore, it seems advisable to define normatively some *optimum* methods of communication. A good safeguard would be that the universities take the initiative. In this context, the universities could pose significant problems to the government in the area of long-term problems, while the government could propose research on short-term problems to the university.

One very practical suggestion made by this working group was in dealing with the need to phrase research findings in such a way that they can be easily communicated not only to the politicians and administrators but also to the wider community. It was suggested that roundtable discussions be organized with political leaders, administrators, community leaders, and others both to inform these persons of the implications of policy for research and to obtain feedback for orienting the particular findings or future research schemes towards policy. Such discussions, it was felt, might profitably be instituted under the auspices of established pressure groups and political parties. Advisory groups or mixed teams of academics, political leaders, and administrators were also proposed as a means of working on specific problems for short periods of time, a technique which might effectively be used in probing areas of policy and related research focus. These techniques, as they point out, have the advantage of providing the possibility of working outside, but not against, the usually rigid bureaucratic structure, and they open up the opportunity for innovation.

In relating the use of the social sciences to government policy, it would be a simple matter to fault officials in both public and private institutions in Latin America for not considering research results and conclusions of the social scientists in setting and executing better policy for urbanization. This might be laid to an impact lag between research and political wisdom; it could even be charged to gross disregard of research in order to protect given interests which would be affected by policy based on such research conclusions. It would be fairer to assert in some cases, however, that research has often been limited in terms of policy implications and that neither of the prior arguments is exclusive.

It is ancient history that the social sciences—especially those considered to be more behavioral in their orientation—have been self-satisfied with research for the sake of pure knowledge, an orientation which cannot be denied its own internal merits. Lynd (A, 1939) referred to this professional orientation of the scholar as "impersonal objectivity," "aloofness from the strife of rival values," and the self-justifying goodness of "new knowledge" about anything, big or little. But, as Lynd warned us, the decisions will be made and public policies will be established without the social scientist unless his research results become more relevant. The situation is only too parallel to the thoughts expressed by an anonymous Japanese poet about the philosopher-intellectual: "sitting quietly, doing nothing, spring comes and the grass grows by itself."[11]

One of the great difficulties that social science has encountered has been the struggle to prove itself worthy of the name of "science" in emulation of the physical and biological sciences. Much depreciation and self-deprecation has been poured into the hollow pursuit of this professional ideal. The situation has been rudely contrasted by the physical and biological sciences, which have proven themselves to be of considerable practical use even, often, without complete and totally explainable "theories." This has been aided, unquestionably, by the fact that their research products have had economic value to the productive sectors of society. It can be suggested, however, that the greater use of the social sciences for practical purposes, whereby they evidenced by their particular methods of viewing and analyzing society that they were capable of aiding in the solution of societal problems, would bear substantial fruit in proving that a science is involved. The social sciences are, in fact, becoming increasingly attuned to this approach, largely due to the growth of interest in socially useful activities. As scientists, professionals are becoming aware that they may also hold values which give their intellectual interests a social purpose other than mere knowledge of the verities of the moment.

Inputs to Urban Policy Planning

Much research may take its orientation from identified policy areas which surface in the day-to-day activities of government agencies and private institutions. It may even draw inspiration for policy-relevant areas from the concerns of the political parties which reflect problems in the society for one or more groups of "clients" for whom public policy may be seen as necessary. This is insufficient, however, given the occasional incapacity of bureaucratic professionals to be effective in the search and identification of crucial problem areas for which policy formulation is required. National concern for public intervention in the urbanization process, concern which would help raise the need for policy formulation and the research upon which to base such policy, is an areas of political activity usually lacking in clearly enunciated form.

Thus, concern for public intervention and policies for this intervention may grow out of either considered and intentional activity for the development of policy or out of an informal process by which policies are derived in the simple procedure of dealing with specific issues as they arise. The latter informal process is more likely to develop where traditional urban planning is based upon isolated and seemingly fragmented crises; the former intentional concern results from an ability to see urbanization as a national process affecting most towns and cities in similar ways and calling for a systematic approach to the resolution of common problems—not a case-by-case patchwork approach. The patchwork approach is also reinforced by the fact that the resolution of problems growing out of urbanization almost always cuts across agency responsibilities. These separate jurisdictions typically deal only with limited functional areas, and the precise juridical and budgetary ways in which these responsibilities and the separate roles of the agencies are defined prevents greater flexibility in the formulation and implementation of programs and projects. Difficulties of interagency cooperation for the resolution of local urban problems, notorious in any society, only compound normal tendencies which thwart the resolution of problems that are structurally complex.

Urbanization, as a result, tends to be approached from the standpoint of limited functional elements—housing, health, education, transportation. Without question, this makes agency action more manageable and subject to easier and quicker project formulation and implementation because only limited functions have to be considered. Policy, too, of course, becomes immediately simplified, and the task of the social scientist engaged in research which can guide this type of limited policy-making is reduced to satisfying less complex requirements, those of simple and direct functional need. It can be argued that there is, nonetheless, a role here for social science research that helps to provide simple end-products such as housing, but such aid largely ignores the more complex nature of housing in its relationship to employment, transportation, and the like.

Social scientists, however, are only too keenly aware that it is not always possible or practical to treat more than a few of these functional elements fully in research useful to policy formulation. This tendency to simplify will be further reinforced by a desire to be theoretically or hypothetically neat in the formulation of the problem and research. Contributions to policy are, nonetheless, needed which are based upon as many crucially relevant aspects as possible in order to illuminate relationships among the elements in the essential problem structure and to suggest needed changes in institutional organization and behavior, and in policy and indicated programs. This is especially so in those cases where effective solution really depends on more than one element.

It should become the special task of the social science researcher concerned with urban policy-relevant research to investigate the possibility of advancing problem areas not consistently or seriously treated by government, at least in clearly designed policy terms, and to demonstrate, where this is the case, the way in which key elements are linked in the problem matrix. By this means he can help raise the problem area to the level of discussion and consideration by the government, show how the elements may be linked, and what importance this may have for policy-making. He may serve an additional social role in pointing out how present institutional arrangements may be inadequate for tackling the problem and indicate possibilities for how they might be restructured to do so.

Research Areas: Fixations and New Directions

There is no intent to belittle the more purely intellectual interests of theory-building and basic knowledge for each of the social sciences as these interests have more than negligible implications for policy. An examination can be made of these sciences, however, in terms of their past relevance for the more practical aspects of their use and in terms of present needs for immediate social utility. A brief and only very partial review, then, is offered in this section for various social science disciplines as a guide to the potential that is offered for challenging and worthwhile inputs to planning whether it be for policy, programs, or projects.

The Historian

On the side of historic studies, it is in the nature of the field that major work will have been in the less than recent past in most cases. It is also understandable that the history of urbanization, settlement patterns, and specific urban places represents a topic generally treated as part of broader historical studies. One is occasionally able to determine from these some of the forces which have influenced urban growth in each country but this is seldom treated as a theme apart. Some exceptions include, e.g., Cuauhtemoc Cardenas, *Crecimiento Económico y Urbanización en México* (I, n.d.) and Angel Palerm (L, 1955).

The historian has, probably more than any other social scientist, the ability to be interdisciplinary in outlook and to maintain a multicausal view of the historical process of human behavior, yet it is amazing how little his broad outlook and talents are used for applied purposes. This is due both to his own reticence to get involved and to the reticence of functional-action institutions to use his special attributes. Generally they are considered too broad and of interest intellectually only in their "historic" sense. Yet as Stanley J. Stein suggests (L, 1964: 114), the historian "must constantly review the broad issues and generalizations of Latin American history and test them at all levels, preferably at the local level—village, municipal, state, provincial, or departmental—searching for primary materials." Such a search could have, e.g., very practical uses in the policy area of centralization and decentralization in government and adminis-tration. Valid results might ferret out the advantages and disadvantages inherent in given distributions of power, experimentations with their exceptions within the culture, and the like. There are too many generalizations about this one aspect of national life alone which lack detailed evidence and which have grown into a body of myths and the too easy acceptance of expectations about the values of given power distribution systems.

The Geographer

In Latin American geography there has been an almost exclusive concern for the regional-continental or national study of climates, geomorphology, soils, and ecology of the type typically of interest to agriculturalists, mineralogists, and archeologist-historians. If not based primarily on purely physical geography, studies have dealt with cultural and historical patterns. In contrast, there has been very little work in contemporary economic geography of a more sophisticated brand, a situation which has begun to change, however, as interest in governments for the promotion of regional economic development has grown. Study in this area has been initiated, as Fernandes implied would happen (Diegues and Wood, B, 1967), by government interest, not by some spontaneous professional orientation, and a large part of the work has or is being done by economists, not geographers.[12]

As James J. Parsons (J, 1964: 59) stated about the field,

one cannot but be impressed with the paucity of even descriptive economic studies or studies of the causes and consequences of uneven distributions of population, not to mention the absence of any efforts to seek such principles and probability statements as may derive from the austerity spatial approach of the new school of quantitative economic geographers.

With respect to urbanization itself, he added,

the neglect of the phenomenon of urbanization by students of Latin America generally and by geographers in particular has been striking. As the organization center of human society, exercising powerful influences on the use of surrounding space, and as a geographical phenomenon of interest for its own sake, whether in terms of historical evolution, layout and morphology, or internal and external linkages, the Latin American city offers a multitude of significant and unexplored geographical themes.

A certain few studies have added some knowledge in this area but far below that of the interest devoted to urban evolution and morphology in other parts of the world. Some of the Latin American studies include Stanislawski's essay "Early Spanish Town Planning in the New World" (L, 1947), the survey of South American cities by Wilhelmy (L, 1952), and the four volume study of São Paulo by Azevedo et al. (J, 1958). On the other hand, central place theory and economic base studies of cities have hardly been touched. Since 1960, *Aspectos de geografia Carioca* (Associação dos Geógrafos Brasileiros, J, 1962) and the periodical work of the Associacão have added studies on the urban and hinterland geography of a number of small urban places in Brazil.[13]

Neither has the study of political geography contributed much to a knowledge of the spatial characteristics of politics, political parties, regional movements, differential government administration and services, and so on in the Latin American nations. As Parsons (J, 1964: 62-63) indicated,

> The significance of the size and shape of nations and their provincial subdivisions, the nature and function of boundaries (mostly passing through sparsely settled areas), the geography of voting habits, of political awareness, and of civil disobedience and *violencia,* along with many other themes, remain to be seriously considered from the geographical point of view.[14]

The Anthropologist

In anthropology, a fixation in research developed at the stage of the infancy of anthropology itself, with the result that a preponderance of anthropological work has been done among exotic, primitive, rural communities. Such studies cannot be ignored because they often have importance in better understanding the rural immigrant and his social organization in the urban community, a fact which Oscar Lewis has pioneered in his studies (Lewis, H, 1952 onwards). Whiteford, too, has presented a notably excellent study, *Two Cities of Latin America: A Comparative Description of Social Classes* (H, 1960), which is a useful model in describing the receptivity for economic change in two communities, one of which is positively structured for change and the other blocked by tradition. The first corresponds to what has been referred to elsewhere as a "social growth pole."

Although there is a fair and respectable body of anthropological literature on Latin America, the urban socioanthropological study is rare. Carlos Delgado in this book and elsewhere (H, 1960; H, 1965), William Mangin (H, 1967), and Richard W. Patch (H, n.d.) have written on the topic at various times, more especially with respect to the squatter settlements. And, Lisa Peattie (H, 1968) has given us a valuable insight in *The View from the Barrio* to an entire community in the throes of rapid change and major government intervention through planning for the development of a new regional urban industrial center in the Venezuelan Guayana. It is especially to be recommended in terms of policy and planning.

Peattie's study is, in part, an answer to Arnold Strickon's question, "Where is the social anthropological study of the Venezuelan oilworker, the Bolivian tin miner . . . ? The lack of studies of various urban groups very obviously represents a major disciplinary gap" (G, 1964: 150). He suggests that

> studies might focus on such groups or voluntary organizations, occupational groups or categories, and others that we know are critical to the organization of urban peoples in other parts of the world. Similarly, kinship as a means of structuring economic and political elites might come in for study. A critical group in the economic or political life of a community might be isolated as a focus of interest. It would be merely the stage upon which we could see the myriad of connections (both within and without the locality) among the people, their organization, and various categories of cultural phenomenon.

Strickon has exposed an idea which should be central to anthropological studies in the city, that is, that the study of a neighborhood, less than that of a rural community, cannot be made in isolation from the larger community of which it forms a part. Individual and social behavior and economic and social problems in a neighborhood are, in an important way, a response or result of the urban community beyond the vague boundaries of the barrio itself. Gideon Sjoberg expressed surprise during the Seminar at the generally low priority given to the ecological dimensions of urban life within communities and to the outside and suggested that this should constitute a major focus of research interest in sociology and anthropology, as well as among other disciplines. For policy purposes it is essential to be knowledgeable about the internal and external (existing or potential) change agents which further improve the total environment for the less favored individuals and social groups "out there."

A particularly significant new approach in the anthropological study of urban places is that of Clifford Geertz (H, 1965), *The Social History of an Indonesian Town.* Although it is not a study of a Latin American community, it can be recommended as a model of anthropological research useful for urban policy. In brief, it presents a picture of the interaction of ecological, economic, sociocultural, and welfare factors in shaping the life of the community and in giving it form through "penetrating to the forces that shape social action." Since the viability of any policy is crucially dependent upon policy and program congruence with social forces, knowledge of this interaction represents an awareness useful to policy formulation. Another model for research has been advanced recently by Anthony Leeds (G, 1970) which may prove to be valuable as a research vehicle for policy input. Basically, it deals with localities as the loci of certain forms of power and with supralocal structures (institutions and organizations functioning for multiple localities) as loci of other forms of power. Knowledge about the variety of oppositional, cooperative, complementary, and other types of relationship between these two forms of power is assumed to be useful for developing theories of change and resistance to change, as well as for preparing practical policies to aid in change.

The Political Scientist

If one is to believe Merle Kling (B, 1964: 168), political science research in Latin America is in a dismal state and concerned with some rather traditional areas of intellectual probing: formal procedures, written prescriptions, governmental structures, stated (versus actual) public policy, and so on. In effect, too much emphasis has been placed on form and not on process. The political science researcher should be wary of falling into the same trap when dealing with research on urban politics and national politics relevant to urban centers in Latin America. The formulation of research projects along purely formalistic-legalistic lines could, at best, be assiduously avoided.

As Kling indicated, this traditional political science focus was changing in the first part of the sixties, and an orientation was developing toward studies of power, interests, parties, groups, elections, processes of decision-making, operational rules of the game, and the like. Certainly the trend has continued even within the area of the urban political structure as demonstrated by Francine F. Rabinovitz et al. (K, 1969). It must be said, however, that the trend during the sixties towards the military takeover of constitutional government and the suppression of political interests in many Latin American countries has not favored political science research. Further, it has drawn such interest as does exist away from the urban to the national front. It has also made it more difficult for the political scientist to make policy inputs.

Even with a growth of interest in political topics with less formal content, much more is needed. This is especially true in the area of depth of knowledge about the functioning of the public administration as part of the political system, how it approaches urban problem resolution, what are the failings and why, how it balances the interests of different groups, how power is exerted for alternative allocations, who has it, and so forth. The importance of this area cannot be overlooked. The management of the national government with respect to urban problems and project allocations is a key area of investigation, given that central government spends up to ninety-eight percent of all government monies in some Latin American countries. If there is an urban crisis in the provision of the basic amenities and health safeguards in the Latin American city, how is this crisis being met politically? The problem is not only economic; it is in large measure also political and institutional. Political scientists could shed much light on this dark, Stygian region.

Research focused on the urban problem could also lead to a clarification of knowledge about the general political system. Administrative decisions are not purely and exclusively technical; there is a large measure of the political. The often-asserted statement that urban politics is basically national in content is not without merit when one considers the facts of political power distribution, but it should not be overlooked that there *is* "a politics of the urban sector" which is found at the national level, most frequently in the administration of the central government. A far better understanding of that politics is essential for overcoming urban difficulties and altering existing political structures and policies. It seems crucially necessary for achieving improved decision-making for implementation. Daniel Goldrich suggested during the Seminar that the political scientist might profitably seek out those cases where major reforms have occurred to see how these reforms have affected the urban process. Cuba is cited as one case.

In terms of the spatial distribution of power within a country, a great deal more information is needed as well. Are the elected representatives, for example, of one region truly representing the interests of their constituents or is the regional political base used merely as part of the scramble for party domination at the center? If so, this may reenforce trends that give undue importance in political decisions to the center, delay the spatial development of the nation, and create an imbalance in its urban growth. Or, is the situation the reverse—that is, that regional interests are so strongly determining that allocations of central monies are inefficient and delay, in the short run, national growth and, in the long run, the growth of all regions?

Kling (B, 1964: 204-205) phrased the issue very well:

> In the case of Latin America political scientists continue to ascribe "power" to abstract, evidently monolithic entities—the landowners, the army, the president. Yet, we have not made a series of empirical studies to determine the process by which specific decisions have been reached. Is there anything distinctive about Latin American policy-making processes? In general, who takes the initiative in pushing policy measures and in generating support (consensus building)? What are the veto groups on different types of policy? It is true that public decision-making in Latin America seems characterized by lower visibility than in the United States; but studies of the formation of specific public policies, if feasible, might make it possible to associate the concept of "power" more meaningfully with particular groups and institutions in Latin America.[15]

As one example, one could ask how a major public investment decision, such as the metropolitan rapid transit system in Santiago, Chile, could reach the construction contract stage without significant public information or discussion? What groups or individuals are involved? Was there substantial tacit agreement or consultation with nongovernment party leaders who may be responsible for carrying out the twenty-year construction if the present government party is not continuously in power during this period? Were alternative uses of the money considered? A more profound knowledge about the workings of such decisions can yield a great deal on how the political process actually works and, indeed, what the informal political structure not spelled out by formal institutions, procedures, groupings, or roles actually is which determines power exerted.

The Economist

Research or intellectual interest has hardly been noticeable in the field of urban economics in Latin America, aside from purely fiscal policy and taxation and even this has been minimal. It should be added, of course that this is a field still in formation in the United States. What interest has been shown has developed only recently and is still quite local. As a research interest it is being developed in large part by Latin American professionals who have had some training or contact with it in the United States. Still, in some research areas almost nothing has been done.

There are a number of nagging questions which are beginning to surface and which beg greater knowledge and guidance. Can and should certain fiscal decisions or resources be decentralized to local government or local-regional branches of central government? What decisions are economically appropriate for decentralization and how may it be accomplished? These are, appropriately, areas of interest for the economist, the political scientist, the public administration expert, and the lawyer; they demonstrate very clearly the necessity for an integrated approach to urban policy research.

More knowledge from economists is crucially needed for input to urbanization policies. In fact, it is probably fair to say that the lack of such policies is due in fair measure to inadequate concern and guidance from professionals in this field. Evaluations and cost-benefit studies of urban growth alternatives are nonexistent. Such alternatives are usually posed by geographers, political scientists, sociologists and planners on the basis of urban system theories, presumed economic efficiency, or social objectives other than those dealing with economics. As urban infrastructure expenditures increase both in quantity and as a proportion of total government investments, however, it becomes more urgent to assure greater efficiency in the use of these resources.

It is curious, but understandable, that the situation has arisen in many countries of the world, as well as in Latin America, where careful consideration is given to the scale and location of investment, say, in national energy or heavy industry as a national policy issue, but little attention is devoted to such basic questions as how much should be invested in urban infrastructure and where this investment should occur. The fragmentation of urban investment decisions, the decision-making and budgetary jealousies of responsible government agencies, and the lack of any national committee, council, ministry, or joint ministerial committee to consider these questions, form policy, and guide urban development are all contributing.

More economists in Latin America need to be attracted away from the professional interest in GNP to that of urban and regional economics. There are sufficient intellectual attractions there if the professional will but look. The employment opportunities will have to be created in part by his interest and by his persuasion of the public agencies that the questions to be examined are important questions. The Latin American city, for example, in its hyper-urbanized form, is woefully short of jobs in the secondary (manufacturing) sector in contrast to cities in developed countries. Some economists have argued for an expansion of the urban construction industry, especially housing, as a means of generating employment and, through it, a demand for consumer products. What are the overall effects of investing in these types of activities over investment in capital-intensive projects? Laughlin Currie (I, 1966) advances the argument that between sixty and seventy percent of the working force in many developing countries should really be included in the disguised unemployment category, and that the rate of growth in per capita production is a highly unsatisfactory goal of development and policy. As an ameliorative measure and holding higher employment as a bona fide political and economic goal, he suggests a breakthrough plan based upon construction of urban facilities and housing. This type of unknown effect needs greater probing.

Furthermore, economists need to have their professional curiosity piqued by the question of urban land economics under situations of rapid urbanization. The Secretary-General of the United Nations has often sounded the alarm, for example, about the adverse effects of uncontrolled urban development on land costs, a phenomenon which has led to an increasing capitalization of land that is forcing, through elevated land costs, high density uses with social consequences of crowding, noise, and enforced anonymity. A related variable in terms of policy and practical development alternatives is the question of transportation economics. Much needs to be done to bring these factors into greater harmony at the project stage.

Knowledge about urban economies and diseconomies of scale, the external and agglomeration economies, the efficiency of programmed infrastructural investment alternatives, urban economic base analysis as a basis for planned future investment, methods and means of financing, recouping social investments which are self-funding over time, the economic role of given urban centers under varied conditions for regional development, the influence of income gaps between regions and urban centers on migration,[16] and alternative locations of productive activities as influential for population settlement patterns are only suggestive of the multitude of questions to which the economist could address himself in assisting policy formulation.[17]

The Sociologist

Generally, sociology and demography have made important contributions to knowledge about urban social processes in Latin America, although certain areas remain quite incomplete in their coverage and contemporary relevance. This can be laid in part to what Rex Hopper (G, 1964) has identified as the emergence in recent years of the new school of sociology and the fact that the number of "new sociologists," those who study real problems with empirical research, is still inadequate.

The work of Argentine sociologist Gino Germani, Luis Costa Pinto, and J. Matos Mar is representative of some of the urban sociology which has been done. An essay guide for research by Germani (A, 1960), can still be examined for current use. More attention, however, needs to be given to research (1) at the urban neighborhood level, and (2) in the sociology of urban institutions or of those dealing with urban problems—together with the political scientists and the public administration experts. Attention in these areas would suggest practical research programs and projects rather than a sometimes too exclusive concern for the study of urbanization at the national and continental-regional level.

It is interesting to note that an essay by T. Lynn Smith (G, 1970) on the development of sociological studies of Latin America in the United States is almost exclusively descriptive of either rural or broad national social studies. In this sense, it parallels the early concentration of anthropology on the rural sector.

Considerable research direction and training for specific urban problems is actually being provided in Latin America, however, by such research and education groups as the Centro Latinoamericano de Pesquizas em Ciências Sociais in Rio de Janeiro, FLACSO (Facultad Latino Americana de Ciencias Sociales), and CELADE (Centro Latino Americano de Demografía, in Santiago. FLACSO has, for example, used as one of its research models, under the category of the process of economic and social development, the investigation of "urban socialization through local groups." More specifically it refers to the "socialization of rural immigrants through participation in formal groups created on an ecological basis and working towards better personal and social conditions of the inhabitants of the local urban area."

Hopper (G, 1964) points out, as has been done here,

> that a research program focussed on the sociology of development be directed toward large-scale research on centrally crucial social questions. *These problems should be identified by our Latin American sociologists rather than by "outsiders."* There will be thus greater stimulus for research. I am proposing that research strategy in Latin America could well be pointed toward providing aid in the techniques of translating social problems into researchable sociological problems. [Emphasis added.]

In the area of socioeconomic differentiating among regions, provinces, and communities, Armand Matellart (H, 1965; Matellart and Garreton, H, 1969), a Belgian demographer, has presented two studies which have advanced a better understanding of spatial distinctions within Chile. The *Atlas Social de las Comunas de Chile* and *Integración Nacional y Marginalidad: Ensayo de Regionalización Social de Chile* represent social characteristics of the nation on a spatial basis which existed before almost exclusively only at the national level or for selected communities. These are studies of a type useful to national urban policy and regional development planning.

The Legal Professional

There is probably no area of intellectual exercise more out of joint with the social needs of that discipline itself than that of jurisprudence. Even though there have been moves away from a strict and dry deductive analysis of the civil-law system and the application of new legislation and interpretation based on strict conformity to the annotated guides of past codes, there is still remarkably little interest in an examination of the legal system from the point of view of its function in the face of new social conditions. This applies as well to the area of administrative regulations (devised by the legal profession) which often constitutes such a detailing of responsibilities and constraints on action that the purpose of the agency, itself, may often be hamstrung by its own structured juridical nature. And an examination is rarely made of the accumulated legal detritus (*tramites*) of the past, which effectively prevent action.

It is a fact that many renters or purchasers of public housing in Latin America are so discouraged in their efforts to make payments on the property that they delay payments for months and, even, eventually give up because of the bureaucratic red tape and difficulties forced on them. This points up what Kenneth L. Karst (K, 1964: 293) has emphasized—that is, that "research in Latin American law seems best oriented toward institutions and not toward a comparison of rules or principles." Unless legal scholars become concerned with how the legal system complicates the work of the social institutions and prevents the efficient and effective implementation of the programs they are supposed to carry out, the profession of law will not be able to understand adequately one of the principal reasons for the development and use of the legal system. Greater knowledge is needed about the actual effects of legislation; too much is based upon a normative legalistic idea of what it ought to do. The two, on hindsight, may be dramatically different. Much could be done in the legal area dealing with urban problems. In what sense, for example, do existing constitutional provisions, legislation, and administrative regulations affect the actual solution of urban problems, either as local matters or as matters of national concern?

As Karst (K, 1964: 303) put it,

A high degree of centralization characterizes all Latin American governments, despite the formal federation of some of them. It would be rewarding to study existing local governments—their structure, their functions, and their financing—at least in part in order to see whether there is any possibility of using local government as a means of educating citizens in responsible participation in public affairs.

Another very critical area is the examination of legislation relative to urban physical development. How does such legislation prevent rational land use and expansion? How can necessary expropriation for renewal and the provision of public services be improved? Is urban land reform a growing necessity and, if so, how can it be achieved? And what are the legislative provisions which prevent local government from providing its citizens with basic urban services?

Seminar Recommendations on Urban and Regional Research

Preliminary Note

An important objective of the Jahuel Seminar was the formation of work groups at the conclusion of the Seminar. These groups proposed recommendations for social scientists and institutions interested in the field of urban research and urban policy planning in Latin America. The groups were concerned with four principal areas: Urban and Regional Research; Training and Education

Programs for Urban and Regional Development; Experimental Research Projects on Urban and Regional Development; and Improved Communications in Urban and Regional Development: International, Inter-American, and University-Government.

For the relevance that the report of the Urban and Regional Research Work Group Report has for the theme of this book, it is included in its entirety. It is followed by a brief extract from the report of the Working Group on Experimental Projects for Urban and Regional Development in Latin America. Observations and recommendations from the other reports are introduced at pertinent points elsewhere in this chapter [—Ed.] .

Work Group Report on Urban and Regional Research[18]: Introduction[19]

The present report is divided into three main parts. In the first section, some general research themes are identified as important for understanding urbanization processes in Latin America, as well as for policy and planning. In the second section, specific projects are considered which would build an adequate "infrastructure" for urban research. Finally, a number of issues relating to organization for urban research are considered.

Some general issues should be mentioned which relate to many of the proposals described further on.

Conceptual clarity. Some critical concepts for urban research and theory remain to be clarified. One of these is a distinction between "rural" and "urban" relevant to the Latin American context. Greater conceptual clarity is also required with respect to what someone has called the "largely heterogeneous urban universe." Moreover, such categories should be rendered more meaningful in the context of national societies. The very notion of urbanization needs to be more fully explored. Obviously, however, we must proceed with research even though these questions are not finally settled.

Historical focus.[20] Historical research on all major themes of interest to urban planning and development should be encouraged. Social scientists must now generate historical background studies for their individual projects; it would be preferable for them to be able to draw upon coherent bodies of broad-ranging and comparative historical research. Of particular interest would be the historical analysis of urban systems; patterns of ethnic and class relationships; forms and characteristics of urban entrepreneurship; local government; and patterns of migration and assimilation of immigrants.

Criteria for assigning priorities. This was a subject of considerable discussion. One suggestion was that priorities should reflect the magnitude of problems as determined by the size of the population affected and by their larger national significance. A more elaborate view was that we need "a strategy for identifying significant research topics where significance implies a reasonable chance of yielding useful returns." When studying urban systems, we are dealing with exceedingly complex domains, and our natural inclination is to impose order on the initial chaos of complexity by either

(1) creating typologies; or

(2) establishing developmental sequences.

Under each of these headings we could outline a substantial checklist of substantive research inquiries, and bring the two streams together by assaying whether or not there are relationships between the typologies and sequences. For example, it is quite important to examine whether there is a unidimensional "urban-regional-national" development sequence, and whether types of socio-economies simply reflect stages on such a sequence. A hypothesis of this kind was basic to several of the papers presented at the Seminar, but obviously needs testing. On the other hand, we also live in a world in which public policy is of increasing importance to the nature and performance of urban systems. An alternative way of identifying significant research tasks and originating priorities is therefore in relation to the instruments and objectives of public policy.

In general, we feel that whatever the abstract merits of priorities for research, the allocation of funds should take into account what might be called the law of opportunity. This means that research support should be adjusted to the interests and ideas of capable individual researchers or research institutions in addition to reflecting policy priorities where these can be identified.

Research Themes

There are a number of broad research themes related to urbanization and regional development in Latin America which, though extremely important in themselves and from a policy standpoint, have not yet received proper attention. As formulated here, the themes do not constitute specific projects; rather they suggest areas and directions of research within which particular projects may be identified for detailed treatment. Each theme is illustrated with reference to specific examples. It is in no way intended, however, that these examples should in themselves constitute suitable research topics without first undergoing substantial reformulation.

Theme 1. Development problems of major Latin American metropolitan regions. An effort should be made to accumulate and store relevant data on metropolitan structure, functions, ecological, and other variables in a standardized and readily accessible form for a number of major metropolitan regions in Latin America. Within the context of these studies, special attention might be given to:

(a) Research on "urban land reform" including problems in using expropriation, taxation, and legalized "squatting" policies as instruments for achieving a more desirable distribution and utilization of urban land.

(b) Research on the internal patterns of urban land occupance and their changes over time. Emphasis might be given to the resulting physical form of metropolitan areas in relation to their social evolution and the introduction of new technologies at different points in time. Similarities of Latin American metro-regions to North American, European, Asian, and African centers might also deserve attention.

(c) Research on changes in the distribution of occupations of the urban labor force. Trends in un- and underemployment should be investigated for their effects on political, administrative, and social organization and behavior. The functioning of the metropolitan labor market should also be carefully analyzed.

(d) Research on the social origins of migrants in relation to their gradual assimilation into urban society.

(e) Research on types of housing submarkets for different socioeconomic groups: their structure, operation and efficiency.

(f) Research on the history, performance, ups and downs, and problems experienced by official housing agencies in various Latin American countries. A survey of the experience of major Latin American cities with "master plans" would also be instructive.

(g) Experimentation with new approaches to metropolitan research adapted to the needs of Latin American cities and the research capabilities of the institutions doing research.

Theme 2. Consequences for regional and urban development of alternative policies for achieving Latin American integration. This would include continuation and refinement of the Stöhr-Pedersen type of studies (reported in this volume) on the implications of alternative integration policies on regional development. The possible consequences of presently evolving integration policies for the growth of very large cities and for presently underdeveloped regions (such as the Northeast of Brazil) should receive special attention.

Theme 3. Patterns and consequences of the areal distribution of powers. Planning operates within a complex power structure: It is crucial to understand this structure, and to have some continuing indices of changes in the system. Some major reasons for this are:

(1) All planning requires taking into account conditions of power structure and their changes.

(2) Specifically, it is important to trace changes in class structure in major urban regions.

(3) The planning operation itself works within a power structure, and it can be more effective if it is carried out with this knowledge available to it.

The effects of different patterns of decision-making power on economic and political development merits special consideration in this context.

Theme 4. Political consequences of accelerated urbanization in relation to national development.[21] This would include subthemes such as measures of the changes in urban "marginal populations" in relation to changes in party organization, political doctrine, and voting behavior; frequency of occurrence, types, and overt (or hidden) meaning of urban conflict situations; analysis of the "crisis of participation" which may appear in certain countries as a result of accelerated urbanization, and of the different ways in which attempts have been made to deal with this crisis; the effect of accelerated urbanization on social ethos (for example, consumption versus production orientation; collectivism versus individualism; egalitarian-cooperative norms versus competitive norms) and compatibility of this ethos with the objective demands of national development.

With regard to participation and conflict, particularly at the city level, new tools of observation, new concepts, and new data are needed. Existing instruments may not be adequate to Latin American societies and, in any case, existing indicators are still rather gross. Specifically, two research topics have been singled out as particularly important: (1) How do urban complex variables affect not only the level but also the structure, channels, intensity, and direction of social participation? Are cities really integrative factors? (2) How can different forms of conflict be detected in Latin American cities? What do these conflicts mean in terms of the national system? How are conflicts affected by urban conditions and policies?

Some specific approaches, within the major theme, were also suggested. In the first place, the need was mentioned of taking into account the role of the international power structure as a meaningful independent variable in the study of urban life. Another important aspect concerns the national political conditions under which urban life becomes more humane. Specific cases should be selected in which such effects could be detected and analyzed.

Theme 5. Urban social and political organization and the capacity to innovate (research on "city personality" or "city style"). Urban development policy includes an effort to channel resources to those urban areas which have a demonstrated or potential capacity for innovative effort. Within the framework of this theme, research should be undertaken to study the validity and usefulness of "bureaucratic" and "innovative" organizational models of urban life; the conditions under which such models would be verified; and the factors which contribute to reinforcing one or the other model. Other dimensions of the model which might be emphasized include: degree of social conflict or harmony; role of paternalistic versus upstart (or foreign) elites; and degree of permeability of social structure. Special emphasis might be given to studies that would focus on critical "turning points," as a city changes from bureaucratic-traditional to innovative-democratic structures.

Theme 6. Frontier settlement (new colonization). This research would emphasize subthemes such as rate and form of city formation on the settlement frontier, development potential of these cities, political and social structures and organization in formation, attractive power of the frontier for population and capital, major incentives of frontier settlement on a large scale (especially major new road systems, such as the Carretera Marginal de la Selva), the role of cities in frontier settlement, and sequence of stages in frontier occupance and consolidation.

Theme 7. The urbanization of the countryside. This theme would stress such topics as impact of cities on rural society, forms of urbanization—mass media, syndicates and cooperatives of rural workers—impact of these forms of urbanization on traditional rural values, impact of urbanization on agricultural production, income, and on the pattern of rural settlement, impact of urbanization on the scale, selectivity, and direction of rural emigration, and finally, impact of rural emigration on the economic organization of agriculture.

Theme 8. The social process of the formation of new and developing urban settlement districts. This would include giving attention to patterns of social organization emerging in different types of new and developing urban settlement districts, political attitudes and behavior associated with these districts, evolution of settlement districts over time (consolidation, incorporation or degeneration), capacity for innovation and self-help, anomie, migration among different settlement types within a city related to the family life cycle and improvements in economic or social status, and the significance of land-ownership as an instrument of socialization of the poor into the dominant society.

Infrastructure of Urban Research

Urban research projects require varying amounts of preliminary work and, in general, would benefit immensely from the creation of data banks and processing facilities that could be used by many different projects. The following are necessary steps to build such a minimum infrastructure:

(a) To develop and distribute basic series of historical data, using comparative categories whenever possible, with special emphasis on *recent* data (nineteenth/twentieth centuries). Sample subjects to be covered would be population, urbanization rates, internal and international migration, and changes in the occupational structure by economic sector. Obviously, preparation of basic historical data can and should include other types of data that may not be the central core of interest to urban researchers. In this sense, what may be needed is a recovery of entire censuses and other types of historical data, rather than of data pertaining specifically to urbanization.

(b) To create conditions for a more efficient use of census data by promoting and generalizing the use of census samples, by attempting to influence national census bureaus and the Census of the Americas Organization in order to expand conventional census information and include information on topics that are of relevance for sociological and urban research. One such possibility would be, for instance, to collect data on the father's education or occupation in order to assess intergenerational mobility. Efforts should also be made to ensure greater

comparability both in data collection, by means of using identical categories, and in census reporting, by means of publishing a minimum amount of descriptive data and analytical tables that are the same in different countries. As steps in this direction have already been taken by a number of agencies (for instance, CELADE and the Census of the Americas Organization), it is suggested that support be given to these initiatives and that attempts be made to supplement them, instead of setting in motion an entirely separate process.

(c) To compile inventories of scientific findings that would summarize the existing empirical knowledge in urbanization, using both published and mimeographed materials.

(d) To train personnel for systems programming, preferably those with some background in the social sciences. The physical existence of computational facilities is not enough, and adoption and development of computer programs are needed.

(e) To support the establishment of data banks and other facilities that would make existing data more accessible and useful.

Aspects of Organization for Urban Research in Latin America

In considering how to promote research along the lines indicated in the preceding pages, a number of principles or considerations of a general character may be considered. They are included here either as straightforward normative statements on what ought to be done or, alternatively, as issues which should be carefully thought about.

(1) "Urban studies" are not unique. They are not only a concern of centers bearing this title but also constitute a promising focus of research for more traditional disciplinary centers. In an urbanizing Latin America, the importance of studies focusing on cities, systems of cities, and the social, economic, cultural, and political changes engendered in city, region, and nation by urbanization should be increasingly recognized by *all* the social sciences.

(2) The newly constituted Latin American Social Science Research Council (CLACSO) can serve as an important institution for the coordination of urban research efforts by acting as a clearing house of information about ongoing research, supporting research infrastructure services, promoting interinstitutional contacts, and in other ways.

(3) Much urban research is best carried out through multidisciplinary efforts. Nevertheless, this characteristic should not detract from the importance which research along single disciplinary lines may have for certain types of urban research. Multidisciplinary (or interdisciplinary) research should not be allowed to become a fetish.

(4) Much progress can be made in urban research by concentrating efforts in individual countries. Greater generality may be obtained by carefully

designed comparative studies, either within a single country (among cities) or between two or more countries. Grand Latin American approaches should be avoided.

(5) The preparation of personnel for research careers in urban studies should not be neglected. At the moment, this objective does not appear to be within reach in Latin America. Fellowship programs should be considered that will allow a limited number of Latin American students to pursue advanced urbanization studies at the doctoral level overseas.

(6) Research funds generally go to those institutions most capable of doing sophisticated research. Nevertheless, urban research should, to a limited extent, be promoted also in other university centers. Some thought might be given to linking such (secondary) research to the more important urban research programs at major universities in each country. An example of this type of cooperation is the recent agreement between CIDU at the Catholic University of Chile and the Universidad Austral (Valdivia) for a joint research endeavor.

(7) International agencies should consider funding a portion of the local costs of urban research and using available funds as "seed money" for promoting strategic lines of investigation in hitherto unexplored fields.

(8) To the extent possible, urban research should be integrated with teaching efforts. In this way, new generations of Latin American students can be brought up who not only will have close familiarity with research thinking and problems of conducting urban research but who will also have gone through a period of apprenticeship to senior professors.

Experimental Projects: A Resumé

The Working Group on Experimental Projects for Urban and Regional Development in Latin America[22] suggested various criteria which might aid in research project design along experimental lines. They defined, in very general terms, an experimental project as

a set of propositions, techniques and resources (human, physical, financial) that are [sic] organized with the object of submitting to proof one or various elements and for examining their behavior under determined circumstances. The projects should be directed, consequently, to the testing of previously conceived hypotheses about the form of achieving determined objectives which are of importance for urban and regional development.

In the actual conditions of Latin America, every experimental project for urban regional development, they felt, should present certain basic characteristics that assure relevance and efficiency. These characteristics include:

(a) An innovating purpose, that is to say, that they are destined to the introduction, diffusion, or institutionalization of novel solutions in the treatment of the problems of urban and regional development.

(b) The projects have to be sufficiently representative of a wide set of cases so that the results of the experiment can be generalized.

(c) The projects should be conceived in such a manner that their cost is proportional to the foreseen utility of their results.

(d) All projects of this type should be conceived in terms of an important area of problems and, in order to reduce the risks of isolation and duplication, they should be part of a previously defined line of investigation.

(e) The elements or variables in the experiment should be duly identified and they should constitute manageable units so that the project can be duly evaluated and adjusted.

(f) The project should be oriented in such a way that it is possible to identify and reveal the possible obstacles to the innovation that is proposed.

(g) The project should be organized so that the resultant impact of its normal application can be foreseen, and it should take into account the existing restraints, principally economic and political, to its wider application.

(h) The project should be designed in such a way that it is possible to stimulate, capture, and develop a collective participation in the most efficient manner possible, for which it is essential to integrate the corresponding social groups in the process of decision-making in the project (—Ed.).

Latin American Centers for Education and Research in Urban Affairs

Can A University Education be Interdisciplinary? And Problem-Oriented?

New interdisciplinary and problem-oriented systems of education are being instituted in North America as well as Latin America, and much interest will focus on results over the next few years. A modest beginning in the United States in terms of the structuring of an entire university has been made, e.g., on the University of Wisconsin's Green Bay (UWGB) campus. There, an innovative approach to education aimed at serving the society directly and intimately rather than serving for the accumulation of knowledge has been inaugurated. The guiding philosophy of what the chancellor terms the "communiversity" is aimed at creating an integration of the social and natural sciences around the problem foci in the community rather than at the formation and management of an institution separated in activity and basic "interest" from the community. (Ricardo Jordan suggested, too, at Jahuel that the Latin American university has a specific role in communicating with the society, and that it should also serve as the critical conscience of that society.)

Chancellor Weidner defends the development of disciplinary skills and interests but within an orientation toward what the youthful clients of university education have termed relevance.

The UWGB catalog itself states:

Sharpening the student's thought processes and helping him examine his values are basic responsibilities of a university. But liberating the student's spirit is fruitless and even dangerous if at the same time the problems brought into focus by values and thought processes are not grasped more effectively. The relevant curriculum heightens the meaning of higher education by leading to a renewed emphasis on problem-solving and creating a habit of mind that is usefully extended to the community at large.

On the basis of this guiding philosophy and convictions, the UWGB academic plan focuses with special emphasis on ecology—the study of man in relation to his surroundings and the crises which stem from man's relation to and use of his environment—on interaction among men, and on man's perceptions of his place in the biosphere.

An ecological focus demands an interdisciplinary—indeed, a pan-disciplinary—focus. Artificial boundaries of disciplines restrict rather than enhance understanding of the several environments of man. The study of any type of environment intersects many disciplines and involves all branches of knowledge—the physical, biological, and behavioral sciences and the humanities.

The University, as a consequence, has not been organized along traditional disciplinary lines but rather within the framework of environmental themes.

Two colleges select certain types of environment for attention. The College of Environmental Sciences emphasizes the problems of the natural environment. The College of Community Sciences focuses on the social environment.

The College of Community Sciences has two concentrations—urban analysis and regional analysis.

If the description of this new experiment has been overly lengthy, it has been made to demonstrate the possibility of seeking and establishing new and creative approaches both to education and to the use of it. It is clear that this view represents a wind of change in university education. If the present members of the separate traditional disciplines are unable to bridge the artificial limits of their training created both by a narrow professionalism and what Myrdal calls "an unnecessarily elaborate and strange technology," then the present generation of "relevancy"-oriented students—coming, in part, from experiments such as the one at UWGB—may be able to do so. It suggests, though, that a rigorous preparation in disciplinary skills is still justified and necessary, a fact which Kenneth D. Roose has ably demonstrated (A, 1969). The large mass, seeming almost amorphous at times, must be broken into smaller segments in order to be manageable, but segmentation does not necessarily mean division into disciplinary fields without cross-fertilization in the approach to problem definition, research, and policy-making for the urban social process.

Universities in Latin America are only now beginning to break forth from a professional faculty orientation (in which all knowledge is taught students within the cloistered precincts of each faculty) into an arrangement which makes it possible for the student to take courses in disciplines and faculties outside his own. It is likely that the pathology of the urban organism will hasten a less rigid approach to social science education, much as the pathology of the human organism did for medical education. While it may be premature to suggest that more drastic changes will occur of the order that is built around problem-focused and interdisciplinary structures, it may also be suggested that the winds of change in Latin American university education have only begun to blow.

Latin American Urban Studies and Research Centers

While urban studies have emerged within the past two decades as a major focus for university education and research in the United States, they have only begun to achieve a certain modicum of support and interest in Latin American universities. As in the United States, some of this new interest derives from the demand of practicing urban (physical) planners, urban planning educational programs, and government agencies working on social, economic, and physical problems in the cities. Economics, sociology, and anthropology have been the disciplines most closely linked to this movement, but of late it has also drawn in a few political scientists, lawyers, educational planners, geographers, public administrators, public health researchers, and social work (community development) professionals. In a turn away from the more traditional philosophical concerns of the various disciplines on one side and away from the purely technical contribution (as of engineers) on the other, members of these disciplines are increasingly beginning to view the practical implications of their disciplinary "intelligence" as a part of the input needed for the resolution of complex problems found in modern urban life and to understand the need to cast their research in terms of greater relatedness to the work of other disciplines.

Such an understanding is still, nonetheless, building, and any appreciation of the value of integrated efforts or, indeed, of the value of focusing on urban studies as a disciplinary interest is only slowly making itself present in the consciousness of educators and research centers in spite of the extensive discussion about urbanization. Ralph Gakenheimer has pointed out that planning professionalism came first in the United States, and the planners became by necessity (as their need to be more knowledgeable expanded), "urban" social scientists. Almost the reverse is true in Latin America. The development of social science and its gradual involvement in urban matters occurred prior to, and is now continuing to accompany, the formation and growth of urban studies and research centers.

How can these interests be awakened in education even more and channelled into the proper entry points? What is (are) the most appropriate educational mechanism(s)? As the Jahuel Seminar Working Group on Training and Education Programs for Urban and Regional Development[23] in Latin America indicated:

There is substantial controversy concerning the content of educational programs for urban and regional development. The field is changing and we do not believe that any single approach offers the solution. We do suggest, however, that throughout the world—and certainly in the leading university programs dealing with these problems—the emphasis is shifting to broad gauged approaches. In some cases, special courses are being established dealing with the urban and regional aspects of such traditional disciplines as economics, sociology, anthropology, geography, and political science. In other cases, programs in city and regional planning are being broadened to include national and international aspects of urban and regional development as well as the inclusion of specialists from many disciplines to provide a richer background in the social sciences, engineering, computer technology and some of the more sophisticated and promising research methodologies. As a consequence, a variety of specialists are emerging with interests in the economic, the social, the physical or urban design aspects of urban and regional development. Still others prefer to work as generalist planners.

One indication of the rapid growth of professional interest in urban-regional development planning as an interdisciplinary/multidisciplinary field is the change in the composition of the membership of the Inter-American Planning Society. In 1969 almost one-half of the membership (48%) was composed of economists, sociologists, lawyers, medical doctors, public administrators, and the like. This is in contrast to the membership of a short four to five years before, when it was almost exclusively a professional society for physical planners (architects and engineers).[24]

Yet, as much with the urban organism as with the human organism, the mere increase in numbers of specialists in each discipline who study either the urban or human organisms is an insufficient condition. Where would the treatment of the ills of the human being be, for example, if the fields of biology and chemistry, or of psychiatry and physiology, had not combined with that of the medical (interdisciplinary) profession to minister to man? The same integrated effort may also be said to be necessary for resolving urban problems by educating newly socializing members of the separate disciplines in some integral fashion and by carrying out research in the same way. Given the general historic tendency of Latin American universities to break into isolated faculties, the mere proliferation of urban courses in each faculty falls short of the mark of optimal use of resources or optimal opportunities for cross-fertilization. A better understanding of the process involved in urbanization and the interrelations which aid or prevent problem resolution and the attainment of social goals is not ideally furthered by disciplinary "blinders."

It can be suggested that urban studies need some formal mechanical-structural device which aids in the better understanding of the contribution of the varied disciplines to an integrated body of urban knowledge. Even modest beginnings can be made which constitute an improvement over the present situations in some universities. The creation of a Center for Urban Studies and Research, for example, in given universities seems an obvious proposal, yet it may often be rejected offhand as a result of professional jealousies. Faculties of medicine were created, on the other hand, to treat the human condition and over time they gradually brought together persons specialized in biology, physiology, psychology, and chemistry. It is very doubtful if modern medicine would have developed its present competence without this convergence. This has not meant, however, that each of these disciplines was not developing separately because it, obviously, also serves purposes other than human medicine.

The proposal for the initial and modest establishment of Centers for Urban Studies and Research could mean, as an example, that in the first stage all university courses in the social and physical sciences which deal specifically and concretely with urban problems be listed as part of the educational program of the Center. Students of the different faculties who are interested in concentrating on urban studies within their discipline could be permitted to take especially relevant courses in other disciplines, a procedure which would not require major institutional reform or financing. It would require, however, guidance from a small core of dedicated professionals. In fact, some existing centers already conform, in part, to this model.

The Jahuel Seminar Working Group on Training and Education Programs for Urban and Regional Development in Latin America has observed, for instance, that

for many years existing universities in a number of Latin American countries will not be in a position to develop independent centers or programs for training in urban and regional development. They may, however, encourage the establishment of a few courses in urban and regional development which should complement existing programs in economics, sociology, engineering and the like. Such courses might even be established in universities in countries with advanced training programs (in urban studies). This would encourage students to enter the field of urban and regional studies. Many of these students would then be able to get jobs in this field even if they do not continue their education. Still others might pursue more advanced work at other existing centers in Latin America. In addition, the established centers in urban and regional development in Latin America might assist some of the universities in these countries which now lack advanced programs. They can do this by providing short term specialized courses for public officials and specially qualified students until more adequate programs can be established.

During the next decade, Latin American universities can be expected to institute the creation of research and policy centers whose function will be to serve the society in varied ways on matters related to urbanization. Much could be gained by bringing together the efforts of certain faculty members and researchers, often widely dispersed over a series of weakly or presently unrelated work, to concentrate upon key urban problems. In many Latin American countries university education constitutes a much higher proportion of total government expenditures for education than is true for the United States and Western Europe. If for no other reason than this, universities would seem to have an obligation and responsibility to the society to focus a greater share of their interests and activities directly upon those issues which are of national import.

Urbanization—a better understanding of it, and assistance in the alleviation of its more distressing symptoms—represents one such area.

Actually, there is a strong possibility, if the universities can develop serious research and policy centers aimed at resolving many of those problems to which government policy must or should address itself, that their usefulness will come to be appreciated by the government in ways which will bring access, request for assistance, and collaborative efforts.

Regional Social Science Collaboration

At the regional level, significant trends are being established. CLACSO (Consejo Latino Americano de Ciencias Sociales—the Latin American Council of Social Sciences) was formed in 1966 as a permanent organization charged with coordinating the development of the social sciences in Latin America. Members include various centers and institutions of social science, and it has as its principal objective the development of the social sciences in Latin America. This is to be achieved through the promotion and strengthening of institutions dedicated to research or research and teaching in the area and through the continuous improvement of the formation of Latin American social scientists. It also supports individual research and *the application of the social sciences to concrete problems of reality and to the social and economic development of Latin America, including that of Latin American integration.*

CLACSO functions through the promotion of the interchange of information between members regarding research and teaching programs in each of the centers. It acts as a center of interchange of information in relation to studies and programs in the project stage and between its members, as well as with others. It fulfills the same function in relation to personnel, basic data, methodology, work experiences, publications, and so on. It acts as a forum for the examination and comparison of programs and projects of members and promotes cooperation in the execution of projects of common interest. It also promotes research and teaching projects of special importance for the region, thereby stimulating the interest and cooperation of members and others.

In addition, CLACSO advises its members in the formulation and development of programs and projects of research and teaching, facilitates the intraregional mobility of the social scientist and the better use of his service, promotes the realization of scientific meetings, puts the social scientists in Latin America in contact with those of other areas and countries, maintains contact with the International Council of Social Sciences, stimulates the consideration of problems of Latin American integration in the programs of research and teaching, and stimulates individual research through scholarships, prizes, subsidies, and other incentives.

As an indication of the importance to social science of the process of urbanization, the Comisión de Desarrollo Regional y Urbano (Urban and Regional Development Commission) has been formed as an integral part of CLACSO. This commission is charged with doing for the social scientist interested in the problem of urbanization and regional development what the larger body does for the social scientist in general. The commission is composed of approximately twelve research and education centers dealing with urban and regional development in Latin America.

Among recent regional moves to foment the advance of teaching and research for urban development in Latin America can be cited the Technical Meeting on Urban Development sponsored by the Secretary General of the Organization of American States with the support of the College of Mexico (March 17-21, 1969). Recommendations made there are indicative of the state of awareness for regional collaboration in the improvement of the institutional framework for teaching and research and of the need for an examination of study plans, research priorities, interinstitutional relations, Latin American resources, external assistance, and measures for immediate action at the inter-American level. This was demonstrated by recommendations calling for:

(1) the strengthening of existing education and research centers with regard to the quality of personnel and "improved" knowledge;

(2) stimulation in the formation of new national and regional centers for education and research, and the establishment of a net of centers in Latin America;

(3) an intensification in the centers of efforts for exchange and complementarity;

(4) an intensification on the part of assistance organizations, the nations, and the centers of efforts destined to create stimuli and conditions that would facilitate the return of national experts who are working abroad, as well as the absorption of national specialists who are not now, or are only marginally, dedicated to the urban development field;

(5) the encouragement of international organizations in the support of long-term basic research;

(6) the fostering among external aid entities of greater flexibility in their programs, in the sense of making them more adequate for the objectives and goals of the centers; and

(7) a search for additional financing for the expansion of already existing nets of cooperation among the centers of CLACSO with other existing centers or centers in the process of formation.

It was also recommended that the Secretary General of the OAS carry out, in collaboration with CLACSO and other centers and entities, an analysis of the necessities for specialists in the field of urban development in the region and the preparation of an integrated plan to cover these necessities until 1975 and 1980.

A clear demonstration of the urgent need for improved personnel for urban development planning in Latin America has also come from the medical profession. The Asociación Colombiana de Facultades de Medicina sponsored a regional seminar on urbanization in 1969 which pointed out the extreme scarcity of specialized personnel in urban and regional planning and the "vital importance of preparing interested professionals in specializations in the field." It called specifically for universities, municipalities, the central governments, and intermediate levels of government to offer scholarships for this purpose.

Existing Centers

Among education and research centers for urban affairs that serve Latin America can be mentioned PIAPUR (Programa Interamericano de Planeamento Urbano y Regional) in Lima, a master's degree-granting center for all of Latin America sponsored by the OAS, the Universidad Nacional de Ingenieria, and the Peruvian government. The Escuela Latinoamericana de Ciencias Políticas (FLACSO) in Santiago is also involved in research on the problems of urbanization throughout the region.

National centers include CEUR (Centro de Estudios Urbanos y Regionales), associated with the Torcuato di Tella Institute in Buenos Aires, an urban-regional research center with a professional staff making important contributions. CIDU (Centro Interdisciplinario de Desarrollo Urbano y Regional) is an educational, research, technical assistance, and publications center founded in 1966 in the Catholic University, Santiago, which is making important inputs of personnel, research, and technical assistance to Chilean governments at the national and urban level. Other centers include the Colegio de Mexico, Mexico City; the Instituto de Estudios Peruanos, Lima; and the Centro de Estudios Nacionales del Desarrollo (CENDES), of the Universidad Central de Venezuela, Caracas.

An Urban Research Center has also been created at the Brazilian Institute of Municipal Administration (IBAM), a private, nonprofit organization which is devoted to the improvement of local government and urban services in Brazil. The center will provide IBAM with information and data on urban problems needed for the execution of its programs and assistance to local, state, and federal governments for urban development action and policies. In 1968, the Institute provided direct technical aid to one-half the municipalities existing in Brazil in that year.

In housing research, a new National Center of Housing Research (CENPHA) has been established in Brazil through an agreement between the National Housing Bank, the Catholic Pontifical University of Rio de Janeiro, and the Federal Housing and Urban Agency.

All of these centers are interdisciplinary in teaching and research and are attracting to themselves each year a few more professionals of higher caliber from each of the social sciences, as well as students who are interested in the problem approach of the centers and the use of their own discipline in efforts of integrated collaboration. There are deficiencies, nonetheless, which prevent the centers from being more effective and from demonstrating their usefulness, especially to private and public institutions. These institutions increasingly need more and better-trained personnel to cope with the burgeoning tasks of guiding urbanization and deciding priorities for resource allocation.

The Jahuel Seminar Working Group on Training and Education Programs for Urban and Regional Development in Latin America set out various recommendations for overcoming these deficiencies.

(1) A fellowship fund should be established and administered by a respected organization—perhaps the Latin American Council of Social Sciences. The fund should:

(a) help able students from different Latin American universities to attend one of the major one-year graduate training programs in Latin America dealing with urban and regional development;

(b) help exceptionally qualified students or practitioners to obtain advanced training in Europe or North America;

(c) facilitate the interchange of professors among the Latin American and other centers, so that each of the centers might from time to time be able to take advantage of a wider range of educational resources.

(2) Fellowship, teaching, and travel funds must be obtained to help finance short-term (two- to three-month) training programs in specialized fields such as transportation, urban economics, housing problems, and policies. These special courses could also serve practitioners from various Latin American and other countries, not only nationals.

(3) Special funds are also needed to permit professors, research specialists, and professionals in government and administration at all levels to attend lectures, congresses, seminars, and other meetings devoted to the analysis of regional development or urbanization problems.

(4) There is also a need for a clearing house to identify urban and regional specialists who could contribute to action, training, and applied research programs in Latin America. This could facilitate the movement of many highly trained European and North American professionals who would like to work in this region and whose services might be desired.

Special emphasis was placed by the Working Group on assistance from the United States and the OAS, as well as from foundation, national, and international technical assistance agencies. Such assistance could take the form of matching funds, finances for special purposes and, otherwise, the creation of a budgetary environment which would attract competent national and international professionals to the centers and make it possible for these centers to compete for the availability of social scientists now engaged in other activities.

In a move to address itself to the future of advanced education in urban and regional affairs in Latin America, the Jahuel Seminar Working Group on Training and Education Programs for Urban and Regional Development in Latin America recognized that

at the present time, existing Latin American centers dealing with urban and regional planning and development do not offer graduate programs beyond the equivalent of the master's degree. It is probably wise to have Latin American institutions provide the bulk of the training in the field up to this level—partly because of the advantages of training professors and researchers in the social setting in which they must work, partly because of the greater expense of training abroad, and partly because of the inability of foreign universities to serve the increasing demand for such training. Eventually, however, it will be necessary to establish an advanced graduate training program in Latin America. We believe that the leaders of the major educational programs in urban and regional development in Latin America should consider when and how such an extension of their existing programs might be effectively developed—as well as the physical, human and financial requirements this would entail and the kinds of assistance such a major enterprise might require from international agencies as well as universities abroad.

Publications

A not unimportant aspect of improved knowledge about urban and regional affairs is the diffusion of information which can have wider use and application outside any given center or nation. Several recent publications are now filling what was formerly a complete vacuum in this respect in Latin America.

The Interdisciplinary Center of Urban and Regional Development (CIDU) of Catholic University, Santiago, has recently begun the publication of a journal of Latin American urban-regional research (*Revista Latinoamericana de Estudios Urbanos Regionales*) for CLACSO. It is intended as a means of communicating research results of social scientists which have relevance for urban-regional policy and planning. This and other centers have also begun an interchange of professionals. CIDU has even inaugurated a program to bring advanced students and faculty from the United States to its program for a period of research and study.

A recent publication series in this field is the *Latin American Urban Annual* of Sage Publications, Beverly Hills. This series will publish research efforts on selected aspects of Latin American urbanization as an aid to researchers and policy planners in better systematizing comparisons of the many dimensions of cities and urbanization in Latin America. It is proposed that each volume will contain an overview essay on recent urban research on Latin America reviewing theoretical studies and field investigations of significant urban problems and programs. In addition, it will also include a series of articles on various dimensions of urban structure, policy, and process (including models and typologies for the study of Latin American cities and urbanization); reports of work on institutional, cultural, and environmental conditions; and studies of policies, decisions, or events, as well as a bibliographical review discussing recent publications of interest to those specializing in urban affairs within Latin America.

The professional journal of the Inter-American Planning Society (SIAP), *Revista de la Sociedad Interamericana de Planificación,* should not be overlooked, either in terms of its contribution to a wider distribution of urban affairs research or as a vehicle of communication for social scientists working in this area.

An entire field of extremely valuable support for urban development on the part of the social scientists is the preparation of technical manuals and documents which can aid municipal and national governments in improving the quality of administration and planning for urban development. FUNDA COMUN (Fundación para el Desarrollo de la Comunidad y Fomento Municipal), for example, in Venezuela, has produced a series of such especially for this purpose. They are scientific and technical works in the various areas of planning and development aimed at contributing to an increase in the knowledge of technicians for dealing with urban development problems. They cover property evaluation for tax collection as a means of improving municipal finance positions (Huck, F, n.d.), housing administration (Carazo, F, n.d.), municipal budget procedures (Cabezas, F, n.d.b), municipal accounting (Cabezas, F, n.d.a), community development methods (Acedo, F, n.d.), and municipal structure in Venezuela (Castro, K, n.d.). A similar publication for regional development planning purposes has recently been published by CIDU (Centro Interdisciplinario de Desarrollo Urbano y Regional) of the Catholic University, Santiago, for the Chilean national planning office (CIDU, F, 1970).

The availability in Spanish and Portuguese of worthwhile books on urban problems in other languages or of new scholarly contributions within Latin America is always a problem for the professional. This will begin to be partially remedied shortly, however, through the use of a grant from the Ford Foundation to SIAP for the annual publication of four pertinent books not otherwise available in the tongues of Cervantes and Camões. Such seemingly minor efforts may seem minuscule in the general flow of new publications in all fields, but the general dissemination of some forty significant books in the languages of the region over a ten-year period among individuals and institutions engaged in dealing with urbanization will be, undoubtedly, an important catalyst for understanding and coping with urban issues.

In short, the past five years have seen the welling up of interest, new centers, and new communications networks focused on urban development that could hardly have been foreseen five years before. And the end is nowhere in sight, since the social need for and understanding of the contribution of these and future new centers will inevitably rise with the level and intensity of urbanization in Latin America.

NOTES

1. A recent publication concerned with the policy implications of the social sciences is Heilbroner (C, 1969). This collection of essays is an examination of the present conditions of economic science, regarding both its claim to be a science and its applicability to contemporary problems. An article by Adolph Lowe, especially, contends that economics as presently constituted requires a thoroughgoing reorientation if its relevance for policy-making is to be reestablished. "Instrumental economics" is proposed.

2. Other books addressing themselves to the issue of values in social research include Kelman (A, 1968), in which he considers the social scientist as producer of social forces, as experimenter and social thinker, and as participant in social action; Beals (C, 1969). Dilemmas involving values and goals and impinging inevitably upon research are discussed in Part IV of the recent second edition of *The Planning of Change,* edited by Warren G. Bennis, Kenneth D. Beane, and Robert Chin (C, 1969).

3. Silvert (B, 1961) stresses the point of culturally derived blindness on the part of Americanists in terms of their examination of political institutions. As one example, Victor Flores Olea (Diegues and Wood, B, 1967: 157) criticizes the political development framework offered as a basis for analysis by Kling (B, 1964: 194-196) as full of value judgments and prescriptions for political action which need to be, as he says, examined critically. Validity in the use of value judgments is not denied, but knowledge of how well they fit the culture is desired.

4. Mack (A, 1969) has pressed for a recognition of theoretical and substantive biases which he has identified as: (1) ethnocentrism, including the aggrandizement effect; (2) tool bias, or problem selection on the basis of tool availability; (3) fiduciary drift, or monetary magnetism in problem selection; (4) the debunking bias; (5) theory-shyness, or false modesty copout; and (6) theoretical inefficiency, or the use of labels and other nonvariable frames of reference.

5. Publications which have dealt with the topic of new directions in higher education based upon relevance or problem orientation include Axelrod et al. (A, 1969); Mayhew (A, 1969).

6. Psychoeconomics is perhaps the most recent bridging effort. In the words of its proponents, it is a "new dimension" which "strives to illuminate the whole man in his active or passive involvement with the daily demands of his economic life." Its central thesis is that the individual (the "soul" of human action) is nation's secret weapon and that the total economy, therefore, can be best understood through the economic experiences of the individual! See Sharron and Alkin (C, 1968).

7. See Neutze (E, 1965) as one attempt to examine the cost of city size and Youngson (I, 1967) for a general discussion in terms of development and a treatment of infrastructure (overhead capital) investments. Stanford Research Institute et al. (I, 1968) has also completed a case study of India involving the costs of urban infrastructure for industry as related to city size.

8. An interesting and important treatment of the social sciences as a single science is Kuhn (A, 1963).

9. For further readings on interdisciplinary education and research efforts touching on urban problems, see Sherif and Sherif (A, 1969). See especially in this book, chapters by Marvin W. Mikesell, "The borderlands of geography as a social science," pp. 227-248; Arnold A. Rogow, "Some relations between psychiatry and political science," pp. 274-291; Sidney H. Aronson, "Obstacles to a rapprochement between history and sociology: a sociologist's view," pp. 292-304; and Donald T. Campbell, "Ethnocentrism of disciplines and the fish-scale model of omniscience," pp. 328-348.

10. This Working Group was composed of the following: José A. Silva Michelena (rapporteur), Julio Cotler, René Eyheralde, Guillermo Geisse, Leonardus Klaassen, Antoni Kuklinsky, Poul Pedersen, Colin Rosser, and Ernest Weissmann.

11. Quoted in *The Man of Many Qualities: A Legacy of the I Ching,* by R. G. H. Siv (Cambridge, Mass: MIT Press, 1968).

12. See, for example, Chile Corporación de Fomento (J, 1967).

13. See also Guarda (L, 1968).

14. See as one example Cruz Coke (J, 1952).

15. Two early studies of local decision-making include those of Form and D'Antonio (K, 1959) and Klapp and Padgett (K, 1960).

16. The macroeconomic analysis of internal migration posited by Simon Rottenberg's income hypothesis can be cited as one example (Rottenberg, I, 1959).

17. A whole series of economic research questions are ably posed by Wingo (E, 1969), and the reader would profit by an examination of this excellent questioning essay. The same is also true of a research prospectus for the United Nations by Lloyd Rodwin (I, 1970) on the economics of urbanization.

18. Members of this Work Group included Gino Germani (rapporteur), Richard Adams, Brian Berry, Robert Daland, Carlos Delgado, Carlos Fortín, John Friedmann, Daniel Goldrich, Rose Goldsen, Albert Hirschman, and Richard Morse.

19. This report is presented as a discussion document. It is the result of one morning's brainstorming session during which ideas were generated; in the afternoon, a unified document was prepared by several members of the work group and submitted in the evening to all of the members. Subsequently, the document was revised on the basis of comments made during its formal presentation at a plenary session of the Seminar. Nevertheless, the present document should not be considered in any way definitive.

20. See a prior discussion of historical research in this chapter.

21. See also "Fixations of Research: The Political Scientist" in a prior section of this chapter.

22. Members of this Working Group included Eduardo Neira (rapporteur), Fernando Aguirre, William Mangin, Aníbal Quijano, and Walter Stöhr.

23. Members of this Working Group included Ricardo Jordán (rapporteur), Calvin Blair, Ralph Gakenheimer, Ralph Harbison, Jorge Hardoy, Armando Méndez, Lloyd Rodwin, Thomas Sanders, and Gideon Sjoberg.

24. *Sociedad Interamericana de Planificación Newsletter,* March-April, 1969.

REFERENCES

A. Social Sciences: General

AXELROD, JOSEPH et al. (1969) Search for Relevance: The Campus in Crisis. San Francisco: Jossey-Bass.

BAUER, RAYMOND A. [ed.] (1966) Social Indicators. Cambridge, Mass.: MIT Press.

BOULDING, KENNETH E. (1970) Social Dynamics. New York: Free Press. (Overview of patterns of social change from an interdisciplinary perspective.)

BRODBECK, MAY [ed.] (1968) Readings in the Philosophy of the Social Sciences. New York: Macmillan.

BROWN, ROBERT (1963) Explanation in Social Science. Chicago: Aldine.

GERMANI, GINO (1963) "Problems of establishing valid social research in the under-developed areas." Pp. 373-392 in Bert F. Hoselitz and Wilbert E. Moore (eds.) Industrialization and Society. Paris: UNESCO.

——— (1960) "Problems and strategies of research in less developed countries: Latin America." Presented to the North American Conference in the Social Implications of Industrialization sponsored by UNESCO, September, University of Chicago.

GLASER, BARNEY (1963) "The use of secondary analysis by the independent researcher." Amer. Behavioral Scientist 6 (June): 11-14.

——— and ANSELM L. STRAUSS (1966) The Discovery of Grounded Theory: Strategies for Qualitative Research. Chicago: Aldine.

GREER, SCOTT (1969) The Logic of Social Inquiry. Chicago: Aldine. (Relevance of social science to broad philosophical questions and to major questions covering the human situation.)

HOMANS, GEORGE C. (1967) The Nature of Social Science. New York: Harcourt, Brace & World.

HUGHES, E. C. (1959) "The dual mandate of social science: remarks on the academic division of labor." Canadian J. of Economics and Pol. Sci. 25: 401-410.

International Conference on Comparative Social Research in the Developing Countries [Buenos Aires, 1964] (1965) Papers presented. América Latina 8 (January-March): 3-100, 175-183.

KELMAN, HERBERT C. (1968) A Time to Speak on Human Values and Social Research. San Francisco: Jossey-Bass.

KUHN, A. (1963) The Study of Society: A Unified Approach. Homewood, Ill.: Dorsey Press. (An interesting and important treatment of the social sciences as a single science.)

LIPTON, MICHAEL (1969) Interdisciplinary Studies in Less Developed Countries. Presented at Society for International Development Eleventh World Conference, New Delhi, November 14-17, 1969.

LYND, ROBERT S. (1939) Knowledge for What? The Place of Social Science in American Culture. Princeton, N.J.: Princeton Univ. Press. (Especially Chapters IV and V: "The social sciences as tools" and "Values and the social sciences.")

MACK, RAYMOND W. (1969) "Theoretical and substantive biases in sociological research." Pp. 52-64 in Muzafer Sherif and Carolyn W. Sherif (eds.) Interdisciplinary Relationships in the Social Sciences. Chicago: Aldine.

MacKENZIE, NORMAN [ed.] (1964) A Guide to the Social Sciences. New York: New American Library. (Especially "Introduction" by the editor, pp. 7-34.)

MAYHEW, LEWIS B. (1969) Colleges Today and Tomorrow. San Francisco: Jossey-Bass.

MILGRAM, STANLEY (1969) "Interdisciplinary thinking and the small world problem." Pp. 103-120 in Muzafer Sherif and Carolyn W. Sherif (eds.) Interdisciplinary Relationships in the Social Sciences. Chicago: Aldine.

MYRDAL, GUNNAR (1969) Objectivity in Social Research. New York: Pantheon.

O'TOOLE, RICHARD [ed.] (1969) The Organization, Management and Tactics of Social Research. Cambridge, Mass.: Schenkman.

POPENOE, DAVID (1969) "Urban studies centers in institutions of higher education: some thoughts on their structure, functions and problems." Urban Affairs Q. 5 (December): 143-150.

——— (1963) "Education for urban studies." Amer. Behavioral Scientist 6 (February): 14-20.

ROOSE, KENNETH D. (1969) "Observations on interdisciplinary work in the social sciences." Pp. 323-327 in Muzafer Sherif and Carolyn W. Sherif (eds.) Interdisciplinary Relationships in the Social Sciences. Chicago: Aldine.

SHERIF, MUZAFER and CAROLYN W. SHERIF [eds.] (1969) Interdisciplinary Relationships in the Social Sciences. Chicago: Aldine.

SILVERT, KALMAN (1965) "American academic ethics and social research abroad: the lessons of Project Camelot." Background 9, 3 (November).

VAN NIEUWENHUIJZE, C. A. O. (1962) Society as Process: Essays in Social Sciences Method. The Hague: Mouton.

VICKERS, Sir GEOFFREY (1968) Value Systems and Social Process. New York: Basic Books.

WAX, MURRAY L. (1969) "Myth and interrelationship in social science: illustrated through anthropology and sociology." Pp. 77-99 in Muzafer Sherif and Carolyn W. Sherif (eds.) Interdisciplinary Relationships in the Social Sciences. Chicago: Aldine.

WOOD, BRYCE and CHARLES WAGLEY (1961) The Social Sciences, Parochial or Cosmopolitan? Reflections on the Inter-American Conference on Research and Training in Sociology. Social Science Research Council Items 15 (no. 4, December).

B. Social Sciences in Latin America

ADAMS, RICHARD (1963) "Some supplemental notes on the work of anthropology in Latin America." Presented to the Seminar on Latin American Studies of the American Council of Learned Societies and the Social Science Research Council, Center for the Advanced Study in Behavioral Sciences, Stanford, California, July.

BAZZANELLA, WALDEMIRO (1963) "Priority areas for social research in Latin America." In Egbert De Vries and José Medina Echavarría (eds.) Social Aspects of Economic Development in Latin America, I. Paris: UNESCO.

BLAIR, CALVIN P., RICHARD P. SCHAEDEL, and JAMES H. STREET (1969) Responsibilities of the Foreign Scholar to the Local Scholarly Community: Studies of U.S. Research in Guatemala, Chile, and Paraguay. New York: Education & World Affairs.

BLASIER, COLE [ed.] (1968) Constructive Change in Latin America. Pittsburgh: Univ. of Pittsburgh Press. (Development examined from the perspectives of anthropology, economics, literature, political science, and sociology.)

BONILLA, FRANK and JOSE A. SILVA MICHELENA [eds.] (1967) A Strategy for Research on Social Policy. Cambridge, Mass.: MIT Press. (See especially José A. Silva Michelena, Chapter 4: "The Venezuelan bureaucrat"; and Frank Bonilla, Chapter 7: "The national perspectives of Venezuelan elites.")

DIEGUES, MANUEL, Jr., and BRYCE WOOD [eds.] (1967) Social Science in Latin America. New York: Columbia Univ. Press.

FERRER, ALDO (1969) Consejo Latinoamericano de Ciencias Sociales: Información Básica. Buenos Aires.

GODOY URZUA, HERNAN (1960) Orientación y organización de los estudios sociológicos en Chile. Santiago: Universidad de Chile.

JOHNSON, JOHN J. [ed.] (1964) Continuity and Change in Latin America. Stanford: Stanford Univ. Press. (Essays of interdisciplinary aspects of social science in Latin America.)

KLING, MERLE (1964) "The state of research on Latin America," Pp. 168-213 in Charles Wagley (ed.) Social Science Research on Latin America. New York: Columbia Univ. Press.

MARSAL, JUAN F. (1967) Cambio social en América Latina: crítica de algunas interpretaciones dominantes en las ciencias sociales. Buenos Aires: Solar Hachette.

MEDINA ECHAVARRIA, JOSE (1963) "A sociologist's view." In Social Aspects of Economic Development in Latin America. II. Paris: UNESCO.

NAYLOR, R. A. (n.d.) "Research opportunities in modern Latin America. I: Mexico and Central America." Americas 18: 353-365.

Organization of American States, General Secretariat (1968) Inter-American University Cooperation: A Survey of Programs of Cooperation Between Institutions of Higher Education in the United States and Latin America. Washington, D.C.: Pan American Union.

ROBSON, WILLIAM ALEXANDER (1961) La enseñanza universitaria de las ciencias sociales: ciencia política: informe. Washington, D.C.: Pan American Union.

SILVA MICHELENA, J. A. (1960) El Estado Actual de las Ciencias Sociales en Venezuela. Rio de Janeiro: Centro Latino-Americano de Investigaciones en Ciencias Sociales.

SILVERT, KALMAN (1961) The Conflict Society. New Orleans: Hauser.

VILLALBA VILLALBA, LUIS (1961) El Primer Instituto Venezolano de Ciencias Sociales. Caracas: Asociación Venezolana de Sociología.

WAGLEY, CHARLES [ed.] (1964) Social Science Research on Latin America. New York: Columbia Univ. Press.

ZIMMERMAN, IRENE [comp.] (1961) A Guide to Current Latin American Periodicals: Humanities and Social Sciences. Gainesville, Fla.: Kallman.

C. Policy Uses of the Social Sciences

BAUER, RAYMOND and KENNETH J. GERGEN [eds.] (1968) The Study of Policy Formation. New York: Free Press.

BEALS, RALPH L. (1969) Politics of Social Research: An Inquiry into the Ethics and Responsibilities of Social Scientists. Chicago: Aldine.

Behavioral and Social Sciences Survey Committee (1969) The Behavioral and Social Sciences: Outlook and Need. Englewood Cliffs, N.J.: Prentice-Hall. (Suggests ways in which social science research can contribute knowledge and techniques useful to those responsible for the planning and execution of social policy.)

BENNIS, WARREN G., KENNETH D. BENNE, and ROBERT CHIN [eds.] (1969) The Planning of Change. New York: Holt, Rinehart & Winston.

BEUTEL, K. F. (1957) Some Potentialities of Experimental Jurisprudence as a New Branch of the Social Sciences. Lincoln, Neb.: Univ. of Nebraska Press.

BRAYBROOKE, DAVID and CHARLES E. LINDBLOM (1963) A Strategy of Decision: Policy Evaluation as a Social Process. New York: Free Press.

DAHL, ROBERT A. (1961) "The behavioral approach in political science: epitaph for a monument to a successful protest." Amer. Pol. Sci. Rev. 55, 4: 763-772.

DROR, YEHEZKEL (1969) "Accelerated development and policymaking improvement." Civilisations (Brussels) 19, 2: 209-215.

——— (1968) Public Policymaking Reexamined. San Francisco: Chandler. (Proposes a new interdisciplinary field "for accelerating the discovery of policy knowledge and for increasing the actual use of such knowledge in policymaking.")

EULAU, HEINZ (1963) The Behavioral Persuasion in Politics. New York.

GERMANI, GINO (1965) "Estratégia para estimular la movilidad social." In J. A. Kahl (ed.) La Industrialización en América Latina. Mexico City and Buenos Aires: Fondo de

Cultura Económica. (Also in Egbert De Vries and José Medina Echavarría (eds.) Social Aspects of Economic Development in Latin America, I. Paris: UNESCO.

――― (1963) "Uses of social research in developing countries." In Bert F. Hoselitz and Wilbert E. Moore (eds.) Industrialization and Society. Paris: UNESCO.

HEILBRONER, ROBERT L. [ed.] (1969) Economic Means and Social Ends: Essays in Political Economics. Englewood Cliffs, N.J.: Prentice-Hall.

ISARD, WALTER (1969) General Theory: Social, Political, Economic and Regional, with Particular Reference to Decision-Making Analysis. Cambridge, Mass.: MIT Press.

KAHN, ALFRED J. (1969) Theory and Practice of Social Planning. New York: Russell Sage Foundation.

LASSWELL, HAROLD D. (1951) "The policy orientation." Pp 3-15 in Daniel Lerner and Harold D. Lasswell (eds.) The Policy Sciences. Stanford: Stanford Univ. Press.

LERNER, DANIEL and HAROLD D. LASSWELL (1965) The Policy Sciences. Stanford: Stanford Univ. Press.

LIPSET, SEYMOUR MARTIN [ed.] (1969) Politics and the Social Sciences. New York: Oxford Univ. Press.

LIVINGSTON, ARTHUR (1969) Social Policy in Developing Countries. New York: Humanities Press.

MILLIKAN, MAX F. (1959) "Inquiry and policy: the relation of knowledge to action." Pp. 158-180 in Daniel Lerner (ed.) The Human Meaning of the Social Sciences. Cleveland: World Publishing.

MYRDAL, GUNNAR (1965) The Political Element in the Development of Economic Theory. Cambridge, Mass.: Harvard Univ. Press.

PEATTIE, LISA R. (1958) "Interventionism and applied science in anthropology." Human Organization 17 (Spring): 4-8.

PODGORECKI, ADAM (1962) "Law and social engineering," Human Organization 21 (Fall): 177-181.

RANNEY, AUSTIN [ed.] (1962) Essays on the Behavioral Study of Politics. Urbana, Ill.: Univ. of Illinois Press.

REIN, MARTIN (1970) Introduction to Social Policy: Issues of Choice and Change. New York: Random House.

ROSE, ALBERT (1965) "The role of government in promoting social change." In Murray Silverman (ed.) Proceedings of a Conference Sponsored by the Columbia University School of Social Work. New York: Arden House.

SCHNORE, LEO F. (1960-1961) "Social problems in the underdeveloped areas: an ecological view." Social Problems 8 (Winter): 182-201.

SHARRON, ARTHUR and E. DEBORAH ALKIN (1968) Psycheconomics and Its Applications. New York: Psycheconomics.

SHERIF, M. (1967) "If basic research is to have bearing on actualities." in M. Sherif, Social Interaction. Chicago: Aldine.

SIMEY, T. S. (1969) Social Science and Social Purpose. New York: Schocken.

SJOBERG, GIDEON [ed.] (1970) Ethics, Politics, and Social Research. Cambridge, Mass.: Schenkman.

United Nations. Economic Commission for Latin America (1969) Tendencias Sociales y Política de Desarrollo Social en América Latina. Presented at the Special Meeting of UNICEF in Santiago, May 19-20.

VAYDA, ANDRES P. (1967) "On the anthropological study of economics." J. of Economic Issues 1 (June): 86-90.

D. Urban Research in the Social Sciences: General

ARENSBERG, CONRAD M. (1954) "The community study method." Amer. J. of Sociology 2: 109-124.

BELL, GWEN and PAULA MacGREEVEY (1970) Behavior and Environment: A Bibliography of Social Activities in Urban Space. Exchange Bibliographies 123. Monticello, Ill.: Council of Planning Librarians.

BELL, WENDELL (1948) "The utility of the Shevky typology for the design of urban sub-area field studies." J. of Social Psychology 47: 71-83.

DAVIS, KINGSLEY (1961) "Foreword: urban research and its significance." Pp. xi-xxii in Jack P. Gibbs (ed.) Urban Research Methods. Princeton, N.J.: Van Nostrand.

GUTMAN, ROBERT and FRANCINE F. RABINOVITZ (1966) "The relevance of domestic urban studies to international urban research." Urban Affairs Q. 1 (June): 45-64.

HALL, ROBERT B. (1947) Area Studies: With Special Reference to Their Implications for Research in the Social Sciences. Social Science Research Council Pamphlet 3. New York.

HATT, PAUL (1946) "The concept of natural area." Amer. Sociological Rev. 11: 423 ff.

HAUSER, PHILIP M. [ed.] (1964) Handbook for Social Research in Urban Areas. Paris: UNESCO.

JAKLE, JOHN A. (1970) The Spatial Dimensions of Social Organization: A Selected Bibliography for Urban Social Geography. Exchange Bibliographies 118. Monticello, Ill.: Council of Planning Librarians.

LAMPARD, ERIC E. (1961) "American historians and the study of urbanization." Amer. Historical Rev. 67 (October): 49-61.

——— and LEO F SCHNORE (1961) "Urbanization problems." Pp. 1-63 in Research Needs for Development Assistance Programs. Washington, D.C.: Brookings Institution.

ORLEANS, PETER (1966) "Robert Park and social area analysis: convergence in urban sociology." Urban Affairs Q. 1 (June): 5-19.

SCHNORE, LEO F. (1961) "The myth of human ecology." Sociological Inquiry 31, 2. (Reprinted in Paul Meadows and Ephraim H. Mizruchi [eds.] Urbanism, Urbanization, and Change: Comparative Perspectives. Reading, Mass.: Addison-Wesley.)

——— and ERIC E. LAMPARD (1967) "Social science and the city: a survey of research needs." Pp. 21-47 in Leo F. Schnore and Henry Fagin (eds.) Urban Research and Policy Planning. Beverly Hills: Sage Publications.

SHEVKY, ESHREF and WENDELL BELL (1955) Social Area Analysis: Theory, Illustrative Applications and Computational Procedures. Stanford: Stanford Univ. Press.

STEWARD, JULIAN H. (1950) Area Research: Theory and Practice. Social Science Research Council Bulletin 63. New York.

STRAUSS, ANSELM L. (1967) "Strategies for discovering urban theory." Pp. 79-98 in Leo F. Schnore and Henry Fagin (eds.) Urban Research and Policy Planning. Beverly Hills: Sage Publications.

WILMOTT, P. (1967) "Social research and new communities." J. of Amer. Institute of Planners 33 (November): 387-398.

YUJNOVSKY, OSCAR et al. (n.d.) La Urbanización como Campo de Investigación de las Ciencias Sociales. Buenos Aires: Centro Editor de América Latina.

E. Urban Research for Policy and Planning

BLUMENFELD, HANS (1969) "The rational use of urban space as national policy." Ekistics 27 (April): 269-273.

BOYCE, CHARLES P. (n.d.) "Desarrollo de los procesos de planificación local en Venezuela." Plerus 2, 1. (University of Puerto Rico, Graduate School of Planning.)

CASIMIR, JEAN (1967) "Duas cidades no Nordeste do Brasil: sua estrutura social e sua importância para a planificação econômica regional." América Latina 10 (January-March): 3-48.

CEDUG (1966) "Transportation study for the state of Guanabara." Ekistics 21 (April).

CHOMBART DE LAUWE, PAUL-HENRY (1963) "The social sciences, urbanism and planning." International J. of Comparative Sociology 4: 19-30.

Companhia do Metropolitano de São Paulo (n.d.) Metro. 2 vols. (A very complete publication of the subway planning for São Paulo.)

CUEVAS, MARCO ANTONIO (1966) "Análisis de tres áreas marginales de la ciudad de Guatemala y su incidencia en una política urbana nacional." Economía (Guatemala) no. 10 (January-April): 7-16.

DROR, YEHEZKEL (1967) "Policy analysts: a new professional role in government service." Public Administration Rev. (September).

EARWAKER, FRANK (1969) "Programación del desarrollo urbano en Chile." Pp. 119-150 in John Friedmann (ed.) Contribuciones a las Políticas Urbanas, Regionales y Habitacionales–Chile: La Década del 70. Santiago: Ford Foundation.

ERBER, ERNEST [ed.] (1970) Urban Planning in Transition. Part 3: "The professional planner's role," including "The need for planners trained in policy formulation" by Herbert J. Gans. New York: Grossman.

FAGIN, HENRY (1965) The Policies Plan: Instrumentality for a Community Dialogue. Pittsburgh: Univ. of Pittsburgh, Institute of Local Government.

FALETTO, ENZO (n.d.) "Los aspectos políticos de la planificación." Boletín Informativo de PLANDES (Santiago) no. 30.

GAKENHEIMER, RALPH A. (1969) "El desarrollo metropolitano de la década del 70." Pp. 151-174 in John Friedmann (ed.) Contribuciones a las Políticas Urbanas, Regionales y Habitacionales–Chile: La Década del 70. Santiago: Ford Foundation.

GARCIA, PATRICIO (n.d.) "El enfoque interdisciplinario en planificación: la participación del sociólogo." Boletín Informativo de PLANDES (Santiago) no. 30.

GODOY, HORACIO and MARCOS KAPLAN (n.d.) "Planificación y ciencia política." Boletín Informativo de PLANDES (Santiago) no. 30.

GYARMATI, GABRIEL (n.d.) "Algunas reflexiones sobre relaciones entre planificación y sistemas políticos." Boletín Informativo de PLANDES (Santiago) no. 30.

MANN, LAWRENCE D. (1966) "Research for national urban development planning." Pp. 1042-1067 in Sam Bass Warner, Jr. (ed.) Planning for a Nation of Cities, Vol. II. Cambridge, Mass.: MIT Press.

MICHAEL, DONALD N. (1965) "Urban policy in the rationalized society." J. of Amer. Institute of Planners 31 (November): 283-288. (Although it deals with the United States, it is illustrative of a series of problems to be faced at the urban policy level.)

MICHELSON, W. (1968) "Urban sociology as an aid to urban physical development." J. of Amer. Institute of Planners 34 (March): 105-108.

NEUTZE, G. M. (1968) "The process of urban development: a research project outline." Growth (February): 22-26.

——— (1965) Economic Policy and the Size of Cities. Canberra: Australian National University.

PADRON, MANUEL and ROBERT BRASWELL (1969) "Planning of rapid transit in Caracas." Traffic Engineering (July).

PERIN, C. (1967) "Some interests of the city planner in social science research." J. of Amer. Institute of Planners 33 (March): 114-116.

PERLMAN, R. (1966) "Social welfare planning and physical planning." J. of Amer. Institute of Planners 32 (July): 237-241.

Process Planning: Symposium (1965) "Urban policy in the rationalized society" and "New directions in social planning." J. of Amer. Institute of Planners 31 (November).

RODWIN, LLOYD (1961) "Metropolitan policy for developing areas." Daedalus (Winter).

ROSSI, PETER H. (1960) Social Science and Community Action. East Lansing, Mich.: Michigan State Univ. Press.

SCHEIBER, WALTER A. (1967) "Evolving a policy process for a metropolitan region." Public Administration Rev. (September).

SCHULTZ, T. W. (1966) "Urban development and policy implications for agriculture." Economic Development and Cultural Change 15 (October).

Sociedad Interamericana de Planificación (San Juan, Puerto Rico). Newsletter.

——— (San Juan, Puerto Rico). Revista de la Sociedad Interamericana de Planificación (Cali, Colombia).

TEITZ, MICHAEL B. (1968) "Toward a theory of urban public facility location." Papers of the Regional Science Association, no. 21. Philadelphia.

WEISSMANN, ERNEST (1967) "The role of the United Nations in urban research and planning." Pp. 553-581 in Leo F. Schnore and Henry Fagin (eds.) Urban Research and Policy Planning. Beverly Hills: Sage Publications.

WILMOTT, P. and E. COONEY (1963) "Community planning and sociological research." J. of Amer. Institute of Planners 29 (May).

WINGO LOWDON (1969) "Latin American urbanization: plan or process?" Pp. 115-146 in Bernard J. Frieden and William Nash (eds.) Shaping an Urban Future. Cambridge, Mass.: MIT Press.

F. Social Science Contributions to Planning Tools

ACEDO MENDOZA, CARLOS (n.d.) Desarrollo Comunal Promoción Popular. Caracas: Fondo Editorial Común.

CABEZAS M., RAMIRO (n.d.a) Manual de Contabilidad para Gobiernos Municipales. Caracas: Fondo Editorial Común.

––– (n.d.b) Manual del Presupuesto para Gobiernos Municipales. Caracas: Fondo Editorial Común.

CARAZO, RODRIGO (n.d.) Administración de Vivienda. Caracas: Fondo Editorial Común.

CIDU [Centro Interdisciplinario de Desarrollo Urbano y Regional] (1970) Manual de Planificación Regional. Santiago: CIDU, Catholic University.

HARDOY, JORGE E. (1968) "Política urbanística y política del suelo urbano y suburbano en América Latina." Planificación (Mexico), no. 3.

––– RAUL OSCAR BASALDUA and OSCAR MORENO (1967) "Mecanismos de regulación de la tierra urbana y sub-urbana en América del Sur." Revista de la Sociedad Interamericana de Planificación 1, 3: 37-44.

HARDOY, JORGE E. et al. (1968) Política de la Tierra Urbana y Mecanismos para su Regulación en América del Sur. Buenos Aires: Instituto Torcuato di Tella.

HARDOY, JORGE E. et.al. (n.d.) Urban Land Policies and Urban Land Control Measures in South America. New York: United Nations, Centre for Housing, Building and Planning.

HIRSCH, WERNER Z. and SIDNEY SONENBLUM (1970) Selecting Regional Information for Government Planning and Decision-Making. New York: Frederick A. Praeger. (Role of information system combined with program budgeting and benefit-cost analyses which results in a dialogue between decision makers and analysts and allows decision makers to arrive at valid policy and program decisions.)

HUCK, ROBERT. (n.d.) Manual General de Avaluos. Caracas: Fondo Editorial Común.

HUGHES, J. T. and J. KOZLOWSKI (1968) "Threshold analysis–an economic tool for town and country planning." Urban Studies 5 (June): 132-143.

VAZQUEZ, FRANCISCO (1969) "Un sistema de información para una política habitacional." Pp. 223-258 in John Friedmann (ed.) Contribuciones a las Políticas Urbanas, Regionales y Habitacionales–Chile: La Década del 70. Santiago: Ford Foundation.

G. Urban Anthropology, Demography, and Sociology in Latin America

(See also Chapters 7 and 8: References.)

ADAMS, RICHARD (1963) "Some supplementary notes on the work of anthropology in Latin America." Presented to the Seminar on Latin American Studies of the American Council of Learned Societies and the Social Science Research Council, July, Center for the Advanced Study in Behavioral Sciences, Stanford, California.

Anuario Indigenista [Mexico] (1967) Special Issue on the Integration of Anthropological Education and Research in Latin America. Vol. 27 (December).

BROWNING, HARLEY L. (1967) "The demography of the city." In Glenn H. Beyer (ed.) The Urban Explosion in Latin America. Ithaca, N.Y.: Cornell Univ. Press.

HEINTZ, PETER (1962) "Research models for Latin America." Presented to Second Inter-American Meeting of Sociologists, Princeton, New Jersey, Sept. 10-12 (mimeo).

HOPPER, REX (1964) "Research on Latin America in sociology." Pp. 243-289 in Charles Wagley (ed.) Social Science Research on Latin America. New York: Columbia Univ. Press.

LABBENS, JEAN (1969) "The role of the sociologist and the growth of sociology in Latin America." International Social Sci. J. 21, 3.

LEEDS, ANTHONY (1970) "Locality power in relation to supra-local power institutions." In Aidan Southall and Edward Bruner (eds.) Urban Anthropology. Chicago: Aldine.

MACK, RAYMOND W. (1969) "Theoretical and substantive biases in sociological research." Pp. 52-64 in Muzafer Sherif and Carolyn W. Sherif (eds.) Interdisciplinary Relationships in the Social Sciences. Chicago: Aldine.

SMITH, T. LYNN (1970) Studies of Latin American Societies. Garden City, N.Y.: Doubleday Anchor Books. (Especially Chapters 2 and 16: "The development of sociological studies of Latin America in the United States" and "Possibilities and pitfalls in the transplantation of socio-cultural traits, complexes, and systems, with special reference to Latin America.")

——— (1951) "Sociology." Pp. 234-238 in Francisco Aguilera (ed.) Handbook of Latin American Studies, no. 17. Gainesville: Univ. of Florida Press.

La Sociología en la América Latina: Problemas y Perspectivas. (n.d.) Buenos Aires: Editorial Universitaria de Buenos Aires.

STRICKON, ARNOLD (1964) "Anthropology in Latin America." Pp. 125-167 in Charles Wagley (ed.) Social Science Research on Latin America. New York: Columbia Univ. Press.

H. Anthropology, Demography, Sociology in Latin America: Urban Case Studies

(See also Chapters 7 and 8: References.)

CAPELO, J. (1895-1902) Sociología de Lima, 4 vols. Lima.

DELGADO, CARLOS (1965) Estudio Socio-Económico de la Barriada El Hermitaño. Lima: Instituto de Investigaciones Económicas de la Universidad Nacional Mayor de San Marcos.

——— (1960) Barriadas de Lima metropolitana. Lima: Fondo Nacional de Salud y Bienestar Social.

GEERTZ, CLIFFORD (1965) The Social History of an Indonesian Town. Cambridge, Mass.: MIT Press.

GERMANI, GINO (1960) "Inquiry into the social effects of urbanization in a working class sector of greater Buenos Aires." Pp. 206-233 in Philip H. Hauser (ed.) Urbanization in Latin America. Paris: UNESCO.

KAHL, JOSEPH A. (1968) The Measurement of Modernism: A Study of Values in Brazil and Mexico. Austin: Univ. of Texas Press.

LEWIS, OSCAR (1961) The Children of Sanchez: Autobiography of a Mexican Family. New York: Random House.

——— (1959) Five Families: Mexican Case Studies in the Culture of Poverty. New York: Basic Books.

——— (1952) "Urbanization without breakdown: a case study." Scientific Monthly 75: 31-41.

MacLEAN Y ESTENOS, R. (1951) "Sociología de la ciudad en el Nuevo Mundo." Pp. 277 ff. in Proceedings of the Fourteenth International Congress of Sociology, August 30-September 3.

MANGIN, WILLIAM (1967) "Latin American squatter settlements: a problem and a solution." Latin American Research Rev. 2 (Summer): 65-98.

MATELLART, ARMAND (1965) Atlas Social de las Comunas de Chile. Santiago: Editorial del Pacífico.

——— and MANUEL A. GARRETON (1969) Integración Nacional y Marginalidad. Santiago: Instituto de Capacitación e Investigación en Reforma Agraria.

MATOS MAR, J. (1961) "The barriadas of Lima: an example of integration into urban life." In Philip M. Hauser (ed.) Urbanization in Latin America. Paris: UNESCO.

PATCH, RICHARD W. (n.d.) "Life in a callejón: a study of urban disorganization." West Coast and South American Series 13, 6. American University Field Staff.
PEATTIE, LISA (1968) The View from the Barrio. Ann Arbor, Mich.: Univ. of Michigan Press.
Peru, Oficina Nacional de Planeamiento y Urbanismo (1967) Plan de Desarrollo Metropolitano Lima–Callao, Esquema Director 1967-80. Lima.
SILVERT, KALMAN (1961) The Conflict Society. New Orleans: Hauser.
WHITEFORD, ANDREW W. (1960) Two Cities in Latin America: A Comparative Description of Social Classes. Beloit, Wis.: Logan Museum of Anthropology, Beloit College.

I. Urban Economics in Latin America

(See also Chapters 4 and 5: References.)

BIRD, RICHARD (1963) "The economy of the Mexican Federal District." Inter-American Economic Affairs 17 (Autumn): 19-51.
CARDENAS, CUAUHTEMOC (n.d.) Crecimiento Económico y Urbanización en México. Buenos Aires: Centro Editor de América Latina.
CURRIE, LAUGHLIN (1966) Accelerating Development: The Necessity and the Means. New York: McGraw-Hill.
DIEGUES, MANUEL, Jr. (1966) "Urban employment in Brazil." International Labour Rev. 93 (June): 643-657.
FITZGIBBON, RUSSELL H. (1952) "The economy of Montevideo." Inter-American Economic Affairs 6 (Autumn): 70-88.
GOETZE, ROLF with JOHN F. C. TURNER (1968) Developing Incentives to Guide Urban Autonomous Growth. New York: Asia Society.
HEILBRONER, ROBERT L. [ed.] (1969) Economic Means and Social Ends: Essays in Political Economics. Englewood Cliffs, N.J.: Prentice-Hall.
HIRSCH, WERNER Z. (1959) "Expenditure implications of metropolitan growth and consolidation." Rev. of Economics and Statistics 41 (August): 232-241.
ISARD, WALTER and ROBERT COUGHLIN (1957) Municipal Costs and Revenues. Wellesley, Mass.: Chandler-Davis.
MORSE, RICHARD M. (1954) "São Paulo in the twentieth century: social and economic aspects." Inter-American Economic Affairs 8 (Summer): 3-60.
——— (1951) "São Paulo in the nineteenth century: economic roots of the metropolis." Inter-American Economic Affairs 5, 3: 3-39.
MOSK, SANFORD A. (1954) "Indigenous economy in Latin America." Inter-American Economic Affairs 8 (Winter): 3-25.
OLDMAN, OLIVER, HENRY J. AARON, RICHARD M. BIRD, and STEPHEN L. KASS (1967) Financing Urban Development in Mexico City: A Case Study of Property Tax, Land Use, Housing, and Urban Planning. Cambridge, Mass.: Harvard Univ. Press.
PIKE, FREDERICK B. (1960) "Aspects of *cabildo* economic regulations in Spanish America under the Hapsburgs." Inter-American Economic Affairs 13 (Spring): 67-83.
RHOADS, WILLIAM G. and RICHARD M. BIRD (1967) "Financing urbanization in developing countries by benefit taxation: case study of Colombia." Land Economics (November): 403-412.
RODWIN, LLOYD (1970) First Stage Research Prospectus on the Economics of Urbanization prepared for the Centre for Housing, Building and Planning, United Nations, New York. Cambridge, Mass.: Special Program for Urban and Regional Studies of Developing Countries, MIT.
ROTTENBERG, SIMON (1959) Notes on the economics of urbanization in Latin America. Prepared for the Seminar on Urbanization in Latin America, July 6-18. Pp. 8-11 in United Nations document E/CN.12/URB6 - UNESCO/SS/URB/LA/6 (September 30).
SHAPIRO, HARVEY (1963) "Economics of scale and local government finance." Land Economics 39 (May): 175-186.

Stanford Research Institute et al. (1968) Costs of Urban Infrastructure for Industry as Related to City Size in Developing Countries. Palo Alto: Stanford Research Institute. (India case study.)

STEIN, STANLEY J. (1954) "The Brazilian cotton textile industry, 1850-1950." Inter-American Economic Affairs 8 (Summer): 69-91.

TERNENT, JAMES ANTHONY S. (1967) "Algunas consideraciones económicas sobre una política urbana para Colombia." Unpublished. Bogotá, July.

THOMPSON, WILBUR R. (1967) "Toward an urban economics." Pp. 135-159 in Leo F. Schnore and Henry Fagin (eds.) Urban Research and Policy Planning. Beverly Hills: Sage Publications.

TIEBOUT, CHARLES M. (1960) "Economics of scale and metropolitan governments." Rev. of Economics and Statistics 42 (November): 442-444.

YOUNGSON, A. J. (1967) Overhead Capital: A Study in Development Economics. Edinburgh: Edinburgh Univ. Press.

J. Urban Geography in Latin America

(See also Chapter 4: References.)

ABREU BERGO, MARIA STELA DE (1952) Estudo Geográfico da Cidade de Campinas. Presented to the Tenth Brazilian Congress of Geography.

AB'SABER, AZIZ NACIB (1953) "A cidade de Manaus: primeiros estudos." Boletim Paulista de Geografia, no. 15.

ALONSO, WILLIAM (1964) "The form of cities in developing countries." Papers of the Regional Science Association 13.

AMATO, PETER (1970) "Elitism and settlement patterns in the Latin American city." J. of Amer. Institute of Planners 36 (March): 96-105.

––– (1969) "Environmental quality and locational behavior in a Latin American city." Urban Affairs Q. 5 (September): 83-101.

––– (1968a) An Analysis of the Changing Patterns of Elite Residential Areas in Bogotá, Colombia. Latin American Studies Program Dissertation Series. Ithaca, N.Y.: Cornell University.

––– (1968b) "Patrones de ubicación en una ciudad Latino-americana." Revista de la Sociedad Interamericana de Planificación 2 (December): 38-45.

ARAUJO, JOSE DE SOUSA AZEVEDO PIZARRO (1945) Memórias Históricas do Rio de Janeiro. Vol. 1: Bibl. Popular Brasileira, no. 4. Rio de Janeiro: M.E.S., Instituto Nacional do Livro.

ARBOS, PHILIPPE (1946) "Petrópolis, esbôço de geografia urbana." Boletim Geográfico (Rio de Janeiro) 4, 37-38: 18-25, 133-146.

Associação de Geógrafos Brasileiros (1958) A cidade de São Paulo: estudo de Geografia urbana. São Paulo: Ed. Nacional.

Associação dos Geógrafos Brasileiros Secção Regional do Rio de Janeiro (1962) Aspectos da Geografia Carioca. Rio de Janeiro.

AZEVEDO, AROLDO DE et al. [ed.] (1958) A cidade de São Paulo: estudos de geografia urbana. 4 volumes. São Paulo.

––– (1957a)"Cuiabá: estudos de Geografia urbana." Anais da Associação de Geógrafos Brasileiros 7, 2: 9-66.

––– (1957b) "Vilas e cidades do Brasil colonial: ensaio de Geografia Humana retrospectiva." Anais da Associação de Geógrafos Brasileiros, 1954-1955 (São Paulo) 9, 1: 83-168.

BATAILLON, CLAUDE (1964) "La geografía urbana de la ciudad de Mexico." América Latina 7 (October-December): 71-88.

BERGO, MARIA ESTELA DE ABREU (1952) "Estudo geografico da cidade de Campinas." Anais do Congresso Brasileiro de Geografia, 10th (Rio de Janeiro) 3: 641-694.

BERNARDES, LISIA MARIA CAVAL CANTI (1951) "Notas sobre a cidade de Diamantina e seus habitantes." Boletim Carioca de Geografia (Rio de Janeiro) 3, 2-3: 26-47.

BERRY, BRIAN J. L. (1965) "Research frontiers in urban geography." Pp. 403-430 in Philip M. Hauser and Leo F. Schnore (eds.) The Study of Urbanization. New York: John Wiley.

BITTENCOURT, AGNELO (1949) "Manaus." Boletim Geográfico (Rio de Janeiro) 7, 76: 385-395.

Brazil Instituto Brasileiro de Geografia e Estatística (1957-1958) Enciclopédia dos Municípios Brasileiros. Rio de Janeiro.

CARDOSO, MARIA FRANCISCO T. C. (1955) "Aspectos geográficos da cidade de Cataguases." Revista Brasileiro de Geografia 17, 4: 423-446.

CASTRO, JOSUE (1948) Fatôres de Localização da cidade do Recife; um ensaio de Geografia urbana. Rio de Janeiro: Impr. Nacional.

CHAPIN, F. S., Jr. (1964) "Selected theories of urban growth and structure." J. of Amer. Institute of Planners 30 (February).

Chile Corporación de Fomento (1967) Geografía Económica de Chile. Santiago: CORFO.

COLE, J. P. (1957) Estudio Geográfico del Gran Lima. Lima: Oficina Nacional de Planeamiento y Urbanismo.

COUTO E SILVA, GOLBERY DO (1967) Geopolítica do Brasil. Rio de Janeiro: José Olympio.

Conselho Nacional de Geografia, Diretório Regional de Santa Catarina (1958) Atlas Geográfico de Santa Catarina.

CRUZ COKE, RICARDO (1952) Geografía Electoral de Chile. Santiago: Editorial del Pacífico.

DEFFONTAINES, PIERRE (1938) "The origin and growth of the Brazilian network of towns." Geographical Rev. 28 (July): 379-399.

DOMINGUES, ALFREDO JOSE PORTO and ELZA COELHO DE SOUSA KELLER (1958) Bahia. Rio de Janeiro: Conselho Nacional de Geografia.

DYER, DONALD R. (1967) "Research on geography presented at Latin American regional conference." Latin American Research Rev. 2, 2: 55-75.

HARDOY, JORGE E. (1969) "El paisaje urbano de Suramerica." Revista de la Sociedad Interamericana de Planificación 3 (September): 27-42.

HAWTHORN, HARRY B. and AUDREY HAWTHORN (1948) "The shape of a city: some observations on Sucre, Bolivia." Sociology and Social Research 33: 87-91.

HAYNER, NORMAN S. (1945) "Mexico City: its growth and configuration." Amer. J. of Sociology 50 (January): 295-304.

――― (1944) Oaxaca: city of Old Mexico." Sociology and Social Research 29: 87-95.

HILL, A. DAVID (1967) "Spatial relations and socioeconomic change: a preliminary study of differentiation of places in the Sabana de Bogotá, Colombia." Professional Geographer 19 (May): 136-143.

HOYT, HOMER (1963) "The residential and retail patterns of leading Latin American cities." Land Economics 39 (November).

Instituto Panamericano de Geografia e Historia (1968) Simposio de Geografía Urbana 274. Rio de Janeiro.

――― (1960) Apuntaciones para una geografía urbana de Quito. Mexico, D.F..

LOPES, RAIMUNDO (1956) Antropogeografía. Rio de Janeiro.

MATOS, DIRCEU LINO DE (1956) "Principais aspectos da geografia urbana de Belo Horizonte." Anais da Associação de Geógrafos Brasileiros, 1949-1950 (São Paulo) 4, 2: 7-35.

MAYER, HAROLD M. (1969) "Cities and urban geography." J. of Geography (January).

――― (1967) "Urban geography and city and metropolitan planning." Pp. 221-238 in Leo F. Schnore and Henry Fagin (eds.) Urban Research and Policy Planning. Beverly Hills: Sage Publications.

――― (1965) "A survey of urban geography." Pp. 81-114 in Philip M. Hauser and Leo F. Schnore (eds.) The Study of Urbanization. New York: John Wiley.

MELO, MARIO LACERDA DE (1958) "Tipos de localização da cidades em Pernambuco." Boletim Carioca de Geografia (Rio de Janeiro) 11, 3-4: 5-32.

MONBEIG, PIERRE (1954) "Aspectos geográficos do crescimento da cidade de São Paulo." Boletim Paulista de Geografia (São Paulo) no. 16: 3-29.

MULLER, NICE LECOCQ (1958) "Campina Grande: notas de geografia urbana." Anais da Associação de Geógrafos Brasileiros (São Paulo) 6, 2: 13-34.

PARDO VALLE, NAZARIO (1966) Poligrafía de Bolivia: resumen físico, político-administrativo, cultural y económico del pais. La Paz.

PARSONS, JAMES J. (1964) "The contribution of geography to Latin American studies." Pp. 33-85 in Charles Wagley (ed.) Social Science Research on Latin America. New York: Columbia Univ. Press.

PAZ-SALDON, C. E. (1957) Lima y Sus Suburbios. Lima: Universidad Nacional de San Marcos de Lima.

PELUSO, VICTOR A., Jr. (1956) "Tradição e plano urbano: cidades protuguêsas e alemães no estado de Santa Catarina." Boletim Geográfico (Rio de Janeiro) 14, 133: 325-357.

PINTO, MARIA MADALENA VIEIRA (1960) "Nucleos urbanos." In Grande região Centro-Oeste. Rio de Janeiro: Conselho Nacional de Geografia.

PRESCOTT, J. R. V. (1969) The Geography of State Policies. Chicago: Aldine.

PRESTON, JAMES (1947) "Belo Horizonte e Ouro Preto: estudo comparativo de duas cidades brasileiras." Boletim Geográfico (Rio de Janeiro) 4, 48: 1598-1609.

ROCHE, JEAN (1955) "Pôrto Alegre, metrôpole do Brasil meridional." Boletim Paulista de Geografia (São Paulo) no. 19: 31-51.

ROCHEFORT, MICHEL (1959) "A organização urbana da Amazônia Média." Boletim Carioca de Geografia (Rio de Janeiro) 13, 3-4: 15-29.

SANTOS, ELINA (1956) "Ponta Grossa, capital regional do Oeste do Paraná." Boletim, Paulista de Geografia (São Paulo) no. 24: 57-77.

SANTOS, MILTON (1959) O Centro da Cidade de Salvador. Salvador: University of Bahia, Laboratory of Geomorphology and Regional Studies.

SCHNORE, LEO (1965) "On the spatial structure of cities in the two Americas." Pp. 347-398 in Philip Hauser and Leo Schnore (eds.) The Study of Urbanization. New York: John Wiley.

SILVA, MOACIR M. F. (1946) "Tentativa de classificação das cidades brasileiras." Revista Brasileira de Geografia (Rio de Janeiro) 8, 3: 283-314.

SOARES, TERESINHA SEGADAS (n.d.) "O conceito geográfico de bairro e sua exemplificação na cidade do Rio de Janeiro." Boletim Carioca de Geografia (Rio de Janeiro)11, 3-4: 47-68.

THOMLINSON, RALPH (1969) Urban Structure: The Social and Spatial Character of Cities. New York: Random House.

VALVERDE, ORLANDO (1944) "Dois ensaios de geografia urbana: Pirapora e Lapa." Revista Brasileiro de Geografia (Rio de Janeiro) 6, 4: 509-533.

K. Urban Government-Administration, Political Science and Law in Latin America

(See also Chapters 6 and 7: References.)

BASALDUA, RAUL O. and OSCAR A. MORENO (1969) "Institucionalización de un área metropolitana en Argentina." Revista de la Sociedad Interamericana de Planificación 3 (March-June): 39-43.

CASTRO GUEVARA, JULIO (n.d.) Esquema de la Evolución Municipal en Venezuela. Caracas: Fondo Editorial Común.

FORM, WILLIAM H. and WILLIAM V. D'ANTONIO (1959) "Integration and cleavage among community influentials in two border cities." Amer. Soc. Rev. 24 (December): 804-814.

International Union of Local Authorities (1968) Urbanization in Developing Countries. IULA Publication 93. La Haya. (Discusses the role of local authorities and planning. See especially H. J. Cole, "Integrated metropolitan development in Brazil.")

KARST, KENNETH L. (1964) "The study of Latin American law and legal institutions." Pp. 290-333 in Charles Wagley (ed.) Social Science Research on Latin America. New York: Columbia Univ. Press.

KLAPP, ORRIN E. and L. VINCENT PADGETT (1960) "Power structure and decision-making in a Mexican border city." Amer. J. of Sociology 65, 4: 400-406.

KLING, MERLE (1964) "The state of research in Latin America: political science." Pp. 168-213 in Charles Wagley (ed.) Social Science Research on Latin America. New York: Columbia Univ. Press.

MOUCHET, CARLOS (1968) "Aspectos de las áreas metropolitanas." Revista de la Sociedad Interamericana de Planificación 2 (March-June): 61-65.

RABINOVITZ, FRANCINE F. et al. (1969) Latin American Political Systems in an Urban Setting: A Preliminary Bibliography. Gainesville: University of Florida, Center for Latin American Studies.

L. Urban History In Latin America

(See also Chapters 1 and 4: 1/References.)

ADAMS, ROBERT M. (1966) The Evolution of Urban Society, Early Mesopotamia and Pre-Hispanic Mexico. Chicago: Aldine.

ALEMPARTE, JULIO (1966) El Cabildo en Chile Colonial. Santiago: Editorial Andres Bello.

BARATA, M. (1959) "Formação histórica das cidades brasileiras." Habitat 10 (November).

BERMUDEZ MIRAL, OSCAR (1966) Orígenes Históricos de Antofagasta. Santiago: Editorial Universitaria.

BISHKO, C. J. (1956) "The Iberian background of Latin American history: recent backgrounds and continuing problems." Hispanic American Historical Rev. 36: 50-80. (A bibliographical essay of great value.)

CARDOSO, FERNANDO HENRIQUE (1965) "The structure and evolution of industry in São Paulo: 1930-1960." Studies in Comparative International Development 1, 5.

COARACY, VIVALDO (1955) Memórias da Cidade do Rio de Janeiro. Rio de Janeiro.

CRESPO R., ALBERTO (1961) Historia de la Ciudad de La Paz, Siglo XVII. Lima.

DAVIS, KINGSLEY (1960) "Colonial expansion and urban diffusion in the Americas." International J. of Comparative Sociology 1: 43-66.

FERREIRE LORIA HECTOR (1954) Evolução Industria de São Paulo. São Paulo: Livraria Matins Editora.

GAKENHEIMER, RALPH (1966) Effects of the Municipality on the Growth and Pattern of the XVIth Century Peruvian City. Presented at the Thirty-seventh International Congress of Americanists, Mar del Plata, Sept. 4-10.

——— et al. (1967) "Conclusions and evaluation of the symposium on 'the process of urbanization in America since its origins to the present time.'" Latin American Research Rev. 2, 2: 76-90.

GARCIA, JUAN AGUSTIN (1937) La Ciudad Indiana. Buenos Aires.

GIL MUNILLA, LADISLAO (1955) "La ciudad de Hispanoamérica." Estudios Americanos 10 (September): 307 ff.

GLAAB, CHARLES N. (1967) "Historical perspective on urban development schemes." Pp. 197-219 in Leo F. Schnore and Henry Fagin (eds.) Urban Research and Policy Planning. Beverly Hills: Sage Publications.

GOYCOOLEA I., ROBERTO (1968) "Plan regulador: historia del urbanismo en Concepción." AUCA no. 13: 25-29.

GUARDA, GABRIEL (1968) La ciudad chilena del siglo XVIII. Buenos Aires: Centro Editor de América Latina.

——— (1967) Influencia militar en las ciudades del Reino de Chile. Santiago: Academia Chilena de la Historia, Pontificia Universidad Católica de Chile.

HANDLIN, OSCAR (1963) "The modern city as a field of historical study." Pp. 1-26 in Oscar Handlin and John Burchard (eds.) The Historian and the City. Cambridge, Mass.: MIT Press and Harvard Univ. Press.

HANKE, LEWIS (1958) "Luis Capoche and the history of Potosí, 1545-1585." Inter-American Economic Affairs 12, 2: 19-51.

HARDOY, JORGE (1968) Urban Planning in Pre-Columbian America. Planning and Cities Series. New York: Goerge Braziller.

——— (1964) Ciudades Precolombinas. Buenos Aires: Ediciones Infinito.

IANNI, OCTAVIO (1966) "Las ciudades pioneras del Brasil." Desarrollo Económico (New York) 3, 1: 17-21.

LUBOVE, R. (1967) "Urbanization process: an approach to historical research." J. of Amer. Institute of Planners 33 (January): 33-39.

MARTINEZ, CARLOS (1967) Apuntes sobre el urbanismo en el Nuevo Reino de Granada. Bogotá.

MORSE, RICHARD M. (1966) "Cities and society in XIX century Latin America: the illustrative case, Brazil." Presented at the Thirty-seventh International Congress of Americanists, Mar del Plata, Sept. 4-10.

——— (1962) "Some characteristics of Latin American urban history." Amer. Historical Rev. 67 (January): 317-338.

——— (1958) From Community to Metropolis. Gainesville: Univ. of Florida Press.

——— (1951) "São Paulo in the 19th century: economic roots of the metropolis." Inter-American Economic Affairs 5 (Winter).

NECTARIO MARIA (1966) Historia de la Conquista y Fundación de Caracas. Caracas: Comisión de Obras Culturales, Comisión Nacional del Cuatrocentenario de la Fundación de Caracas.

PALERM, ANGEL (1955) "The agricultural basis of urban civilization in Meso-America." In Julian H. Steward et al. (eds.) Irrigation Civilization: A Comparative Study. Washington, D.C.

——— and E. WOLF (1961) "La agricultura y el desarrollo de la civilización en Mesoamérica." Revista Interamericana de Ciencias Sociales (Washington) 1, 1.

PALM, ERWIN WALTER (1951) "Los orígenes del urbanismo imperial en América." Pp. 258 ff. in Contribuciones a la Historia Municipal de América. Mexico City.

PENA OTAEGUI, CARLOS (1944) Santiago de Siglo en Siglo. Santiago: Empresa Editora Zig-Zag.

RANDLE, PATRICIO (1966) "Cities and frontiers (1779-1879): a century of urbanizing the desert of Buenos Aires." Presented at the Thirty-seventh International Congress of Americanists, Mar del Plata, Sept. 4-10.

RINALDINI, JULIO (1954) "Buenos Aires." Pp. 382-400 in German Arciniegas (ed.) The Green Continent. New York: Alfred A. Knopf.

RIVET, PAUL (1960) Maya Cities. New York: G. P. Putnam.

ROCA, JULIO CESAR DE LA (1966) "Biografía de un pueblo: síntesis monográfica de Quetzaltenango: interpretación de su destino." Guatemala: Editorial "José de Pineda Ibarra."

SCOBIE, JAMES R. (1968) "Buenos Aires of 1910: the Paris of South America that did not take off." Inter-American Economic Affairs 22 (Autumn): 3-14.

——— (1966) "Changing urban patterns: the Porteña case, 1880-1910." Presented at the Thirty-seventh International Congress of Americanists. Mar del Plata, Sept. 4-10.

SMITH, ROBERT C. (1955) "Colonial towns of Spanish and Portuguese America." J. of Amer. Society of Architectural Historians 14 (December): 3-12.

STANISLOWSKI, DAN (1950) The Anatomy of Eleven Towns in Michoacan. Austin: Univ. of Texas Press.

——— (1947) "Early Spanish town planning in the New World." Geographical Rev. 37: 94-105.

——— (1946) "The origin and spread of the grid-pattern town." Geographical Rev. 36: 105-120.

STEIN, STANLEY J. (1964) "Latin American historiography: status and research opportunities." Pp. 86-124 in Charles Wagley (ed.) Social Science Research on Latin America. New York: Columbia Univ. Press.

VICUNA MacKENNA, BENJAMIN (1938) Historia Crítica y Social de la Ciudad de Santiago, 2 vols. Santiago: University of Chile.

VISCAYA CANALES, ISIDRO (1969) Los Orígenes de la Industrialización de Monterrey (1867-1920). Monterrey: Instituto Tecnológico y de Estudios Superiores de Monterrey.

WILHELMY, HERBERT (1952) Südamerika im Spiegel seiner Städte. Hamburg.

WORMALD CRUZ, ALFREDO (1968) Frontera Norte. Santiago: Editorial Orbe.

ZAPATA GOLLAN, AGUSTIN (1966) "Urbanization of old Santa Fe." Presented at the Thirty-seventh International Congress of Americanists, Mar del Plata, Sept. 4-10.

Appendices

Appendix I

Jahuel Seminar Summary

KALMAN H. SILVERT

Recent rigorously empirical studies of the sociology of conferences indicate that the most ungrateful position is that of the caboose. To occupy this position is to be talking about the past when everyone's mind is in a mobile future. Another problem is that to provide an integrating conclusion necessarily means to attempt to reconstruct what has happened not in an analytical, but in a synthetic, fashion. Yet each one of us necessarily has his own reality, making the concentration of our differing perceptions a literal impossibility. Nothing could be more banal in the social sciences that that statement, and yet nothing could be more absolutely true. As Lawrence Durrell put it—and I paraphrase him rather badly—two paces to the East or two paces to the West and our perception of reality changes totally. So I would ask you to bear with me concerning a reality that is mine but will not necessarily be yours.

One of the better ways, at least for me, to begin this synthesis is to get into what has been generally subterranean, but has surfaced at least part of the time: the differences in stances and ideologies, and in learning experiences and occupations that have characterized the entire discussion. Obviously my own point of departure is that of the theoretician and academician, as opposed to or different from the stance of the practitioner. I should like to develop some of these dualistic propositions concerning stance through a number of different dimensions. Let me say, however, that I will make ideal-type statements and that we complex and ornery humans will not absolutely fit any one of these ideal-type statements. I will approach the subject by suggesting a number of different oppositions or dichotomies because I am attempting the construction of a typology.

The opposition between practitioner and theorist is obviously an old one, even going back to the differences between Plato and Aristotle. So nothing I say should be taken as very original, but I hope my remarks will gain freshness by specific reference to this Seminar. In a puristic way, the practitioners, it appears to me, have tended to be physical planners; they have tended to talk about spatial relations, of course, but they have assumed policy as a given, and if they voiced complaints about politics and social structure and the rest, they were the complaints of the old economic developers who see social structure and politics and such other manifestations of human behavior as simple impediments to development. Somehow or another, if the whole messy social thing would go away, then our planning could be clean, pure, exact, and proper as we know that it can and should be. Next, the practitioner bids the academic to be relevant, complaining in so many words about ivory towers. The planner's orientation is usually, but not necessarily, one of rather short-term problem-solving. He tends to see the problem of the city as a problem in poverty. He thus leans toward the use of micro-variables, so to speak, of variables smaller than total societies or communities. This group also tends toward ahistoricism, because taking a historical point of view necesarily implies taking a comparative point of view, which by definition is theoretical. To compare what was the past with what is the present for us, one has to be theoretical, and to be theoretical is to surrender to the fuzzy head of the academic—an obviously undesirable practice. Nevertheless, the practitioner always talks about how experience should be transferred, so he is not truly as ahistorical as he would like to think himself. Indeed, very often he sets up complicated mechanisms for sometimes the very expeditious and useful lateral transfer of experience. Another characteristic of the practitioner, too, is his sense of urgency, a sense that speed is required, that there are certain changes for which we can no longer wait.

The academic-theoretical person sometimes acts in ways opposed to the practitioner. The speed of the academic's work does not bother him unless a promotion is on the horizon—or not, as the case may be. How fast he goes is nothing he would relate directly to the social process. The academic tends to be rather more "macro" than the practitioner in his approach, but nevertheless there is a strong conflict inside the academic community between micro-theorists and macro-theorists, a disagreement possibly more bitter and profound than any confrontation between practitioners and theoreticians. The theoretician also tends to take into consideration questions of "grand" politics—not as opposed to "small" politics, but, rather, grand politics in the Platonic sense. He usually thinks in ideological terms even though, of course, he argues that ideology should somehow be controlled in the research process. He synthesizes, in addition to being analytical; the practitioner is more analytical than synthetic, if, indeed, he is ever synthetic.

The academic often argues that finding immediate relevance is not his job. Thus a gulf exists between the academic researcher and the person skilled in translating academic findings into relevant and applicable terms for other persons. If speed is not the academic's criterion, sometimes lassitude is. Some research projects necessarily take eight, ten, twelve, or fourteen years, and therefore the work of the academic-theoretician or the academic-researcher sometimes has to escape the confines of immediate social need which the practitioner has ever before him as his legitimate reason for being. I do not mean to say that the academic does not have feelings of social need, but rather that he inhabits an institutional setting that makes it difficult for him to translate his feelings of need into practice. And there, I think, is one of the greatest differences between the two groups. The institutional situs of the practitioner is, by and large, government or a government-related agency. The institutional setting of the academic is, of course, a university or a private research institution. Such bridging agencies as the Brookings Institution in the United States, the Di Tella Institute in Argentina, or the Vargas Foundation in Brazil have inherent disabilities built into them by the very fact that they are indeed bridges. The argument is sometimes advanced, then, that such organizations stain both functions.

Clearly, however, there are overlaps between practitioners and academics; their separation is not absolute. First, it is obvious that practitioners are not without theory. They may not make their theories explicit, but implicitly they certainly hold premises that may be very highly articulated and organized. In other cases, they may hold mere prejudices that they do not allow to appear, keeping them hidden under the guise of the necessity of acting as technical and apolitical persons—in itself, of course, a political stance.

The mutually beneficial symbiotic relationship between a practitioner and an academic should, it appears to me, be evident. If each one of us is held in a particular professional institutional location, each one of us also is framed within more general institutional settings, causing us to interact whether we will it or no. This Seminar is a case of an overlapping institutional setting; but so, of course, is the nation-state, or any central or local government. As a matter of fact, so is a trolley car, the institution of marriage and the family, and everything else binding us into a sense of community and the necessity for accepting sets of patterns of interaction. The issue is the closeness and the easiness of the interactions, not whether they exist.

There have been other obvious divisions in this group. I will mention them much more briefly than I have treated the practitioner-academic dichotomy. One of them is the break between lefts and rights in simple, straightforward political terms. This division does not, I suggest, correlate very highly with whether one is a practitioner or an academic. Certainly there are practitioners here who are on the left, and practitioners on the right, and academics to left and right. Indeed, these splits show themselves daily. For example, an academic dryly suggested that we should respect people occupying the lower levels in society, and, of course, somebody who is a practitioner with an academic background (the usual combination) could not but say defensively, "We are populist, too."

That brings us to yet another split: the elitist vs. the populist. But, naturally, we have elitist populists and pluralist populists, so that this dichotomy breaks itself up into a four-cell arrangement. Yet another break, a subdivision of the ideological schism, is between those who are political and those who pretend to be apolitical. Some argue that our every action must necessarily be guided by a political end; still others say they have no politics at all; sophisticates may argue that every action must have a political referent, and that good politics permits some men to be apolitical in certain circumstances. This particular confrontation offers possibilities for many schismatic patterns. If I may add a footnote, perhaps the ability to differentiate clearly among many differing citizenship functions is a measure of modernization; the ability to discriminate professional from political, and from political-professional functions is a mark of the complex modern man.

The next division may be labeled an interesting and subtle culturological one: it is the division among Europeans, Latin Americans, and North Americans. The usual split in such conferences as this is between Latin and North Americans. The differences crop up in many ways. A sample divergence is over whether there is a social science for Latin America. Is social science, like physics, one for all societies? My personal opinion would be, "Of course, let us by all means have a social science relevant for Latin America." If it really is so, it should also be relevant for everyplace else, in differing degrees—but that is another statement. Nevertheless, what has been of interest to me, as an only partially participant observer, is the subtlety of the European, Latin American, and North American break in this meeting. I will not enter into detail, but I imagine that others have observed from their own stances these culturological differences in approach.

There is one last way in which I suggest that we could group ourselves: there are those who believe in idealistic planning, and those who believe in pragmatic planning. This dichotomy is another way of separating the academics from the theoreticians, but is perhaps more refined than suggested above. I would guess that here we would indeed find a correlation—the academic who wants to be relevant will tend to idealistic planning, and the practitioner, in his search for immediate relevance, will lean toward pragmatic planning. However, I think Mr. Hirschman is somebody who does not fit these boxes, an example that none of these categories is all-inclusive. If we take them all together, however, I think we might have some interesting typologizing of the participants, and perhaps a way of explaining what some of the cross-currents have been and why the appearance of some arguments has been extremely short-lived. Obviously we have not wanted to touch each other in certain points. As Mr. Germani said, everyone thought about priorities but said little, because the issue is a sensitive one. One might well ask why we have been so delicate with one another.

The second major set of Seminar matters I should like to attempt to sum up returns us to the factual content of the discussion. What are some of the major themes of the Seminar? In the following listing, I have made no attempt to follow the titles of papers or the order of discussion. Instead, I have done what I have been bidden to do—I have attempted to find essential themes, and thus I have had to scramble, reorder, and, at times, rethink.

Put again in simple dualistic fashion, the principal dichotomy has been between the rural and the urban. I suggest that, as Professor Germani remarked, the difference has never really been defined; we have not reached collegiate agreement on what an urban life style is as contrasted with a rural one. We have always presumed that there is such a difference, however, and we have treated the matter in dialectical fashion. We have also seen a distinction drawn between urban and regional *organization,* specifically described from a number of different viewpoints in several papers.

The differences between local and national organization have also been mentioned, but I consider it of crucial significance that almost all the discussion has been about local organization, local government, local problems, or municipal problems, and that practically none of the talk has concerned the very complex relationships between local and national problems. When such issues were introduced, the theme was always ideological, always concerning what it may be possible to do at the local level given the nature of the national scenes in the several Latin American republics. This confrontation has not been an even-handed one.

Another dichotomy, again bubbling under the surface and only every now and then appearing, is the contrast between the national (now including the local) and the international scenes. That theme also arose ideologically, not surprisingly paralleling the confrontation between local and national governments in Latin America. Let me illustrate: If we use the word "pueblo" in a group of this nature, it is to refer to lower classes. But if we employ the word pueblo when confronting Latin America with the United States, then we mean everybody in Latin America. What we are doing, of course, is saying that the superordinate government somehow is an impediment, an evil, that it does not permit decent things to happen, and that it is the lower order that is somehow better and more valuable. Therefore, it is with that lower order that we should work. But the moment that we think globally, we transpose that feeling of identification with local communities to the total national scene, and then say something negative about the international scene. Again, however, this argument has not been a structured one in this Seminar.

Another general duality has opposed national organization (again defined as including local) to Latin American integration. Clearly all these oppositions could be, and, indeed, in some papers have been, scrambled. In the Pedersen-Stöhr presentation, for example, we are given a combination of the rural-urban dichotomy and Latin American integration. I do not want to suggest, then, that these simple dichotomies exhaust the possibilities of the cross-tabulations, so to speak.

A second major topic for discussion is the sociological role of cities. I have picked two quotes to emphasize two different points of view. One is that "rapid urbanization will sooner or later lead to more participant societies." Another comes from a participant who said that he does not believe that automatic consequences stem from large-scale urbanization, but also that large-scale urbanization will obviously not leave Latin America unaffected. That is to say, one point of view is that the mere fact of an urban agglomeration creates a specific set of all-embracing consequences for the persons who live in that agglomeration.

The other view is much more probabilistic, holding that urban concentrations in any part of the world can lead to a very broadly varied set of human reactions. This theme impregnates all of the literature on urbanization. Undoubtedly, ever since Pirenne nobody has been able to escape the question of what may be the qualitative social results of given kinds of physical/spatial/material/human relationships. We certainly could not have been expected to come up with good answers to this question in any conference, for the social sciences as a whole are not yet able to satisfy our curiosity on this subject. But if I, for one, were forced to plump for any approach, it obviously would be in the direction of the great variability of human cultural response to the simple facts of human ecology.

A third stream, I should suggest, concerns the range of effective choice open to individuals and social groups under any particular set of given situations. This subject is closely related to the second theme above. One group of us has been very deterministic, assuming that under given conditions the range of human choices is very narrow. Another group has been extraordinarily relativistic, and has presumed that under any given set of conditions one can carry out not an infinite, but a very wide array of social acts. With respect to this question, issues have been raised concerning specific policies to be adopted, and what the particular obstacles may be. Ideologies reared their heads again concerning the question of speed, although the relationship between simple velocity and the quality of human events has not arisen. Very important to this question of the effective range of choice have been those persons describing their actual experiences.

Even though the papers sometimes have not been consciously adjusted to the question of what the range of effective choice may be, it is clear that their meaning for the theoretical as well as the empirical portions of this Seminar has to do with what it is that can be done in any particular Latin American situation. This subject is what Mr. Delgado is referring to in Lima. How much social "play" is there? Given the room for maneuver that there may be, what is the relationship among social-structural, normative, and institutional factors? Again we have come up with no structured responses, but certainly this area is one that all of us have grappled with here at one time or another.

Another question left much more implicit than explicit, but again bubbling throughout almost everybody's presentation, was an inability to handle well the question of what effect the order of change may have on the quality of change. A few of us mentioned order quite explicitly, of course, but again the Seminar has come to no specific conclusions.

A fifth and last question concerning the sociology of cities is what we should now do. This applied question has slipped from the unguarded lips of the academics as much as from the more harried and worried pursed lips of the practitioners. The matter concerns not only projections into the far future, but the questions of politics, urban organization, and questions of human misery now—not tomorrow, but now. It is precisely here in this feeling of a close identification with human needs that academics and practitioners really came together time after time. That is to say, at certain moments, we all acted as citizens throughout the discussions, no matter what the particular stances or occupations may have been that we brought to the meeting with us.

A third general area was, of course, exemplified today in the search for a straight definition of professional needs. I will do little more than list these needs, and then add a small appendix. The requirements mentioned are in the areas of research training, practice, relations among persons and agencies, available resources, the time we have for working, and, last, the definition of priorities. If I may repeat the statement that I made hurriedly and rather futilely earlier, I say that it is perhaps the priorities question that most severely puts to the test the seriousness of our statement of needs. That is, the question of how we arrive at priorities is the area in which we must demonstrate the symbiotic relationship between academic persons and practitioners. Both groups need ordered priorities, for nobody can escape decision as to what to do first, second, third, fourth, or fifth, even if the decision is made upon a convenient or casual or accidental basis. (Those, too, are reasons for making decisions.) If we are truly to become professional, truly to put under disciplined control that which we are doing, may I suggest that we must emerge from the specifics of our activities to the broader area of the total range of what we might possibly do. In the act of that emergence, in the act of making an honest decision about what the order of priorities is, academicians and practitioners need each other desperately.

I should like rapidly to make a few suggestions as to how these diversities and divergences in approaches, disciplines, and personality can find common areas so that we do not continue scattered and, in effect, wasted efforts. I do not make these suggestions with any absolute surety, for I am not certain of the validity of what I am about to say. On the other hand, I would not like to conclude this synthesis without any expression at all of other areas of our common beliefs and purposes. I have indicated that I think the proper way to establish priorities certainly is in itself one area best served by common endeavor. But in terms of the intellectual content of what it is that we are about, I pick up from Gideon Sjoberg his feeling that one of those areas in which we obviously all have a common interest is the simple one of ecology, which I mentioned earlier. The relationship among space, the human occupancy of space, and the quality of human relationships as against that space variable has been a universal theme. Another area in which every one of us is interested—and absolutely has to be interested—is the question of social structure. Social structure may be approached from a stratification viewpoint (basically occupational), or from a power viewpoint (basically political), but in any event, what we are all talking about is the distribution of income, the distribution of political participation, pecking orders, and so on. We have not been talking among ourselves of ideas as ideas, but rather of ideas as *effective* instruments for change or resistance to change. Effectiveness—or power—is, of course, a function of social structure. In all our research and application, there can be no escape from somehow handling the question of effectiveness.

Another area in which we all share a common interest is that of social values and ideologies—the meaning persons give to the power they possess and the acts they perform. It is true of us all that everyone has some ability and some effectiveness. At the very least, for example, we can always tell the state to kill us if it wants to, thus withdrawing our tacit consent. Every one of us has some power, and every one of us has ideas concerning the meaning of that power. These statements are human universals. They need to be put into our equations in order to control our actions vis-à-vis the persons we deal with, as well as in order to be competent and decent practitioners and professionals in dealing with urban development.

A last area of human behavior that I think we must all be consciously concerned with is what so many people at the Seminar have time and again referred to—simple, ordinary, routine, human behavior: what people learn to do, what they are able to do, how much they themselves voluntaristically can do, and what they do as a plain matter of human practice. The reasons for emphasizing all four of these areas—ecology as an academic problem in itself, the question of social structure, ideologies and values, and behavior patterns—is to permit us to accord full respect to the true complexity of the human situation. Involved in this suggestion is also an explicit argument against any kind of lineal determinism.

In conclusion, let me take a leap. Let us ask ourselves—without regard to the material or physical facts of the matter—what is the urban condition? Perhaps the urban condition can best be described by some hackneyed and yet hallowed concepts coming from certain of the more liberal parts of the social sciences. I think that the urban condition can be described as what most of us think of as the modern condition: contract in public relationships; impersonality and a certain freedom in the structuring of personal relationships; something as mundane and as delicious as choice and variety in the human experience. We are also dealing with merit selection instead of ascription, of course, as has been said so many times, as well as with the equality of individuals before the institutional structures of society. We are speaking of access to communications and to institutional structures, of the ways in which individuals *as individuals* can be freed to become as highly variable as they possibly can and choose to be. When we speak of urbanization as making for participant societies, what has been assumed is some set of criteria of this nature. The urban condition is somehow the libertarian condition. What is now being made available to us technologically and ideologically is the ability to start treating human beings simultaneously as individuals and as members of society.

The Authors

ROBERT T. DALAND *is Professor of Political Science at the University of North Carolina, Chapel Hill. He has published a book and several articles on Brazilian planning and development administration, and recently edited* Comparative Urban Research: The Administration and Politics of Cities. *He has served as a Fulbright research professor in Brazil during which time he concluded a study of development orientations among national government administrators.*

CARLOS DELGADO, *social anthropologist, is Director of Social Planning, Institute of National Planning, in Lima, Peru. Formerly he was Visiting Professor to the Interdisciplinary Center of Urban and Regional Development (CIDU) at Catholic University, Santiago de Chile, and Head of the Social Studies Department, Metropolitan Development Plan Office, Lima. His research and publications cover topics ranging from education, social problems and planning, and social mobility in Peru to problems of the Peruvian family and youth.*

JOHN FRIEDMANN *is Professor and Chairman of the Urban Planning Program in the School of Architecture and Urban Planning of the University of California, Los Angeles. He was Director of the Ford Foundation Urban and Regional Development Advisory Program in Chile at the time of the Jahuel Seminar. He is the author of several books and numerous articles on regional development and planning, and on urban aspects of national development. Among these are* Regional Development Strategy: A Case Study of Venezuela *and* Venezuela: From Doctrine to Dialogue.

RALPH A. GAKENHEIMER *is Professor of City and Regional Planning at the Massachusetts Institute of Technology. He was formerly editor of the* Journal of the American Institute of Planners, *Adviser on Metropolitan Development for the Ford Foundation in the Ministry of Housing and Urban Development of Chile, and Professor of City and Regional Planning at the University of North Carolina, Chapel Hill.*

JOHN MILLER *is a doctoral candidate at the Massachusetts Institute of Technology. He was formerly Program Specialist in regional development with the Ford Foundation Urban and Regional Development Advisory Program in Chile and has served as consultant in regional community development and American Indian housing for private and public policy purposes.*

383

RICHARD M. MORSE *is Professor of History and Chairman of the Council on Latin American Studies at Yale University. Among his numerous publications are included two historical studies of Brazil:* From Community to Metropolis: A Biography of São Paulo, Brazil *and* The Bandeirantes: The Historical Role of the Brazilian Pathfinders. *He has also served on the board of editors to the* Hispanic American Historical Review *and* Caribbean Studies.

POUL OVE PEDERSEN *is Professor of Regional Development at the Technical University of Denmark, Copenhagen. Formerly he served in the same capacity at Catholic University, Santiago de Chile. He has published various articles on the structure and development of metropolitan areas and is currently doing research on diffusion processes in urbanization in Latin America.*

KALMAN H. SILVERT *is currently Professor of Government and Director of the Ibero-American Center at New York University, as well as Program Advisor in Social Sciences and Humanities, Latin America, to the Ford Foundation. He has served on the Advisory Board of Editors to* Comparative Politics, American Behavioral Scientist, Trans-Action Monograph Series, *and* Desarrollo Económico *(Buenos Aires). His books include* The Conflict Society: Reaction and Revolution in Latin America *and* Chile Yesterday and Today. *In addition, he has written extensively as editor and contributor to numerous books and is author of a wide selection of articles on Latin America dealing with socio-political aspects of that cultural region.*

WALTER STOHR *is Professor of Geography at McMaster University, Hamilton, Ontario. Prior to this position he served as Program Specialist in regional development for the Ford Foundation Urban and Regional Development Advisory Program in Chile. He received his doctorate in economics at the Vienna School of Economics and was formerly chief economist of the Austrian Institute of Regional Planning in Vienna. He has worked extensively on problems of regional analysis and planning, with particular attention to underdeveloped regions.*

Participants in the Jahuel Seminar

FERNANDO AGUIRRE. Director, Oficina de Planificación Nacional (ODEPLAN) (National Planning Office), Santiago.

BRIAN J. L. BERRY. Professor, The Center for Urban Studies, The University of Chicago.

HARRY J. COLE. Director, Servicio Federal de Habitação e Urbanismo (Federal Housing and Urban Services), Ministerio do Interior, Rio de Janeiro.

JULIO COTLER. Professor, Instituto de Estudios Peruanos (Institute of Peruvian Studies), Lima.

ROBERT T. DALAND. Professor, Department of Political Science, The University of North Carolina, Chapel Hill.

CARLOS DELGADO. Visiting Professor, Comité Interdisciplinario de Desarrollo Urbano (CIDU) (Interdisciplinary Committee of Urban Development), Universidad Católica de Chile, Santiago.

CARLOS FORTIN. Director of Research, Facultad Latino Americano de Ciencias Sociales (FLACSO) (Latin American Faculty of Social Sciences), Santiago.

JOHN FRIEDMANN. Director, Urban and Regional Development Advisory Program in Chile. The Ford Foundation, Santiago.

GUILLERMO GEISSE. Assistant Director, Comité Interdisciplinario de Desarrollo Urbano (CIDU) (Interdisciplinary Committee of Urban Development), Universidad Católica de Chile, Santiago.

GINO GERMANI. Monroe Gutman Professor of Latin American Affairs, Department of Social Relations, Harvard University, Cambridge, Mass.

JORGE HARDOY. Director, Centro de Estudios Urbanos y Regionales (CEUR) (Center of Urban and Regional Studies), Instituto Torcuato di Tella, Buenos Aires.

ALBERT O. HIRSCHMAN. Professor of Political Economy, Department of Economics, Harvard University, Cambridge, Mass.

EDITORS' NOTE: *Positions occupied by the Seminar Participants and Observers as given here are those existing at the time of the Jahuel Seminar, April 22-25, 1968.*

ALBERT O. HIRSCHMAN. Professor of Political Economy, Department of Economics, Harvard University, Cambrdige, Mass.

RICARDO JORDAN. Director, Comité Interdisciplinario de Desarrollo Urbano (CIDU) (Interdisciplinary Committee of Urban Development), Universidad Católica de Chile Santiago.

LEONARDUS KLAASSEN. Director, Nederlandsch Economisch Institut (Netherlands Economic Institute), Rotterdam.

ANTONI R. KUKLINSKY. Director, Regional Development Program, United Nations Research Institute for Social Development, Geneva.

WILLIAM MANGIN. Chairman, Department of Anthropology, Syracuse University, Syracuse, N.Y.

ARMANDO D. MENDES. Professor, Universidade Federal do Pará, Belém, Brazil.

RICHARD M. MORSE. Professor, Department of History, and Chairman, Council on Latin American Studies, Yale University, New Haven, Conn.

EDUARDO NEIRA ALVA. Urban Development Advisor, Inter-American Development Bank, Washington, D.C.

POUL O. PEDERSEN. Visiting Professor, Comité Interdisciplinario de Desarrollo Urbano (CIDU) (Interdisciplinary Committee of Urban Development), Universidad Católica de Chile, Santiago.

ANIBAL QUIJANO. Division of Social Affairs, Economic Commission for Latin America, United Nations, Santiago.

LLOYD RODWIN. Chairman, Faculty Committee, MIT-Harvard Joint Center for Urban Studies, Cambridge, Mass.

JOSE AGUSTIN SILVA MICHELENA. Professor, Centro de Estudios del Desarrollo (Center for Development Studies), Universidad Central de Venezuela, Caracas.

KALMAN H. SILVERT. Program Advisor. Social Sciences, The Ford Foundation, New York.

GIDEON SJOBERG. Professor, Sociology Department, University of Texas, Austin.

CLAUCIO A. DILLON SOARES. Professor, Department of Sociology and Political Science, MIT, Cambridge.

WALTER STOHR. Regional Planning Advisor, Urban and Regional Development Advisory Program in Chile, The Ford Foundation, Santiago.

ERNEST WEISSMANN. Senior Advisor on Regional Development, Office of Technical Co-operation, United Nations, New York.

LIST OF PARTICIPANT OBSERVERS

MANUEL ACHURRA. Assistant Director, Oficina Nacional de Planificación (ODEPLAN) (National Planning Office), in charge of Regional Division, Santiago.

RICHARD ADAMS. Professor, Department of Anthropology, University of Texas, Austin.

JUAN ASTICA. Director of Urban Planning, Ministerio de la Vivienda y Urbanismo (Ministry of Housing and Urban Development), Santiago.

PETER BELL. Acting Representative, The Ford Foundation, Rio de Janeiro.

CALVIN BLAIR. Consultant in Economics and Administration, University of Texas, Austin.

FRANK BONILLA. Professor, Department of Political Science, MIT, Cambridge.

FRANCIS EARWAKER. Urban Development Policy Advisor, Urban and Regional Development Advisory Program in Chile, The Ford Foundation, Santiago.

RENE EYHERALDE FRIAS. Advisor in Rural Housing and Facilities, Urban and Regional Development Advisory Program in Chile, The Ford Foundation, Santiago.

CHARLES FRANKENHOFF. Advisor in Housing Policy, Urban and Regional Development Advisory Program in Chile, The Ford Foundation, Santiago.

PETER FRAENKEL. Representative, The Ford Foundation, Lima.

RALPH GAKENHEIMER. Metropolitan Development Advisor. Urban and Regional Development Advisory Program in Chile, The Ford Foundation, Santiago.

JULIO GIANELLA. Assistant Director, Plan de Desarrollo Metropolitano (Metropolitan Development Planning Office), ONPU, Lima.

BRUCE L. GIBB. Assistant to the Representative. The Ford Foundation, Santiago.

DANIEL GOLDRICH. Program Advisor in Political Science, The Ford Foundation, Santiago.

ROSE GOLDSEN. Professor, Department of Sociology, Cornell University, Ithaca, N.Y.

VICTOR GUBBINS. División de Estudios, Promoción Popular (Research Division, National Community Development Office), Santiago.

NORA L. HAMILTON. Local Staff Assistant, The Ford Foundation, Santiago.

RALPH HARBISON. Assistant to the Representative, The Ford Foundation, Bogotá, Colombia.

NITA MANITZAS. Program Officer, Social Sciences, The Ford Foundation, New York.

JOHN MILLER. Regional Planning Advisor, Urban and Regional Development Advisory Program in Chile, The Ford Foundation, Santiago.

JOHN P. NETHERTON. Representative and Program Advisor in Education, The Ford Foundation, Santiago.

COLIN ROSSER. Director of the Metropolitan Planning Project, The Ford Foundation, Calcutta, India.

THOMAS SANDERS. Institute of Current World Affairs, Santiago.

JOHN STRASMA. Program Advisor in Social Science, The Ford Foundation, Santiago.

FRANCISCO VAZQUEZ. Advisor in Information Systems, Urban and Regional Development Advisory Program in Chile, The Ford Foundation, Santiago.

AUTHOR INDEX

GEOGRAPHIC INDEX

SUBJECT INDEX

Accessibility, -production curve of, 92-93; and economic development, 44, 47-49, 55, 92-93, 97, 99; to employment, 288-90; iso-accessibility lines of, 86-91; intra-metropolitan, 272, 284-85, 290; physical, 85-86, 94, 96, 98-101, 178; political, to centers of decision, 236, 240

Achievement orientation, 257; of political leaders, 245; of urban migrant groups, 259

Agrarian reform in El Salvador, 46, 51

Airline linkages, most frequent, in South America, 78-79

Allocation of resources, see Investment allocation

Andean, Common Market, 57-58; Group, 57-58, 85, 96

Anthropology, anthropologist, 313, 318, 322, 330-31, 347-48; social, 319; economic, 319

Associación Colombiana de Facultades de Medicina, 351

Associational groups (community associations), 235; see also Community development

Barriadas, 223, 286, 297 n. 11; characteristics of, 276-79, 297 n. 9; definition of, 280; high-density –internal (slums), 281, 287-88; –peripheral (slums), 281-82, 287, 289, 292-93; internal settlements –in incipient consolidation, 281-83; –in advanced consolidation, 281-83; peripheral settlements –in advanced consolidation, 281, 283; –in incipient consolidation, 281, 283; –in rural areas, 281, 284-85; recent peripheral settlements, 281, 283; see also settlements

Barrios marginales, see Settlements

Birth rate, crude, in Latin America, 22-23

Border (frontier) zone integration, see Integration

Budgets, government, in Latin America, 217-20

Bureaucracy, bureaucratization, 122, 124, 147, 174, 206, 215, 225, 238-39, 265, 324, 326, 341

Capital, 114; concentration of, 112; input for integral Latin American development policy, 99-100; preferential treatment in receipt of, among Latin American nations, 96; see also Diffusion of capital

Carretera Marginal de la Selva, 45-46, 61-63, 342

Carretera Transandina (Chile-Argentina), 67

Cartagena Agreement, 43, 57-58

Caribbean Coastal Highway, 63, 65

CELADE (Centro Latino Americano de Demografía), Santiago, Chile, 336

CENDES (Centro de Estudios Nacionales del Desarrollo), Caracas, 352

CENPHA (National Center of Housing Research), Rio de Janeiro, 352

Center-periphery:, national, 118, 124-25, 137-38, 142, 147, 150, 152, 172, 177, 212; metropolitan, 133, 273, 280; see also Periphery

Central American Bank of Economic Integration (BCIE), 53-54

Central American Common Market, 43, 45, 48-49, 51-54

Centralization: budgetary, 216-17; bureaucratic, 183, 237; governmental-political, 118, 133, 137, 148, 151, 214-17, 246, 253, 255-56, 329, 337; Spanish colonial, 47; see also Center-periphery, Concentration, Decentralization, Deconcentration, Devolution; Primate-capital cities

Centro Latinoamericano de Pesquizas em Ciéncias Sociais (Rio de Janeiro), 336

CEUR (Centro de Estudios Urbanos y Regionales), Buenos Aires, 352

Cholos, 150, 152, 287

CIDU (Centro Interdisciplinario de Desarrollo Urbano), Santiago, 344, 352, 354-55

Cities, South American, 132-38; commercial, 67, 111, 115; industrial, 112, 121; mining, 99, 115; physical expansion of, 15; as political-administrative centers, 73, 111, 115, 120; port, 44, 55, 65, 67, 85, 111, 115, 190, 194; as terminals for foreign trade, 73; see also Primate-capital cities, Role of cities, and individual cities in Geographic Index (under nations)

City size, 253; distribution, 14; economic, 146, 320, 356 n. 7

CLACSO (Latin American Social Science Council), 343, 350-52, 354

Classes, socioeconomic, low-income (popular), 206, 239, 248, 270, 277-78, 283, 286-87; middle-income, 118, 121, 197, 238-41, 245, 264-65; see also Urban social groups

Colegio de México, 351-52

"Colonial" dependence, internal, of Latin American nations, 99, 109, 128

Colonization, 122, 130; areas, 29, 63, 341-42; policies, 15, 129, 137, 146; see also Settlement policy

Communications, flow, 45, 121; in government, 256; and modernization, 197, 264; policies, 100; system, 170, 194; –Central America, 55; –in a model of urbanization and political development policies, 251, 255, 257-58; in urban areas, 29, 241; and urbanization, 247; variables, 23-25

Communists, 242-43

Community development, 132, 221-25, 252, 336; professionals, 347

393